Experience the California Coast
Beaches and Parks from San Francisco to Monterey

COUNTIES INCLUDED
MARIN · SAN FRANCISCO · SAN MATEO · SANTA CRUZ · MONTEREY

CALIFORNIA COASTAL COMMISSION

Experience the California Coast
Beaches and Parks from San Francisco to Monterey

COUNTIES INCLUDED
MARIN · SAN FRANCISCO · SAN MATEO · SANTA CRUZ · MONTEREY

State of California
Edmund G. Brown, Jr., *Governor*

California Coastal Commission

Peter Douglas, *Executive Director*   Susan Hansch, *Chief Deputy Director*

Steve Scholl
Editor and Principal Writer

Erin Caughman
Designer and Co-Editor

Jonathan Van Coops
Mapping and GIS Program Manager

Gregory M. Benoit
Principal Cartographer

John Dixon, Ph.D.   Melissa Kraemer
Jonna Engel, Ph.D.   Sylvie B. Lee
Lesley Ewing, P.E.   Christiane Parry
Tamara Gedik   Cassidy Teufel
Mark Johnsson, Ph.D.   Jonathan Van Coops

Contributing Writers

Jo Ginsberg
Consulting Editor

Woodcuts by Tom Killion

Linda Locklin
Coastal Access Program Manager

University of California Press
Berkeley   Los Angeles   London

University of California Press, one of the most distinguished
university presses in the United States, enriches lives around the
world by advancing scholarship in the humanities, social sciences,
and natural sciences. Its activities are supported by the UC Press
Foundation and by philanthropic contributions from individuals and
institutions. For more information, visit www.ucpress.edu.

University of California Press
Berkeley and Los Angeles, California

University of California Press, Ltd.
London, England

Library of Congress Cataloging-in-Publication Data

Beaches and parks from San Francisco to Monterey: counties included, Marin,
San Francisco, San Mateo, Santa Cruz, Monterey / Steve Scholl, editor and
principal writer ... [et al.].
     p. cm. — (Experience the California coast ; 4)
  "California Coastal Commission."
  Includes bibliographical references and index.
  ISBN 978-0-520-27157-9 (paper : alk. paper)
  1. Pacific Coast (Calif.)—Guidebooks. 2. California—Guidebooks.
  3. Beaches—California—Pacific Coast—Guidebooks.
  4. Parks—California—Pacific Coast—Guidebooks. 5. Marin County
  —(Calif.)—Guidebooks. 6. San Francisco—(Calif.)—Guidebooks.
  7. San Mateo County (Calif.)—Guidebooks. 8. Santa Cruz County (Calif.)—Guidebooks. 9. Monterey County (Calif.)—Guidebooks.
  I. Scholl, Steve. II. California Coastal Commission.

  F868.P33B43 2012

  917.904—dc23

                          2011028664

Printed in China.

19 18 17 16 15 14 13 12 11

10 9 8 7 6 5 4 3 2 1

The paper in this publication meets the minimum requirements of
ANSI/NISO Z39.48-1992 (R 1997) (Permanence of Paper).

Contents

Features

Wilder Coast, Santa Cruz County, *original print 10 x 13 inches*

Introduction

MANY OF CALIFORNIA'S most alluring coastal attractions are described in this guidebook. Point Reyes National Seashore, San Francisco's waterfront, Golden Gate National Recreation Area, Santa Cruz Beach Boardwalk, Monterey Bay Aquarium, and Point Lobos: these and many more are found within these pages. Along with numerous deservedly popular destinations are sites that are less well known, if equally enticing. Even travelers on California's coastal highway could easily miss some strikingly beautiful beaches located mere steps away, yet out of sight. In all, some 350 shoreline destinations are thoroughly described here, including every known publicly accessible beach along the coast of Marin, San Francisco, San Mateo, Santa Cruz, and Monterey Counties. Here too are wildlife reserves, marinas, aquariums, public parks, and other attractions.

From San Francisco Bay to Monterey Bay and beyond, California's coast bears traces of the region's colorful history. The days of Spanish settlement, Mexican ranchos, and gold rush–era immigration are reflected in historic settlements, many of them still flourishing, while others have vanished. Some of California's earliest shoreline resorts were born along this stretch of the state's central coast. Natural treasures of the coast, including geologic formations, wildflowers, tidepools, and spacious beaches, are everywhere and are thoroughly described in this book.

The California Coastal Commission, along with the State Coastal Conservancy, the Department of Parks and Recreation, and the Department of Fish and Game, is charged with conserving, enhancing, and making available to the public the beaches, accessways, and resources of the coast. The Coastal Commission's responsibilities under the law known as the California Coastal Act include providing the public with a guide to coastal resources and maintaining an inventory of paths, trails, and other shoreline accessways available to the public. This book furthers those purposes, as do the first three books in the California Coastal Commission's guidebook series: *Experience the California Coast, A Guide to Beaches and Parks in Northern California*; *Beaches and Parks from Monterey to Ventura*; and *Beaches and Parks in Southern California*, as well as the previously published *California Coastal Resource Guide* and *California Coastal Access Guide*.

The state of California owns all tidelands, submerged lands, and the beds of inland navigable waters, holding them for "public trust" uses that include fishing, navigation, commerce, nature preserves, swimming, boating, and walking. Tidelands consist of the area on a beach or rocky coastline that is between the mean high tide line and the mean low tide line. The California Constitution guarantees the public's right of access to tidelands. The state of California (or other managing agency), however, may place restrictions on the time, place, and manner of use of tidelands.

Private property exists along the California coast in many locations, inland of the tidelands. The public generally does not have a right to cross private property without permission to get to tidelands, although easements and other legal provisions allow public use of some private shoreline properties; see entries that follow for more information.

The California Coastal Commission, the State Coastal Conservancy, local governments, and nonprofit land trusts in the five-county region addressed by this book continue to press for increased opportunities for legal, safe access to the beach. This guidebook tells you what coastal resources are at each location and what you might do there. The book is meant to encourage all coastal visitors, whether equipped with beach blanket, binoculars, or bodyboard, to explore the richness and diversity of the California coast.

Dogs enjoy an outing to the coast, but their inquisitive nature can create hazards for coastal wildlife. In state parks, dogs must be kept on leashes that are no more than six feet long and in a tent or enclosed vehicle at night. Except for guide dogs, pets are not allowed in state park buildings, on trails, or on most beaches. Although allowed in some city and county beach parks, dogs may be subject to leash requirements. Please observe posted signs regarding dogs on trails and beaches and in parks. For more information on beaches described in this guide that allow dogs either on- or off-leash, check the index for "dog-friendly beaches." Glass containers and alcoholic beverages are prohibited on most urban beaches, and some communities prohibit smoking on the beach; check individual entries for more information.

Numerous commercial outfitters sell or rent surfboards, kayaks, bicycles, and other recreational gear; some are listed here, as space allows. Check local yellow pages or Internet search services for more. The editors welcome suggestions for future editions (see p. 300).

For an economical overnight stay, this guide lists hostels, publicly owned campgrounds, and, as space permits, private campground facilities. Campsites in public or private parks include family camps, group camps, sites with RV hookups, walk-in environmental campsites, hike or bike sites, and enroute (overflow) spaces. Many can be reserved in advance. Visitors are encouraged to check with clearinghouses such as the local visitor bureaus for additional campground listings; for more information, see the introduction for each county.

Information about market-rate hotels, inns, eating establishments, and other visitor destinations is available from numerous guidebooks and websites.

Enjoy your visits to California's spectacular coast. Keep safe by observing posted restrictions along hazardous stretches of shoreline. Remember that sleeper waves are a factor on the California coast. When strolling the beach or checking out tidepools, make it a general rule not to turn your back on the ocean. Remember that large waves may wash over what look like safe spots on rocks and bluffs. When possible, swim near a lifeguard. Lifeguards patrol many parts of the central California coast year-round, although lifeguard towers on the sand are very limited and are generally staffed daily only during the summer.

Natural conditions along the California coast are always changing, and the width of beaches and shape of bluffs can be altered by the seasonal movement of sand or by erosion. Coastal access and recreation facilities can be damaged by these forces, and trails, stairways, parking areas, and other facilities may be out of service or may be closed due to budget constraints. When planning any trip to the coast, check ahead of time to

For general information on state parks, including a list of camping and day-use fees and campgrounds available without a reservation, see: www.parks.ca.gov.

For state park camping reservations, call: 1-800-445-7275 (available 24 hours), or see: www.reserveamerica.com.

For other camping opportunities, see individual entries that follow.

For information on Hostelling International's facilities, see: www.hiusa.org.

make sure that your destination is currently accessible. Some facilities, such as park visitor centers, are run by volunteers and are open only limited hours; call ahead to check open times. Facilities such as running water are limited or not available at some parks and shoreline accessways; it is a good idea on a coastal trip to bring water, food, layered clothing, and sunscreen. Bring change for parking meters. There is room here for only limited information about public transit lines that serve beaches; check with local transit providers for details.

This guide's purpose is to contribute to a better understanding of the importance of coastal resources, both to the quality of life for people and to the maintenance of a healthy and productive natural environment. This book is offered with the knowledge that a wide appreciation for the coast among Californians plays an important role in the protection and restoration of coastal resources.

Seal Rock Overlook, San Francisco

Using This Guide

Each group of sites is accompanied by a map and a chart of key facilities and characteristics. The "Facilities for Disabled" chart category includes wheelchair-accessible restrooms, trails, campsites, or visitor centers; text descriptions note where restrooms are *not* wheelchair accessible. The "Fee" category refers to a charge for entry, parking, or camping. Check the index for surfing spots, beaches with lifeguard service, and other recreational highlights. Most parks and recreational outfitters maintain websites, but URL

addresses may change and space here is limited; use any popular Internet search engine to look for more information on facilities listed in this guide.

Brief introductions to coastal environments such as beaches, rocky shore, and the vast Monterey Submarine Canyon are included, along with highlights of plants, animals, and other resources that you may see there. For more information about the California coast, consult the Bibliography and Suggestions for Further Reading found on p. 308.

Natural Bridges State Beach, Santa Cruz County

Caring for the Coast

C AN YOU IMAGINE California without the coast? Our state is in many ways defined by its coastline, which provides us with endless enjoyment, beauty, solace, and adventure. It is easy to take this for granted. But what have you done for the coast lately? You can contribute to its good health by developing an awareness of how it is affected by your everyday actions, and striving to act in ways that will have beneficial results. Here are some tips. For more ideas and to take the Coastal Stewardship Pledge, visit www.coastforyou.org or call 1-800-COAST-4U.

Stash Your Trash

Each year, thousands of marine animals die after becoming entangled in or ingesting debris. Plastic is particularly harmful because it does not biodegrade. When exposed to the elements, plastic breaks up into smaller and smaller pieces, but these particles persist. Researchers have found alarming quantities of small plastic pieces in the open ocean, where they circulate continuously unless and until consumed by a bird, fish, or marine mammal.

Most of this debris comes from land and was carried to the ocean by rain, tides, or wind. Avoid contributing to this problem by always disposing of trash properly and by practicing the three "Rs"—**reduce** the waste you generate, buy **reusable** items, and **recycle** trash when possible. When going to the beach or out on a boat, bring a bag and pick up the debris you come across. Each piece you collect is one less hazard for a marine animal. Another way to help is to volunteer for a beach cleanup activity, such as Coastal Cleanup Day or the Adopt-A-Beach Program.

Volunteers on an excursion from Fresno participating in a beach cleanup at Monterey Beach

Coastal Wetlands

In California, population growth and associated coastal development have destroyed or degraded most of our coastal wetlands. Those that remain provide critical wildlife habitat and are a tremendous public resource. Wetlands can serve as a refuge for wild-life and for human visitors, too—a place to go for a respite from urban life, where you can experience nature. This book describes many of these wetlands and the recreation-al opportunities available there. Take care when visiting wetlands; they are susceptible to damage if vegetation is disturbed by foot traffic, and sensitive wildlife species are vulnerable to disturbance by humans, dogs, and horses. When visiting wetlands, stay on prescribed pathways and boardwalks, and pay close attention to rules imposed by land managers. Where dogs are allowed, keep them leashed.

Tidepool Etiquette

Tidepools offer the opportunity to see fascinating marine creatures at close range. However, given the sensitivity of tidepool plants and animals to human contact, there is a real danger of these remarkable ecosystems being quite literally loved to death. It is critical that all visitors learn proper "tidepool etiquette." Please follow these rules when visiting tidepools, and help to educate other visitors as well.

• Watch where you step. Step only on bare rock or sand.

• Don't touch any living organisms. A coating of slime protects most tidepool animals, and touching the animals can damage them.

• Don't prod or poke tidepool animals with a stick. Don't attempt to pry animals off of rocks.

• Leave everything as you found it. Collecting tidepool organisms is illegal in most locations and will kill them. Cutting eelgrass, surfgrass, and sea palm is prohibited.

Tidepools exposed at low tide at James V. Fitzgerald State Reserve

Marine Protected Areas

California's designated marine protected areas include "no-take" marine reserves, where all marine life is protected, as well as marine conservation areas and marine parks, where the catch of certain species with specified types of fishing gear is allowed. For maps and regulations, which are different for each site; see: http://www.dfg.ca.gov/mlpa/. Or, contact the California Department of Fish and Game by e-mail at: AskMarine@dfg.ca.gov or call: 831-649-2870.

Watching Wildlife

Observing wild animals in their natural environment is a rare treat. To ensure that the encounter results in no harm to either the animal or the human observer, keep your distance and watch quietly. Stay clear of mothers with young, and never surround an animal, or trap an animal between a vessel and shore. Leave pets at home, or keep them on a leash and away from wildlife. Never feed wild animals. If a marine mammal appears sick or a pup appears to be abandoned, resist the temptation to "save" it. Instead, seek help from a professional. Contact the Marine Mammal Center: 415-289-SEAL.

Sensible Seafood Choices

Increasing consumer demand for seafood has led to overfishing. Some fishing practices destroy habitat and harm non-target fish and animals. Use your purchasing power to support healthy oceans by selecting seafood that is harvested in a sustainable and environmentally responsible manner. For a pocket guide to sensible seafood choices, visit www.montereybayaquarium.org/cr/seafoodwatch.asp.

Non-point Source Pollution

Another way that people affect the health of the coast is through non-point source pollution, which gets flushed into the ocean by stormwater runoff. Minimize your contribution to this problem by taking simple actions; for example, use least-toxic gardening products, maintain your car to prevent oil leaks, and pick up after your dog.

Whale Tail License Plate

California drivers can help the coast by purchasing a Whale Tail License Plate. The plate funds coastal access trails, beach cleanups, habitat restoration projects, and coastal and marine education programs throughout California, including grants to local groups. The Whale Tail License Plate got a fresh new look in 2011. The new Whale Tail Plate was designed by California artists Elizabeth Tyndall and Bill Atkins.

For information, call: 1-800-COAST-4U, or visit www.ecoplates.com.

New whale tail plate design

Map Legend

TRANSPORTATION

———————— Major Road
———————— Minor Road
——————[1]—————— California State Highway
——————{101}—————— United States Highway
══════[580]══════ Interstate
+-+-+-+-+-+-+-+-+ Railroad

SHORELINE AND HYDROGRAPHY

———————————— Shoreline
———————————— Rivers and Streams

Pacific Ocean, Bays
Lakes, and Ponds

TRAILS AND BIKE WAYS

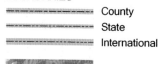

Hiking Trail
Hiking Trail Along State Highway
Hiking Trail Along Road

Pacific Coast Bicentennial
Bike Route
Bike Route Along State Highway
Bike Route Along Road

TOPOGRAPHY AND BATHYMETRY

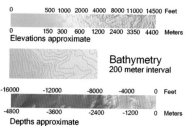

0   500 1000 2000 4000 8000 11000 14500 Feet

0   150 300 600 1200 2400 3350 4400 Meters
Elevations approximate

Bathymetry
200 meter interval

-16000   -12000   -8000   -4000   0 Feet

-4800   -3600   -2400   -1200   0 Meters
Depths approximate

BOUNDARIES

═══════════ County
─────────── State
─────────── International

Los Padres NF — Public Land

Hunter Liggett Military Reservation — Military Land

NORTH ARROW AND BAR SCALE

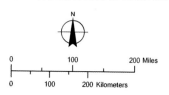

N

0   100   200 Miles

0   100   200 Kilometers

MARINE PROTECTED AREAS

Marine Protected Areas along the central California coast have been designated by the California Department of Fish and Game. For maps and information about fishing restrictions, see: www.dfg.ca.gov/mlpa or call: 831-649-2870.

DATA AND INFORMATION SOURCES

California Coastal Commission
California Department of Fish and Game
California Spatial Information Library
U.S. Geological Survey

Protected open space data is from the California Protected Area Database (CPAD) provided by GreenInfo Network, 2009

Page opposite: Tomales Point, Marin County

Marin County

Marin County

ALTHOUGH CLOSE to population centers of the Bay Area, Marin County is largely rural. Parks and agricultural and open space lands dominate the coast; small villages and scattered ranch houses dot the landscape. Once-upon-a-time plans for a city in the Marin headlands and freeways through the coastal hills never came to pass, and now west Marin County boasts three national parks and monuments, three state parks, and numerous county parks and open space preserves, along with conservation lands managed by nonprofit entities. Beaches, bays, rocky shore, and forests invite visitors to explore the coast.

Outdoor activities span the seasons in Marin. Whale watching is popular from fall through spring. From spring into summer, coastal visitors enjoy viewing wildflowers on Point Reyes and hiking trails throughout the coastal area. Autumn brings the southerly migration of hawks, falcons, eagles, and other birds of prey, and Marin offers exceptional opportunities to view them. Many raptors prefer to fly over land rather than the sea, and as they head south, they tend to funnel over the Marin Headlands. The Golden Gate Raptor Observatory counts and monitors the birds from year to year at a location off Conzelman Road in the Golden Gate National Recreation Area known as Hawk Hill. Visitors are welcome at the site, where occasional talks and banding demonstrations are offered from September through November; for information, call: 415-331-0730.

Annual events include the Western Weekend parade and barbecue in Point Reyes Station in June and the Fourth of July beach tug-of-war by residents of Bolinas and Stinson Beach. Yacht races on Tomales Bay, open artists' studios in springtime, and the Labor Day sand sculpture contest at Drakes Beach are recurring activities. For information on local events and visitor attractions, contact the West Marin Chamber of Commerce in Point Reyes Station at 415-663-9232 or the Marin County Visitors Bureau at 415-925-2060. The West Marin Stagecoach provides limited transit service from San Anselmo along Sir Francis Drake Blvd. to Olema, Point Reyes Station, and Inverness, and from Marin City at Hwy. 101 to Stinson Beach and Bolinas; call: 415-526-3239. The San Francisco Municipal Railway provides bus service to the Marin Headlands on Sundays and holidays; call: 415-701-2311.

The Marin County coast is home to long-established surf shops and recreational outfitters, including:

Point Reyes Surf, 11101 Shoreline Hwy., Point Reyes Station, 415-663-8750;

Live Water Surf Shop, Stinson Beach, 415-868-0333;

Stinson Beach Surf and Kayak, 415-868-2739;

Proof Lab on Shoreline Hwy. off Hwy. 101, Mill Valley, 415-380-8900.

2 Mile Surf Shop, Brighton Ave., Bolinas, 415-868-0264.

Kayaking equipment and tours:

Blue Waters Kayaking, offering rentals, tours, and camping trips to remote beaches in the Point Reyes National Seashore; locations at 19225 Shoreline Hwy., Marshall, and 12938 Sir Francis Drake Blvd., Inverness, 415-669-2600.

Point Reyes Outdoors, 11401 Shoreline Hwy., offering kayak, bicycle, and hiking tours; call: 415-663-8192.

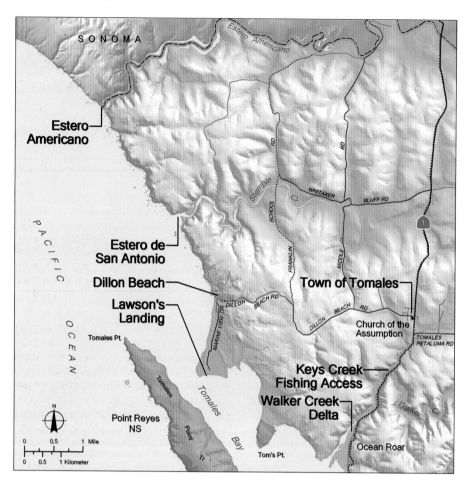

Dillon Beach

Tomales / Dillon Beach

	Sandy Beach	Rocky Shore	Trail	Visitor Center	Campground	Wildlife Viewing	Fishing or Boating	Facilities for Disabled	Food and Drink	Restrooms	Parking	Fee
Estero Americano												
Estero de San Antonio												
Dillon Beach	•	•					•		•	•	•	
Lawson's Landing	•				•	•	•		•	•	•	
Town of Tomales							•		•	•	•	
Keys Creek Fishing Access							•			•	•	
Walker Creek Delta						•						

ESTERO AMERICANO: *Off Hwy. One, 9 mi. N.W. of Tomales.* Americano Creek winds through rolling coastal hills, forming the fjord-like Estero Americano. The creek lies in a "drowned valley," the term for an area gradually flooded by a relative rise in sea level. The change in sea level came about either through an actual rise of ocean waters as glaciers melted and sea water warmed after the last Pleistocene Ice Age, through the land's subsidence, or through a combination of these factors. The estero is a shallow body of mixed salt and fresh water; the saltwater influence extends up to three miles inland. In summer, reduced freshwater flow allows a sandbar to build, blocking the mouth of the estero and creating heightened salinity behind the bar. The long, narrow configuration of the estero is unusual among California estuaries.

ESTERO DE SAN ANTONIO: *Off Hwy. One, 5 mi. N.W. of Tomales.* The Estero de San Antonio, lying in the drowned valley of Stemple Creek, is a long, narrow estuary similar in form to the Estero Americano. Wading birds feed and rest here. Waterfowl such as pintails, American wigeons, canvasbacks, and ruddy ducks can be found here, but generally in smaller numbers than at the neigh-

Estero Americano

Estero de San Antonio

boring Estero Americano, which has greater open water area. Western pond turtles commonly bask in the sun along the margins of the Estero de San Antonio. There is no public access to the estero, which is surrounded by private land, but the upper end of the estero may be seen from Whitaker Bluff Road.

DILLON BEACH: *End of Dillon Beach Rd., 4.1 mi. W. of Tomales.* Rows of modest cottages dating from the 1920s line the narrow streets of this resort community. Day use of the privately owned sandy beach is available for a fee. Clinging to the rocks at the north end of the beach is a rich assortment of intertidal species, such as sea palms, sea anemones, California mussels, goose barnacles, and ochre sea stars. Picnicking, crabbing, clamming, and fishing are popular; leashed dogs allowed on beach. Call: 707-878-2094.

LAWSON'S LANDING: *5 mi. W. of Tomales, off Hwy. One, S.W. of Dillon Beach.* Take the road south from Dillon Beach through sand dunes, some of which are 150 feet high, to this privately operated resort on a wide sandy beach at the mouth of Tomales Bay. Beach

sagewort plants may be seen among the dunes, harbor seals haul out on the sandy shore, and tule elk may be seen on Tomales Point across the narrow bay. Picnic tables, fire rings, and trailer and tent camping are available in meadows surrounded by sand dunes; call ahead in wet weather, when the campground may be closed. RV dump stations available. Dogs allowed on leash. Car day-use and camping fees apply.

Boating facilities include self-launch, launching service by tractor, boat rentals, fuel, and repairs. Popular area for gaper clamming. Pier fishing for perch, smelt, and crabs during daylight hours, usually February through October. Salmon and halibut fishing are generally best from mid-June through August. The boathouse offers bait and tackle, propane, firewood, and fishing licenses; open limited hours during December and January. Call: 707-878-2443.

TOWN OF TOMALES: *Hwy. One, 4.5 mi. S. of the Sonoma County line.* The village of Tomales was once an ocean port and one of Marin County's most important towns.

The first European settler was an Irishman named John Keys, who, beginning in 1850, built a house and store. Other businesses followed, along with a line of warehouses, which served the ships that carried butter, hogs, beef, and potatoes down Keys Creek to Tomales Bay and thence to San Francisco. Within 20 years the creek bed had silted in, and ships could sail no closer to Tomales than Ocean Roar at the mouth of Keys Creek. When the North Pacific Coast Railroad reached Tomales in 1875, linking the area to the rail-ferry wharf in Sausalito, transportation of farm produce was greatly improved. A number of 19th century structures remain near the intersection of Main St. and Dillon Beach Road. The Church of the Assumption, located just south of the present business section, was built in 1860 and restored after the 1906 earthquake.

KEYS CREEK FISHING ACCESS: *Milepost 44.07 on Hwy. One, 1.6 mi. S.W. of Tomales.* This small public fishing access area has picnic tables and restrooms. A trail leads from the almost-hidden gravel parking lot down to the bank of Keys Creek, where coho salmon and steelhead are caught from late fall until spring.

WALKER CREEK DELTA: *2 mi. S. of Tomales, W. of Hwy. One.* Walker Creek with its tributary, Keys Creek, is the second largest of the streams feeding Tomales Bay. Although its flow is reduced by siltation, the stream still supports runs of coho salmon and steelhead, and efforts have been made by land managers to improve the habitat for fish. The Walker Creek delta includes over 100 acres of marsh and mudflats where salt marsh plants predominate. Shorebirds use the marsh, including whimbrels, short-billed dowitchers, and occasional long-billed curlews. The delta is managed by Audubon Canyon Ranch, a land preservation and education organization, and access to the marsh is reserved primarily for educational and scientific purposes and is by appointment only; for infor-

Town of Tomales

The San Andreas Fault zone, visible in the linear form of Tomales Bay (looking southeast)

San Andreas Fault

THE SAN ANDREAS FAULT, perhaps the most famous fault in the world, slices through California from the Gulf of California to Cape Mendocino. North of Pacifica, the fault runs along the coast, intermittently passing on and offshore, between Bolinas Lagoon and Shelter Cove. The fault separates rocks of the Pacific Plate on the west from rocks of the North American Plate to the east. The Pacific Plate is sliding northward along the fault at the rate of about two inches per year, although most of the motion occurs suddenly during major earthquakes that occur at intervals of about 400 years. For example, the Pacific Plate lurched 24 feet to the north in the Olema area during the 1906 San Francisco Earthquake, offsetting fences, opening cracks in the ground, and shaking the earth sufficiently to level much of San Francisco.

The fault has left its mark on coastal geography. The rocks near the fault are highly fractured and sheared as a result of hundreds of such earthquakes, repeated over geologic time since the fault first became active about 30 million years ago. These fractured rocks are eroded more easily than the more coherent rocks away from the fault, and for this reason the trace of the fault is often marked by long, linear valleys that cut across the land. Tomales Bay is one such valley, in this case flooded by the sea.

The Point Reyes area is an excellent place to observe the San Andreas Fault. The fault trace is readily visible not just at Tomales Bay, but also as the long valley running between Point Reyes Station and Stinson Beach, along Highway One. The Earthquake Trail, a half-mile-long paved loop that starts at the Bear Valley headquarters of Point Reyes National Seashore, lets you observe the fault up close. The trail's many interpretive panels describe the geology of the area and explain how the fault has shaped the landscape.

Offset fence at Olema after 1906 earthquake

View from San Francisco Bay toward Ferry Building and City burning after 1906 earthquake

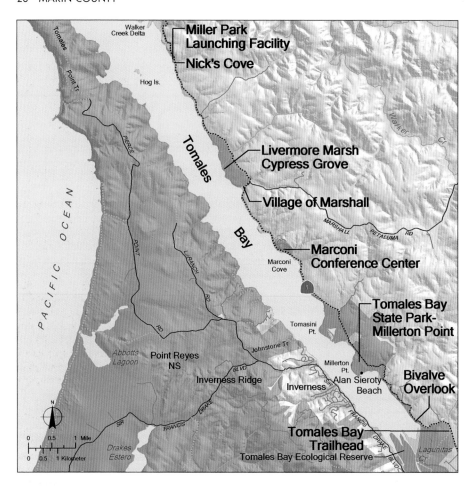

Village of Marshall

Tomales Bay/East Shore

	Sandy Beach	Rocky Shore	Trail	Visitor Center	Campground	Wildlife Viewing	Fishing or Boating	Facilities for Disabled	Food and Drink	Restrooms	Parking	Fee
Tomales Bay	•	•				•	•	•	•	•	•	
Miller Park Launching Facility							•	•	•	•	•	•
Nick's Cove						•	•		•	•	•	
Livermore Marsh/Cypress Grove						•						
Village of Marshall							•		•	•	•	
Marconi Conference Center							•		•	•	•	•
Tomales Bay State Park–Millerton Point	•	•				•	•			•	•	
Bivalve Overlook						•				•		
Tomales Bay Trailhead			•			•				•		

TOMALES BAY: *N.W. of Point Reyes Station.* When Spaniard Sebastián Vizcaíno sailed homeward from Cape Mendocino on a voyage of exploration in 1603, he mistook the mouth of Tomales Bay for the outlet of a great river and named it Río Grande de San Sebastián. It was not until 1793 that another Spaniard, Captain Juan Matute, scouted the interior of the bay, where he was greeted by peaceful Miwok Indians who lived in shoreline settlements.

The bay is 13 miles long, one mile wide, and very shallow; the south end is less than ten feet deep, and wide expanses of mudflats are exposed at low tide. The bay is fed not by a great river, but rather by small streams, of which Walker/Keys Creek, Lagunitas Creek, and Olema Creek are the largest. The amount of fresh water entering the bay is modest, and the bay is not a true estuary, where substantial mixing of fresh water and salt water takes place. Localized estuarine conditions do exist at scattered points along the shoreline, however, and both salt and freshwater marshes are found here.

Nearly 100 species of water-associated birds have been identified at Tomales Bay. Shorebirds commonly seen include marbled godwits, black turnstones, and willets. Waterfowl seen include surf scoters, buffleheads, and ruddy ducks. Great egrets wade in shallow bay waters in search of fish.

Tomales Bay

Oyster farming began in California following the Gold Rush, when prospectors from the East Coast craved the shellfish from home. They tried the native oyster, the Olympia oyster (*Ostrea conchaphila*, also called *Ostrea lurida*) that local Native Americans ate, but these were smaller and more strongly flavored than the ones that were familiar to them. So entrepreneurs began importing live oysters and transplanting many of them into shallow water around San Francisco Bay, keeping and growing them until they were ready to eat.

These oyster beds were a temptation to oyster pirates—enterprising poachers who would steal oysters being farmed and then sell them to an appreciative public for below market prices, which were high due to a monopoly in the oyster-growing business. In the early 1890s before he became a renowned author, Jack London was first an oyster pirate and later a patrolman hired to catch oyster thieves. He wrote about oyster theft in several stories, including *John Barleycorn*: "There it was," says the narrator, "the smack and slap of the spirit of revolt, of adventure, of romance, of the things forbidden done defiantly and grandly. . . . To-morrow I would be an oyster pirate, as free a freebooter as the century and the waters of San Francisco Bay would permit."

Once very plentiful, native oysters declined in number in the first part of the 20th century, likely due to pollution and increased sediment in the water, overharvesting, and perhaps the arrival of the Atlantic oyster drill, a non-native predator. Some environmental groups are working to restore reefs of native oysters, because they provide habitat for fish and shellfish (whose abundance also helps the birds and mammals that eat them) and improve water quality through their filtering actions. Clearer water, in turn, promotes the growth of aquatic plants including native eelgrass, which also supports a wide food web and serves as a nursery for herring and other young marine life.

Today, Marin County ranks second in California behind Humboldt Bay in the production of oysters. In Tomales Bay, seed oysters are imported from the Pacific Northwest and East Coast because local waters are too cold for the non-native varieties (Pacific, Eastern, and Kumamoto oysters) to reproduce naturally. The seed oysters are suspended from racks, where they grow to harvestable size. Rows of racks are visible at low tide at several points along the east shore of the bay, and oysters are offered for sale along Highway One.

Oysters in production in Marin county include (from top to bottom) Eastern, Pacific, and Kumamoto oysters.

MILLER PARK LAUNCHING FACILITY: *Hwy. One, 3.6 mi. N. of Marshall.* This county park has a pier, jetty, concrete boat launch ramp, paved parking, and restrooms. The park offers fishing in Tomales Bay or picnicking in a grove of trees overlooking Hog Island and Inverness Ridge. Fee for parking.

NICK'S COVE: *Hwy. One, 3.6 mi. N. of Marshall.* A restaurant and inn occupy historic buildings on the Tomales Bay shoreline; there is public access to the pier during business hours.

LIVERMORE MARSH / CYPRESS GROVE: *Marshall-Petaluma Rd., Hwy. One intersection.* The marsh is managed by Audubon Canyon Ranch, a land preservation and education organization. Access is reserved primarily for educational and scientific purposes and is by appointment only; for information, call: 415-663-8203.

VILLAGE OF MARSHALL: *Hwy. One, 10 mi. N. of Point Reyes Station.* In the 19th century, this was an important transfer point between ocean-going schooners and the North Pacific Coast Railroad, which ran along Tomales Bay. Today Hwy. One occupies the old railroad right-of-way at Marshall. Commercial and recreational fishing continues in the area; boat repair and service facilities are located just south of town. Kayak rentals and instruction are available at Blue Waters Kayaking at 19225 Shoreline Hwy. in Marshall; call 415-669-2600.

MARCONI CONFERENCE CENTER: *E. of Hwy. One, 1 mi. S. of Marshall.* A Miwok Indian village once occupied the cove at Marconi. The 28-room Marconi Hotel was built in 1913 by the Marconi Wireless Company in the style of an Italianate villa to house workers at what was the first transpacific radio transmission facility. Only a year before, the prompt rescue of survivors of the wreck of the Titanic in the North Atlantic Ocean had been made possible by Marconi's application of the new technology of wireless communication to marine transportation. Radio equipment at the Marconi site included a mile-long antenna held aloft by 270-foot-high towers; both international and ship-to-shore communications were conducted at the site. In 1929, Radio Corporation of America moved parts of the radio operation to a site on the Point Reyes Peninsula that was better suited to the new shortwave radio technology, and radio operations at Marconi ceased in 1939.

On the blufftop above the cove at Marconi, the site of the old Marconi Hotel is now a state park, used as a conference center. Use for meetings and conferences is available for groups, by reservation only. Overnight accommodations are also offered, on a space-available basis, to travelers not attending a conference; reservations are taken three days in advance. Call: 415-663-9020.

TOMALES BAY STATE PARK–MILLERTON POINT: *Hwy. One, 5.4 mi. N. of Pt. Reyes Station.* This unit of Tomales Bay State Park juts into Tomales Bay opposite the village of Inverness. Walk to the point for views of the bay as well as across the water to forested Inverness Ridge. A small salt marsh borders the beach, known as Alan Sieroty Beach, near an osprey platform built to encourage nesting. Near the gravel parking area are picnic tables, grills, and restrooms that are wheelchair accessible with assistance. Dogs on leash allowed only on the fire road running on high ground from the parking lot. Tomasini Point, which is undeveloped state park property, is located one mile to the north of Millerton Point. An opening in the fence at Tomasini Point allows pedestrian access to a trail running down to the shore of the bay; no dogs allowed. For information, call: 415-669-1140.

BIVALVE OVERLOOK: *Milepost 31.50 on Hwy. One, 3.2 mi. N. of Pt. Reyes Station.* A fine view of the southern end of Tomales Bay is available from a gravel pull-out along Hwy. One. The site is known as "Bivalve" from the days when it was a stop on the North Pacific Coast Railroad which operated along the shore of Tomales Bay. The railroad's original embankment can be seen cutting diagonally across the marsh.

TOMALES BAY TRAILHEAD: *Edge of Tomales Bay Ecological Reserve, 2.2 mi. N. of Pt. Reyes Station.* A trail leads from Hwy. One to the southern tip of Tomales Bay at the edge of the Tomales Bay Ecological Reserve. Small gravel parking lot.

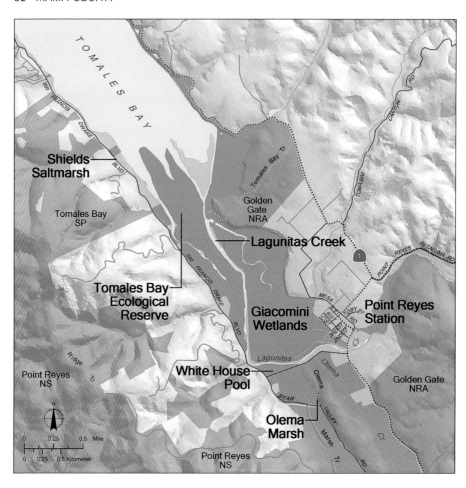

Point Reyes Station

Point Reyes Station

	Sandy Beach	Rocky Shore	Trail	Visitor Center	Campground	Wildlife Viewing	Fishing or Boating	Facilities for Disabled	Food and Drink	Restrooms	Parking	Fee
Lagunitas Creek						•						
Point Reyes Station							•		•	•	•	
Giacomini Wetlands		•				•						
Olema Marsh		•				•				•		
White House Pool		•				•	•	•		•	•	
Tomales Bay Ecological Reserve		•				•	•					
Shields Saltmarsh						•					•	

LAGUNITAS CREEK: *Hwy. One at Pt. Reyes Station.* Lagunitas Creek, also called Paper Mill Creek, drains the northern slopes of Mount Tamalpais and flows through redwood forest and riparian woodland before entering the south end of Tomales Bay. Lagunitas Creek is the largest of the streams feeding Tomales Bay. Its significance for salmon and steelhead trout, which return to deposit eggs on the gravelly bottom of the stream, far outweighs the modest scale of Lagunitas Creek. Fishery experts estimate that, historically, some 4,000 adult coho salmon swam up the creek and its tributaries to spawn. The number of returning salmon dropped by 1998 to perhaps 250, recovered in the following few years to more than 2,000, then plummeted by 2009 to only a few dozen. As of 2010, twenty-one dams within the watershed blocked salmon migration. Drought and barriers such as road crossings jeopardize the coho salmon population. The National Marine Fisheries Service has prepared a Coho Recovery Plan that sets a target for returning fish of 2,600 adults per year. The Salmon Protection and Watershed Network, or SPAWN, carries out environmental education and habitat restoration programs; for information, call: 415-663-8590. Lagunitas Creek is also habitat for the endangered California freshwater shrimp, which live only in a few creeks in Marin, Sonoma, and Napa Counties.

POINT REYES STATION: *Hwy. One at Pt. Reyes–Petaluma Rd.* Point Reyes Station was originally a stop on the North Pacific Coast Railroad, which linked Sausalito in southern Marin County to northern Marin and Sonoma Counties. In 1875 the line reached the town of Tomales, and by 1877 it extended north to the lumber mills on the Russian River. Southeast of Point Reyes Station, the tracks (originally narrow-gauge) ran through dense redwood forest along Lagunitas Creek; north of town the tracks ran mostly on a trestle along the eastern shore of Tomales Bay. The railroad hauled lumber, farm produce, commuters, and weekend sightseers on trips that were not without their mishaps; more than one locomotive left the tracks and landed in the creek or upside down in the bay mud.

The townsite of Point Reyes Station was laid out in 1883, and the town grew up around the railroad station. Many early immigrants

Point Reyes Station, The Western Hotel

Lagunitas Creek tributary

came from northern Italy or Italian-speaking Switzerland, and the names of local geographical features and dairies reflect this heritage. Buildings on the south side of "A" Street (Hwy. One) date from around the turn of the century, including the red brick Mission Revival–style Grandi Building at the corner of 2nd Street. After train service to Point Reyes Station ceased in 1933, commercial structures were built on the north side of "A" Street on the former railroad right-of-way; the old depot now serves as the post office. Other buildings in town are named for their original functions: the Old Creamery Building, the Livery Stable, the Hay Barn. Today, Point Reyes Station is the commercial center of west Marin, with a bank, grocery store, and hardware store, as well as restaurants, galleries, and gift shops. Public restrooms and children's play equipment are on Mesa Rd. at Toby St.

GIACOMINI WETLANDS: *W. of Point Reyes Station.* A substantial historic marsh at the south end of Tomales Bay was once diked off for grazing land as part of the former Giacomini Ranch. The property was acquired

by the National Park Service in 2000, and wetland restoration began in 2007. Restoration is occurring on some 560 acres of formerly diked pastures, an amount equivalent to more than ten percent of central California's lost coastal wetlands. Anticipated benefits include the capture of significant amounts of sediment, thus improving the quality of water in Tomales Bay; improved passage for coho salmon that return to spawn in streams feeding Tomales Bay; and increased diversity of birds that depend on marshes, such as the rarely seen California black rail. Long-term monitoring of the restoration project's effects will take place, and adjustments to the project may take place if required. Spur trails that overlook the restored wetlands begin at 3rd and C Streets in Point Reyes Station. For information on public field seminars and volunteer work days, call: 415-464-5227.

OLEMA MARSH: *Sir Francis Drake Blvd. and Bear Valley Rd. intersection, S.E. corner.* This 40-acre wetland, the largest of the freshwater marshes around the edge of Tomales Bay, is formed by Olema Creek upstream from its junction with Lagunitas Creek. The marsh is bordered by dense willow thickets, and public entry is not permitted, but many birds may be seen from the roadside along Sir Francis Drake Blvd. or from a small parking area off Bear Valley Rd. Over 150 species of birds have been observed, including the yellow warbler, the Virginia rail, and the sora, an uncommon relative of the rail. Kingfishers and red-winged blackbirds are common among the cattails, and during fall and winter migratory water birds including American coots use the marsh. Western pond turtles are found in abundance. The marsh is part of the Point Reyes National Seashore; no facilities.

WHITE HOUSE POOL: *Sir Francis Drake Blvd. and Bear Valley Rd. intersection, N.E. corner.* White House Pool is a public fishing access point near the junction of Lagunitas and Olema Creeks. Good birding opportunities among the willow thickets along the creeks.

TOMALES BAY ECOLOGICAL RESERVE: *Southern portion of Tomales Bay.* A large wetland and marsh complex is found at the shallow southern end of Tomales Bay where Lagunitas Creek enters the bay. Some 500 acres of wetlands are included in the Ecological Reserve managed by the Department of Fish and Game. Waterfowl hunting and fishing are permitted in the reserve with a valid hunting or fishing license; for more information, call: 707-944-5500. Pedestrian access to the reserve from White House Pool parking lot; walk north along the levee. The land area is closed from March 1 through June 30 to protect nesting birds; fishing access from Shoreline Hwy. on the east side of the bay is open all year.

SHIELDS SALTMARSH: *Sir Francis Drake Blvd., 3 mi. N. of Pt. Reyes Station.* Views of the marsh are available from an overlook with a bench and interpretive displays. Bring field glasses to spot distant birds or wildlife across the grassy plain. Limited parking in roadside pull-out. The area is managed by Audubon Canyon Ranch, an organization devoted to preservation, research, and education with wildlife reserves near Bolinas Lagoon and elsewhere; call: 415-663-8203.

Tomales Bay Ecological Reserve

Mosses, Fungi, and Lichens

MOSSES, FUNGI, AND LICHENS are remarkable groups of organisms often overlooked because they tend to be small and to occupy ecosystem "nooks and crannies." Typically, mosses are found in moist pockets, fungi are below ground just puncturing the surface, and lichens are on bare rock or branches. Mosses are primitive plants in the Kingdom Plantae. Fungi are different from both plants and animals, warranting their own Kingdom, the Fungi. And lichens are a combination of two Kingdoms: Plantae and Fungi. All three groups are found throughout the world.

Mosses are the most common members of the Division Bryophyta, which also includes hornworts and liverworts. Fossil evidence indicates that bryophytes are among the earliest plants. Bryophytes do not have flowers or fruits; instead of producing seeds, they reproduce by single-celled spores. Unlike the majority of plants, bryophytes lack a system of vascular tissue (the xylem and phloem found in roots, stems, and leaves) for transporting fluids. Bryophytes generally have wider geographic ranges than vascular plants, and they grow on a wide variety of substrates, including exposed soil, rocks, and trees; some are completely aquatic. Extreme environments, such as mountain tops, arctic and Antarctic tundra, and deserts, are home to certain bryophytes. Because they lack woody tissue for support, most of them are quite small.

All plants have life cycles with an alternation of generations between a diploid sporophyte form (containing a full set of genes) and a haploid gametophyte (half the genes), but bryophytes are the only plants that have a dominant gametophyte generation. The sporophytes grow attached to the gametophytes and are dependent on them for taking in water and other materials. Hornworts get their name from an elongated horn-like structure, which is the sporophyte. The flattened, green plant body of a hornwort is the gametophyte plant. Mosses have an erect shoot that bears tiny leaf-like structures arranged in spirals. Liverworts are typically less than three inches in diameter and have a leathery body that grows flat on moist soil, or, in some cases, the surface of still water.

Remarkably, molecular studies of cells indicate that animals, not plants, are the closest relatives of fungi; fungal cells have more in common with our cells than with plant cells. Fungi, including the yeasts and molds, hold a unique ecological role as decomposers; fungi digest food outside of their body by secreting powerful enzymes called exoenzymes. Scientists estimate that there are roughly one and a half million species of fungi, and we can thank fungi for the bread and beer we enjoy, the ability to recycle trash, and the capability of plants to extract nutrients from soil. Most fungi are constructed of tiny filaments called hyphae that enable them to absorb food digested outside of their body. Hyphae form an interwoven mat called a mycelium. The familiar mushroom cap is the reproductive part of the fungus where spores are formed.

Lichens are actually two organisms in one, the result of a symbiotic relationship between fungi and algae (more rarely, cyanobacteria) which each carry out functions that the other could not provide on its own. "Alice algae took a lichen to Freddie fungus" is a mnemonic for remembering the nature of lichens. The fungal hyphae form most of the lichen tissue and provide the algae with a place to live; algae, in turn, provide the fungus with food. Lichens live in places where neither fungi nor algae could live alone, and over 25,000 species have been described to date. Some lichens are thousands of years old and are among the oldest organisms on earth. Lichens are important pioneers on newly cleared rock and soil surfaces, such as burned forests and volcanic flows. Lichens absorb most of the minerals they need either from dust in the air or from rain.

The **scented liverwort** (*Conocephalum conicum*) is a "thallose" (leaf-lacking) liverwort that gets its common name because when it is crushed it exudes a faint sweet scent. *C. conicum* is very common and can be found along stream banks and forest floors throughout the Northern Hemisphere. It can be identified by its flattened and spotted plant body. *C. conicum* is "dioecious," meaning that male and female gametes are borne on separate plants; the male receptacles are sessile, or stalkless, and slightly purple, and the female receptacles are like tiny umbrellas, sometimes reaching lengths of four inches. *C. conicum* grows well in a terrarium when provided with moist, well shaded soil.

Scented liverwort

The **black morel** (*Morchella elata*) is an edible mushroom that is considered a delicacy by many fungal enthusiasts. One of the easiest ways to enjoy morels is by gently sautéing them in butter and then sprinkling them with salt and pepper. Morels can be found along the coast in early spring in coniferous woodlands in disturbed areas including campgrounds, road edges, and recently logged areas. They are often found in large numbers following forest fires. The black morel is recognized by its dark, ridged and pitted, conical-shaped cap and its creamy-white stipe, or stalk-like structure. The morel has many nicknames, of which one of the more interesting is "dryland fish," because when it is cut lengthwise, breaded, and fried, it looks like a fish.

Black morel

Caloplaca coralloides is a species of lichen that lives in the upper intertidal zone. It is classified as a marine lichen because it is restricted to the seashore and is directly influenced by spray or waves. It ranges from Baja California to Oregon and can be found at Hopkins Marine Station growing on exposed surfaces of granitic rocks. Salt spray is the main factor that influences where marine lichens live within the intertidal zone; another important factor is light exposure. *C. coralloides* contains the pigment parietin, which functions as a sunscreen and enables *C. coralloides* to withstand high light exposure. Parietin absorbs high-frequency light waves in the blue and ultraviolet range; the fact that *C. coralloides* is orange makes sense, because these are the light waves it reflects.

Caloplaca coralloides

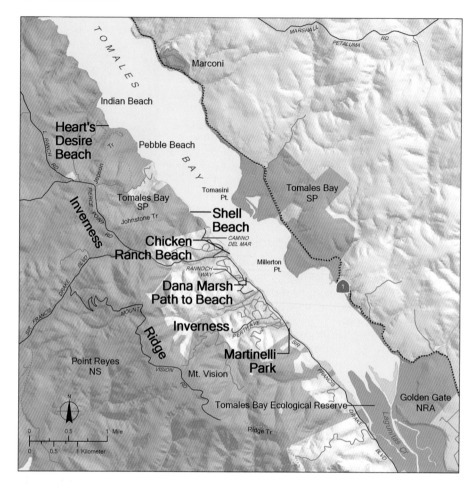

Tomales Bay near Inverness

Tomales Bay/ West Shore

	Sandy Beach	Rocky Shore	Trail	Visitor Center	Campground	Wildlife Viewing	Fishing or Boating	Facilities for Disabled	Food and Drink	Restrooms	Parking	Fee
Martinelli Park						•			•	•		
Inverness							•	•	•	•	•	
Dana Marsh / Path to Beach	•					•						
Chicken Ranch Beach	•					•				•	•	
Inverness Ridge			•									
Shell Beach	•	•								•	•	
Heart's Desire Beach (Tomales Bay State Park)	•	•				•	•			•	•	•

MARTINELLI PARK: *Sir Francis Drake Blvd., Inverness.* A small park adjacent to Tomales Bay with fine views of the water and forested ridge.

INVERNESS: *Sir Francis Drake Blvd., 3.1 mi. N. of Bear Valley Road.* Originally a summer resort on the wooded slopes of Inverness Ridge overlooking the waters of Tomales Bay, Inverness is now both a year-round and seasonal community. The village offers several points of public access to the shore of the bay, along with overnight accommodations and a handful of eating establishments.

DANA MARSH / PATH TO BEACH: *Sir Francis Drake Blvd., .25 mi. N. of Inverness.* Dana Marsh is a small restored wetland adjacent to Tomales Bay. There is an unpaved path to a small bay beach, accessible from Sir Francis Drake Blvd. at the foot of Rannoch Way. Adjacent private property; do not trespass.

CHICKEN RANCH BEACH: *Sir Francis Drake Blvd., .5 mi. N. of Inverness.* This small sandy beach on Tomales Bay is reached via a bridge over a creek. There is limited street parking; chemical toilet, not wheelchair accessible.

INVERNESS RIDGE: *W. of Tomales Bay.* The steep, forested Inverness Ridge that runs parallel to the drowned rift valley of the San Andreas Fault beneath Tomales Bay presents a sharp contrast to the rolling grassy hills on the east side of the bay. The highest point on Inverness Ridge is Mount Wittenberg, elevation 1,407 feet, located southwest of Point Reyes Station. A dense canopy of Douglas-fir covers the southern end of Inverness Ridge, while bishop pine grows on the northern end.

Inverness

Forest near Shell Beach

Near the point where Sir Francis Drake Blvd. crosses the crest of the ridge is a dwarf bishop pine forest where severely acidic soils cause stunting; the trees here, however, are not as dwarfed as those in the Mendocino pygmy forest. Found in association with the bishop pine forest on Inverness Ridge is the rare Mount Vision ceanothus; this is the only known location for this species of plant. The forest on Inverness Ridge harbors the southernmost colony in the coastal range of the native mountain beaver, an elusive, cat-sized, nocturnal rodent. Ospreys nest in snags on the ridge, and blue Steller's jays are abundant. Pygmy nuthatches may be seen among the trees, and king bolete mushrooms may be found here. Much of the bay side of Inverness Ridge is privately owned; Point Reyes National Seashore and units of Tomales Bay State Park compose the rest.

An undeveloped unit of Tomales Bay State Park is located on the ridge above Inverness.

Starting from the top of Perth Ave., there are hiking trails through the forest that connect to Mount Vision in the Point Reyes National Seashore. Check at the Heart's Desire park headquarters for more information, or call: 415-669-1140.

SHELL BEACH: *End of Camino del Mar, off Sir Francis Drake Blvd., 1 mi. N. of Inverness.* This small unit of Tomales Bay State Park includes a sandy curve of bay beach at the base of a hillside cloaked with dense bishop pine forest. The quarter-mile-long trail from the parking lot winds downhill through trees festooned with moss and surrounded by ferns and huckleberry. Bright orange lichens cover the north-facing boulders along the beach, and heart cockles inhabit the sand. Day use only; dogs are not allowed on the beach. From Shell Beach, the 4.3-mile-long Johnstone Trail leads north through the forest to the Heart's Desire Beach unit of Tomales Bay State Park.

HEART'S DESIRE BEACH: *Pierce Point Rd., 2 mi. N. of Inverness*. This is the main facility of Tomales Bay State Park. Heart's Desire Beach is popular for picnicking, clamming, and boating. The beach is sandy and gently sloping, and the shallow bay waters invite swimming. Nearby are picnic tables and restrooms with running water. A separate larger picnic area including several group sites and offering fine filtered views of Tomales Bay through the pine trees is located at the vista point, a few hundred yards south of Heart's Desire. Dogs on leash are allowed in the vista point picnic area, but not on trails or at the beach. No camping allowed.

Several short to moderate hiking trails start at Heart's Desire. A half-mile-long nature trail starts at the north side of the cove and leads north through bishop pine and oak forest to Indian Beach. Along the path are interpretive signs explaining the uses of plants such as coffeeberry, bracken fern, and poison oak by the Coast Miwok people who once lived in small villages along this shoreline. On Indian Beach are replicas of Miwok houses. From the south side of Heart's Desire Beach, the Johnstone Trail leads 4.3 miles to Shell Beach, along the way passing small secluded Pebble Beach and the Jepson Trail, which winds through a particularly fine stand of virgin bishop pine. The forest along the trails is fragrant with California bay and pine, and huckleberry and thimbleberry crowd the path. Animals that inhabit the area include foxes, raccoons, badgers, weasels, squirrels, rabbits, deer, bobcats, and gopher and garter snakes. Birds include chestnut-backed chickadees, goldfinches, and woodpeckers, and monarch butterflies may be found here.

Heart's Desire Beach

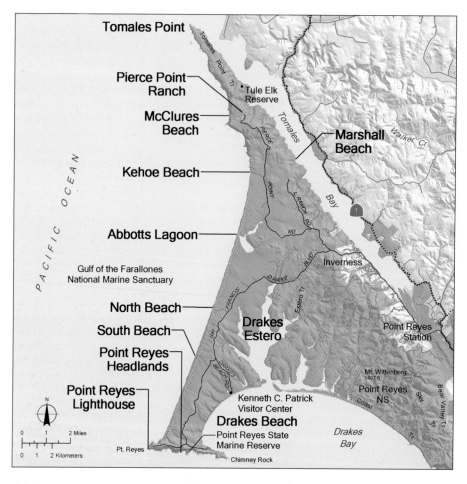

Tomales Point

Pierce Point Ranch

Tule Elk Reserve

McClures Beach

Marshall Beach

Kehoe Beach

Abbotts Lagoon

PACIFIC OCEAN

Gulf of the Farallones National Marine Sanctuary

Inverness

North Beach

South Beach

Drakes Estero

Point Reyes Headlands

Point Reyes Station

Mt. Wittenberg 1407 ft

Point Reyes NS

Point Reyes Lighthouse

Kenneth C. Patrick Visitor Center

Drakes Beach

Point Reyes State Marine Reserve

Drakes Bay

Pt. Reyes

Chimney Rock

Tomales Point Tr.

PIERCE POINT RD

L RANCH RD

RD

Tomales Bay

Walker Cr

BLVD

DRAKE

Estero Tr

SIR FRANCIS

DRAKES BEACH RD

Coast

Sky Tr

Bear Valley Tr

Tr

N

0   1   2 Miles

0   1   2 Kilometers

Point Reyes National Seashore Tule Elk Reserve, Tomales Point

Tomales Point to Point Reyes Lighthouse

	Sandy Beach	Rocky Shore	Trail	Visitor Center	Campground	Wildlife Viewing	Fishing or Boating	Facilities for Disabled	Food and Drink	Restrooms	Parking	Fee
Marshall Beach	•		•			•				•	•	
Tomales Point / Pierce Point Ranch	•	•	•			•	•			•	•	
McClures Beach	•	•	•			•	•			•	•	
Kehoe Beach	•		•			•	•			•	•	
Abbotts Lagoon	•		•			•	•	•		•	•	
Drakes Estero			•			•	•			•	•	
North Beach and South Beach	•						•			•	•	
Point Reyes Headlands		•	•				•			•	•	
Point Reyes Lighthouse		•	•	•		•	•			•	•	
Drakes Beach	•		•				•		•	•	•	

MARSHALL BEACH: *"L" Ranch Rd., off Pierce Point Rd., 1.3 mi. N. of Sir Francis Drake Blvd. junction.* A steep trail leads to this Tomales Bay beach, which is part of Point Reyes National Seashore. Small dirt parking lot; restrooms available.

TOMALES POINT / PIERCE POINT RANCH: *End of Pierce Point Rd., 7 mi. N. of Inverness.* Pierce Point Rd. winds north through the hills from Sir Francis Drake Blvd., past historic dairy ranches established in the 1860s. The road climbs in elevation toward the end, offering water views that alternate between Tomales Bay and the ocean. At the end of the road is a cluster of buildings from the historic Pierce Point Ranch, preserved by the National Park Service but no longer in operation as a dairy. In the 19th century, each cow in the Pierce Ranch's herd typically produced one pound of butter per day, for shipment via schooner to San Francisco and other points in California. Visitor facilities at Pierce Ranch include a self-guided trail with

Pierce Point Ranch

McClures Beach

interpretive signs about the history of the ranch and the buildings.

The northern four miles of Tomales Point, including the Pierce Point Ranch buildings, are within the National Seashore's Tule Elk Reserve. The reserve was created in 1978 to restore to the elk some of the habitat originally theirs before the introduction of dairy farming on the peninsula. Some 3,000 acres are available for the elk to roam; they may be seen year-round. Tule elk share the Point Reyes Peninsula with native black-tailed deer. A three-mile-long trail leads from the parking area at Pierce Ranch through grasslands inhabited by badgers and California voles to the north end of Tomales Point, with striking views of Tomales and Bodega Bays and the ocean; no beach access.

MCCLURES BEACH: *End of Pierce Point Rd., 9 mi. N. of Inverness.* Exposed to the full force of storms and waves rolling in off the open ocean, this is one of the most dramatic sections of the Marin coast; it is also extremely unsafe for swimming. Backed by steep bluffs, the beach is a broad sandy crescent; portions are covered with rocks smoothed by the surf. A smaller sandy beach to the south is reachable through a cleft in the rocks, at extreme low tides.

Cormorants, brown pelicans, and common murres may often be seen on the granite sea stacks off the south end of the beach, and black oystercatchers may be spotted on the offshore rocks. Surf scoters ride the ocean waves. Red-tailed hawks sometimes hang nearly motionless, riding the wind, above the high bluff backing the beach. Abundant intertidal life, including giant green anemones and ochre sea stars, is found among the rocks on the beach. A steep half-mile-long trail used by hikers and equestrians leads from the parking lot to the beach; dogs are not permitted. In summer, look for sticky monkeyflowers blooming along the trail.

KEHOE BEACH: *Trail off Pierce Point Rd., S. of McClures Beach.* A half-mile-long trail to the beach runs beside Kehoe Marsh, a freshwater pond that supports migratory waterfowl and year-round bird residents. Spring wildflowers include California poppies, baby blue eyes, wild hollyhock, phacelia, and cream cups. Most of the trail is wheelchair negotiable. Restrooms available; parking along road shoulder. Kehoe Beach is nesting habitat for western snowy plovers, a threatened bird species. From about mid-March to early September, the beaches remain open to visitors, although breeding areas may be roped off and dogs are prohibited from near Kehoe Beach south to near the Point Reyes Beach North parking lot; leashed dogs allowed at other times.

ABBOTTS LAGOON: *Off Pierce Point Rd., 3.4 mi. N.W. of Sir Francis Drake Blvd.* An easy 1.5-mile-long trail leads from the parking lot to the lagoon, where hikers may continue to the sand dunes and the beach. Western grebes and pied-billed grebes are frequently sighted in the lagoon; Caspian terns may be seen in the summer. Look also for common yellowthroats. Canoeing is permitted.

DRAKES ESTERO: *Estero Trail off Sir Francis Drake Blvd., 4 mi. W. of Inverness.* This is the largest of the saltwater lagoons along the Marin coast. The shallow estero receives freshwater flow only from small streams; culverts beneath two road crossings were replaced in 2008 to allow native steelhead

trout to migrate upstream to spawn. Broad mudflats are exposed at low tide. Giant geoduck clams live in the mudflats, along with abundant phoronids, or "stringworms." The rocky intertidal area of the estero is inhabited by limpets, sea anemones, ochre sea stars, and several varieties of crabs. The estero harbors rays and leopard sharks and also serves as a nursery for fish such as lingcod. A large harbor seal breeding colony can be seen at Drakes Estero. The mile-long Estero Trail leads downhill from Sir Francis Drake Blvd. to the water's edge.

Aquaculture has been practiced in Drakes Estero for perhaps a century, first by Johnsons Oyster Company and later by Drakes Bay Oyster Company. Pacific oysters have been raised singly or in clusters grown on "mother" oyster shells. Due to excellent water quality, oysters have been harvested year-round, some sold live in their shells and some shucked in containers.

NORTH BEACH AND SOUTH BEACH: *Off Sir Francis Drake Blvd.* This 12-mile-long beach is sandy, windy, and often wild. The surf here is undiminished by offshore reefs or islands, and the horizon seems extra-large. The cold waters do not invite swimming, nor are the currents safe for doing so. Huge breakers pound this windward shore; when strolling, look out for hazardous sneaker waves.

Elephant seals hauled out at Pt. Reyes Headlands

Two main access areas are served by parking lots. In the wide dune field behind the beach are stands of endangered Point Reyes lupine. Dogs on leash and campfires allowed on the beach. North Beach supports nesting snowy plovers during spring and summer, when dogs are prohibited from near the North Beach parking area to near Kehoe Beach; leashed dogs allowed at other times.

POINT REYES HEADLANDS: *End of Sir Francis Drake Blvd., 15 mi. S.W. of Inverness.* The headland extending from the Point Reyes Lighthouse east to Chimney Rock forms a massive granite promontory up to 600 feet high. The submarine topography is similarly steep: depths of 150 feet and more are found close to shore. Along the shoreline at the base of the headland are sea stacks, smooth granite rocks, wave-carved sea caves, and coarse-sand pocket beaches. The variety of surfaces makes the area attractive to many different kinds of clinging plants and invertebrates. The subtidal zone is home to giant green anemones, rose anemones, and red sea urchins. Red abalone fasten to undersea rocks, where they feed on kelp.

Censuses have shown that the headland area is the principal location in the county for breeding birds. Particularly numerous are common murres, thousands of which nest in the summer on the rocks almost directly below the lighthouse, and Brandt's and pelagic cormorants. California sea lions occupy offshore rocks, and there is a breeding colony of Steller sea lions in one of the coves. Since 1981, an elephant seal breeding colony near Chimney Rock has grown to over 1,000 animals; an overlook east of the lighthouse provides views of the animals as they come ashore during the winter breeding period, summer molting period, and at other times. In spring, look for blue-eyed grass and sky lupine blooming in the coastal prairie. The headland and adjoining waters from the lighthouse east to Chimney Rock are within several marine protected areas, where public entry is prohibited and no plants or animals may be taken. The waters off the Point Reyes Peninsula are part of the Gulf of the Farallones National Marine Sanctuary and the adjoining Cordell Bank National Marine Sanctuary.

POINT REYES LIGHTHOUSE: *End of Sir Francis Drake Blvd., 15 mi. S.W. of Inverness.* The tip of the Point Reyes Peninsula, thrusting seaward some 20 miles from the main shoreline and subject to persistent winds and fogs, has been the site of numerous ship-

Point Reyes Lighthouse

Drakes Beach and Kenneth C. Patrick Visitor Center

wrecks. The earliest recorded was in 1595 when the *San Agustín*, a Spanish galleon loaded with cargo from the Philippines and captained by Sebastián Rodríguez Cermeño, went aground in what is now called Drakes Bay. In 1870 the Point Reyes Lighthouse was built on the bluff face 294 feet above sea level. An automated light and foghorn were installed in 1975, although the original lighthouse and Fresnel lens remain. The point receives up to 2,700 hours of fog annually, but it gets relatively little rainfall, less than 20 inches per year.

Gray whales pass near Point Reyes on their annual winter migration south to Baja California, where calving takes place in warm lagoons. Point Reyes is a favorite whale-watching spot between January and early May; prime viewing months are mid-January (southbound animals) and mid-March (northbound), with the last cows and calves heading north from April to early May.

Parking at the lighthouse is limited; during peak whale-watching months, the National Park Service operates a fee shuttle from the Drakes Beach parking area, weekends and holidays only. From the parking area, a half-mile-long paved path leads to the Point

Reyes Light Visitor Center, view platform, and 300-step stairway leading down to the lighthouse. Special parking and drop-off areas and arrangements for visitors with limited mobility are available. Interpretive walks are led through the lighthouse; Visitor Center open Thursday through Monday, 10 AM to 4:30 PM; the stairs are closed when wind and weather conditions warrant. For information, call: 415-669-1534.

DRAKES BEACH: *Drakes Beach Rd., off Sir Francis Drake Blvd.* A popular broad sandy beach with chalk white cliffs; swimming and beach fires permitted. Moon jellies and by-the-wind-sailors sometimes wash ashore here. The Kenneth C. Patrick Visitor Center has interpretive displays and ranger-led walks. Open daily except Wednesday and Thursday during summer months, and open weekends and holidays all year, 10 AM to 5 PM. Facilities include snack bar, picnic tables, and restrooms. Call: 415-669-1250.

Near the visitor center is a monument to English explorer Francis Drake, thought by some historians to have landed near here in 1579. The white cliffs and summer fogs match the descriptions brought back to England by Drake's expedition.

Point Reyes from Double Point, *detail, original print sized 13 x 15 inches* © 2012, Tom Killion

The Ocean

THE OCEAN is the largest reservoir of water on the planet, holding 97 percent of the earth's water and covering over 70 percent of the earth's surface. Of the remaining three percent of water, a little more than two percent is frozen in glaciers and ice caps while less than one percent is fresh. We all know that the ocean is salty, but have you ever wondered why? Most of the ocean's salts, which are dissolved minerals, come from geologic processes. Those processes include the breakdown of rocks by wind and by the process known as "weathering." The resulting mineral particles are swept to sea in streams. Some of the ocean's salts have been dissolved from rocks and sediments on the ocean floor. Still other sources of salts are solid and gaseous materials in the atmosphere and volcanic eruptions.

The most common dissolved salts in the ocean are chloride, sodium, magnesium, sulfur, calcium, and potassium. Sodium chloride (NaCl), or ordinary table salt, is the most abundant substance dissolved in sea water. The presence of salt in the ocean impacts the physical properties of sea water in several ways, including increasing its density, boiling point, electrical conductivity, velocity of sound, and viscosity; and lowering its freezing point. There is so much salt in the ocean that if all of it were dried it would cover the continents to a depth of approximately five feet. Scientists measure the salt content, or salinity, of the ocean in parts per thousand; the symbol for salinity is ‰. Ocean salinity typically ranges between 33‰ and 37‰; a salinity of 33 means that the ocean holds 33 pounds of salt per 1,000 pounds of sea water.

Just as in the terrestrial realm, oxygen is an extremely important element for life in the ocean. As you might imagine, surface waters are well oxygenated. Near the surface, oxygen concentrations are close to that of the earth's atmosphere due to the mixing of air and water and the production of oxygen by phytoplankton through photosynthesis. Oxygen concentration tends to decrease with depth, because oxygen is consumed in the various metabolic processes of plants and animals such as protein synthesis and respiration. The zone where oxygen concentration is at its lowest is called the "oxygen minimum zone," or OMZ. This zone occurs at a depth of about 600 to 3,000 feet, depending on local circumstances. Counter-intuitively, oxygen levels actually increase at water depths below the OMZ. Several factors account for the rise in oxygen concentration below the OMZ: cold water holds more oxygen than warm water; cold, oxygen-rich water at the poles sinks and is the source of deep ocean water; and the rate of oxygen consumption in the deep ocean is low compared to that in surface waters because there is a lot less life in the deep ocean.

In addition to salts and oxygen, many other elements, including gold, silver, copper, and iron, are suspended in sea water. Amazingly, if we could mine all the gold held in the world's oceans, we could give each person on the planet nine pounds.

Temperature, pressure, and acidity (pH), in addition to the substances dissolved in sea water, are physical properties that influence the biological zonation patterns we observe in the ocean. Most organisms are limited to certain areas in the ocean by their tolerance to specific physical factors. For instance, whales and dolphins, seals and sea lions, and turtles are found at a variety of depths throughout the world's oceans and can tolerate a wide range of temperature and pressure. By contrast, phytoplankton, such as diatoms, are found almost exclusively in the ocean photic zone, that is, where light penetrates. The range limits of many invertebrates are determined by their temperature, light, and pressure tolerances, whereas, in general, fish zonation tends to be

more influenced by their habitat preferences, feeding strategies, and predator avoid-
ance adaptations. The temperature of the oceans is highly variable, ranging from less
than 32° Fahrenheit (0° Celsius) at the poles to more than 85° F (29° C) in the tropics.
Sea water remains liquid below the ordinary freezing point of fresh water because of
all the salt it contains. Sea water in Antarctica can be as cold as 28.5° F (-1.9° C), yet
remain liquid. Cold sea water is denser than warm sea water and in certain areas, like
the poles, where surface water becomes very cold, it sinks and initiates the formation of
slow currents called thermohaline currents, which move deep-ocean water throughout
the oceans of the world.

If you were to measure and record the temperature of the ocean at a given location,
from the surface to the bottom (a temperature profile), you would likely find zones
where the temperature changes abruptly; the boundary zone between significantly different temperature layers is called a thermocline. Thermoclines mark the separation
between the mixed layer above, which is influenced by the atmospheric and surface
conditions, and the deep ocean below. In the eastern Pacific off the coast of California,
in those areas not influenced by upwelling, thermocline depth varies with the seasons,
ranging from approximately 150 feet in the summer to over 500 feet in winter. Many
factors influence the presence and depth of thermoclines, including season, latitude,
weather, and phenomena such as the "El Niño Southern Oscillation," a warming of the
ocean current along the coasts of Peru and Ecuador that is generally associated with
dramatic changes in weather patterns around the world.

Like temperature, pressure is another physical feature of the ocean that influences
ocean life. Pressure causes water density to increase, and the boundary zone where
pressure changes are abrupt is called a pycnocline. At the deepest point anywhere in
the oceans, the Mariana Trench off the coast of Japan that is approximately seven miles
deep, the pressure is more than eight tons per square inch, or the equivalent of one
person trying to support the weight of 50 jumbo jets.

Acidity of a solution is indicated by its "pH," a measure on a negative logarithmic scale
of the concentration of hydrogen ions; pH ranges from 1 to 14. Low pH indicates a high
concentration of hydrogen ions (acidic condition), whereas high pH indicates a low
concentration of hydrogen ions (basic condition). The pH of ocean water is naturally
basic and varies from 8.0 to 8.3. Since the beginning of the Industrial Age, the average
pH of the ocean's surface waters has dropped by approximately 0.1 due to human-
caused, carbon dioxide emissions. Because pH is measured on a logarithmic scale, a
drop of 0.1 corresponds to about a 30 percent increase in the concentration of hydrogen
ions in the world's oceans. "Ocean acidification" is the term loosely applied to this phenomenon of elevated hydrogen ion concentration caused by carbon dioxide absorption
in the ocean. Scientific research predicts a further drop in pH of 0.3–0.5 on the scale of 1
to 14 by the end of the 21st century, barring changes in carbon dioxide emissions. This
alteration in ocean chemistry is of great concern, in part, because of impacts to "calcify-
ing" organisms such as corals, coralline algae, shellfish, and pteropods. Formation of
calcium carbonate requires more energy in a low pH ocean and is expected to result
in reduced rates of growth or dissolution of skeletons or shells, leading to important
effects on species growth, survival, and reproduction.

The survival of ocean organisms depends on both natural and anthropogenic phenomena, including geologic processes, climate change, and chemical pollution. While we
do not control natural processes, we can make changes in our lives as individuals and
as members of society to contribute to the survival of ocean life.

The **humpback whale** (*Megaptera novaeangliae*) is a baleen whale that can be seen seasonally off the north-central California coastline. These animals are part of the north Pacific Ocean humpback whale population, one of four distinct regional groups. The humpback whales that visit California's waters undertake one of the longest migrations of any mammal, traveling thousands of miles from summer feeding grounds off Alaska and the Pacific Northwest to winter mating and calving areas in the warmer waters off Mexico and Hawaii. Well known for their "whale songs," all the male humpback whales within the north Pacific Ocean population sing the same unique song, regardless of their particular location. This song slowly changes over the years without repeating and is distinct from that sung by humpbacks from the other three populations.

Humpback whale

The **fin whale** (*Balaenoptera physalus*), is the second largest living animal on the planet. At up to 88 feet long, the fin whale is only slightly smaller than its close relative, the blue whale. Remarkably, these two massive whales feed on some of the ocean's smallest animals, the shrimp-like krill. The fin whale seeks out dense concentrations of this prey to engulf in a single 18,000-gallon gulp and then uses the fine filtering hairs of its baleen to strain out the ocean water. The fin whale is quite speedy for its size, moving at up to 25 miles per hour, and has been known to leap completely out of the water—a good reason to keep your distance when whale watching.

Fin whale

Considered to be the world's largest marine turtle, and one of the largest reptiles, the **leatherback sea turtle** (*Dermochelys coriacea*) has been known to exceed ten feet in length and to weigh more than a ton. The leatherback is the only one of the seven sea turtle species that does not grow a bony outer shell, instead producing the tough leathery skin for which it is named. Long known to be ocean nomads, leatherback turtles have been shown by research using global positioning satellite tags to roam throughout the world's oceans, ranging farther than any other sea turtle and inhabiting both high latitude and tropical waters. Leatherback turtles dive to depths of more than 4,000 feet in search of the jellyfish that are their main food source.

Leatherback sea turtle

Humboldt squid

The **Humboldt squid** (*Dosidicus gigas*) is named for the waters of the Humboldt Current which flows along the western coast of South America. This squid has been observed in recent years in large numbers off California. Reports of Humboldt squid in the area, along with climatic and oceanographic changes, have led scientists at the Monterey Bay Aquarium Research Institute to believe that the Humboldt squid may be undergoing a range expansion. Given that a Humboldt squid is an aggressive predator, consuming small fish, shrimp, and other species of squid, and can reach six feet in length and 110 pounds during its one-to-two year lifespan, the species' expansion could result in a substantial change to the ocean food chain.

Brown pelican

The **Brown pelican** (*Pelecanus occidentalis*) is one of the state's largest marine birds, weighing approximately ten pounds and measuring about four feet from bill to tail with an average wingspan of seven feet. The brown pelican's 12-inch bill and pouch make it unmistakable. These birds can often be observed gliding in single file just above the surface of the ocean or dramatically plunge-diving for fish. Brown pelicans dropped precipitously in number in the 1960s. Their decline was the result of the pesticide DDT, which was present in the ocean food chain and caused thinning of eggshells. Thin eggshells were especially problematic for pelicans because they incubate their eggs with their webbed feet, warming them by standing on them. DDT was banned in the U.S. in 1972, and the brown pelican was removed from the endangered species list in November 2009.

Stylaster californicus

Stylaster californicus is one of the most beautiful creatures you will ever encounter underwater. It is a hydrocoral, with an internal structure in the form of canals. The tubular canals make the coral much less dense and hard compared to stony corals. These canals house all of the coral polyps and aid in food distribution. *S. californicus* can form encrusting or branching colonies that can be bright pink, purple, or orange. *S. californicus* is found off the coast of California in waters from 30 to 300 feet deep. It makes a living by filtering planktonic organisms and is most abundant on exposed rock pinnacles characterized by high water motion.

Pteropod, which means "winged foot," is a term for an open ocean, or pelagic, snail (Gastropod). Pteropods include the Gymnosomata, or **"sea angels"** and the Thecosomata, or "sea butterflies." The sea angel has a distinct head with antennae and a mouth with specialized hook sacs and a jaw. The "wings" of a sea angel are small; when the animal swims, the wings beat rapidly in comparison with those of the sea butterfly. Although a type of snail, the Gymnosomata lack shells. Sea angels, such as *Clione limacina*, are active predators of sea butterflies. *C. limacina* is found in cold and temperate waters in oceans around the world to depths of 1,800 feet. While animals of this species can reach a length of up to three inches, off the West Coast of North America they are typically less than one inch long.

Sea angel, *Clione limacina*

Sea butterflies, such as *Corolla calceola*, have wing-like extensions of the foot that enable them to drift passively. A sea butterfly secrets a mucous sheet, up to six feet in diameter in *C. calceola*, to gather planktonic food particles. The Thecosomata have shells, and ocean acidification poses a serious threat to these pteropods. Research has shown that a small decrease in the ocean's pH, meaning an increase in acidity, causes dissolution of sea butterfly shells. *C. calceola*, in the suborder Pseudothecosomata, lacks an external shell; however, it does have a thin internal shell that provides skeletal support and protection.

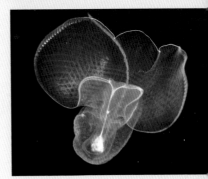

Sea butterfly, *Corolla limacina*

Diatoms are single-celled planktonic algae, or phytoplankton, found in both fresh and salt water. *Pseudonitzschia* is the genus name for more than a dozen marine diatom species, a subset of which are responsible for toxic phytoplankton "blooms" that occur off the coast of California. These population explosions occur when certain species of *Pseudo-nitzschia* multiply rapidly and produce the neurological toxin domoic acid. When concentrated through the food chain, domoic acid can lead to sickness or death in seabirds and marine mammals and, in humans, amnesic shellfish poisoning. Much research has been directed toward understanding the factors that promote toxic blooms. Changes in physical and chemical conditions, such as high nutrient concentrations, from river discharges and coastal upwelling have been implicated, although the exact relationships between the growth of *Pseudonitzschia* species, the production of domoic acid, and specific environmental factors are still unknown.

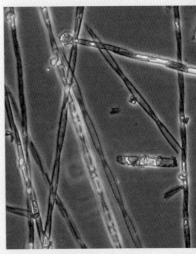

Diatom, *Pseudo-nitzschia*
approximate magnification 100 x

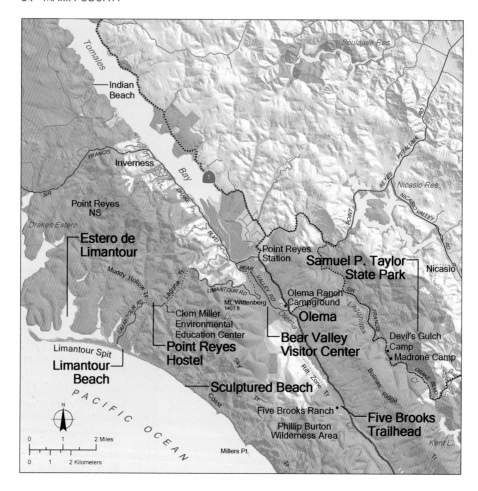

Estero de Limantour trail

Limantour Beach/ Olema Valley

	Sandy Beach	Rocky Shore	Trail	Visitor Center	Campground	Wildlife Viewing	Fishing or Boating	Facilities for Disabled	Food and Drink	Restrooms	Parking	Fee
Estero de Limantour			•			•	•			•	•	
Point Reyes Hostel			•					•		•	•	•
Limantour Beach	•		•				•			•	•	
Sculptured Beach	•		•									
Olema			•	•			•		•	•	•	
Bear Valley Visitor Center			•	•			•			•	•	
Samuel P. Taylor State Park			•		•		•			•	•	•
Five Brooks Trailhead			•				•			•	•	

ESTERO DE LIMANTOUR: *End of Limantour Rd.* Extending along the north side of the two-mile-long Limantour Spit is the sheltered Estero de Limantour. Pickleweed grows in the salt marsh on the margin of the lagoon, and eelgrass grows in deeper water. Water birds such as white pelicans and brant feed and rest in the estero, and harbor seals haul out on shore. Numerous invertebrates are found in the mudflats, including blue mud shrimp and Lewis's moon snails. The 500-acre estero is a state marine reserve, where viewing of wildlife is allowed, but State Department of Fish and Game regulations prohibit the take of all marine life.

POINT REYES HOSTEL: *Off Limantour Rd., 7 mi. from Bear Valley Rd.* The hostel has 41 beds, including family rooms and bunkhouse space for groups; wood stoves; and a full kitchen. A wheelchair ramp leads from the parking lot to the main house. Overnight fees are charged. Advance reservations are strongly recommended year-round. For information, write P.O. Box 247, Point Reyes Station 94956, or call 415-663-8811 from 7:30–10:00 AM or 4:30–9:30 PM only.

LIMANTOUR BEACH: *End of Limantour Rd.* A long sandy crescent backed by grassy dunes stretches east from the mouth of Drakes Estero. Due to the sheltering effect of the Point

Limantour Beach

Olema

Point Reyes National Seashore was created to protect wild lands, natural ecosystems, and open space close to the urban centers of the San Francisco Bay Area. Recreational activities in the National Seashore include beachcombing, hiking, kayaking, bicycling, and wildlife viewing. Some 80 miles of unspoiled coastline are preserved in the park, and there are beaches, grasslands, forests, and estuaries to explore.

About half of the 71,000-acre National Seashore has been designated the Phillip Burton Wilderness Area, composed of a patchwork of tracts interspersed among grazing and other private lands. A network of foot trails leads through the wilderness area; there are no structures or pavement. Horses are allowed on wilderness trails; no bicycles or motorized vehicles permitted.

Camping in the National Seashore is permitted at four walk-in camps and at boat-in beaches on the west side of Tomales Bay north of Indian Beach, all by reservation only. Camping permits are available at the visitor center daily or by phone from 9 AM to 2 PM, Monday through Friday; call: 415-663-8054. There is no car camping available in the park. Dogs, which must be leashed, are allowed in the Point Reyes National Seashore only on South Limantour Beach, North and South Point Reyes Beaches, and Kehoe Beach; seasonal closures may apply. National Seashore information is available at the Bear Valley Visitor Center, or call: 415-464-5100 or 415-464-5137.

The Point Reyes National Seashore Education Program offers classes and field seminars on environmental education and natural history, and a summer youth camp. The Clem Miller Environmental Education Center, an overnight facility available to groups for educational purposes, features hiking trails and interpretive programs. For information or reservations for field programs or the Clem Miller Center, write: Point Reyes National Seashore Association, Point Reyes Station 94956, or call: 415-663-1200.

Reyes Headlands, wave action is generally calmer here than on the west-facing beaches of the Point Reyes Peninsula. A wheelchair-accessible trail runs along the lagoon southeast of the main access road (watch for sign). The beach can also be reached via the Coast Trail from Palomarin at the southeast end of the national seashore.

SCULPTURED BEACH: *6 mi. from Bear Valley via trail.* A sandy beach backed by colorful eroded bluffs is located three miles south of Limantour Beach, accessible by trail from the Bear Valley Visitor Center or from Palomarin. Sculptured Beach can also be reached from points north or south along the shore at very low tide. For National Seashore information, including recorded weather, trail, and tide conditions, call: 415-464-5100.

OLEMA: *Hwy. One at Sir Francis Drake Blvd.* Olema retains the look of the 19th century stagecoach stop that it once was. The building occupied by the Olema Inn at the corner of Hwy. One and Sir Francis Drake Blvd. dates from 1876, and a handful of other historic buildings give the village its old-time flavor. Olema never grew large; when the North Pacific Coast Railroad was constructed through West Marin in the 1870s, Olema was bypassed in favor of nearby Point Reyes Station.

Tent and RV camping are available at Olema Ranch Campground, which has 187 sites, some with full or partial hook-ups. RVs up to 50 feet long can be accommodated; dump station available. The campground offers hot showers, a general store and laundromat, play area and recreation hall, mountain bike rentals, wireless Internet access, and a post office. Group camping facilities available. Dogs allowed on leash. Reservations recommended during summer months; call: 415-663-8106.

BEAR VALLEY VISITOR CENTER: *Bear Valley Rd., .5 mi. N.W. of Olema.* The visitor center,

Bear Valley Visitor Center

housed in a modern high-ceilinged wooden structure, features a bookstore and exhibits about park attractions. Open 9 AM–5 PM weekdays, 8 AM–5 PM weekends and holidays (closed December 25). Nearby facilities include a Coast Miwok Indian village, a wheelchair-accessible Earthquake Trail, and a Morgan horse farm. Trails from the visitor center span the park, leading to beaches, lagoons, and forests.

SAMUEL P. TAYLOR STATE PARK: *Sir Francis Drake Blvd., 5.2 mi. E. of Olema.* 2,600 acres of wooded canyons along Lagunitas (or Paper Mill) Creek. The park is the former site of the first paper mill on the Pacific Coast, built in 1856. The park features picnic areas, trails, and campgrounds. There are 60 developed family sites, an area set aside for hike or bike campsites, and about 30 enroute sites. Five group camping areas are available, two at Madrone and three primitive sites (one for equestrians) at Devil's Gulch, located one mile north of the other camping areas. Group campers must check in at the main park entrance. For camping reservations, call: 1-800-444-7275. Picnic areas, campground restrooms, and six family campsites are wheelchair accessible; there are four miles of paved trails. Streams in the park are closed to fishing and boating year-round; there is a children's swimming area in the creek. Paved and unpaved cycling paths available. Call: 415-488-9897.

FIVE BROOKS TRAILHEAD: *Hwy. One, 3 mi. S. of Olema.* A network of trails begins here for the southern part of the Point Reyes National Seashore. Many trails lead over wooded Inverness Ridge to beaches in the Phillip Burton Wilderness Area of the National Seashore. Trails also lead to the Coast Trail and to walk-in campsites. Check with the Bear Valley Visitor Center for trail conditions; trail maps available at all park visitor centers. Parking and restrooms at the trailhead; the main trail is partially wheelchair accessible with assistance. For park and trail information, call: 415-464-5100 or 415-464-5137. Five Brooks Ranch offers horseback riding lessons and trail rides; for information, call: 415-663-1570.

Farms and ranches dominate the coastal landscape of northern and central California. Half of Marin County's land is devoted to agriculture, and Marin's dairies produce 20 percent of the Bay Area's milk. In 1862, Marin County already provided one-quarter of the state's butter, which, when salted, was less perishable than milk for shipment to market in the days before refrigeration. In addition to butter and cheese, Marin County farms produced potatoes, beets, peas, wheat, and barley, which were loaded onto ships at Bolinas or Tomales or onto the North Pacific Coast Railroad for transport to San Francisco's growing population. Hay grown in Marin helped fuel the state's horse-drawn transportation facilities.

Raising potatoes on slopes in northwestern Marin County resulted in sediment clogging coastal streams. Look at Keys Creek and try to imagine even a small ocean-going schooner making its way upstream to the village of Tomales. Today, farming practices have changed, and the raising of cows, calves, and sheep, along with dairy operations, are predominant in Marin County. Specialty products, including organic ice cream, cheese, and yogurt, are on the increase. Production of fruit, vegetables, and wine grapes increased between the years 2000 and 2009.

Although there are now fewer dairy operations in Marin County than in the 1950s, those that remain are larger and produce more milk per cow. Most operations remain family-owned, and nearly all farmers want to continue farming, despite often slim economic returns. The preservation of agriculture is encouraged by county ordinances that discourage creation of residential subdivisions in farming areas. Some 40,000 acres of land on over 60 family farms and ranches in Marin County have been permanently protected for agriculture through conservation easements held by the Marin Agricultural Land Trust. Established in 1980, the trust was the nation's first private nonprofit set up specifically to preserve farmland. Grazing co-exists with recreation and resource protection in the Point Reyes National Seashore and Golden Gate National Recreation Area, which include 32,000 acres of land leased to farmers.

In 2009, some 18,000 acres of land in Marin were farmed using organic methods. The Straus Family Creamery on the east side of Tomales Bay was the first organic dairy in the western United States. Some ranches in Marin County produce pasture-raised chickens and pork and grass-fed beef, lamb,

and goats without the use of antibiotics or growth hormones. Natural forage production in the generally moist coastal environment is up to six times higher than in the arid interior of California.

The Grown in Marin marketing program, as well as local farmers markets throughout the North Coast, allow visitors to sample the outstanding products of this evolving industry, which forms an enduring part of the character and economy of the California coast. The popular Point Reyes Station Farmers Market takes place at Toby's Feed Barn on Saturday mornings from June to November. The larger Civic Center Farmers Market in San Rafael operates on Thursday and Sunday mornings, year round.

Farm stays and tours are available in many locations; check tourism offices, University of California Cooperative Extension offices, or farm bureaus for more information.

Dairy land at Tomales Point

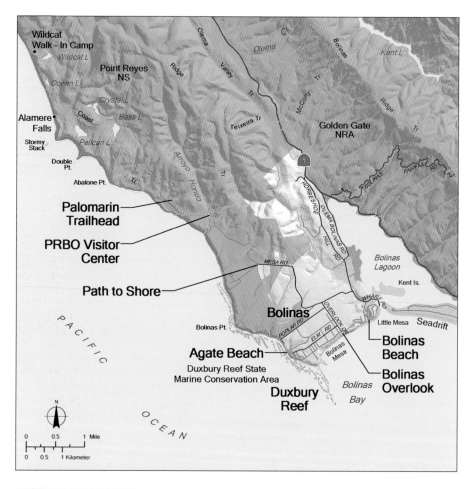

Wildcat
Walk - In Camp
Wildcat L
Point Reyes
NS
Ocean L
Ridge
Olema
Olema
Valley
Tr
Cr
Bolinas
Kent L
McCurdy
Tr
Ridge
Tr
Crystal L
Coast
Bass L
Teixeira Tr
Golden Gate
NRA
Tr
Alamere
Falls
Pelican L
Stormy
Stack
Double
Pt.
Arroyo Honda
Tr
HORSESHOE
Abalone Pt.
Tr
Tr
OLEMA BOLINAS HILL RD
BOLINAS
FAIRFAX RD

**Palomarin
Trailhead**

**PRBO Visitor
Center**

MESA RD
Bolinas
Lagoon
Kent Is.

Path to Shore

WHARF RD
Bolinas
OVERLOOK DR
Little Mesa   Seadrift

PACIFIC
Bolinas Pt.
POPLAR RD
ELM RD
**Bolinas
Beach**

Agate Beach
Bolinas
Mesa
Duxbury Reef State
Marine Conservation Area
Bolinas
**Duxbury
Reef**
Bolinas
Bay
**Bolinas
Overlook**

OCEAN

N

0   0.5   1 Mile
0   0.5   1 Kilometer

Alamere Falls

Bolinas

	Sandy Beach	Rocky Shore	Trail	Visitor Center	Campground	Wildlife Viewing	Fishing or Boating	Facilities for Disabled	Food and Drink	Restrooms	Parking	Fee
Palomarin Trailhead			•			•				•	•	
PRBO Visitor Center			•	•		•	•			•	•	
Path to Shore	•	•	•			•					•	
Agate Beach		•					•				•	
Duxbury Reef		•				•				•	•	
Town of Bolinas	•						•		•	•	•	
Bolinas Overlook		•									•	
Bolinas Beach	•	•				•	•			•	•	

PALOMARIN TRAILHEAD: *End of Mesa Rd., 5 mi. N.W. of Bolinas.* The Palomarin Trailhead provides access to the southern end of the Point Reyes National Seashore. A network of trails leads along the bluffs and to lakes, beaches, and walk-in camps. At Double Point, two Monterey shale outcroppings enclose a small bay, where acorn barnacles and California mussels cling to the reef. Purple and giant red sea urchins lie in the crevices, and red rock crabs are common. Rocks north and south of Double Point, particularly Stormy Stack off North Point, are important feeding and roosting sites for Brandt's cormorants, common murres, grebes, and California brown pelicans. On top of the bluff is Pelican Lake, drained by a stream flowing down to the beach. Four nearby freshwater lakes, named Bass, Crystal, Ocean, and Wildcat, contain small marshy areas and provide habitat for waterfowl. Alamere Falls cascades down the bluff north of Double Point. The Coast Trail continues north along a roadless stretch of shoreline to Sculptured Beach and beyond.

PRBO VISITOR CENTER: *Mesa Rd., 4.5 mi. N.W. of Bolinas.* Formerly known as the Point Reyes Bird Observatory, PRBO Conservation Science carries out research and education focused on protecting birds and other wildlife. PRBO research activities have helped lead to creation of the three national marine sanctuaries that touch Marin County's coast: the Gulf of the Farallones, Cordell Bank, and Monterey Bay National Marine Sanctuaries. Visitors are welcome to view some of the research activities, including the bird-banding process in which birds are safely captured in a fine net, examined, and released. Banding takes place in the morning, Tuesday through Sunday, from May 1 through Thanksgiving, and on Wednesdays and weekends the remainder of the year, weather permitting. Drop-in visitors in groups of 10 or fewer are welcome to view the mist-netting process; for information on scheduling a school or community group tour, or to check conditions, call: 415-868-0655.

A small visitor center with displays of the observatory's research projects is open from early morning to 5 PM; a half-mile-long self-guided nature trail leads through coastal scrub habitat and the small canyon of Arroyo Hondo. Monthly bird walks are offered year-round by PRBO, to locations throughout Marin County, including Bolinas Lagoon, Muir Beach, Point Reyes, and Limantour Estero. For information, call: 415-868-1221.

PATH TO SHORE: *451 Mesa Rd., N.W. of Bolinas.* A half-mile-long trail leads from Mesa Rd. to the shoreline; part of Point Reyes National Seashore. For information, call: 415-464-5100. A second unimproved path to the shoreline is located a quarter-mile north, near mile marker 2.68 on Mesa Road.

AGATE BEACH: *End of Elm Rd., Bolinas.* This county park includes a northwest-facing beach at the edge of Duxbury Reef. The park is small, but it provides access to nearly two miles of shoreline at low tide. Rocks around the beach that are splashed by the waves hold associations of algae and invertebrates. The nearshore waters north and south of Agate Beach are part of the Duxbury Reef State Marine Conservation Area, where the take of all living marine resources is prohibited except the recreational take of finfish from shore and abalone. Call: 707-875-4260.

DUXBURY REEF: *S.W. perimeter of Bolinas Mesa.* Duxbury Reef is California's largest exposed shale reef. The reef lies at the base of the headlands known as the Bolinas Mesa, formed of Monterey shale. At low tide, a mile-long stretch of reef is exposed. The shape of the reef is continuously changing, as the waves erode the edges of the reef and the adjacent cliffs. The relatively soft shale is habitat for an unusual assemblage of rock-boring clams and worms.

To view the reef up close, park at Agate Beach at the end of Elm Road. Shallow gravel tidepools contain a type of acorn worm that is apparently unique to Northern California, and a small burrowing anemone is known only from here and San Juan Island in Washington State. The intertidal area includes gooseneck barnacles, ochre sea stars,

Duxbury Reef

Town of Bolinas, Smiley's Bar

and huge beds of California mussels. Regulations prohibit the take of all living marine resources except the recreational take of finfish from shore and abalone; check Dept. of Fish and Game rules, or call: 707-875-4260.

TOWN OF BOLINAS: *End of Bolinas-Olema Rd., off Hwy. One.* When San Francisco grew explosively after the discovery of gold in 1848, Bolinas shared the boom in a modest way. Redwoods on the hills surrounding Bolinas were cut to build the wooden row houses of San Francisco, and smaller trees were cut for household fuel. From sawmills near the shore, lumber was loaded on flat-bottomed lighters in Bolinas Lagoon and transferred to ships anchored offshore. In the U.S. Census of 1850, the first to include California, two-thirds of Marin County's few hundred residents lived in the Bolinas area. Some 19th century buildings remain, particularly near the old downtown along Wharf Road. Part of Smiley's Bar dates from 1852, the Bigson House building dates from 1875, and St. Mary Magdalene Catholic Church from 1878. Masses of monarch butterflies

once overwintered in Bolinas, but since the 1990s numbers have declined sharply.

BOLINAS OVERLOOK: *End of Overlook Dr., Bolinas.* A spectacular view of the southern portion of Duxbury Reef, the ocean, and San Francisco in the distance is available from a small pull-out at the end of Overlook Drive.

BOLINAS BEACH: *Ends of Brighton and Wharf Aves., Bolinas.* Bolinas Beach curves around the headland known as the Little Mesa, and the beach can be reached from two street ends. At the end of Brighton Ave., a gated concrete ramp leads to a sand and pebble beach popular with surfers. At high tide, the beach is narrow. A small county park with restrooms and tennis courts is located on Brighton Ave. near the beach. The second entrance to Bolinas Beach is from the end of Wharf Ave., which has very limited parking and no turn-around at the end. The mouth of Bolinas Lagoon, which is only a narrow channel at low tide, separates Bolinas Beach from the Seadrift sandspit. Brown pelicans, gulls, and waterfowl can be seen at the entrance to the lagoon.

Northern California's National Marine Sanctuaries

THE 1972 National Marine Sanctuaries Act authorizes the protection of marine areas that include coral reefs, fish habitats, historic shipwrecks, and whale breeding grounds. The U.S. has 13 national marine sanctuaries; California's four are Cordell Bank, Gulf of the Farallones, Monterey Bay, and Channel Islands.

"Sanctuary" implies protection, and such is the goal of national marine sanctuaries. National marine sanctuaries are intended to protect marine life and the diversity of habitats in our oceans, which have been affected by over-fishing, whaling, and climate change. The marine sanctuaries are vital places for learning—for young students on their first ocean field trip and for experienced research scientists. Marine sanctuaries are also places for commerce and recreation. Ships pass through California's marine sanctuaries, carrying goods to and from foreign shores; commercial and recreational fishing takes place; and, in nearshore waters, surfers ride the waves. Each marine sanctuary has regulations governing various activities. Restrictions typically prohibit mining; the discharge of waste into sanctuary waters; and disturbance of historic shipwrecks, marine mammals, seabirds, or the ocean floor.

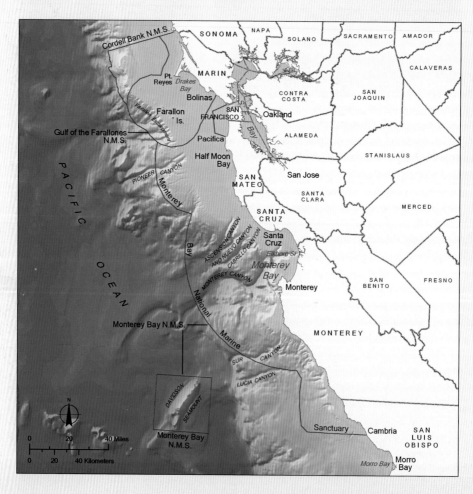

Cordell Bank National Marine Sanctuary encompasses an "underwater island" some nine miles long and five miles wide off Point Reyes. Its granite "peaks" are submerged, but just barely; some pinnacles have less than 130 feet of water over them. Cordell Bank is crowded with sponges, anemones, hydrocorals, and barnacles that thrive in the relatively shallow and bright conditions. Rich supplies of nutrients are provided by upwelling, the wind-driven process that brings deep water and organic material to the surface. The California Current's vigorous upwelling pattern is one of only a few like it in the world. Nutrient-laden waters support tiny phytoplankton and zooplankton, which are consumed in turn by larger organisms, forming the marine food web.

The Gulf of the Farallones refers to the waters partly enclosed by the curve of coastline extending from Point Reyes to the San Francisco Peninsula, with the Farallon Islands to the west. The Gulf of the Farallones National Marine Sanctuary encompasses 1,279 square statute miles, including nearshore waters such as Tomales Bay and the ocean out to and beyond the Farallon Islands. The broad continental shelf, with water above it measuring only about 200 feet deep, slopes gradually westward from the mainland; beyond the Farallon Islands the seafloor plunges to a depth of 6,000 feet.

Endangered blue and humpback whales travel thousands of miles every year to the Gulf of the Farallones to feed on tiny shrimp-like krill that are abundant due to upwelling. Gray whales migrate through the national marine sanctuary; their numbers have increased to the point that they are no longer considered threatened. In late summer and fall, white sharks are drawn to the Gulf of the Farallones, where they feast on seals and sea lions. California sea lions and the larger, scarcer Steller sea lions breed in the sanctuary, as do harbor seals and elephant seals. Leatherback sea turtles occasionally come from warmer, more southerly waters to the Gulf of the Farallones, where they feed on jellyfish. In spite of sanctuary protections, continuing threats to marine organisms come from vessel traffic, polluted runoff, and plastic waste swept out to sea from San Francisco Bay Area cities.

Monterey Bay National Marine Sanctuary was created to protect the marine resources of the area centered on Monterey Bay and its colossal undersea canyon, and to provide opportunities for study and education. The Monterey Bay National Marine Sanctuary is the largest of the nation's marine sanctuaries, encompassing over 5,300 square miles. It is inhabited by 33 species of marine mammals, 94 species of seabirds, and nearly countless numbers of other organisms.

Coastal visitor centers, including the Monterey Bay Aquarium, stock books, maps, and posters about California's national marine sanctuaries. The Gulf of the Farallones Visitor Center is at Crissy Field in San Francisco; call: 415-561-6625. A Monterey Bay National Marine Sanctuary Exploration Center is planned in Santa Cruz; call: 831-420-3664.

Humpback whale, Gulf of the Farallones

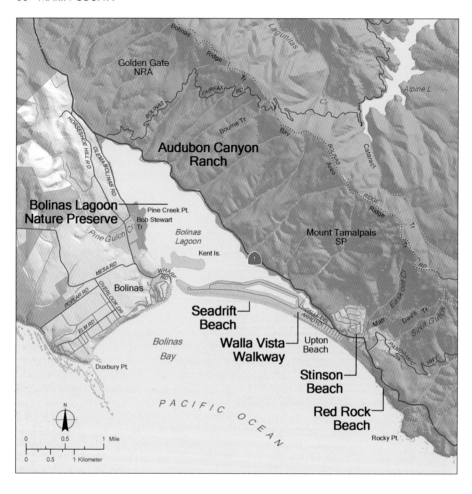

Bolinas Lagoon, view from Mt. Tamalpais State Park

Stinson Beach

	Sandy Beach	Rocky Shore	Trail	Visitor Center	Campground	Wildlife Viewing	Fishing or Boating	Facilities for Disabled	Food and Drink	Restrooms	Parking	Fee
Bolinas Lagoon Nature Preserve			•			•					•	
Audubon Canyon Ranch			•	•		•	•			•	•	
Seadrift Beach	•											
Walla Vista Walkway	•										•	
Town of Stinson Beach	•							•	•	•	•	
Stinson Beach	•								•	•	•	
Red Rock Beach	•	•	•								•	

BOLINAS LAGOON NATURE PRESERVE: *Along Hwy. One and Olema-Bolinas Rd.* Bolinas Lagoon is a county-owned preserve that includes over 1,200 acres of sheltered water, salt marsh, and mudflat. The lagoon is a major stopover point for migrating shorebirds and other waterfowl, including sandpipers, plovers, geese, and ducks. As many as 35,000 birds have been counted, representing over 60 species. Herons and egrets are resident year-round and are abundant on the mudflats. Surf scoters, ruddy ducks, greater scaups, avocets, and pintails are also commonly seen along with black-necked stilts. Uncommon, but occasionally present, are Virginia rails.

Bolinas Lagoon is home to a colony of harbor seals, which can be seen at low tide hauled out on the mudflats, often far out in the lagoon. Bring field glasses for a closer look; do not attempt to approach these shy creatures. The lagoon also serves as a nursery for fish such as starry flounder, cabezon, and several varieties of perch. Pickleweed grows along the margin of the lagoon, and western pygmy blue butterflies may be seen in the area. The shallowness of the lagoon has resulted from siltation due, in part, to historic logging on the surrounding hills. There are excellent vistas of the lagoon from numerous pull-outs along Highway One; view wildlife respectfully from a distance. The Bob Stewart Trail is a quarter-mile loop that leads through an alder forest at the mouth of Pine Gulch Creek into the nature preserve; dogs must be leashed. Call: 415-499-6387.

AUDUBON CANYON RANCH: *Hwy. One, 3 mi. N. of Stinson Beach.* Inland of Hwy. One near Bolinas Lagoon are several heavily wooded canyons separated by grass-covered ridges. High in the redwood trees in one of the canyons is a large nesting colony of great blue herons and great egrets. Audubon Canyon Ranch, a nonprofit environmental preservation, education, and research organization, operates the Bolinas Lagoon Preserve. A half-mile-long trail leads to an overlook on the hill where fixed telescopes allow close-up views of all the activities of a nesting colony of great blue herons, including courtship, mating, incubation, feeding, and fledgling flights. Two three-mile-long loop trails and a self-guided nature trail into other canyons are also available.

Facilities at Audubon Canyon Ranch include an exhibit hall, nature bookshop, and picnic area adjacent to the 1875 home of Captain

Great blue heron

Peter Bourne. The ranch is open to the public during the nesting season on weekends and holidays, from the second weekend in March through the second weekend in July, from 10 AM to 4 PM. Courting displays of the birds take place early in the season, while eggs and chicks are visible in April and May or later. Visits to the preserve are self-guided. Blinds for viewing nesting birds, picnic tables, the display hall, and the bookstore are wheelchair accessible. In a neighboring canyon, the ranch operates a wildlife education center in another ranch house built in the 1870s. School and other groups may visit Tuesday through Friday by appointment. Dogs other than service animals not allowed in the preserve. No fee for entry, but donations are encouraged. Call: 415-868-9244.

SEADRIFT BEACH: *N.W. of Stinson Beach.* The mile-and-a-half-long Seadrift sandspit curves upcoast from Stinson Beach, where the generally south-facing shore and nearby mountains create a relatively warm, shel-tered beach environment. Although the roads in the Seadrift subdivision are for residents only, the beach from the water's edge inland to 60 feet from the private seawall is open to the public.

WALLA VISTA WALKWAY: *Calle Del Arroyo, off Hwy. One.* A public pedestrian accessway leads from Calle del Arroyo, outside the Seadrift Subdivision gate, along the west side of Walla Vista, a short lane leading to the beach. Turn right to Seadrift Beach, or turn left to the Marin County–maintained Upton Beach; for county policy regarding dogs on Upton Beach, call: 415-499-6387. Limited road shoulder parking on Calle del Arroyo, on the north side only.

TOWN OF STINSON BEACH: *Hwy. One, .3 mi. N. of Panoramic Hwy.* Early settler Alfred D. Easkoot promoted Stinson Beach as a destination for campers and swimmers; his 1875 house, now restored, is located on Highway One just west of the village center.

Some 40 years ago, Bolinas Lagoon faced a fate far different from the serene beauty enjoyed by today's visitors. In the early 1960s, a freeway was slated for construction at sea level along the east side of the lagoon, paralleled on the ridge above by a "parkway" that would have sliced through the forested slopes. Bolinas Lagoon was proposed to be dredged for an enormous marina, to be sited next to a heliport and a hotel built on filled land in the lagoon (located atop the San Andreas Fault). Inevitably, the highways would have brought urban development on a massive scale to the quiet valleys of West Marin, with a catastrophic loss of wildlife habitat and natural values. Alarmed citizens campaigned against the development plans and raised funds to acquire key parcels of land in and around the lagoon. In the end, the freeway plans were dropped, the Bolinas Harbor District was disbanded, and open space was protected.

Bolinas Lagoon is now a nature preserve maintained by Marin County, and Audubon Canyon Ranch operates an adjacent preserve centered on a magnificent heron and egret rookery. The Golden Gate National Recreation Area and Mount Tamalpais State Park encompass neighboring slopes and are managed for protection of wildlife and scenic beauty and for public recreation.

Bob Stewart Trail, Bolinas Lagoon

Around 1900, a summer tent colony called Willow Camp appeared in the dunes near the beach. Cabins and houses began to be built after a subdivision was created by Nathan H. Stinson in 1906. Early day visitors to Stinson Beach arrived by stagecoach or buggy via a road around the north side of Mount Tamalpais; a 1911 plan to extend the Mount Tamalpais and Muir Woods Railway from Mill Valley was never carried out.

Introduced eucalyptus and Monterey pine trees in the village are winter resting areas for colonies of monarch butterflies. Easkoot Creek, bordered by dense riparian vegetation, flows through the center of town and feeds Bolinas Lagoon. The former creek mouth was located on the beach, emptying directly into the bay. Efforts are under way to restore the creek's habitat value for steelhead trout. Galleries, eating places, and a few small inns are located in the village.

STINSON BEACH: *W. of Hwy. One, N. of Panoramic Hwy.* Probably California's most popular beach north of San Francisco, Stinson Beach offers sunbathing, volleyball, surfing, and other recreational pursuits. Air and water temperatures are often milder along this broad, sandy stretch than on other northern California beaches because it faces south and is sheltered by coastal mountains. Lifeguards are on duty at the beach from late May to mid-September.

The main part of the beach, parking area, and support facilities lie within the Golden Gate National Recreation Area (GGNRA). There are picnic tables and barbecue grills set among willows and cypress trees, a snack bar (open summer only), restrooms, and showers. The vehicle entrance gate is open from 9 AM to about sunset; check current closing time upon entry. Volleyball equipment and a beach wheelchair can be borrowed from the main lifeguard tower. No pets allowed on the beach. Call: 415-868-1922. Upton Beach, extending two-thirds of a mile upcoast from the Golden Gate National Recreation Area beach, is maintained by Marin County; call: 415-499-6387.

RED ROCK BEACH: *Hwy. One, 1 mi. S. of Stinson Beach.* From an unpaved parking lot at milepost 11.45, a trail leads down the steep, red chert bluff to a remote, clothing-optional beach within Mount Tamalpais State Park. Springs seeping from the cliff face support wildflowers, and giant boulders are scattered on the beach.

Stinson Beach

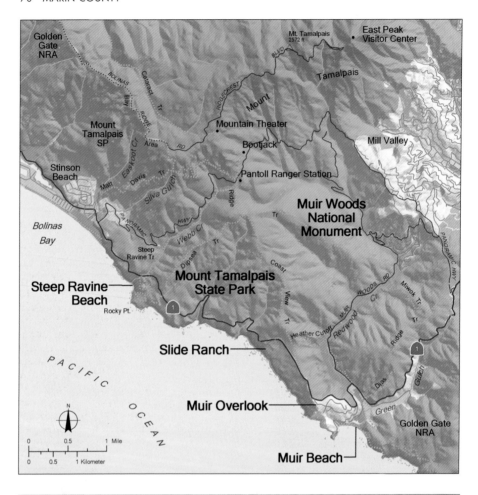

Steep Ravine Beach

Muir Beach Area

	Sandy Beach	Rocky Shore	Trail	Visitor Center	Campground	Wildlife Viewing	Fishing or Boating	Facilities for Disabled	Food and Drink	Restrooms	Parking	Fee
Steep Ravine Beach	•	•	•		•			•		•	•	•
Mount Tamalpais State Park			•	•	•	•		•		•	•	•
Slide Ranch		•	•	•	•	•		•		•	•	•
Muir Overlook		•						•		•	•	
Muir Beach	•	•					•	•		•	•	
Muir Woods National Monument			•	•				•	•	•	•	•

STEEP RAVINE BEACH: *Hwy. One, 2 mi. S. of Stinson Beach.* Nine rustic cabins overlook the sea from a marine terrace within Mount Tamalpais State Park. Cabins have wood stoves, picnic tables and benches, sleeping platforms, and outdoor barbecues, but no running water or electricity. Primitive toilets, water faucets, and firewood are nearby. Seven primitive campsites, each with table, firepit, food locker, and space for a tent, are located a few hundred yards from the parking area. No showers available. A maximum of one vehicle and five people are allowed per cabin or campsite; no pets. One campsite and one cabin are wheelchair accessible.

Reservations are required for all Steep Ravine sites, which book up well in advance; call: 1-800-444-7275. Campers with reservations may drive to a parking area a quarter-mile down the road leading to the beach; beach day users must park elsewhere and walk down the road.

MOUNT TAMALPAIS STATE PARK: *Off Panoramic Hwy.* More than 6,000 acres of parkland in Mount Tamalpais State Park adjoin recreational land holdings of the Golden Gate National Recreation Area, and other entities, linked by trails and scenic roads. From the top of 2,571-foot Mount Tamalpais, once reached by a winding railroad line and now accessible by road or trail, visitors have a panoramic view of the Farallon Islands offshore, the towers of San Francisco, and parts of the Coastal Range. Astronomy evenings with a talk by an astronomer and a look through volunteer-provided telescopes are held at the Mountain Theater one Saturday evening per month from April to October; for recorded information or updates due to cloudy weather, call: 415-455-5370.

Some 250 miles of trails link the beaches with the top of Mount Tamalpais and the town of Mill Valley. The Steep Ravine and Cataract Trails follow streams with waterfalls. Trail maps are available at the visitor center on the summit of the mountain's east peak and at local bookstores. The Mount Tamalpais Interpretive Association offers volunteer-led hikes featuring a variety of park resources and attractions; for recorded information, call: 415-258-2410. Horses are allowed on fire roads, paved roads, and on posted equestrian trails; bicycles are allowed on fire roads and paved roads only. Dogs are not permitted on trails or in undeveloped areas of the state park.

Pantoll Campground on Panoramic Hwy. has 16 campsites with tables, rock barbecues, food lockers, and space for a tent; running water, restrooms, and parking are nearby; no reservations taken. There is also an enroute campground at Pantoll in the lower parking lot, where self-contained RVs can be accommodated on a one-night basis between 6 PM and 9 AM only. Panoramic Hwy. is narrow and winding, and motor homes over 35 feet in length are not recommended. Alice Eastwood Group Camp, located off Panoramic Hwy., and Frank Valley Group Horse Camp, on Muir Woods Rd., accept reservations for group camping, call: 1-800-444-7275. For information on campgrounds, call Pantoll Ranger Station: 415-388-2070. Fees apply for camping and for day-use parking within Mount Tamalpais State Park at Pantoll, Bootjack, and East Peak.

SLIDE RANCH: *Hwy One, 1 mi. N. of Muir Overlook.* Slide Ranch is a nonprofit environmental education center located within the Golden Gate National Recreation Area, on a steep slope of Mount Tamalpais. Educational programs and summer day camps emphasize agriculture and sustainability. Wildlife, such as bobcats, red-tailed hawks, and lizards, use the property, along with domestic animals that include goats, sheep, and ducks. Hiking trails and tidepools on the site are used to teach about resource conservation.

Programs are offered to families and groups, with an emphasis on elementary school-age children. Family programs include camp-outs, toddler's days, and family farm days. Daytime and overnight programs for school and community groups include exploration, campfires, and experience with farm chores. Pre-registration is required; fees charged, but scholarships may be available for those with limited income; call: 415-381-6155.

MUIR OVERLOOK: *Off Hwy. One, 1 mi. N. of Muir Beach.* Spectacular views of steep serpentine cliffs are available from this bluff

Muir Beach

high above the sea. Offshore due south is the Potato Patch Shoal, where the sea at low tide is little more than 20 feet deep, causing turbulence and occasional freak waves that threaten boaters. Picnic tables, restrooms, and paved parking available.

MUIR BEACH: *Hwy. One at Muir Woods Rd.* Redwood Creek drains the southern slopes of Mount Tamalpais and flows through Frank Valley to the ocean, adjacent to the community of Muir Beach. The creek is a spawning stream for steelhead and coho salmon. Big-leaf maple trees, with leaves that turn golden in the fall, grow along the stream as do red alders.

Where Frank Valley and Green Gulch meet at the shoreline is a lagoon formed by Redwood Creek and a large beach with rocky areas and tidepools at both ends. Between mid-October and mid-March, monarch butterflies overwinter in a grove of introduced Monterey pines near the entrance to the Golden Gate National Recreation Area parking lot. The sandy beach is popular for fishing, picnicking, and sunbathing.

MUIR WOODS NATIONAL MONUMENT: *Off Hwy. One, 3 mi. N. on Muir Woods Rd.* Muir Woods, a 554-acre grove deep in Redwood Creek valley, contains the only remaining old-growth redwood forest near San Francisco. Although its loop trails are very popular with visitors, Muir Woods connects to less-crowded trails that lead throughout Mount Tamalpais State Park and the Golden Gate National Recreation Area. The Pantoll Trail leads west to Stinson Beach on the coast, and the Dipsea Trail, which passes near the Muir Woods visitor center, leads west to Steep Ravine Beach and east to Mill Valley.

From the main entrance to Muir Woods, a wheelchair-accessible boardwalk leads along Redwood Creek into the woods; there are interpretive signs and exhibits including living examples of redwood-like tree species from around the world. Leopard lilies bloom in summer in the shaded forest; look for huckleberries in late summer. Facilities include a visitor center, a bookshop, a café, and restrooms; nature walks are available. The monument is open every day; for recorded information, call: 415-388-2595.

Steep Ravine 1960

Dorothea Lange and her camera seared the faces of 1930s-era migrant farm families into the nation's consciousness. During World War II she photographed shipbuilders in Richmond, California, and interned Japanese-Americans, and she traveled with husband Paul Taylor to Asia, South America, Egypt, and India, taking photos everywhere they went. A childhood bout of polio left her with a life-long limp but failed to hinder her creative power. Dorothea Lange was on the faculty of the California School of Fine Arts (now the San Francisco Art Institute), lived most of her life in Berkeley, and died in 1965.

Dorothea Lange's large circle of relations, stepchildren, and close family friends included photographer Imogen Cunningham; Cunningham's son, Rondal Partridge; and his daughter, Elizabeth. In *Dorothea Lange: A Visual Life*, a volume of images and essays,

Elizabeth Partridge remembers:

Summers we often went to Steep Ravine. There, in Paul and Dorothea's little cabin perched on a cliff hanging over the Pacific Ocean, we shed most of our clothes, and all sense of time. We had nothing but the vastness of the ocean and tiny shell of a cabin, which cradled us all gently when the sun and wind wore us out. Here Dorothea walked slowly through the wet sand, the wind blowing in off the ocean, the ever-present Pentax camera hanging from her neck. Inside the cabin she hung her camera on a nail by the door, ready to take photographs indoors or out. Here the worries that tugged perpetually at adults didn't seem to bother them, and we kids ate and quarreled and slept happily together like a litter of puppies.

Copyright the Dorothea Lange Collection, Oakland Museum of California, City of Oakland. Gift of Paul S. Taylor.

Farallon Islands, *detail, original print sized 7 x 10.5 inches*

Farallon Islands

SITUATED 27 miles outside the Golden Gate, the Farallon Islands, or Farallones, comprise several small rugged islets and numerous exposed rocks clustered in three groups and spread over about six and a half miles of ocean. The largest island, the 77-acre Southeast Farallon Island, combined with the smaller Maintop Island and the rocks that surround it make up the South Farallones. Just under two miles north, the 200-foot-diameter Middle Farallon Island (known as "the pimple") protrudes about 20 feet from the sea, while a cluster of seven exposed rocks several miles farther northwest make up the North Farallones.

The Farallon Islands are composed of granite that was created at great depth, many hundreds of miles to the southeast. Movement of these rocks along the several faults of the San Andreas Fault system, which separates the Pacific Plate from the North American Plate, has carried them far to the north. They continue to slide northwestward at the rate of about two inches per year—or about the rate at which your fingernails grow. Subsequent uplift, probably along an inactive southeast-to-northwest fault, has exposed them above the sea's surface.

During the last Ice Age, some 18,000 to 20,000 years ago, when sea level was about 400 feet lower than today because of the vast amount of water locked up in the continen-

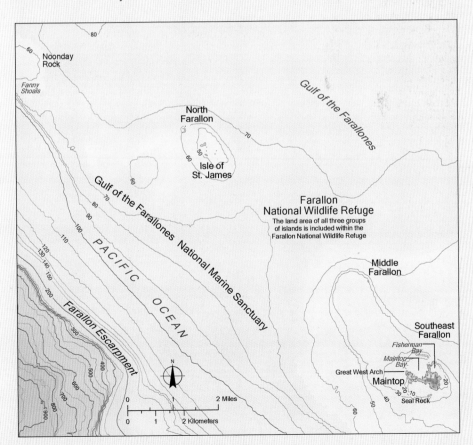

tal ice sheets, most of what is now the continental shelf off California was dry land. One could have hiked from San Francisco to the Farallon Islands, although the 50-mile round trip would have made a challenging backpack trip.

Northwest of the Farallon Islands is Cordell Bank, a rocky feature that has been called an "underwater island." Cordell Bank rises from the continental shelf much as the Farallon Islands do, although the bank is entirely submerged. It is the site of great biological productivity at depths of as little as 130 feet, as compared to a water depth of about 650 feet at the edge of the continental shelf. Cordell Bank is the largest of several such banks lying northwest of the Farallon Islands and defining a linear submarine ridge.

The land area of all three groups of islands is included within the Farallon National Wildlife Refuge. The surrounding waters are part of the Gulf of the Farallones National Marine Sanctuary. All the islands except Southeast Farallon Island are also included within the federally designated Farallon Wilderness. Cordell Bank and adjacent waters are designated as the Cordell Bank National Marine Sanctuary.

These overlapping layers of federal protection have been added to the Farallon Islands and Cordell Bank over the years in recognition of their value for wildlife and in response to significant threats from human activities. From their initial discovery by Europeans in 1579, when the famed English explorer Francis Drake landed on the islands to harvest seabird eggs and seal meat, the Farallones have attracted intrepid sailors interested in braving the notoriously rough seas to take advantage of the diverse and abundant wildlife that inhabits the area. By the mid-1800s, small industries developed that focused on exploiting the northern fur seal and common murre colonies on the islands. Modest fortunes were made in San Francisco from the sale of murre eggs for food and fur seal pelts for foreign trade and clothing. As demand for these products grew in rapidly-expanding San Francisco, the seal and seabird populations on the Farallones crashed. After several decades of intense harvest, the northern fur seal colony, which once included an estimated quarter of a million fur seals, had been completely wiped out, and the historic population of 500,000 common murres was coming dangerously close to a similar fate. Throughout the 1900s, however, recognition and appreciation of the islands' uniqueness, fragility, and ecological importance began to blossom.

Southeast Farallon Island hoist

Southeast Farallon Island

Stringent conservation measures were developed to protect both the islands and the numerous species that they support.

After decades of protection, monitoring, research, and active conservation by dedicated biologists and volunteers with the Point Reyes Bird Observatory (now called PRBO Conservation Science), Gulf of the Farallones National Marine Sanctuary, and Farallon National Wildlife Refuge, the Farallones are slowly showing signs of recovery. Northern fur seals have returned to the islands to establish breeding colonies after an absence of over 150 years. The common murre population has rebounded to nearly 200,000 breeding individuals. The world's largest breeding colonies of western gulls and ashy storm-petrels occur on the islands along with breeding colonies of ten other seabird and shorebird species. In all, the islands support the largest number of breeding seabirds in the lower 48 states, while five marine mammal species haul out on the islands: northern elephant seal, California sea lion, harbor seal, Steller sea lion, and northern fur seal. In the late summer and fall, between 30 and 100 white sharks are attracted by the growing population of marine mammals.

Although the islands' sensitivity restricts access to a small number of research personnel and technicians, the sea around them is a popular destination for boat-based tours out of San Francisco and Half Moon Bay that highlight whale-watching, birding, fishing, and even cage-diving with white sharks. The islands also serve as an invaluable resource for biologists. As California's only true islands outside the Southern California Bight, the Farallones provide researchers with a tremendous opportunity to observe a number of species from the California Current Large Marine Ecosystem, some of them notoriously difficult to study. Seabird, marine mammal, and white shark research carried out on the Farallon Islands over the years has dramatically increased our understanding of marine species and ecosystems and contributed substantially to their conservation. Considering all this, it's no wonder the islands have been nicknamed "California's Galapagos."

Bird rock goldfields

Bird rock goldfields, (*Lasthenia maritima*), also known as maritime goldfields, is by far the most successful plant species growing on the stony Farallon Islands. This plant produces an abundance of showy yellow flowers in the springtime that give away its family relationship to daisies and sunflowers. In addition to providing a splash of color to the dark rocky islands, *L. maritima* is also an important resource for some of the seabirds that nest on the islands. Although many of these birds brood their eggs in rocky crevasses and burrows, other species such as the western gull and Brandt's cormorant prefer to collect bird rock goldfields by the beakful for use in padding their nests.

Farallon arboreal salamander

Believed to have arrived on the Farallon Islands over 10,000 years ago when the lower sea level provided land access, the **Farallon arboreal salamander** (*Aneides lugubris farallonensis*) is the only native terrestrial vertebrate known to inhabit the Farallon Islands year-round. The Farallon arboreal salamander is closely related to a tree-dwelling species found at Point Reyes. Although trees are rare on the islands, the Farallon arboreal salamander has retained the strong claws and prehensile tail that serve as climbing aids for its mainland cousin. Despite its name, the Farallon arboreal salamander inhabits burrows in the ground, typically emerging only at night and using its strong jaws and large teeth to capture and eat small insects.

Northern fur seal

The **northern fur seal** (*Callorhinus ursinus*), known mostly from the North Pacific, Bering Sea, and Sea of Okhotsk off eastern Russia, is also found around California's offshore islands. This eared seal exhibits strong sexual dimorphism—the males are often over four times heavier than the females—and can also be identified by several unique characteristics of its flippers. The hind flippers are the longest of any eared seal species due to very long cartilaginous flaps that extend well beyond their small claws and aid in swimming, and the fore flippers are bald and have a distinct line where the fur begins near the wrists. Once the target of an international industry for their thick coat and dense fur, northern fur seals have been slowly increasing in number since the North Pacific Fur Seal Convention was adopted in 1911.

Found throughout the world's oceans, the **white shark** (*Carcharodon carcharias*) can often be seen cruising off Southeast Farallon Island between September and December, during the elephant seal breeding season. Known to grow to over 20 feet in length and more than 5,000 pounds in weight, white sharks use their size and strength to prey on a variety of marine mammals and fish—including the elephant seals that come close to matching them in size. White sharks are some of the ocean's most successful predators. When females give live birth to their young after 11 to 18 months of pregnancy, the shark pups have already honed their survival skills—developing white sharks are known to exhibit intrauterine cannibalism, whereby the more quickly growing sharks feed on their weaker siblings while still in the womb.

White shark

The subspecies of common murre found along the West Coast, the **California common murre** (*Uria aalge californica*) spends most of its life at sea, only returning to land in the springtime to nest in large, densely packed colonies. The common murre can dive to depths of over 600 feet and stay submerged for several minutes, propelled by its wings and feet. This ability allows the common murre to access a larger foraging area than seabirds that feed only on the ocean's surface. Common murres feed mostly on small fish such as sardines and anchovies. It is said that during the height of the breeding season, this colony resounds with a "murring" sound, as the birds let out a moaning call.

California common murre

The **ashy storm-petrel** (*Oceanodroma homochroa*) is a seabird of very limited population (approximately 10,000 individuals) found almost exclusively off California's coast. Over half of the global population is thought to nest on the South Farallon Islands. Because of predation by other birds such as western gulls and burrowing owls, ashy storm-petrels have adapted to come and go from their colonies at night. The ashy storm-petrel spends much of its life at sea, foraging miles offshore for small fish, squid, and krill that it plucks from the sea surface in mid-flight. Similar in size and coloration to several other storm-petrel species, the ashy storm-petrel can be identified by its quick, shallow wing-beats that rarely extend beyond horizontal at their apex.

Ashy storm-petrel

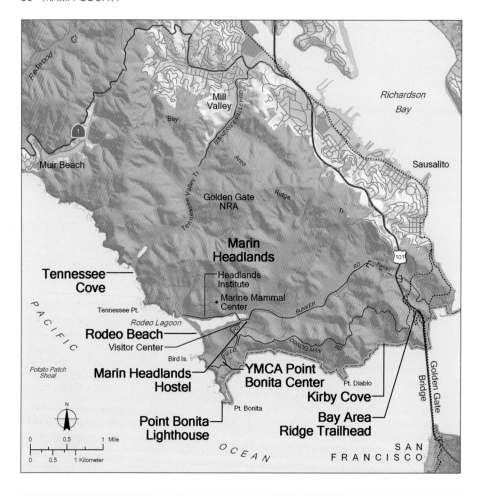

California brown pelican

Marin Headlands

	Sandy Beach	Rocky Shore	Trail	Visitor Center	Campground	Wildlife Viewing	Fishing or Boating	Facilities for Disabled	Food and Drink	Restrooms	Parking	Fee
Tennessee Cove	•	•	•		•			•		•	•	
Rodeo Beach	•	•	•	•				•		•	•	
Marin Headlands Hostel				•				•		•	•	•
Point Bonita Lighthouse			•	•				•		•	•	
Marin Headlands	•	•	•	•	•	•		•		•	•	
YMCA Point Bonita Center				•				•		•	•	•
Kirby Cove	•	•	•	•		•		•		•	•	
Bay Area Ridge Trailhead			•					•		•	•	

TENNESSEE COVE: *Tennessee Valley Rd., off Hwy. One in Mill Valley.* Gently sloping valley, part of the Golden Gate National Recreation Area; hiking trails lead north to Muir Beach and south to Rodeo Beach. A two-mile-long trail leads from the end of Tennessee Valley Rd. to the beach at Tennessee Cove, where a coarse-sand beach is flanked by greenstone outcroppings to the north and south. Haypress hike-in campsite has five sites, each accommodating up to four persons. Dogs, other than service animals, are not allowed at Haypress camp or on most trails in Tennessee Valley; for information, call: 415-331-1540. Miwok Livery Stables offers horseback riding instruction and trail rides by appointment; call: 415-383-8048.

RODEO BEACH: *Bunker Rd. off Hwy. 101 (Alexander Ave. exit).* A wheelchair-accessible bridge across a lagoon leads to the edge of pebbly Rodeo Beach. A picnic area and restrooms are available. Trails lead up the bluffs and through Rodeo Valley. For information on guided walks, call: 415-331-1540.

Former barracks house several environmental organizations. The Marine Mammal Center features a bookstore and is open for public viewing of rescued marine mammals from 10 AM to 5 PM daily, except Thanksgiv-

The Golden Gate National Recreation Area, located in San Francisco, Marin, and San Mateo Counties, reflects an effort by the National Park Service beginning in the 1960s to make its facilities more accessible to America's urban population. A number of unrelated events helped provide land for the recreation area, which was created in 1972, including the closure of the federal prison on Alcatraz Island and disposition of surplus military lands such as Fort Mason. Famed photographer Ansel Adams had proposed as early as the 1940s that the Golden Gate be designated as a national monument. Today, the Golden Gate National Recreation Area (known as GGNRA) is one of the national park system's most popular units, drawing some 17 million visitors annually to its attractions located on both sides of the Golden Gate. Visitor centers in Marin County are located at the Marin Headlands (open daily 9:30 AM to 4:30 PM, except Thanksgiving Day and Dec. 25; call: 415-331-1540) and at Muir Woods National Monument (open daily 8 AM to sunset; call: 415-388-7368).

ing Day, Dec. 25, and Jan. 1; educational and interpretive programs for groups are available by prior arrangement. Free entry, but donations are welcome. For information, call: 415-289-7325. The Headlands Institute offers young people a variety of science programs in a natural setting, including day camps and paid environmental internships; call: 415-332-5771.

Rodeo Beach is popular with surfers, and the adjacent highlands offer elevated spots for observers. The beach includes weathered particles of greenstone, red jasper, and orange chalcedony, known as carnelians, from the nearby cliffs. Offshore is Bird Island, a breeding place in springtime for pelagic cormorants. In summer, California brown pelicans roost on Bird Island. Rodeo Lagoon is a brackish water body where uncommon tufted ducks and harlequin ducks overwinter; in summer, western gulls and Caspian terns may be sighted. Observe posted restrictions on dogs.

MARIN HEADLANDS HOSTEL: *Off Bunker Rd., near Rodeo Lagoon.* 60 beds in shared or private rooms, shared kitchens, lounge with piano and wood stove, and recreation facilities; operated by Hostelling International.

For information or reservations between 7:30 AM and 11:30 PM, call: 415-331-2777. To locate the hostel using a mapping service, search for 941 Rosenstock Rd., Sausalito, CA, but note that the facility is not within the town of Sausalito.

POINT BONITA LIGHTHOUSE: *S.W. tip of Marin Headlands, end of Conzelman Rd.* Built in 1877, the lighthouse was manually operated until 1980. It is located on a treacherous point reached only via a tunnel hewn through solid rock and a suspension bridge over crashing surf. Open year-round from 12:30 to 3:30 PM, Saturday, Sunday, and Monday. Guided full-moon walks to the lighthouse are offered monthly, year-round. The walks are free, but space is limited and reservations are essential; call: 415-331-1540.

The original lighthouse at Point Bonita was built in 1855 and proved to be an inhospitable place; seven different tenders were employed in the first nine months of operation. In 1856 an iron cannon was installed as a fog signal, the first on the Pacific Coast. The keeper of the fog signal found his task somewhat onerous, as he was required to fire the cannon every 30 minutes during continuous fogs, which last sometimes for days on end.

Point Bonita Lighthouse

Rodeo Beach

The cannon was abandoned after a couple of years, and a foghorn was built in 1902.

MARIN HEADLANDS: *Off Hwy. One, N. of Golden Gate Bridge.* A series of grassy hills and valleys; former military lands, now part of the Golden Gate National Recreation Area. A wheelchair-accessible visitor center, located in the former Fort Barry chapel, is on Field Rd. off Conzelman Rd. The center features exhibits, books, and maps and is open from 9:30 AM to 4:30 PM daily, except Thanksgiving Day and Dec. 25; call: 415-331-1540. Permits are required for camping at any of the designated campsites in the headlands and are available at the visitor center. Bicentennial campsite has three sites, each accommodating one or two persons. Hawk camp has three sites, each accommodating up to four persons.

The coastline from Tennessee Cove to the Golden Gate Bridge consists of steep sea cliffs with beaches located between rocky outcroppings. Rocks of the Franciscan Complex, formed as many as 150 million years ago, including red chert, greenstone, and a type of sandstone known as graywacke, can be observed in many exposed locations in the headlands.

Chert is a thin-bedded sedimentary rock found in uncharacteristically thick ribbons in the headlands, usually layered and folded in angular patterns. Red chert is exposed in road cuts along Conzelman Rd., which winds along the headlands west of the Golden Gate Bridge. The basalt found in the headlands, called greenstone, is of volcanic origin, often with a greenish cast due to the presence of the minerals chlorite

Kirby Cove

and pumpellyite. Bird Island, the large rock lying just offshore the south end of Rodeo Beach, is a greenstone formation. Cavities in the greenstone are filled with pillow lavas or with various minerals, such as red jasper, visible on the cliffs around the beach at Kirby Cove, or orange chalcedony. Graywacke is a type of sandstone made up of various-sized angular grains, probably formed originally in a deepwater environment. The rocky cliffs at the north end of Rodeo Beach are composed of graywacke, ranging in color from gray at the bottom to a weathered soft brown at the top.

YMCA POINT BONITA CENTER: *Off Field Rd., near Conzelman Rd.* The center offers hikes and educational programs for youth, adults, and families; also available are overnight accommodations, by reservation only, for groups of 20 or more. Trails lead to a small beach also accessible by trail from Battery Alexander. For information about programs and events, call: 415-331-9622.

KIRBY COVE: *Conzelman Rd., off Hwy. 101 (Alexander Ave. exit).* Follow Conzelman Rd. from Hwy. 101 one-half mile to a locked gate; walk one mile down the steep gravel road. From the pebbly beach there are spec-

tacular views of San Francisco, the Golden Gate Bridge, and passing ships. For GGNRA information, call: 415-331-1540.

At Kirby Cove there are four campsites, each accommodating up to ten people. The sites, with picnic tables and barbecue grills, are set in a lovely grove of trees. Be prepared for foghorns in the night. For required reservations, call: 1-877-444-6777.

BAY AREA RIDGE TRAILHEAD: *Conzelman Rd., off Hwy. 101.* A link to the Bay Area Ridge Trail begins at the parking lot on Conzelman Rd. northwest of the Golden Gate Bridge. The Bay Area Ridge Trail system, planned to be 550 miles long, connects Mount Tamalpais State Park, Muir Woods, and Samuel P. Taylor State Park in Marin County, as well as ridgetops, parks, and open space in ten counties around San Francisco Bay. Different segments of the trail accommodate pedestrians, equestrians, and bicyclists. For information, see: www.ridgetrail.org.

The separate San Francisco Bay Trail provides public access near or along the shoreline of the bay; some 290 miles of trail, more than half of the planned system, have been completed. Call: 510-464-7900.

Painting of the *Tennessee*, San Francisco Maritime National Historical Park

"The tidal stream rushes through the [Golden Gate] in mid-channel generally about six knots an hour. . . . By taking advantage of this great tidal speed and of particular winds, which can almost daily be depended upon, blowing either in or out of the channel at certain periods of the day, ships may always safely enter or depart from the bay at all times of the year. An occasional wreck, where ships may have been driven by the strength of the tide or local currents upon the rocky shores, has indeed taken place, but this has generally been traceable to the ignorance or carelessness of the pilot. . . ." So wrote the authors of *The Annals of San Francisco*, a book published in 1855.

Despite the optimism of the *Annals*, finding the entrance to the Golden Gate was a challenge for mariners in the days before modern navigational aids. The *Tennessee*, a steamship of 1,194 tons, was put into service by the Pacific Mail Steamship Company in late 1849 to transport gold-seekers from Panama to San Francisco. The *Tennessee* also carried mail and merchandise such as pistols, watches, jewelry, glassware, cigars, and playing cards, intended for sale in the fledging city of San Fran-

cisco, where gold dust in the pockets of miners created a ready market for luxury goods. But the *Tennessee's* career was a short one: on March 6, 1853, as the ship felt its way through a dense fog toward San Francisco Bay, the crew saw surf ahead. Rather than strike the rocks that loomed up, the captain ordered full speed ahead toward a cove beach, now known as Tennessee Beach. There was no loss of life as the ship went ashore intact, although it later proved impossible to refloat the ship. Some passengers hiked over the hills to Sausalito, where they hired small boats to ferry them to San Francisco, and others waited for rescue ships.

Only a month later, on April 9, 1853, the steamer *Samuel S. Lewis*, owned by Cornelius Vanderbilt, was on approach from Nicaragua when it overshot the entrance to San Francisco Bay and ran aground on Duxbury Reef. The *Samuel S. Lewis* broke up within a day, a total loss like the *Tennessee*. The 385 passengers, including William Tecumseh Sherman, made it safely to the beach, where bonfires were lit to dry their clothes and they awaited rescue. Within two years, a light was constructed at Point Bonita, at the entrance to San Francisco Bay.

Geology of the Golden Gate

THE CONTRASTING rocks found on either side of the Golden Gate tell a geologic story spanning some 200 million years. It is a story of submarine volcanism, deep sea sedimentation, sliding plates, ocean trenches, and submarine landslides. The rocks telling this tale are all members of the Franciscan Complex, a group of sedimentary and volcanic rocks that is distributed widely throughout northern and central California. At many localities, the Franciscan Complex consists mostly of mélange, an unlayered mixture of hard sandstone blocks of varying size in a matrix of fine sheared mudstone. At the Golden Gate, examples of mélange are indeed exposed, but the Franciscan Complex here consists mostly of better-ordered rocks that reflect their complicated history.

The story starts some 200 million years ago at a so-called "spreading center" thousands of miles west of the North American margin. At that location, undersea volcanic action created new oceanic crust, or seafloor, mostly made up of basalt. The new crust that spread to the west became what is known as the Pacific Plate, and the crust that spread to the east made up the Farallon Plate. As the Farallon Plate drifted eastward it was consumed in a "subduction zone" at the margin of the North American continent, where the Farallon Plate dived beneath the North American Plate, forming a deep ocean trench. Thus, a giant basalt conveyor belt carried ocean crust eastward while the whole system also migrated to the east (relative to North America), narrowing the width of the Farallon Plate.

As the basaltic crust atop the Farallon Plate drifted east, it accumulated sediment. When it was far from North America, this sediment accumulated very slowly and consisted of very fine-grained mud alternating with the silica-rich remains of marine plankton such as radiolarian and diatoms, which would become chert as they solidified. As the crust neared the subduction zone, more abundant sediment derived from sources on the North American continent capped the sequence. Owing to their proximity to their land-based sources, these sediments were much coarser, consisting largely of sandstone. As the Farallon Plate was forced beneath the North American Plate, some of these sediments, and even some of the basaltic crust, were scraped off and tacked on to the margin of the North American Plate.

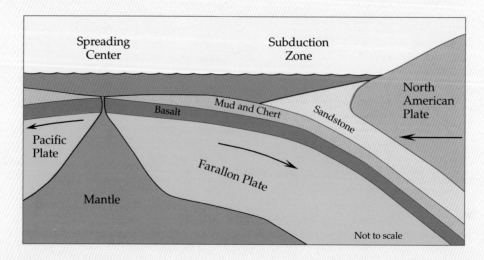

The rocks were added to the North American Plate in distinct slices beginning about 165 million years ago. Succeeding slices were thrust under earlier ones along faults, resulting in a stack of rock units with the youngest on the bottom and the oldest on top. Within each slice, however, the normal stratigraphic succession of younger rocks lying on top of older rocks was maintained. Geologists have identified these distinct slices and call them "terranes." The youngest terrane was accreted about 65 million years ago, and since that time the rocks have been elevated to the positions where we see them today.

The stacked nature of the Franciscan Complex terranes is best seen along the southern side of the Golden Gate, in San Francisco. Indeed, these contrasting terranes and the mélange that separates them are responsible for giving the city its world-famous hills. The faults separating the terranes run from northwest to southeast. The oldest terrane, the Alcatraz Terrane, makes up the northeastern part of the city. Consisting of thick sandstones derived from North America, it is well exposed on Alzatraz Island. If you cannot make it out to the island, you can also see these sandstones on the way up Telegraph Hill to Coit Tower.

Stuffed under the Alcatraz Terrane is the Marin Headlands Terrane, which consists of a fairly orderly succession of basalts overlain by beautiful "ribbon chert," in turn overlain by thick sandstones. The Marin Headlands Terrane is separated from the Alcatraz Terrane by a mélange of less coherent rocks known as the Hunters Point Mélange. (Note that while the various terranes making up the Franciscan Complex are named for San Francisco landmarks, they are not necessarily found only at their named locations.) The Hunters Point Mélange consists mostly of basalt and former basalt that has been altered by hot brines while it was still on the seafloor. The altered basalt was converted into serpentinite, consisting mostly of the mineral serpentine. Good examples of serpentinite can be seen at Fort Point, directly beneath the Golden Gate Bridge. The mélange is susceptible to sliding, and special attention had to be paid to the construction of the south anchorage of the Golden Gate Bridge to ensure its stability.

Tucked beneath the Marin Headlands Terrane is the San Bruno Mountain Terrane, separated by another mélange belt called the City College Mélange. Like the Hunters Point Mélange, the rocks of this mélange consist largely of serpentinite and basalt in a matrix of mudstone, and they are also very susceptible to landsliding. The best exposures of the City College Mélange are along the Coastal Trail at Lands End. The San Bruno Mountain Terrane, the youngest Franciscan terrane exposed in San Francisco, consists mostly of thick sandstone sequences derived from North America. It is well exposed at the site of the former Sutro Baths, below the famous Cliff House.

The headlands on the north side of the Golden Gate include rugged cliffs in which the Marin Headlands Terrane is exposed. When basalt is erupted underwater it forms spheroidal structures known as "pillows." Good examples of such pillow basalt can be seen on the trail leading to the Point Bonita Lighthouse. Excellent exposures of ribbon chert occur along Conzelman Road, and the sandstones can be seen in the bluffs north of Rodeo Beach. A tour of some of the most scenic and interesting sites on both sides of the Golden Gate provides an excellent window to the geologic past.

Because the layered rocks of the Marin Headlands trend at nearly right angles to those of the San Francisco Peninsula, a fault must lie beneath the Golden Gate strait itself. Indeed, weaknesses associated with such a fault, now inactive, might have been responsible for the path chosen for the waters of the San Joaquin and Sacramento rivers—and

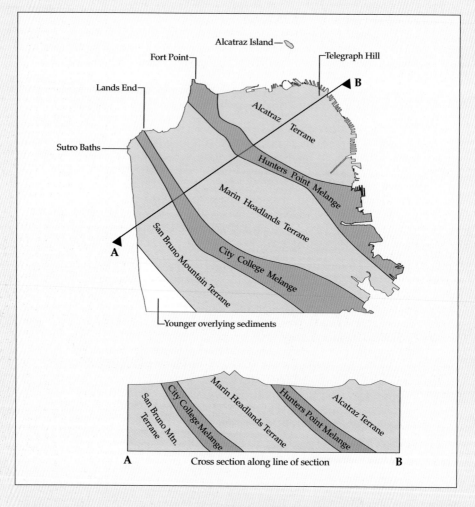

Cross section along line of section

of the Bay itself—to enter the sea. Beneath the waters of the Golden Gate the Franciscan Complex rocks are swept clean of sediment by the powerful tidal currents that sweep under the Golden Gate Bridge. At nearly six miles per hour, these are among the swiftest tidal currents in the world. Caused by the rush of about 25 percent of the volume of the bay through the narrow strait with each tidal cycle, they have carved a channel 370 feet deep floored by bedrock and scattered boulders. As the strait widens seaward, however, the velocity of these currents decreases until, less than a mile west of the bridge, they drop much of their sediment, covering the Franciscan Complex rocks with sheets of sand. This sand is still influenced by the tidal currents, however, which rework it into huge waves, some of which are as much as 30 feet high with wavelengths of over 700 feet. With each ebb tide, the sand waves migrate slightly seaward, carrying sand and gravel brought by rivers and streams through San Francisco Bay to the San Francisco Bar some eight miles outside the Golden Gate, where the sediments are deposited as the currents decelerate further.

Page opposite: 1886 square-rigger *Balclutha* and 1907 steam tug *Hercules* at San Francisco Maritime National Historic Park

San Francisco County

To Santa Rosa

To Sonoma

116

121

SONOMA

37

To Va

MARIN

101

San Pablo
Bay

1

CONTR
COST

580

To Berke

PACIFIC

S. F. Bay

Alcatraz Is

Treasure I

The Presidio of
San Francisco

101

1

Golden Gate Park

SAN

FRANCISCO

Golden Gate NRA

L Merced

280

Oak

Farallon
Islands
(S.F. Co.)

See Inset Below

OCEAN

1

35

280

SAN
MATEO

92

1

North
Farallon

Isle of
St. James

Gulf of the Farallons

Farallon
NWR

Middle
Farallon

PACIFIC

OCEAN

Southeast
Farallon

Maintop

Seal Rock

| 0 | 1 | 2 Miles |

| 0 | 1 | 2 Kilometers |

N

| 0 | 5 | 10 Miles |

| 0 | 5 | 10 Kilometers |

San Francisco County

BEGINNING thousands of years ago with the encampments of California Indians, San Francisco Bay has been a focus of settlement. Exploitation of the bay's abundant marine life supported some of San Francisco's earliest industries after the Gold Rush. Commercial fishing was well established by the time the city built its first Fisherman's Wharf in 1900, in part due to the introduction of the trawling net and lateen-rigged fishing boats by Genoese and Sicilian immigrants. The bay has a 460-square-mile surface area and provides life-sustaining habitat for many species of wildlife, in particular for millions of waterfowl on their annual migrations along the Pacific Flyway.

English expatriate William A. Richardson established a trading post at Yerba Buena Cove in 1835. In July of 1846, the American flag was raised at Yerba Buena, and six months later the outpost was renamed San Francisco—one year prior to the discovery in 1848 of a gold nugget at John Sutter's sawmill on the American River in the Sierra Nevada. Almost overnight the tiny settlement of San Francisco was transformed into an international port of call as gold seekers arrived by the thousands, decamping on the shores of Yerba Buena Cove to make the up-river journey to Sacramento—a day's horseback ride away from the gold fields.

From 1848 to 1849, San Francisco's population swelled with the arrival of more than 40,000 gold seekers, and an "instant city" of tents, shacks, and shanties sprang up at the foot of Telegraph Hill. The invention of the cable car by Andrew Hallidie in 1873 enabled the new "nabobs" such as Leland Stanford, Mark Hopkins, Collis Huntington, and James Flood to erect ostentatious mansions on Nob Hill, most of which were destroyed by the fire that followed the 1906 earthquake.

San Francisco has seen gold-seeking 49ers and is the home of professional football's 49ers. There is the 49 Mile Scenic Drive around the city, and even a magazine called 7x7, referring to the city's shape, roughly seven miles on a side. The city limits of San Francisco, however, encompass the Farallon Islands, located some 27 miles outside the Golden Gate, and Treasure Island within San Francisco Bay. Created for the 1939–1940 Golden Gate International Exposition, Treasure Island was built using landfill, some of which came from the Sacramento Delta. The Delta is fed by rivers that drain former gold mines, perhaps the origin of the island's fanciful name. During World War II, Treasure Island became a U.S. naval base. Following base closure in 1997, the City and County of San Francisco has moved to take over the island and develop a mix of residential, film production, and recreational uses. For information about redevelopment plans, call: 415-274-0660.

Visitors to San Francisco find plenty to do. For myriad ideas, contact the Visitor Information Center on Market St. at the foot of Powell St.; see www.sfcvb.org, or call: 415-391-2000.

Numerous recreational outfitters are located near Crissy Field in the Presidio.

Surf shops near Ocean Beach include: Aqua Surf Shop, 2830 Sloat Blvd., 415-242-9283; Mollusk Surf Shop, 4500 Irving St., 415-564-6300; San Francisco Surf Shop, 3809 Noriega St., 415-661-7873, and Wise Surfboards, 800 Great Hwy., 415-750-9473.

Boat and kayak rentals are available at Pier 40 near South Beach Harbor and also at Pier 39.

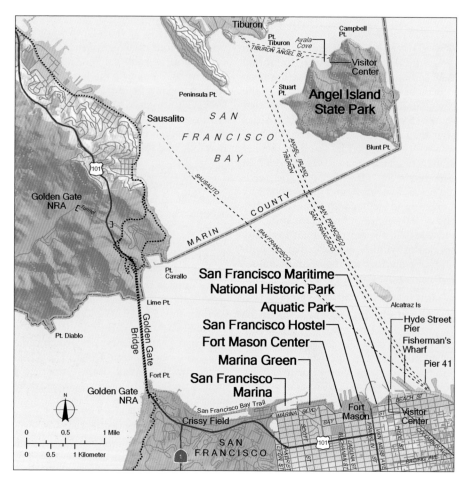

Tiburon

Pt.
Tiburon

Ayala
Cove

Campbell
Pt.

TIBURON ANGEL IS.

Visitor
Center

Peninsula Pt.

Stuart
Pt.

Angel Island
State Park

Sausalito

S A N

F R A N C I S C O

B A Y

Blunt Pt.

101

SAUSALITO

Golden Gate
NRA

Tunnel

C O U N T Y

ANGEL ISLAND
TIBURON

SAN FRANCISCO
SAN FRANCISCO

M A R I N

SAN FRANCISCO

Pt.
Cavallo

**San Francisco Maritime
National Historic Park**

Alcatraz Is

Lime Pt.

Aquatic Park

Hyde Street
Pier

Pt. Diablo

Golden Gate
Bridge

San Francisco Hostel

Fort Mason Center

Fisherman's
Wharf

Fort Pt.

Marina Green

Pier 41

Golden Gate
NRA

**San Francisco
Marina**

N

San Francisco Bay Trail

MARINA BLVD

Fort
Mason

BEACH ST

ST

Visitor
Center

Crissy Field

BAY

SCOTT

VAN NESS AVE

HYDE ST

COLUMBUS

0   0.5   1 Mile

S A N
F R A N C I S C O

BAKER ST

LYON ST

BUCHANAN ST

LAGUNA ST

FRANKLIN ST

PACIFIC AVE.

0   0.5   1 Kilometer

1

101

San Francisco Marina

San Francisco North

	Sandy Beach	Rocky Shore	Trail	Visitor Center	Campground	Wildlife Viewing	Fishing or Boating	Facilities for Disabled	Food and Drink	Restrooms	Parking	Fee
Angel Island State Park	•	•	•	•	•	•	•	•	•	•		•
San Francisco Maritime National Historical Park	•		•				•	•	•	•		
Aquatic Park	•	•	•				•	•	•	•		
San Francisco Hostel								•	•	•	•	•
Fort Mason Center								•	•	•	•	•
Marina Green		•						•	•	•	•	
San Francisco Marina	•	•	•				•	•		•	•	

ANGEL ISLAND STATE PARK: *1 mi. S.E. of Tiburon, Marin County.* Angel Island retains a remote feel, even in the midst of a metropolitan area. The island setting made it well-suited as a one-time immigration station; in the early 20th century, nearly one million U.S. immigrants were inspected, and sometimes detained, on the island. A former quarantine station for those suspected of carrying diseases is located at Ayala Cove. The island's military history began during the Civil War. During World War II, Angel Island was an embarkation point for troops headed for the Pacific theater and a processing facility for prisoners of war.

Blue and Gold ferries to Angel Island depart San Francisco's Pier 41 year-round and Oakland/Alameda and Vallejo seasonally; for recorded schedule, call: 415-773-1188. There is a separate year-round ferry service from Tiburon; call: 415-435-2131. All ferry tickets include state park entry fee. Private boats can dock at the slips at Ayala Cove; mooring fee applies. Service animals only are allowed on the island. Park hours are from 8 AM to sunset.

Ferries land at Ayala Cove, where there is a visitor center (open daily, all year) and a café (open daily from March to November). There are pleasantly sited picnic areas, restrooms, and running water. Seasonal services provided by the Angel Island Co. concessionaire include a summertime oyster bar and cantina, live music, bicycle rentals, and tours by kayak, tram, or Segway; call 415-897-0715. A hike or bike ride on the island's trails or paved roads reveals striking views of San Francisco and the Golden Gate. You may bring your own bicycle on the ferry; an additional fee may apply.

Nine individual environmental campsites and several group campsites are scattered on the island, from 1 to 2.5 miles from the ferry landing. For camping reservations, call: 1-800-444-7275. For state park information, including accessibility for those with limited mobility, call: 415-435-5390.

SAN FRANCISCO MARITIME NATIONAL HISTORICAL PARK: *N. of Beach St. from Van Ness Ave. to Hyde St., San Francisco.* Surrounded by other popular attractions, this unit of the National Park System offers numerous activities that paint a picture of historic life at sea. Many facilities can be enjoyed free of charge.

Start your tour at the visitor center at the foot of Hyde St. The exhibits, which were expanded in 2010, include the first-order Fresnel lens once housed in the lighthouse on the Farallon Islands. Photos show family life of 19th century lighthouse keepers at this isolated post. A large chart of ocean depths around the mouth of the Golden Gate shows an unnerving number of historic shipwrecks. The visitor center is open daily from 9:30 AM to 5 PM; no charge for entry. Call: 415-447-5000. Join in a sea chantey sing on the first Saturday of each month from 8 PM to midnight; for reservations, call: 415-561-7171.

The Hyde Street Pier, once the terminus for Sausalito and Berkeley-bound auto ferries, provides access to the Maritime National Historical Park's collection of historic ships. Pier entry is free; fee applies to board the ships. Open daily from 9:30 AM to 5 PM; last pier entry at 4:30 PM. The pier and some exhibits are wheelchair accessible. A tiny sandy beach and a foot shower are near the beginning of the pier. No dogs allowed on the pier. The Maritime Store with books on nautical topics, scrimshaw artworks, and souvenirs is located at the entrance to the pier.

AQUATIC PARK: *N. of Beach St., from Van Ness Ave. to Hyde St., San Francisco.* Aquatic Park, within the bounds of the San Francisco Maritime National Historical Park, has benches, lawns, and other facilities renovated in 2009–10. Aquatic Park's sandy beach is a favored spot for bay swimming; an outdoor beach shower is at the east end, next to the round observation building. The 1,850-foot Municipal Pier curves into the bay and is a favorite place to fish for smelt, flounder, and sculpin.

The Aquatic Park Bathhouse, completed in 1939 by the City of San Francisco and the federal Works Progress Administration, overlooks the beach. The Streamline Moderne-style structure contains striking public artworks supported by the Federal Arts Project, another New Deal-era federal program. Sea-foam green and white tile mosaics by artist Sargent Johnson face the bay, while interior murals by artist Hilaire Hiler depict fanciful creatures in a turquoise sea. Beginning in 1951, the Aquatic Park Bathhouse housed the National Maritime Museum along with a senior citizens' center. Restoration of the structure commenced in 2006, and maritime exhibits are planned to return to the building by 2012. In the meantime, the building is open daily, 10 AM to 4:30 PM, for viewing of the magnificent artworks.

The Dolphin Club and the South End Rowing Club, both founded in the 1870s, maintain clubhouses on the beach and promote bay swimming and rowing. Public use of the two clubs' facilities is available to swimmers on alternating days from Tuesday through Saturday, 10 or 11 AM, depending on season, to 6 PM; ring the doorbell for entry. Fee applies. The South End Rowing Club conducts an annual Alcatraz swim that is open to the public. Fitness pioneer Jack LaLanne, aged 60 and handcuffed, once swam from Alcatraz Island to Fisherman's Wharf while towing a 1,000-pound boat. For recorded information on San Francisco's beach water quality levels, call: 877-732-3224.

Aquatic Park Bathhouse tile murals by Sargent Johnson

Piers at Fort Mason Center

SAN FRANCISCO HOSTEL: *Fort Mason, near Bay and Franklin Streets, San Francisco.* The Hostelling International facility, also called the San Francisco-Fisherman's Wharf Hostel, occupies a prime site on the San Francisco Bay Trail that connects Fisherman's Wharf, Crissy Field, and other attractions. There are a total of 144 beds in shared and private rooms; café and guest kitchen; dining room, lounge, and outdoor deck; and free WiFi. Facilities are wheelchair accessible. For reservations, call: 415-771-7277. Fee applies.

FORT MASON CENTER: *Marina Blvd. off Buchanan St., San Francisco.* Once a military installation, the waterfront part of Fort Mason now houses galleries, music and theater performance spaces, a conference center, and a restaurant, along with the headquarters of several environmental organizations. Fine bay views from the site. Parking fee applies (first 30 minutes are free.) For current events, see www.fortmason.org.

MARINA GREEN: *N. of Marina Blvd., between Buchanan and Scott Streets, San Francisco.* The large grassy lawn near the breezy Golden Gate is a favorite place for kite-flying. Fitness course facilities are along the perimeter of the park. A snack stand and restrooms

are located near the smaller lawn off Lyon St. Dogs are welcome, if leashed; please pick up after your pet. For information, call: 415-831-5500. South of Marina Blvd. on Lyon St. is the Exploratorium, a science museum housed in the historic Palace of Fine Arts that dates from San Francisco's 1915 Panama-Pacific Exposition.

SAN FRANCISCO MARINA: *N. of Marina Blvd., W. of Fort Mason, San Francisco.* The Marina Yacht Harbor includes some 700 boat slips in two groups, separated by the Marina Green. Guest berths are available on a first-come, first-served basis. A fuel dock is in the East Harbor, and pumpout facilities are in both the East and West Harbors. No fishing or crabbing allowed within the marina. Parking is free, but some spaces are reserved at busy times for slip holders. For marina information, call: 415-567-8880.

At the end of the breakwater reached from Lyon St. off Marina Blvd, near a small sandy beach, is a "wave organ" where high tides produce rumbling sounds audible to visitors. The marina is home to both the St. Francis Yacht Club and the smaller Golden Gate Yacht Club, which in 2010 took possession of the America's Cup sailing trophy.

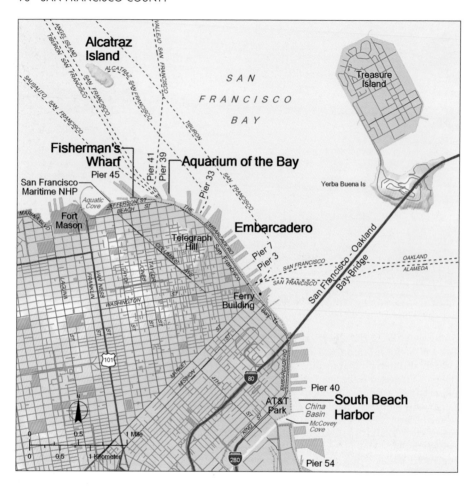

Dungeness crab unloaded at Fisherman's Wharf

San Francisco Northeast

	Sandy Beach	Rocky Shore	Trail	Visitor Center	Campground	Wildlife Viewing	Fishing or Boating	Facilities for Disabled	Food and Drink	Restrooms	Parking	Fee
Alcatraz Island		•	•	•		•				•		•
Fisherman's Wharf			•	•	•	•			•	•	•	
Aquarium of the Bay			•		•		•		•	•	•	
Embarcadero		•				•	•		•	•	•	
South Beach Harbor		•				•	•		•	•	•	

ALCATRAZ ISLAND: *Access via ferry from Pier 33, San Francisco.* The island is one of San Francisco's premier attractions, and there is much more of interest than one might expect at a decaying, one-time place of imprisonment. Alcatraz is a viewing spot for the city's dramatic skyline, prime seabird habitat, and even a garden isle.

The first lighthouse on the Pacific Coast was built on Alcatraz. The island later became a military prison for Civil War, Indian, and World War I prisoners. A maximum-security prison from 1934 to 1963, it housed such notable incorrigibles as Robert Stroud—the "Birdman of Alcatraz"—Al Capone, and Machine-Gun Kelly. In 1969, 80 American Indians landed on Alcatraz, claiming their right to the island on the basis of an 1868 U.S. treaty with the Sioux Nation. The three-year occupation was ended in 1971 when the Indians were evicted by U.S. Marshals. In 1972, "The Rock" became part of the Golden Gate National Recreation Area.

Access to Alcatraz is only by boats operated by Alcatraz Cruises from Pier 33. The first ferry of the day departs at 9 AM; return trips occur throughout the day, until at least 4:25 PM (later departures may be available seasonally). Trips often sell out during the summer and on holiday weekends. Advance reservations are advised; call: 415-981-7625. Entry to the island itself is free, but fee applies for the ferry.

National Park Service staff and volunteers lead island walks highlighting military history, prison inmates who spent time there, and natural history. Visitors may also wander the island independently, taking advantage of interpretive panels at key points; obey posted closures that protect seabird nesting areas. A 45-minute audio tour with reminiscences of Alcatraz prisoners and guards is included in the admission price and is available in the cell house.

Alcatraz is a steep, rocky island; ramps leading from the dock to the cell house rise 130 feet. An electric shuttle runs between the dock and the top of the hill. The ferry from San Francisco and the island's dock area, including restrooms, are fully wheelchair accessible; for information on other accessible

Approaching Alcatraz Island

San Francisco Bay, the region's most prominent feature, seemed doomed to annihilation some 50 years ago. The bay and adjoining marshes were being converted to dry land at a rapid rate. More than three square miles of bay, on average, were filled each year prior to 1965. Public access to the bay was hardly available, or even desirable, given the widespread practice of dumping municipal garbage and treated (or untreated) sewage into it. In 1960, only four out of 276 miles of bay shoreline were accessible for swimming, fishing, and wildlife viewing.

The change in approach from "anything goes" to resource enhancement came about through the efforts of ordinary citizens who glimpsed the threat that government leaders seemed utterly unable to recognize. Activists in communities including Berkeley and Palo Alto lobbied in the 1960s against pending plans to fill yet more bay waters. A widely circulated 1959 report by the U.S. Army Corps of Engineers showed how on-going filling of the bay could lead to its transformation, in places, into something resembling a stream rather than a miles-wide estuary. Years before "climate change" became a widely used term, alarmed residents heard predictions that the Bay Area without a bay would have hotter summers and colder winters.

An upsurge of public interest led to the California legislature's passage in 1965 of the McAteer-Petris Act, arguably the world's first coastal management law. At first temporary, the Bay Conservation and Development Commission, or BCDC, soon became a permanent institution, representing area local governments. Among BCDC's responsibilities are protecting the bay, regulating the filling of bay waters, and enhancing opportunities for public access to and along the shoreline. Limited fill of bay waters is allowed when necessary for essential water-oriented uses, such as ports, but is offset generally by the opening of former diked-off areas to tidal action. For information on BCDC, and a web guide to public accessways around the bay see: www.bcdc.ca.gov.

The bay is larger now than in 1965. Public access is available to more than 200 miles of bay shore; access along 65 miles of shoreline was required by BCDC in connection with waterfront development. The agency has also approved thousands of new boat berths. San Francisco Bay has a thriving shipping economy, anchored by the Port of Oakland (among America's busiest), while BCDC has protected the wildlife habitat values of tens of thousands of acres of saltmarshes, wetlands, and bay waters. The former garbage dump on the Berkeley shoreline is now a grassy park, seasonal home of burrowing owls and the midsummer location of a grand kite-flying festival. Salt ponds in the south bay continue in production, while serving as wildlife refuges. BCDC provided a model for the creation in 1973 of the California Coastal Commission, with its responsibility to protect and enhance the ocean coastline.

San Francisco Bay

facilities, call: 415-561-4900. There is no food service on the island, and eating and drinking, other than consuming bottled water, are not permitted except at the landing dock's picnic area. Smoking on the island is limited to a designated area at the dock.

FISHERMAN'S WHARF: *Jefferson and Taylor Streets, San Francisco.* Originally a harbor lined with fishing boats, the name Fisherman's Wharf now applies to the broader commercial area around the north end of Taylor St. Numerous eating places, commercial attractions, souvenir shops, and street performers can be found here, at what is probably San Francisco's top visitor destination. Although the commercial fishing industry has declined, there are still fishing boats to view and you can arrange a sport fishing or whale watching trip with one of several vendors near Fisherman's Wharf.

Ferries and tour boats leave Piers 41 and 45 for various destinations around San Francisco Bay. At Pier 45 are the Liberty Ship SS *Jeremiah O'Brien* and the USS *Pampanito*, a World War II-vintage submarine that is part of the San Francisco Maritime National Historical Park and is open daily to visitors; fee applies. The Fisherman's Wharf

area also includes Pier 39, which is lined with restaurants and shops. Pier 39 Marina is adjacent. For guest berth information, call: 415-705-5556. The marina has pumpout facilities and a resident population of California sea lions that have commandeered a floating dock and become a visitor attraction of their own.

AQUARIUM OF THE BAY: *Pier 39, the Embarcadero at Beach St., San Francisco.* The aquarium's exhibits focus on the biological riches found in and around San Francisco Bay. Visitors walk through transparent tunnels, surrounded by bay waters and giant seabass, octopus, and schools of anchovies. Touch tanks include marine animals, along with snakes and skinks. Demonstrations include shark feeding, bat ray feeding, and more. Open daily except December 25; hours vary seasonally. Fee for entry. Call: 415-623-5300. The Aquarium of the Bay is affiliated with the Bay Institute, a nonprofit learning and conservation organization.

EMBARCADERO: *Waterfront from Fisherman's Wharf to Pier 40, San Francisco.* San Francisco's northern waterfront rests on landfill composed of rubble and the hulks of abandoned ships left in Yerba Buena Cove after

Pier 7, Embarcadero

1848 as passengers and crew alike rushed to the gold fields. Before landfill extended the waterfront, a sandy beach known as North Beach stretched northwest from Telegraph Hill, then a promontory marking the western end of Yerba Buena Cove.

Before the middle of the 20th century, San Francisco's port was one of the busiest on the West Coast. The Ferry Building's landmark clock tower, completed in 1898 and modeled after Giralda Tower in Seville, Spain, served 40 million ferry passengers a year in its heyday. The opening of the Bay Bridge in 1936 was the beginning of a rapid decline of the ferry system, and by 1958 all commuter ferry service had ceased. Passenger ferries now link San Francisco to Sausalito, Tiburon, Larkspur, Oakland, Alameda, and Vallejo. The Ferry Building thrives again as a culinary destination. There are restaurants, food vendors, and a popular farmer's market.

On the bay side of the Embarcadero, the wide sidewalk bears the name of Herb Caen, long-time San Francisco booster and newspaper columnist. There is excellent access to the bay for viewing and fishing at Pier 7 and also at the foot of Mission St. Public promenades are located on the bay side of some of the pier buildings, such as Pier 3, where there are public restrooms.

The grand pier bulkhead buildings that line the waterfront look much as they did during the port's boom years, although they are no longer devoted to transshipment of cargo. North of the Ferry Building are odd-numbered piers with neoclassical facades, evoking Roman temples. To the south of the Ferry Building the piers bear even numbers, and the facades are more eclectic in design. Embarcadero-area parking meters operate every day, and time limits are strictly enforced. The Municipal Railway's historic streetcars run north from Market Street along the Embarcadero. A separate light-rail line extends south from the underground Embarcadero Station past AT&T Park to the Caltrain railroad station at 4th and King St.

SOUTH BEACH HARBOR: *Between Pier 40 and AT&T Park, San Francisco.* The marina contains 700 slips and a guest dock, adjacent to a pleasant public park. Pumpout stations are on the guest dock; no charge for use. For marina information, call: 415-495-4911. The nearest public boat launch is at Pier 54, about one-half mile farther south along the waterfront.

Next to the marina is bayfront AT&T Park, home of the San Francisco Giants baseball team. The San Francisco Bay Trail runs along the waterfront side of the ballpark.

The year is 1939, and you are an adventurous traveler bound from California to Hong Kong. You might consider making the journey by air: Pan American Airways Clippers offered the first scheduled transpacific passenger service. The planes were huge propeller-driven flying boats; the Boeing B-314 Clipper was the largest passenger craft in the air until the jumbo jet era began, decades later.

At San Francisco, the bay was the runway. The Clippers took off in late afternoon from the waters of the cove between Treasure Island and the newly built Bay Bridge and headed west through the Golden Gate. You would have shared a spacious compartment with a handful at most of other well-off passengers. Elaborate meals were served in the salon, and favored travelers were seated at the captain's table. After dinner, stewards converted seats to berths, and passengers deposited their shoes for an overnight shine. After sunrise the Clipper cruised to a landing on the waters of Pearl Harbor, after as many as 21 hours in the air.

After a comfortable overnight stay at the Royal Hawaiian Hotel, travelers hopped westward on the Clipper from island to island. At virtually uninhabited Midway and Wake Islands, Pan American Airways had built hotels to accommodate its customers; except for the first leg, flights took place only during daylight hours. Additional stops were at Guam, Manila, and Macao. The journey all the way to Hong Kong required more than 60 hours of flying time and six elapsed days (not counting one day gained by crossing the International Date Line). In the late 1930s, passage by ship to China required weeks longer. The 1940 ticket price of $500, roundtrip from San Francisco to Honolulu, reflected the all-first-class nature of the service. Roundtrip to Hong Kong cost $1,368; the fare included hotel stays and meals along the way. Those on board were likely of ample means, perhaps an heiress or two, an ambassador, or maybe writer Ernest Hemingway.

Transoceanic service by flying boat pushed the limits of the era's aviation technology. Immersion in salt water took a toll on equipment, and floating debris was a considerable hazard during take-off and landing. The cabin was not pressurized. The 2,400 miles from San Francisco to Honolulu was traversed at a maximum cruising speed of 150 miles per hour. A stiff headwind coupled with a heavy load of mail sometimes required the captain to leave some passengers behind, or to turn the plane back in mid-flight. And although the cabin was spacious well beyond modern standards, with a high ceiling and large windows, passengers had little to do other than play cards or stroll the grandly named (but short) Promenade Deck.

Pan American Airways Clipper, Boeing B 314

San Francisco Bay and Estuary

ENCOMPASSING more than 1,600 square miles of open water, San Francisco Bay is by far the largest estuary on the west coast of North and South America. The bay's sinuous shoreline, with its tidal channels and river mouths, is some 1,530 miles long, or about two-thirds the length of California's ocean coast.

The bay owes its existence to two splays of the San Andreas Fault system—the San Andreas itself to the west of the bay and the Calaveras, Hayward, and Rogers Creek faults to the east. Although most of the movement along these faults is horizontal slip (that is, one block of the earth's crust is sliding past another), beginning about three million years ago a shift in plate motion introduced an element of compression. This so-called transpressional movement resulted in the uplift of the Santa Cruz Mountains and the East Bay hills. Between them lay the broad Santa Clara Valley. At this time the ancestral Sacramento and San Joaquin Rivers drained to the sea not through what is now the Golden Gate, but rather through an outlet somewhere to the south. We know this because the oldest sediments beneath the Santa Clara Valley and San Francisco Bay are derived only from local rocks rather than from the Sierra Nevada. Beginning only about 600,000 years ago, the Sacramento and San Joaquin Rivers, carrying grains of rock derived from the Sierra Nevada, began to flow into what is now San Francisco Bay.

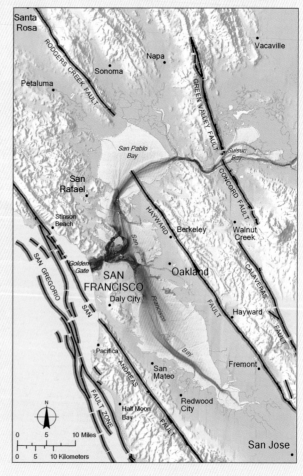

As sea level rose and fell during the past two million years (the Ice Ages), the Santa Clara Valley was alternately flooded by the sea and dry-floored. These oscillations are recorded in alternating bay muds and alluvial sands derived from the local mountains. As recently as 18–20,000 years ago, San Francisco Bay did not exist, and the Pacific Ocean shoreline was located near the continental shelf break west of the Farallon Islands and Cordell Bank. The modern bay only came into existence about 10,000 years ago as it was flooded gradually after the most recent Ice Age, called the Last Glacial Maximum. San Francisco Bay, including the south and central bay, along with San Pablo Bay, Suisun Bay, and the Sacramento and San Joaquin River Delta, then received the run-off from 40 percent of California's surface area. At that time, the extensive complex of bays and tidal and freshwater marshes supported a population of 10 to 20,000 Native Americans, for whom fish and shellfish were an important food source.

After gold was discovered in the foothills of the Sierra Nevada in 1848, California's population exploded, at tremendous cost to aboriginal populations and the natural world in which they lived. Until it was stopped by court injunction in 1884, hydraulic gold mining was practiced in California. This destructive method entailed blasting rock with high pressure jets of water in order to release gold particles. Hydraulic mining fed tens of millions of cubic yards of rocks and earth each year into rivers and streams, devastating salmon habitat, obstructing navigation, and adding enormous quantities of sand and mud to the San Francisco Bay and Estuary.

Commercial fishing in the bay boomed in California's early years and then began its long decline. Eastern species such as striped bass and Atlantic oysters were intentionally introduced in the hopes of commercial exploitation, and shipping accidentally introduced additional non-native organisms. During the same period, the new human arrivals were busy diking and filling marshes for agricultural and other development and dumping their wastes in the bay. Of the 850 square miles of marsh that supported Native Americans for millennia, only about 48 square miles remain. Half the fish species in the marshes are introduced, and hundreds of other exotic plants and animals have invaded the bay. As a result, most of the species of large invertebrates you are likely to observe are not native. The San Francisco Bay and Delta is perhaps the most invaded aquatic system in the world.

Mining, agricultural runoff, and urban waste discharges have added a rich variety of contaminants to bay waters and sediments. And, as the state's population has grown, the demand for water has more than kept pace. Of the 27 million acre-feet of fresh water that flowed into the bay in 1850, over 60 percent is now diverted for human use. Agriculture alone uses over 80 percent of California's managed water supply. Disruption of the natural flow of water by dams and diversions has many negative environmental consequences, the most apparent of which is the decline in many species of fish, such as salmon, striped bass, and delta smelt. Besides the loss or degradation of habitat, many hundreds of millions of juvenile fish are lost by being sucked up by pumps and irrigation siphons. Yet, despite over 150 years of astounding environmental insults, the bay and delta still have incredible biological value, providing habitat for remaining populations of native estuarine species, nursery grounds for native marine fish and invertebrates, and critical habitat for millions of birds migrating along the Pacific Flyway.

Much of the bay is surprisingly shallow—the south bay, for instance, averages only 18 feet in depth. On the other hand, water depth at the Golden Gate is more than 300 feet. The water depth varies with the tides, of course, and in California the so-called mixed semi-diurnal tides result in two unequal high tides and two unequal low tides each day. That is, four times per day the current through the Golden Gate reverses. With each ebb tide, approximately 25 percent of the bay's volume leaves the bay, to be replaced on the subsequent flood tide. The resulting tidal currents are among the strongest in the world and can be a challenge to the novice sailor. It is the mixing of the fresh waters introduced by the rivers and the seawater brought in by the flood tides that creates the diverse environments of this, and any, estuary. Variability in salinity, water depth, and sediment flux creates ecological niches for a diversity of organisms.

Marsh gumplant

As might be guessed from its cheery, daisy-like yellow flowers, **marsh gumplant** (*Grindelia stricta* var. *angustifolia*) is a member of the sunflower family. The name "gumplant" refers to the white sticky latex that protects the developing seeds from predator insects. This two-to-five-foot-tall subshrub with leathery green leaves plays an important role in the ecosystem. During high tides, animals like the salt marsh harvest mouse, clapper rail, and black rail climb up its stems to seek refuge from the inundated lands. Many insects feed on the nectar of the flowers; birds and mice eat the seeds; and some birds nest and roost in its sheltered leafy stems. And of course, people stop to admire the beauty of the flowers, which bloom in late summer.

Suisun thistle

A perennial herb in the sunflower family, the endangered **Suisun thistle** (*Cirsium hydrophilum* var. *hydrophilum*) can be found today in only a few places. Suisun thistle occurs in the upper reaches of undiked tidal marshes, often growing among cattail, American bulrush, saltgrass, and other salt-tolerant, or halophytic, marsh plants. Although each flowering plant may produce hundreds of seed heads, most seeds fail to ripen or are eaten by non-native thistle weevils. Other significant threats to the species include human-caused changes to natural tidal regimes, habitat invasion by the non-native perennial pepperweed, and loss of habitat due to sea level rise.

Great egret

The **great egret** (*Ardea alba*) has a yellow bill and black legs (its smaller cousin, the snowy egret has a black bill and legs and yellow feet). The great egret can be found in both freshwater and saltwater wetlands, marshes, and mudflats, often methodically stalking fish, amphibians, reptiles, and small animals before it quickly thrusts its spear-like bill and swallows its prey whole. Standing over three feet tall with a wingspan of nearly five feet, the great egret not only earns its name for its size, but for its beautiful lacy breeding plumage that extends beyond its tail. Great egrets were once hunted nearly to extinction for these magnificent pure-white feathers, which were used in hats and other fashions. Public outcry led to the birds' protection and eventual recovery, but today the great egret faces new threats as the quality and size of wetland habitats decrease.

A thumb-sized rodent of salt and brackish marshes, the **salt marsh harvest mouse** bears a scientific name (*Reithrodontomys raviventris*) that means "grooved-toothed mouse with a red belly." The northern subspecies (*R. r. halicoetes*) lives in marshes of the San Pablo and Suisun bays, and the southern subspecies (*R. r. raviventris*) lives in marshes of Corte Madera, Richmond, and South San Francisco Bay. Both subspecies depend on dense vegetation for cover from predators, and their preferred habitat is pickleweed. These primarily nocturnal creatures are good swimmers with the ability to drink sea water for long periods. Unfortunately, the species is endangered, having sustained extensive habitat loss. Some of the mouse populations are sustaining themselves in a few marsh areas, such as at Don Edwards San Francisco Bay National Wildlife Refuge.

Salt marsh harvest mouse

The **delta smelt** (*Hypomesus transpacificus*) is a little fish that is endemic to the brackish waters of Suisun Bay and the adjacent confluence of the Sacramento and San Joaquin rivers. The delta smelt spends most of its one-year lifespan feeding where the salt concentration is about two parts per thousand (ocean water is about 33 ppt) and laying eggs nearby in the small branches of freshwater sloughs. Destruction of tidal and freshwater marshlands and the increasing diversion of fresh water to farms and cities have resulted in poorer habitat for the smelt. During the summer period of low flow, massive pumps actually cause the lower river to flow upstream.

Delta smelt

California is home to two of the world's 26 species of sturgeon. Armored with boney plates instead of scales, these fish have changed little in appearance in 200 million years. Like salmon, most sturgeons are anadromous, spending much of their life in the ocean but returning to fresh water to spawn. However, sturgeon spawn many times during a lifetime that may exceed 100 years. The **white sturgeon** (*Acipenser transmontanus*) occurs from the Aleutian Islands to California, where it spawns in the Sacramento River. A favorite target of sport fishermen, the white sturgeon is the largest fish in North America, reaching 20 feet and over 1,500 pounds. White sturgeon are farmed in California, providing a sustainable source of high-quality caviar.

White sturgeon

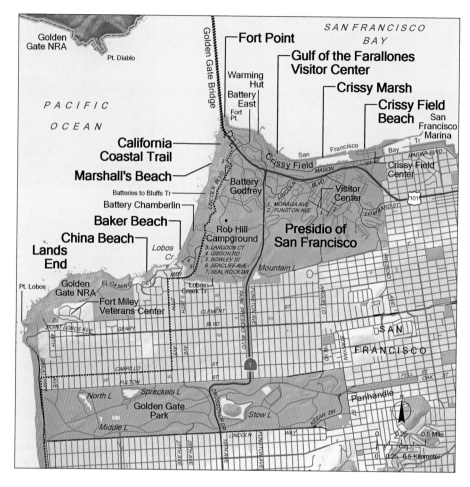

Crissy Marsh

San Francisco Presidio to Lands End

	Sandy Beach	Rocky Shore	Trail	Visitor Center	Campground	Wildlife Viewing	Fishing or Boating	Facilities for Disabled	Food and Drink	Restrooms	Parking	Fee
Presidio of San Francisco	•	•	•	•	•	•	•	•	•	•	•	
Crissy Field Beach	•		•	•		•	•	•	•	•	•	
Crissy Marsh				•		•		•		•	•	
Gulf of the Farallones Visitor Center				•		•		•		•	•	
Fort Point		•	•			•	•	•	•	•	•	
California Coastal Trail			•			•					•	
Marshall's Beach	•	•	•			•	•				•	
Baker Beach	•	•	•				•	•		•	•	
China Beach	•	•					•	•		•	•	
Lands End		•	•			•				•	•	

PRESIDIO OF SAN FRANCISCO: *N.W. corner of San Francisco.* Once a military post under the flags of Spain (1776–1822), Mexico (1822–1848), and the United States (1848–1994), the Presidio is now jointly managed by the National Park Service and the Presidio Trust. The 1,480-acre park contains 11 miles of hiking trails, 14 miles of bicycle routes, spectacular vistas, historic buildings, former coastal defense fortifications, a saltwater marsh, and the Letterman Digital Arts Center, where 21st century films are made. The hilly and forested Presidio is laced with winding streets; to begin your visit, pick up a map at the Visitor Center in the former Officers Club on Moraga Ave. at Arguello Blvd. The building contains a bookshop and exhibit space and incorporates an adobe structure built about 1810–20 as officers' quarters.

High above Baker Beach is Rob Hill campground, renovated in 2010. There are four tent sites open to either families or large groups. Some sites may be in use by the Camping at the Presidio program, which introduces urban kids to a camping experience. Facilities include picnic tables, barbecue grills, campfire circles, and restrooms; there are no showers. Fee for camping; parking is limited. No amplified music or generators allowed; for required reservations, call: 415-561-5444.

CRISSY FIELD BEACH: *W. of San Francisco Marina, N. of Mason St., Presidio, San Francisco.* Crissy Field Beach is located off the Presidio's Mason St., the western extension of Marina Blvd. This long and very scenic beach is a highly popular spot for fresh air, exercise on the San Francisco Bay Trail, and perhaps a toe-dab in the chilly bay water. This is a favored spot to launch a kayak. Picnic tables are located inland of the beach, along with restrooms and beach showers. Near the beach's west end is enormous, grassy Crissy Field, once a landing strip for small aircraft and now suited to vigorous kite-flying. In 1925, two seaplanes departed Crissy Field in a first, and failed, attempt to reach Hawaii nonstop by air; a successful flight took off from the same airstrip two years later. For information on kids' summer camps, call: 415-561-7762. The Crissy Field Center includes a public café; open daily from 9 AM to 5 PM. At 610 Mason St. in the Presidio is a Sports Basement store, offering rentals and sales of recreational equipment.

Park in designated areas only, not on lawns. Observe posted rules for dogs on Crissy Field and adjoining areas; always leash your dog in the parking and picnic areas. No glass containers or fires permitted on the beach. For recorded information on beach water quality levels, call: 877-732-3224.

CRISSY MARSH: *Between Mason St. and the Bay Trail, Presidio, San Francisco.* Restoration of the salt water lagoon and marsh was completed in 2001. The area is a prime site for wildlife viewing. Paved or packed earth paths ring the marsh, and a bridge crosses the eastern neck of the lagoon. Look for shorebirds on the mudflats at low tide, great blue herons and great egrets, and wintertime ducks, such as buffleheads. Anna's hummingbirds and golden-crowned sparrows inhabit the scrub surrounding the marsh.

GULF OF THE FARALLONES VISITOR CENTER: *W. Crissy Field, near Mason St. and Fort Point, San Francisco.* In an old Coast Guard building is a visitor center dedicated to the resources of the Gulf of the Farallones National Marine Sanctuary, located between the Farallon Islands and the mainland. Exhibits show the dozen or so species of whale that frequent the area, including the enormous blue whale, and some 16 shark species, including the basking shark, the white shark's far larger (but less threatening) cousin. Open Wednesday through Sunday, 10 AM to 4 PM. Call: 415-561-6625. Expansion of the visitor center and creation of a new Ocean Climate Center are planned. The Oceanic Society offers public nature cruises to the Gulf of the Farallones to look for seabirds and blue, humpback, and gray whales; call: 415-474-3385.

FORT POINT: *Off Lincoln Blvd., beneath the Golden Gate Bridge, San Francisco.* Fort Point's setting is one of high drama: the towering Golden Gate Bridge, wind-blown waves, great ships sailing by. In Alfred Hitchcock's classic film *Vertigo,* Kim Novak's character in a moment of panic flings herself into San Francisco Bay near Fort Point.

Built between 1853 and 1861, the brick Fort Point is a National Historic Site. Its mighty cannon, trained on the entrance to San Francisco Bay, were never used. Visitors can tour the officers' and enlisted men's quarters, kitchen, and hospital. Members of the American Civil War Association are sometimes present in costume. Winter-time candlelight tours are offered, as are autumn pier-crabbing demonstrations on occasional Saturday mornings; for required reservations, call: 415-556-1693. Fort Point is partially wheelchair accessible. Open Friday through Sunday, 10 AM to 5 PM. On very windy days, park away from the water's edge to avoid a saltwater bath.

Near the shoreline east of Fort Point in Presidio Bldg. 983 is a Warming Hut operated by the Golden Gate National Parks Conservancy. Purchase a hot beverage here or browse in the bookshop. Open daily from 9 AM to 5 PM; call: 415-561-3040. The adjacent torpedo wharf, built in 1908, is now a public fishing pier.

Fort Point

Baker Beach

CALIFORNIA COASTAL TRAIL: *Along the Pacific Coast, from Oregon to Mexico.* The California Coastal Trail enters San Francisco via the Golden Gate Bridge. At the toll plaza, the Coastal Trail heads west and south, past a parking area at Battery Godfrey on Langdon Ct. Southwest of the bridge, bicycles use Lincoln Blvd. From the Golden Gate Bridge, the San Francisco Bay Trail leads east to Crissy Field and beyond. Only the bridge's east sidewalk is open to pedestrians; automatic gates are open generally during daylight hours. Skates and skateboards are not permitted on the bridge; dogs are allowed only on leash.

Bicyclists may cross the bridge toll-free, 24 hours a day, via sidewalk. When the bridge is closed to pedestrians, security staff will buzz bicyclists through the locked gate. Bicyclists generally share the east sidewalk with pedestrians on weekdays and use the bridge's west sidewalk on weekends and holidays. Check signage for complete bridge access information and rules.

For a scenic overlook of the Golden Gate, park at the Battery East parking area 300 yards east of the bridge toll plaza on Lincoln Blvd. The paved, multi-use San Francisco Bay Trail skirts the parking area.

MARSHALL'S BEACH: *W. of Lincoln Blvd., off Langdon Ct., San Francisco Presidio.* A sandy strand bordered by rock headlands lies at the base of a steep bluff, between the Golden Gate Bridge and Baker Beach. Beach access is by foot only, via the Batteries-to-Bluffs Trail, off the California Coastal Trail. From Lincoln Blvd., turn west onto Langdon Ct. one-quarter mile south of the Golden Gate Bridge toll plaza. Park in the gravel lot adjacent to Battery Godfrey and proceed from the south end of the parking area along the Coastal Trail. A series of sturdy wooden steps lead down the slope; the well-signed path is studded with shiny, green outcroppings of serpentinite. No facilities. The parking area at Battery Godfrey offers particularly fine late-afternoon views of the Golden Gate Bridge and Marin Headlands.

BAKER BEACH: *W. of Lincoln Blvd., off 25th Ave., San Francisco.* A mile-long sandy beach, backed by dunes, is a great spot for strolling, shore-fishing, or picnicking. Body-surfing is popular, although the surf can be rough. Two large parking areas at the foot of Gibson Rd. hold more than 160 vehicles; lots close at 7 PM. Restrooms are near the parking areas, and sheltered picnic tables are located among the trees. Observe posted restrictions on dogs; always leash your dog in the parking and picnic areas. The northern portion of the beach is clothing optional.

Battery Chamberlin, at the end of the northern parking lot, is one of many former defense installations around the Golden Gate. The underground facility was completed in 1904, and by the 1920s 16-inch guns had been installed that had a range of 25 miles. During World War II, Battery Chamberlin was on high alert for an enemy attack that fortunately never came. Volunteers are on-site for demonstrations on the first full weekend of each month, from 11 AM to 3 PM; call: 415-561-4323.

Lobos Creek drains the slopes inland of Baker Beach. The creek is the only remaining free-flowing stream in San Francisco. Visitors can explore a dune hollow vegetated with native wildflowers and dune plants, including beach strawberry, lupine , and the rare dune gilia. The Lobos Creek Trail starts on the east side of Lincoln Blvd., south of Bowley St.

CHINA BEACH: *Seacliff Ave. near El Camino Del Mar, San Francisco.* A sandy pocket beach is located between rock outcroppings. There are 40 parking spaces atop the bluff, and a steep paved walkway to the beach. There are restrooms, a sundeck, a picnic area with barbecue grills, and nice views of the shipping channel leading into San Francisco Bay. The surf is too rough for swimming, and the northwest-facing beach can be very windy. No pets, fires, or glass containers. Call: 415-561-4323.

LANDS END: *N. of Fort Miley Veterans Center, San Francisco.* A surprisingly non-urban segment of the California Coastal Trail runs past Lands End. There is parking along El Camino del Mar, north of Seal Rock Dr. The broad-packed earth trail leads through forests of Monterey cypress, overlooking Seal Rocks and the Golden Gate. The first part of the trail is mostly flat and is wheelchair accessible; as it continues north and east, the trail narrows and becomes sandy. Keep on trails; the cliffs are extremely dangerous.

Point Lobos and former Sutro Baths site

California Coastal Trail southwest of Golden Gate Bridge

The California Coastal Trail is planned as a continuous public right-of-way, some 1,200 miles long and located as close as possible to the sea. Not just one pathway, the Coastal Trail is more like a yarn composed of several threads, each one a trail alignment or trail improvement that responds to local terrain or accommodates a particular purpose. One thread may be for beach walkers or equestrians, where a sandy reach of coastline makes this practical. Another segment of the trail may be a paved, urban path for bicyclists, skaters, and wheelchair users. A trail thread may be in use only seasonally, where necessary to skirt a beach on which western snowy plovers nest in spring and summer, or to bypass wintertime high water at a coastal river mouth. An important objective of the Coastal Trail project is to provide a route entirely separate from coastal roads. Because of steep terrain and limited public right-of-way in some locations, however, parts of the trail may require that users share the alignment with vehicles.

Each part of the Coastal Trail has its own character, reflecting the great diversity of environments found along California's varied and dynamic shoreline. About two-thirds of the Coastal Trail has been completed, and work continues. The California Coastal Commission, State Coastal Conservancy, the nonprofit organization Coastwalk, the California Department of Parks and Recreation, and many other groups are working together to make the trail a continuous one and to link parks, ports, communities, schools, trailheads, bus stops, visitor attractions, and more. For information on the Coastal Trail including maps for hikers and other trail users, see: www.californiacoastaltrail.info.

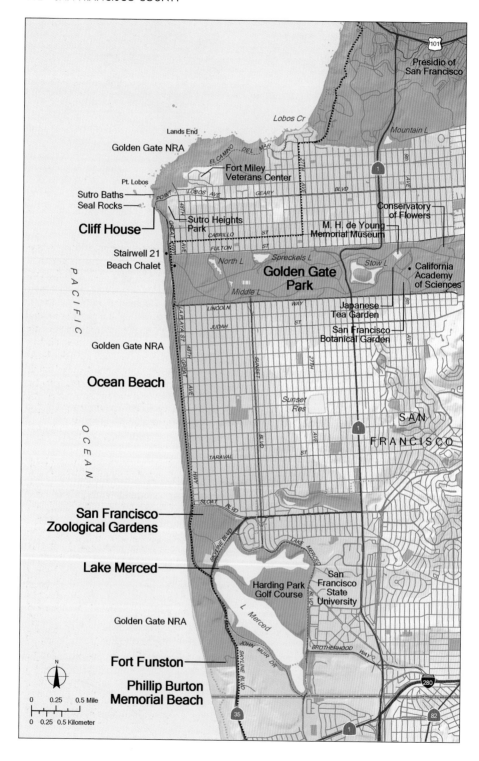

San Francisco West

	Sandy Beach	Rocky Shore	Trail	Visitor Center	Campground	Wildlife Viewing	Fishing or Boating	Facilities for Disabled	Food and Drink	Restrooms	Parking	Fee
Cliff House	•	•	•	•		•			•	•	•	
Golden Gate Park		•	•			•	•		•	•	•	
Ocean Beach	•					•	•		•	•	•	
San Francisco Zoological Gardens				•	•		•		•	•	•	•
Lake Merced			•		•	•	•		•	•	•	
Fort Funston	•		•				•			•	•	
Phillip Burton Memorial Beach	•		•				•					

CLIFF HOUSE: *Point Lobos Ave. and Great Highway, San Francisco.* The first Cliff House, known as Seal Rock House, was a hotel built in 1863. The site was then some seven miles distant from the young city of San Francisco, and it was accessible mainly to those possessed of a private carriage or at least the spirit of adventure. In 1881 Adolph Sutro bought Seal Rock House with the intention of making the seaside site accessible to San Francisco's working-class residents. Sutro was an engineer who had prospered in Nevada's silver mines. In 1888 he built a steam railway from downtown San Francisco to the ocean; the one-way fare to Seal Rock cost a nickel. Fire later destroyed Sutro's roadhouse, as well as a grand Victorian pile built in 1896 to replace it. The present Cliff House was built in 1909 and restored in 2003 by the National Park Service, which owns the site. The Cliff House contains restaurants, gift shops, and public viewing areas.

Seal Rocks, visible offshore from the Cliff House, have been eroded from the mainland by wave action. The rocks are a haul-out area for Steller and California sea lions, the latter distinguished by their raucous barking. Gulls and cormorants also roost here.

Northeast of the Cliff House are the ruins of the Sutro Baths. Built in 1890 by Adolph Sutro, the complex covered more than three acres and consisted of six saltwater swimming pools and a freshwater plunge, a restaurant, conservatories, galleries, and a museum. The baths attracted large crowds who came to see the Roman-like splendor of the public spa. As the popularity of public natatoriums waned, the baths fell into disuse, and in 1937 the largest pool was converted to an ice-skating rink. In 1966 the property was sold to land developers. Within the same year a spectacular fire destroyed all but the foundation walls of the pools, visible today as water-filled ruins. A particularly scenic portion of the California Coastal Trail, uphill to the east of the Sutro Baths, can be accessed by foot. A paved parking lot north of Point Lobos Ave. serves the Cliff House area and the California Coastal Trail, and a new visitor center is planned by late 2011.

Coastal Cleanup Day, Ocean Beach

Sutro Heights Park, at Point Lobos and 48th Ave., is the landscaped grounds of the mansion built by Adolph Sutro in 1879 and since razed. Groves of Monterey pine, fir, and Norfolk Island pine grow on the terrace overlooking the Cliff House and the ocean. For information on the Cliff House area of the Golden Gate National Recreation Area, call: 415-561-4323.

GOLDEN GATE PARK: *E. of Great Highway, between Fulton St. and Lincoln Way, San Francisco.* In 1868, the young city of San Francisco acquired over 1,000 acres of land that extended three-and-a-half miles inland from present-day Ocean Beach. In 1871, William Hammond Hall began development of the park in the English garden style with meadows, lakes, woodlands, and waterfalls. John McLaren took over as park superintendent in 1877 and devoted 56 years of his life to the development and maintenance of Golden Gate Park. A great urban park took form, natural in appearance but created largely from windswept sand dunes.

Within the park are the M.H. de Young Memorial Museum, part of the Fine Arts Museums of San Francisco, and the California Academy of Sciences, which houses a natural history museum with a four-story rainforest, the Steinhart Aquarium, and Morrison Planetarium. Both the de Young Museum and the California Academy of Sciences were completely rebuilt in the first years of the 21st century; the "living roof" of the Academy of Sciences features rolling, dune-like terrain, vegetated with native plants that include beach strawberry, sea pink, and California poppy. Also in Golden Gate Park is the Japanese Tea Garden, a reproduction of a traditional Japanese teahouse and garden built for the "Mid-winter Fair" of 1894. The park's oldest structure is the domed, Victorian-style Conservatory of Flowers, modeled after the glass conservatories in London's Kew Gardens. Built in New York in 1878, it was shipped around Cape Horn in pieces and assembled in San Francisco; major restoration took place from 1999 to 2003. The San Francisco Botanical Garden, in Golden Gate Park at the 9th Ave. entrance, contains spectacular plantings of California native and exotic species. Certain amenities within the park charge an entrance fee.

OCEAN BEACH: *W. of Great Highway, San Francisco.* This long, gently sloping beach is a place of powerful forces: high waves, sometimes wind or fog, always a sense of escape from the city. Surfing and fishing are popular, but swimming is unsafe due to hazardous rip currents. Easiest beach access is at the north end, where large parking areas adjoin the beach and stairs lead to the sand. From Lincoln Way south to Sloat Blvd., multi-purposes paths (one paved) extend along both sides of Great Highway. There is no parking on Great Highway itself, but street parking is on La Playa St. and lower Great Highway, and signalized pedestrian crossings are at every other block. Restrooms are inland of Great Highway at Judah and Taraval Streets. Horses are allowed on Ocean Beach south of Golden Gate Park. Dogs are allowed on parts of the beach; observe posted restrictions. A Snowy Plover Protection Area is designated from Stairwell 21 to Sloat Blvd. to minimize disturbance of wildlife. For recorded information on beach water quality levels, call: 877-732-3224.

SAN FRANCISCO ZOOLOGICAL GARDENS: *Sloat Blvd. at Great Highway, San Francisco.* More than 250 species of animals are on display. Mammals include monkeys, meerkats, and macaques; among the reptiles in the zoo is the endangered San Francisco garter snake. Scheduled feedings of grizzly bears, Magellanic penguins, and white pelicans are among the zoo's popular attractions. Open daily from 10 AM to 4 or 5 PM, depending on season. Fee for entry; wheelchairs and other mobility devices are available for rent. No pets allowed; service animals may enter, except where zoo animals are free-roaming. Call: 415-753-7080.

LAKE MERCED: *E. of Skyline Blvd. and Great Highway, San Francisco.* Lake Merced was a tidal lagoon until formation of a barrier beach closed it off from the sea, creating the five-acre freshwater lake. San Francisco's Harding Park Golf Course separates the two parts of the lake. There is an 18-hole championship course and a 9-hole course, both open to the public. Facilities also include a

Ocean Beach

clubhouse and restaurant. For information, call: 415-664-4690.

In the 1870s, Lake Merced was owned by the Spring Valley Water Company, which once held a monopoly on the city's water supply. The city and county of San Francisco purchased the lake, and it became a popular recreation site. A path for bicycling, walking, and jogging encircles the lake. Parking areas adjacent to the south lake are located off Lake Merced Blvd. and John Muir Dr. and also on the south side of Harding Rd., where there are boats for rent. A large parking area at the foot of Sunset Blvd. adjoins the northern part of Lake Merced; no boating is allowed in this area.

FORT FUNSTON: *W. of Skyline Blvd., .4 mi. S. of John Muir Dr., San Francisco.* This unit of the Golden Gate National Recreation Area is highly popular for dog-walking, hiking, and hang gliding; observe posted restrictions on dogs. The wheelchair-accessible observation deck offers fine views of hang gliders, if present, and on a clear day the Farallon Islands. Paved hiking trails lead along the high bluffs; park personnel and volunteers regularly collect seeds, plant natives, and remove invasive exotics in areas of restored native dune vegetation. Beach access is via sand ladders that lead down the steep, loose slope to an often wild-and-windy beach. Once-numerous but now threatened bank swallows nest in cliff colonies at Fort Funston, one of the few coastal breeding sites for this species left in California. Vehicles enter the parking area from the southbound lanes only of Skyline Blvd. For information, call: 415-561-4323.

PHILLIP BURTON MEMORIAL BEACH: *S. of Fort Funston, San Francisco.* The sandy beach is a popular spot to fish for striped bass and redtail surfperch. San Francisco Congressman Phillip Burton, for whom the beach is named, was instrumental in the creation of the Golden Gate National Recreation Area (GGNRA). Beach access is from Fort Funston in San Francisco County; the beach continues south through the former Thornton State Beach, where road access is closed due to bluff failure, and along the Daly City shoreline. The beach is narrow in places; check predicted tide levels before venturing south of Fort Funston. For information on GGNRA, call: 415-561-4323.

Ocean Beach Seawalls

S AN FRANCISCO'S Ocean Beach stretches from Point Lobos to the Fort Funston bluffs, adjacent to a vast dune system that extends up to six miles inland. The dunes, no longer visible, are locked in place by streets, homes, and other urban development built atop the sand. The high dune fields and nearby bluffs perhaps concealed the entrance to San Francisco Bay for centuries from Europeans who sailed past, including Juan Rodríguez Cabrillo in 1542 and Sebastián Vizcaíno in 1602. In 1765 Gaspar de Portolá's exploring party first saw San Francisco Bay, but their first glimpse was not from the sea but from land, Sweeney Ridge in present-day San Mateo County.

Following the discovery of gold in 1848 at Sutter's Mill, San Francisco's population grew rapidly, with the majority of development occurring near San Francisco Bay rather than near the ocean. Ocean Beach was the city's wild edge, known as the "Outside Lands." Only a few hunters or adventurous picnickers intentionally went there. The first Cliff House was built overlooking Seal Rocks in 1863, and a year later Mark Twain wrote about his harrowing early morning trip along a road still under construction:

> The wind was cold and benumbing, and blew with such force that we could hardly make headway against it. . . . From the moment we left the stable, almost, the fog was so thick that we could scarcely see fifty yards behind or before, or overhead; and for a while as we approached the Cliff House, we could not see the horse at all, and were obliged to steer by his ears, which stood up dimly out of the dense white mist that enveloped him. . . . We could scarcely see the sportive seals out on the rocks, writhing and squirming like exaggerated maggots, and there was nothing soothing in their discordant barking, to a spirit so depressed as mine was.

Within a year of Twain's visit, a toll road (later to become Geary Blvd.) was completed from downtown to the beach. In spite of sometimes challenging conditions, a trip to the ocean became a favorite excursion for San Franciscans and tourists.

In 1868, the city reserved a strip of land at least 200 feet wide for a public highway along Ocean Beach. The City also set aside a 1,000-acre rectangle of land one-half mile wide and over three miles long to be used as an urban park, later to become Golden Gate Park. William Hammond Hall, first park superintendent, discovered after several vain attempts at landscaping that barley would grow on the sand dunes. Once the barley took root, he planted lupine, then grasses, and within three years, trees were growing. Tons of horse manure fertilized the vegetation, and at the western boundary of the park, two Dutch windmills pumped water for irrigation. Finally, a five- to ten-foot-high wall was built along the western boundary to keep wind-blown sand from burying the newly established parkland.

Along the beach, an early sand and dirt trail for horse-drawn carriages was replaced by a paved road. Wind-blown sand was stabilized with sand fencing and tumbled brush. As more of the beach was stabilized, the road was widened farther onto the beach, placing it in the way of storm wave damage. Maurice O'Shaughnessy, appointed City Engineer in 1912, conceived a project to build a seawall, along with a permanent shoreline boulevard and a pedestrian esplanade.

The first section of the seawall project was the 670-foot-long stretch from the Cliff House to the northern corner of Golden Gate Park. The seawall was designed with cross-walls approximately every 150 feet, ensuring that damage to one section would not jeopardize the entire structure. This design also made it possible for O'Shaughnessy to lengthen the seawall whenever the city might appropriate more money. Over a ten-year period, from 1919 to 1929, the city authorized spending $900,000 for a 4,298-foot-long esplanade and seawall, and an additional $450,000 to extend just the Great Highway, minus a seawall, two miles farther south. Although O'Shaughnessy's original plan was to extend the esplanade and seawall along the full distance of the Great Highway, the Great Depression put a halt to public construction along Ocean Beach until the 1940s.

To the beach visitor, the O'Shaughnessy seawall is a great place to enjoy the ocean setting. The seawall provides steps leading down to the beach and wide bleacher seats for picnicking or wave watching. To the coastal engineer, the seawall is a gravity-structure masterpiece that has stood the test of time. The wall is supported by a 27-foot-wide base, with a series of six platforms or bleachers, starting approximately one foot below the level of extreme high tide, and rising to an elevation of 20 feet above the extreme high tide. The highest section of wall includes an early example of a recurved vertical section to reduce wave overtopping. Sheet pile supports extend 13 feet below extreme low tide. Landward of the vertical wall is the esplanade, a 20-foot-wide sidewalk and adjacent landscaped strip. The Great Highway, inland of the esplanade, ranges in width from 150 to 199 feet, with a second sidewalk on the inland side. The Great Highway is protected from wave attack by the seawall, and from flooding by being raised on fill to an elevation of 25.5 feet above mean high water.

South of the O'Shaughnessy seawall, and largely hidden from view by sand, are two other seawalls. One is the 662-foot-long Taraval seawall, built by the city in 1941 to protect a pedestrian underpass, the bluffs, and the Great Highway at the foot of Taraval Street. The top of this wall is almost ten feet lower than the top of the O'Shaughnessy wall. As a result, the Taraval wall is visible only when wave or wind erosion removes the sand that typically covers it.

The other major seawall along Ocean Beach is the Great Highway seawall that was built by the city between 1988 and 1993 to protect portions of a new sewage and storm water collection system. The Great Highway seawall is a 2,900-foot-long vertical wall with an inland pedestrian promenade, extending from Lincoln Way to Sloat Blvd.

O'Shaughnessy seawall, Ocean Beach

Temporary rock revetment installed in 2010 at southern end of Ocean Beach as an alternative to a seawall

In the 20th century, the main response to shoreline erosion was to construct seawalls, that is, the O'Shaughnessy, Taraval, and Great Highway seawalls, extending along 8,162 feet of the northern and central portions of Ocean Beach. The more recent approach to shore protection at Ocean Beach involves regional sediment management. This approach takes advantage of the enormous volume of sand that exists in the littoral system off San Francisco's coast, where some beach areas are characterized by an abundance of sand, while others are starved for sand due to poor distribution.

A crescent-shaped sandbar known as the San Francisco Bar lies outside the entrance to San Francisco Bay. In contrast to the great water depth beneath the Golden Gate Bridge, which exceeds 300 feet, the water depth above the San Francisco Bar measures as little as 20 feet. Modern ocean-going vessels require deep-water channels for navigation safety, and the U.S. Army Corps of Engineers maintains a 55-foot deep shipping channel through the bar by dredging annually some 500,000 to 800,000 cubic yards of sand. Dredged sediments were once placed beyond the main shipping channel, four to five miles from shore. Starting in 1972, the Corps of Engineers instead began to place sand on the south lobe of the San Francisco Bar, where waves could move much of this sand onshore, nourishing the northern half of Ocean Beach. From 1971 to 2004, the northern portion of Ocean Beach expanded in area and volume, adding an annual average of 120,000 cubic yards of material. Almost 85 percent of this sand came from the southern lobe of the San Francisco Bar.

Unfortunately, disposal of sand on the San Francisco Bar has not improved the shoreline erosion situation for the southern portion of Ocean Beach from Sloat Blvd. south to Fort Funston. Over the same time period that the northern beach section was accreting, the southern portion of Ocean Beach either fluctuated in width or continued to erode. By 1997, two recreational parking lots that served the southern portion of Ocean Beach had been lost to erosion. A short-term alternative to a seawall was installed—two rows of quarry stone at the toe of the bluff, followed by a temporary toe protection revetment. These were constructed for a relatively modest cost. By 2010, the southbound lanes of the Great Highway were closed after they were threatened by wave action, and a temporary rubble wall was constructed to protect the remaining highway lanes as well as the underground storm water collection system. At Ocean Beach, as at other urban beaches, the challenge remains: how to maintain roads and other infrastructure located close to a continually evolving ocean shoreline.

Page opposite: Pescadero State Beach, San Mateo County

San Mateo County

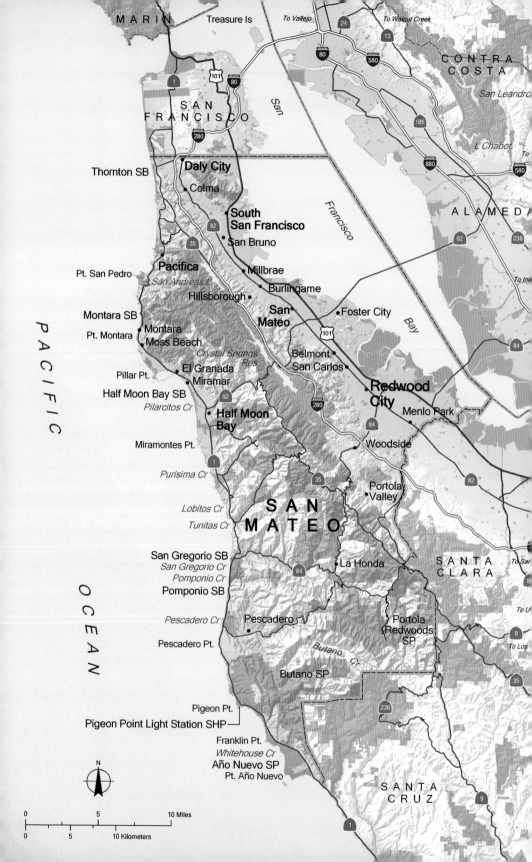

MARIN

Treasure Is

To Vallejo

To Walnut Creek

24

13

80

580

CONTRA COSTA

San Leandro

1

101

80

SAN FRANCISCO

L Chabot

To

280

San

185

880

580

Thornton SB

Daly City

Colma

Francisco

ALAMEDA

South San Francisco

82

San Bruno

92

238

35

Pacifica

Millbrae

To In

Pt. San Pedro

San Andreas L

Burlingame

Hillsborough

Bay

San Mateo

Foster City

Montara SB

Pt. Montara

Montara

101

84

Moss Beach

Crystal Springs Res

Belmont

Pillar Pt.

El Granada

San Carlos

Miramar

Redwood City

Half Moon Bay SB

92

Menlo Park

Pilarcitos Cr

Half Moon Bay

84

Woodside

Miramontes Pt.

1

Purisima Cr

35

Portola Valley

82

SAN MATEO

Lobitos Cr

Tunitas Cr

SANTA CLARA

To Sar

San Gregorio SB

84

La Honda

San Gregorio Cr

Pomponio Cr

To U

Pomponio SB

Pescadero Cr

Pescadero

Portola Redwoods SP

9

To Los

Pescadero Pt.

Butano Cr

35

Pigeon Pt.

Butano SP

236

Pigeon Point Light Station SHP

Franklin Pt.

Whitehouse Cr

Año Nuevo SP

Pt. Año Nuevo

SANTA CRUZ

9

N

1

0   5   10 Miles

0   5   10 Kilometers

San Mateo County

THE OHLONE Indians were the original inhabitants of the San Mateo County coast. The Spanish explorers called them "Costeños" (coast people), and English-speaking settlers mispronounced it as "Costanoans." The Ohlone were made up of forty or so tribelets that migrated seasonally between the interior valley and the coast. They were a nomadic hunting, gathering, and fishing people who lived on abalone, smelt, salmon, mussels, clams, sea urchins, seals, sea otters, and beached whales.

During the Mexican period, from 1822 to 1846, eight ranchos were formed along the San Mateo coast. These were resurveyed and taken over by American settlers in the 1850s and 1860s. Logging in the redwood canyons of the Santa Cruz Mountains followed, along with agriculture on the coastal terrace. Artichokes, first commercially planted in California near Half Moon Bay in 1898, are still an important crop. The growing season averages more than 300 days per year, and cool, foggy summers favor not only artichokes but also Brussels sprouts, mushrooms, and cut flowers. Also grown on the San Mateo coast are snap beans, leeks, and pumpkins. Half Moon Bay's very popular Art and Pumpkin Festival is held every October; call: 650-726-9652. Roadside stands on Hwy. One sell local products, and farmers markets include one in Half Moon Bay on Saturday mornings and an-

other at Rockaway Beach in Pacifica on Wednesday afternoons, both held from May to December. For more information, contact the San Mateo County Convention and Visitors Bureau: 650-348-7600, or the Half Moon Bay Coastside Chamber of Commerce: 650-726-8380.

Wintertime waves reach between 25 and 50 feet in height at the spot known as Mavericks. The Mavericks surf contest brings big wave surfers from around the world to Half Moon Bay. The contest is scheduled on short notice only when conditions are predicted to be just right. Generally, as waves get closer to shore, their base begins to run into the seafloor, slowing the deeper parts of the wave. The shallower part of the wave keeps moving at the same pace, causing the wave to stand up and then pitch forward. This creates the wave face that is so sought after by surfers. Sea-floor maps released in 2007 by the U.S. National Oceanic and Atmospheric Administration revealed why the Mavericks waves form where they do. A long, sloping ramp leads up to the surface under the wavebreak, creating an exceptionally tall wave that holds up for some time before it breaks. Mavericks is located well offshore, largely out of view of those on the beach. Many beaches in San Mateo County have hazardous rip currents and cold water temperatures. Surfing is popular, nevertheless, and a few locations are suited for less experienced surfers.

Surf shops on the San Mateo County coast include:

Log Surf Shop, Pacifica, 650-738-5664

Nor Cal Surf Shop, Pacifica, 650-738-9283

Sonlights, Pacifica, 650-359-5471

Mavericks Surf Shop, Princeton-by-the-Sea, 650-563-9060

Half Moon Bay Board Shop, 650-726-1476

Cowboy Surf Shop, 650-726-6968

Sport fishing and whale watching trips from Pillar Point Harbor:

Captain Smitty, 650-728-8433

Queen of Hearts, 650-728-3377

Huli Cat, 650-726-2926

Captain John's Sportfishing, 650-726-2913

Huck Finn Sportfishing, 650-726-7133

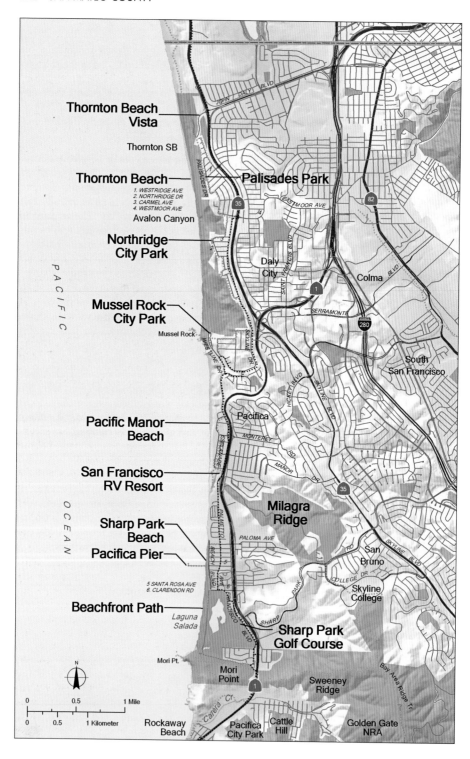

Thornton Beach
Vista

Thornton SB

Thornton Beach
1. WESTRIDGE AVE
2. NORTHRIDGE DR
3. CARMEL AVE
4. WESTMOOR AVE
Avalon Canyon

Palisades Park

Northridge
City Park

Mussel Rock
City Park

Mussel Rock

Pacific Manor
Beach

San Francisco
RV Resort

Milagra
Ridge

Sharp Park
Beach

Pacifica Pier

5 SANTA ROSA AVE
6. CLARENDON RD

Beachfront Path

Laguna
Salada

Sharp Park
Golf Course

Mori Pt.

Mori
Point

Sweeney
Ridge

Golden Gate
NRA

Rockaway
Beach

Pacifica
City Park

Cattle
Hill

PACIFIC

OCEAN

N

0   0.5   1 Mile

0   0.5   1 Kilometer

JOHN DALY BLVD

PALISADES DR

EASTMOOR AVE

Daly
City

Colma   BLVD

SERRAMONTE

SAN FRANCISCO BLVD

SKYLINE DR

WESTLINE DR

Pacifica

MONTEREY RD

HICKEY BLVD

SKYLINE BLVD

MANOR DR

ESPLANADE

PALMETTO

BEACH BLVD

PALOMA AVE

SAN FRANCISCO BLVD

SHARP PARK RD

COLLEGE DR

San
Bruno

Skyline
College

South
San Francisco

Bay Area Ridge Tr

Calera Cr.

35

82

1

280

35

1

Daly City and Northern Pacifica

	Sandy Beach	Rocky Shore	Trail	Visitor Center	Campground	Wildlife Viewing	Fishing or Boating	Facilities for Disabled	Food and Drink	Restrooms	Parking	Fee
Thornton Beach Vista						•		•			•	
Thornton Beach	•											
Palisades Park										•	•	
Northridge City Park										•	•	
Mussel Rock City Park			•			•					•	
Pacific Manor Beach	•	•	•				•				•	
San Francisco RV Resort					•					•	•	•
Sharp Park Beach	•		•			•	•	•	•	•	•	
Pacifica Pier						•	•	•	•	•	•	
Beachfront Path			•			•						
Milagra Ridge			•			•				•	•	
Sharp Park Golf Course									•	•	•	•

THORNTON BEACH VISTA: *W. end of John Daly Blvd., Daly City.* Formerly the vehicular entrance to Thornton State Beach before coastal erosion closed the road, this is still a place to park and enjoy the view. There are fixed telescopes to use while scanning offshore for whales, and the high vantage point affords a clear-day view of the Farallon Islands. Below the parking area, the bluff cascades steeply down to sea level. Despite the lack of vehicle access, the property including the shoreline is still part of the state park system. There is no improved trail system down the bluff, but you might walk south from Fort Funston along the narrow beach, while keeping an eye out for a rising tide.

THORNTON BEACH: *Shoreline W. of Daly City.* Daly City has a long sandy beach, but it is not easily reached due to the extremely high and unstable bluffs. Intrepid hikers might approach from Fort Funston to the north or from Mussel Rock City Park to the south, but must pay close attention to a tide table, as the beach may nearly vanish at high tide. No facilities or improvements.

PALISADES PARK: *Along Palisades Dr. at Westridge Ave., Daly City.* One of two small city parks on the high bluffs of Daly City, Palisades Park is equipped with picnic tables, barbecue grills, and playground equipment. There is also a small dog run. No beach access, but there are nice distant views of the Marin Headlands.

NORTHRIDGE CITY PARK: *Along Northridge Dr. at Carmel Ave., Daly City.* A small city park with picnic and playground facilities and a chemical toilet. No beach access; distant views only of coastal mountains to the north. Access to the shoreline that was once available down precipitously steep Avalon Canyon has been closed for safety reasons.

MUSSEL ROCK CITY PARK: *Westline Dr., off Skyline Dr., Daly City.* A rough-and-tumble park on a high rocky promontory, Mussel Rock is bordered on one side by a solid waste transfer facility and on the other by the spacious blue Pacific. The views are tremendous, even if facilities are lacking. Turn onto Westline Dr. from Skyline Dr. (not the more prominent Skyline Blvd.) and follow it to the end to reach a large paved but uneven parking area. At the north end of the parking lot, informal trails favored by dog-walkers lead down the slope toward the beach far below. The area is also used by paragliders, including members of the Bay Area Paragliding Association, who use terraces along the bluff as launch sites.

PACIFIC MANOR BEACH: *W. of Manor Dr., Pacifica*. Because the bluffs are very unstable, beach access opportunities in this part of Pacifica have come and gone over the years. A public beach access stair located near the north end of the Esplanade was closed in 2009 due to bluff erosion. Following placement of rock riprap on the beach intended to protect the road and blufftop residences, the beach accessway is expected to be reconstructed as a ramp or stair. Farther south, some residences that once stood west of the Esplanade near the end of Manor Dr. have been removed, and the city of Pacifica has made plans for a linear blufftop park in the area. South of Manor Dr., a paved path extends along the top of the bluff seaward of the San Francisco RV Resort, and nice views of the sea can be had from the trail. South of the RV Resort there is a public parking lot, but the steep unimproved path leading down to the beach is virtually inaccessible due to erosion; future plans call for reconstructing a stair at this location. The beach below the bluff is very narrow in any event, and part of it is occupied by rocks placed to slow erosion of the bluff. Enjoy the view, and observe posted safety warnings.

SAN FRANCISCO RV RESORT: *700 Palmetto Ave., Pacifica*. Formerly the Pacific Park RV Resort, this recreational vehicle facility is located on the edge of the coastal bluff, overlooking the ocean waves and an often-narrow sandy beach. Full hookups are available; some sites are pull-through to accommodate large vehicles. Amenities include a heated pool, hot tub, gift shop, laundry, dump station, and free Wi-fi service. Pets welcome. For information, call: 650-355-7093; for reservations, call: 1-800-822-1250.

SHARP PARK BEACH: *From Paloma Ave. to Mori Pt., Pacifica*. A beautiful dark sand beach; a paved pedestrian promenade runs along Beach Blvd. south of Paloma Ave., providing lovely views of coastal mountains and turquoise waters. There is no parking along Beach Blvd., which is one-way southbound. Use caution if walking here on stormy or extra-windy days, when waves can splash over the promenade and onto the roadway. No-fee parking lots are south of the Pacifica Pier, and restrooms are located on the pier. The promenade continues south of the pier and is equipped with benches. The adjoining beach becomes wider the farther south you go, toward Mori Point.

PACIFICA PIER: *Foot of Santa Rosa Ave., Pacifica*. Streets near the pier are all one-way, including Santa Rosa Ave. itself, which is one-way eastbound; approach the pier by vehicle using one of the streets to the north. Viewing and pier fishing are the main activities here. Fishing from Pacifica Pier requires no fishing license, because the facility is a

Pacifica Pier

Milagra Ridge view south to Laguna Salada and Sharp Park Golf Course

municipal pier; catch limits still apply. Pier facilities include restrooms and a café located next to Beach Blvd. The pier is open from 5 AM to 10 PM; dogs not allowed. For information, call: 650-738-7381.

BEACHFRONT PATH: *From Clarendon Rd. to Mori Point, Pacifica.* A wide packed-earth path tops an embankment that overlooks the beach on one side and Sharp Park Golf Course on the other. Within the golf course is Laguna Salada, a freshwater marsh that is a known habitat for the endangered San Francisco garter snake. The path connects to the paved beach promenade near the Pacifica Pier. At the south end of the beachfront path, visitors can climb the slopes of Mori Point, part of the Golden Gate National Recreation Area. The wide beach is composed of fine pebbles with an overall dark-gray appearance; look closely to see an amazing array of colors. Terns roost on the beach, and on a sunny day the nearshore waters are brilliant blue-green in color.

MILAGRA RIDGE: *Sharp Park Rd., E. of Hwy. One, Pacifica.* Turn north off Sharp Park Rd. opposite College Dr. to reach informal roadside parking. A unit of the Golden Gate National Recreation Area, Milagra Ridge has

hiking paths (some paved), spring wildflowers, and spectacular views of the Pacifica shoreline. The federally endangered Mission blue butterfly and San Bruno elfin butterfly inhabit the area, and the threatened California red-legged frog is also present at Milagra Ridge. Look for hawks hunting small prey on the steep slopes. The site includes old defense installations such as a World War II–era gun battery and a Nike missile station dating from the post-World War II period. Remain on the trails; due to rare wildlife, dogs may be restricted or prohibited in some areas. Chemical toilet located along the loop trail, one-quarter mile from parking area. For information, call: 415-561-3034.

SHARP PARK GOLF COURSE: *Sharp Park Rd. and Francisco Blvd., W. of Hwy. One, Pacifica.* This 18-hole golf course, on property owned by the city of San Francisco but located within the city of Pacifica, is open to the public and offers moderate greens fees. The course is situated partly west and partly east of Hwy. One, with a connection via underpass. The course was designed by Alister Mackenzie, known also for the design of the famed Cypress Point course on the Monterey Peninsula. Facilities include a clubhouse and restaurant. Call: 650-355-3380.

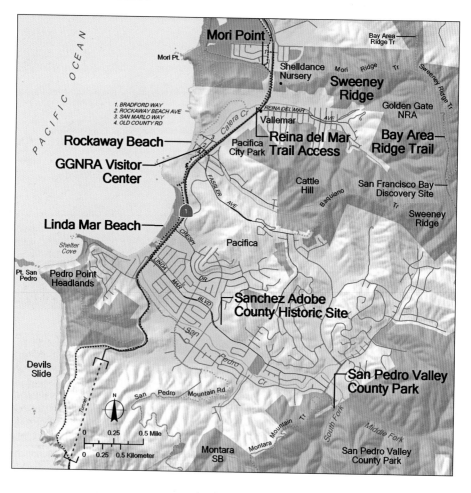

1. BRADFORD WAY
2. ROCKAWAY BEACH AVE
3. SAN MARLO WAY
4. OLD COUNTY RD

Linda Mar Beach

Pacifica

	Sandy Beach	Rocky Shore	Trail	Visitor Center	Campground	Wildlife Viewing	Fishing or Boating	Facilities for Disabled	Food and Drink	Restrooms	Parking	Fee
Mori Point	•		•			•				•	•	
Sweeney Ridge			•			•				•	•	
Bay Area Ridge Trail			•									
Reina del Mar Trail Access			•				•				•	
Rockaway Beach	•	•				•	•	•	•	•	•	
GGNRA Visitor Center				•						•	•	
Linda Mar Beach	•	•	•			•	•	•	•	•	•	
Sanchez Adobe County Historic Site				•						•	•	
San Pedro Valley County Park			•	•		•	•			•	•	•

MORI POINT: *Off Hwy. One, 1 mi. S. of Pacifica Pier, Pacifica.* Mori Point is a spectacular addition, acquired in 2002 with financial assistance from the State Coastal Conservancy, to the Golden Gate National Recreation Area. The high, rocky promontory affords tremendous vistas of sea and rocky coast. A major native plant restoration effort has resulted in fields of colorful spring wildflowers, including Indian paintbrush, tidytips, and goldfields. Goldfinches and white-crowned sparrows are common on the brushy slopes. The endangered San Francisco garter snake and one of its prime food sources, the threatened California red-legged frog, both inhabit restored wetlands on the north side of Mori Point.

Roadside parking is on Bradford Way off Hwy. One. Hikers then have two choices: the more northerly, flat route heads west about one-third mile to the beach, while the more southerly trail climbs the slopes toward the high ground of Mori Point. Observe posted restrictions on dogs on the trails. The old Mori Point Inn stood on a precipice overlooking the sea until it burned in the 1960s. Nearby was a reputed off-loading site for

Mori Point

Canadian whiskey during the Prohibition era. Private land separates Mori Point from Rockaway Beach to the south; to hike or bicycle south from Mori Point, use the California Coastal Trail next to Hwy. One.

SWEENEY RIDGE: *E. of Hwy. One, S. of Sharp Park, Pacifica.* One of the Bay Area's grand vistas is available on Sweeney Ridge. The 360-degree panorama includes the Pacific Ocean, city of San Francisco, and the southern part of San Francisco Bay. The Sweeney Ridge Trail, part of the Bay Area Ridge Trail, runs along the spine of the hills through coastal sage scrub vegetation. In Pacifica, a trailhead with parking and restrooms is located behind the Shelldance Nursery; the entrance off Hwy. One is one-quarter mile south of Sharp Park Rd. but is accessible only to northbound vehicles. The Mori Ridge Trail rises in elevation some 750 feet. Another trailhead, without parking, is located at the end of Fassler Ave. near Rockaway Beach. A third trailhead is located at Skyline College in San Bruno; the trail begins at the southwest end of parking lot "B." Several parking spots there are reserved for GGN-RA use on weekends and holidays. Observe posted restrictions on dogs on the trails.

The so-called San Francisco Bay Discovery Site on Sweeney Ridge is marked with a granite cylinder. There in 1769 members of Gaspar de Portolá's expedition first sighted San Francisco Bay. Of course, Native Americans had lived around the bay for millennia. The monument is reached by a mile-long paved trail starting at the west end of Sneath Ln. off Skyline Blvd. in San Bruno.

BAY AREA RIDGE TRAIL: *Along ridges surrounding San Francisco Bay.* A loop trail some 550 miles long is planned, running all around the greater San Francisco Bay Area. Over 325 miles of trail are currently open for hikers, bicyclists, and equestrians. For information and maps of the trail throughout the Bay Area, see: www.ridgetrail.org.

REINA DEL MAR TRAIL ACCESS: *Off Hwy. One at Reina del Mar Ave., Pacifica.* A paved multi-purpose path, starting at a parking area off Hwy. One, winds along Calera Creek to Rockaway Beach. The trail was constructed by the City of Pacifica. Calera is Spanish for "lime"; a limestone quarry here once furnished whitewash for the newly built Presidio of San Francisco. Good birding along the riparian corridor. No facilities.

ROCKAWAY BEACH: *Foot of Rockaway Beach Ave., Pacifica.* A sandy beach lies in a cove bounded by rocky headlands; popular fishing area. One parking lot is located at the

Rockaway Beach with California Coastal Trail switchbacks in foreground

Linda Mar Beach

end of Rockaway Beach Ave.; a second is at the end of San Marlo Way. During storms, waves may break over the seawall onto the pedestrian promenade. A third parking area is located on higher ground at the south end of Old County Rd.; from there, a paved bicycle path switchbacks over the hill to Linda Mar Beach. Lodging and dining establishments are clustered near Rockaway Beach.

GGNRA VISITOR CENTER: *225 Rockaway Beach Ave., Pacifica.* Maps and visitor information for Pacifica and beyond are available at the center, open daily from 10 AM to 4 PM; call: 650-355-4122.

LINDA MAR BEACH: *Hwy. One between Crespi Dr. and Linda Mar Blvd., Pacifica.* A broad crescent of white sand is easily accessible from a parking area located seaward of Hwy. One (often crowded on weekends) and from the lot inland of Hwy. One at Crespi Dr. Linda Mar is a popular surfing beach; there are waves suitable for surfers of different skill levels. Conditions can be hazardous due to rip currents. Also known as Pacifica State Beach, the area is maintained by the city of Pacifica; call: 650-738-7381.

SANCHEZ ADOBE COUNTY HISTORIC SITE: *Linda Mar Blvd., 1 mi. E. of Hwy. One, Pacifica.* The adobe structure was built between 1842 and 1846 by Francisco Sanchez, a prominent settler who served as alcalde (mayor) of Yerba Buena, later known as San Francisco. A small museum chronicles the history of the site, occupied at one time by Ohlone Indians. Open Tuesday to Thursday from 10 AM to 4 PM, and Saturday and Sunday from 1 to 5 PM; closed on holidays. The historic property is staffed by volunteer docents from the San Mateo County Historical Association; for information, call: 650-359-1462.

SAN PEDRO VALLEY COUNTY PARK: *End of Linda Mar Blvd., Pacifica.* Park facilities include picnic sites with barbecues, group picnic area, visitor center, and a short, self-guided nature trail. The Montara Mountain Trail leads two miles uphill to the summit; others loop through hills and valleys. The south and middle forks of San Pedro Creek, spawning areas for migratory steelhead, flow through the park. No dogs allowed. Day-use fee applies; park opens at 8 AM, and closing time varies seasonally.

Beach Sand

WHEN we think of beaches, we think of sand. Beach sand consists of fragments of rocks and minerals, often mixed with particles of shells, coral, and perhaps bits of wave-smoothed glass. The term "sand" indicates a particle size; sand is coarser than silt and finer than gravel. Depending on the classification scheme, sand consists of grains between 0.06 and 2 millimeters in diameter.

One of the most obvious characteristics of sand is its color. The color of beach sand is greatly influenced by its moisture content; it is usually easy to see where the highest waves have lapped because the wet sand is darker than the dry. Setting aside moisture content, however, sand color is largely determined by the composition of its constituent grains.

The characteristics of sand grains reflect the processes known as chemical and physical weathering. In upland watersheds, far from the shoreline, rocks are broken down by weathering into smaller fragments. Sand is rarely derived directly from rocks, but rather from soils that in turn are formed from rocks. Soils are formed by a complex interplay of processes, but most important in shaping sand composition is chemical weathering. In the process of chemical weathering, exposure to oxygen, carbon dioxide, and water results in changes to the constituent minerals. Minerals that are less stable are broken down faster than more resistant minerals. The extent to which chemical weathering proceeds depends on the steepness of the terrain. Where slopes are steep and the land mass is undergoing tectonic uplift, as is most of coastal California, chemical weathering does not proceed very far before the soils are eroded and the incompletely weathered particles are carried away by rivers and streams.

Sand grains are also subject to physical weathering, such as on the beach where the grains are physically broken and abraded by the powerful action of waves. Some minerals are inherently harder than others, and are therefore more resistant to being broken down in the surf. Sands of different grain size may have different compositions even if derived from the same rocks, because some mineral grains in the source rocks are inherently finer grained than others and are concentrated in sand of finer grain size.

At the shore, waves and currents sort sand grains by size and density, and the finer grains become segregated from the coarser grains. Waves move lighter-weight sands farther up on the beach, leaving heavier sands behind. The result of this sorting process is a streaky appearance on the beach, where dark bands of fine, dense minerals (such as magnetite) are segregated from coarser, less dense minerals (such as quartz).

Montara State Beach

Virtually unseen by beach visitors are the tiny organisms that inhabit the interstices, or spaces, between grains of sand. Called "meiofauna," meaning animals barely visible without magnification, these creatures include ciliate protozoans (one-celled animals with cilia for movement), flatworms, roundworms, polychaete and oligochaete worms, copepods and ostracods, and several inconspicuous invertebrate phyla such as Kinorhyncha, Tardigrada, Rotifera, and Gastrotricha. A scanning electron microscope readily shows Gastrotrichs, which range in size from 0.5 to 4 millimeters in length, such as *Turbanella mustella*. Gastrotrichs feed using cilia on their heads to sweep organic matter into their mouths. Some of the protuberances you see on *T. mustella* are adhesive tubes that enable it to attach temporarily to sand grains. This animal has a very short life, from 3 to 21 days.

Gastrotricha, *Turbanella mustella*, approximate magnification 100x

Grain size may be the most important factor influencing the presence or absence, and the types, of interstitial organisms on a beach. The larger the grain size, the greater the interstitial space available for habitation—and the converse. The mineral nature of the grains, temperature, salinity, and wave action are other environmental factors important in determining the particular composition of a meiofaunal community. Polychaete worms of the species *Eusyllis* are common members of interstitial communities. *Eusyllis* sp. is segmented like all Polychaete worms; each segment has a pair of appendages called parapodia that bear many bristles called setae. Setae are made of chitin, and they assist in movement and attachment.

Polychaete worm, *Eusyllis* sp., approximate magnification 50x

Ostracods are a class of small Crustaceans, sometimes called "seed shrimp" because of their appearance, with over 65,000 known species. They are typically around 1 millimeter long, but can be as small as 0.2 millimeters. Interstitial fauna have specific adaptations that enable them to survive in a harsh habitat. Many animals are elongated so that they can fit between sand grains. Long bodies also provide a better ability to grasp sand grains. Many of the interstitial animals are free-moving, with hooks and claws to fix themselves to sand grains. Many also have either a hard shell or exoskeleton, as do Ostracods, to prevent being crushed.

Ostracod, approximate magnification 250x

White sand
All sand photos are shown at actual grain size

The pure **white** sand at Carmel Beach in Monterey County is composed largely of the mineral quartz. The sand is derived almost exclusively from local granite, which contains roughly equal amounts of quartz, potassium-feldspar, and calcium-sodium feldspars. Compared to quartz, the two types of feldspar are less chemically stable and physically softer. After chemical weathering in the soil, followed by physical breakdown in the surf zone, the sand at Carmel Beach has become enormously enriched in quartz, gaining its brilliant white hue. Quartz sands derived from granite are found elsewhere in California, such as at Montara State Beach in San Mateo County. The deep weathering of bedrock on Montara Mountain, however, has left behind iron oxides that have stained the beach sand grains a buff, rather than a pure white, color.

Black sand

Pure **black** sand is found in irregular streaky deposits on many beaches in California. In most cases, these black streaks are made up of dense, resistant minerals, such as magnetite and ilmenite, that are minor constituents in many rocks. These minerals are particularly abundant in basalts of the Franciscan complex, and are well represented at Ocean Beach in San Francisco and the Marin Headlands beach known as Lower Fishermans, shown here. Magnetite is well named; the most naturally magnetic of any mineral, it is easily picked up by a magnet. Next time you go to the beach, try dragging a strong magnet through the sand—it will likely come back resembling a furry caterpillar, covered with magnetite grains.

Gray sand

Gray sands, such as this example from Pacifica's Sharp Park Beach, are especially common in California. This gray sand is composed not of individual mineral grains, but rather of fragments of source rocks that contain a variety of minerals. These so-called "lithic fragments" contain a great deal of information for the geologist trying to determine the nature of the source rocks. Sands composed of lithic fragments are most common where fine-grained source rocks occur in steep, tectonically active watersheds, where landslides and erosion allow little time for chemical weathering before sand grains reach the shore. These large grains could almost be called "gravel."

Pink sand is fairly rare around the world. Bermuda is famous for its **pink** sand beaches, where the sand is derived from crushed fragments of pink coral. No such coral reefs are found off California, but the state still has its pink sand. In a few spots in Monterey County—at the mouth of the Big Sur River in Andrew Molera State Park and at Pfeiffer Beach in the Los Padres National Forest—"stringers" of brilliant pink sand can be found. This sand is composed of almost pure garnet, which is found in some of the metamorphosed igneous rocks of the Santa Lucia Range. Quickly eroded, after only minor chemical weathering, this garnet is brought by streams to the beach. There it is sorted and winnowed by ocean currents, the mineral garnet being much denser than the average sand grain.

Pink sand

For a real treat, take the one-mile walk down to Kirby Cove in the Marin Headlands. Not only will you get a great view of the Golden Gate Bridge and the San Francisco skyline, but you will see some unusual **red** sands. These sands consist almost entirely of fragments of the red chert that makes up the headlands. When these particles are sorted and washed by the waves, the red color inherent in the chert is accentuated. Look closely among the red particles, however, and notice the presence of other colors. Greenstone derived from basalt found in the headlands has a greenish cast due to the presence of the minerals chlorite and pumpellyite. Graywacke is a type of sandstone made up of grayish-toned, coarse grains.

Red sand

The sand at Monastery Beach south of Carmel has an off-white, or cream, color. Like the sand at Montara State Beach, this sand is locally derived from a weathered granite. Here, however, chemical weathering did not result in iron-staining, probably because of a paucity of iron-bearing minerals in the granite. Because Monastery Beach is a very steep, high-energy beach, only the very coarsest grains stay on the beach. These grains are lithic fragments, as are the gray sands at Pacifica, but in this case they were formed from relatively coarse granite fragments. The granite contains appreciable feldspar (both potassium and sodium-calcium varieties) giving the lithic fragments—and the beach—a creamy color.

Cream color sand

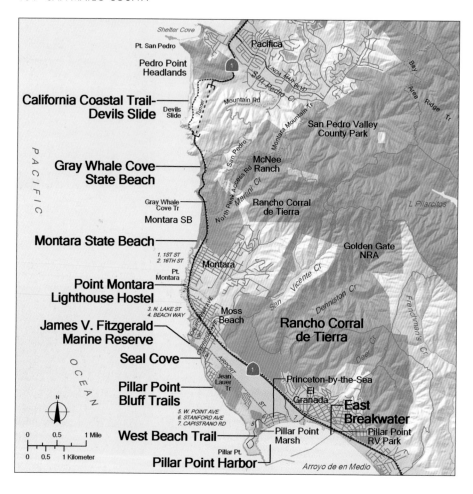

James V. Fitzgerald Marine Reserve

Montara to Pillar Point Harbor

	Sandy Beach	Rocky Shore	Trail	Visitor Center	Campground	Wildlife Viewing	Fishing or Boating	Facilities for Disabled	Food and Drink	Restrooms	Parking	Fee
California Coastal Trail–Devils Slide		•			•				•	•		
Gray Whale Cove State Beach	•	•				•			•	•	•	
Montara State Beach	•	•			•	•			•	•	•	
Point Montara Lighthouse Hostel	•	•		•	•			•	•	•	•	
James V. Fitzgerald Marine Reserve	•	•	•	•	•				•	•		
Seal Cove	•	•			•							
Pillar Point Bluff Trails		•							•	•		
West Beach Trail	•	•	•		•				•	•		
Pillar Point Harbor	•	•		•		•	•		•	•	•	•
East Breakwater		•		•	•					•	•	
Rancho Corral de Tierra		•										

CALIFORNIA COASTAL TRAIL–DEVILS SLIDE:
W. of Hwy. One from 1 mi. S. of Linda Mar Blvd., Pacifica, to .5 mi. N. of Gray Whale Cove State Beach. This spectacular segment in the California Coastal Trail is made possible by the new Hwy. One bypass; the old highway is slated in 2012 to become a trail for pedestrians and bicyclists. Limited parking and restroom facilities are planned at the north and south ends of the new trail segment where it joins Hwy. One.

GRAY WHALE COVE STATE BEACH:
Hwy. One, .5 mi. S. of Devil's Slide, Montara. Gray whales do indeed pass by during their annual migration. The sand is sparkling white, and the nearshore waters are aquamarine. The surf can be very rough. Promontories provide some wind shelter, making the area popular for sunbathing; this is a clothing optional beach.

Beach parking is on the inland side of Hwy. One; use caution in crossing the road. A steep trail and stairway lead down to the shoreline. There is a grassy picnic area equipped with restrooms overlooking the beach. Call: 650-726-8819. The parking area is open 8 AM to sunset. No beach fires; no dogs allowed. Fee for parking; the California State Parks annual day use pass is not accepted.

MONTARA STATE BEACH:
Hwy. One and 1st St., Montara. A half-mile-long white sand beach can be reached via a public stairway located seaward of the restaurant opposite the west end of 1st Street. A public parking lot with unrestricted parking is located 100 feet south of the restaurant. Public beach parking is also available in the restaurant's two lots from 8 AM until 5 PM daily.

Another access to Montara State Beach starts at an unpaved parking area located four-tenths of a mile north of 1st St.; no facilities. Dogs are allowed only on a leash of no more than six feet. No beach fires allowed. For information, call: 650-726-8819.

East of Hwy. One and north of Martini Creek is McNee Ranch, part of Montara State Beach. A steep fire road, accommodating hikers, mountain bikers, and equestrians, leads from Hwy. One to Montara Mountain. A handful of parking spaces on the east side of the highway marks the spot one-half mile north of 1st Street. Montara Mountain, arguably the northern end of the Santa Cruz Mountain range, is composed of 90-million-year-old granitic rock, largely quartz diorite. Montara Mountain can also be reached via the Montara Mountain Trail from San Pedro Valley County Park.

POINT MONTARA LIGHTHOUSE HOSTEL: *Hwy. One and 16th St., Montara.* The historic lighthouse is still an operating aid to navigation, operated by the U.S. Coast Guard, although the facility is now automated. The cast-iron tower that houses the station's light stood originally on Cape Cod in Massachusetts. It was later moved to California and installed in 1928 at Point Montara.

The Point Montara Lighthouse Hostel has shared and private rooms. The communal living room and shared kitchen have nice ocean views. There is access to a secluded cove beach with tidepools. Amenities include free WiFi, free parking, and laundry. Hostelling International operates the accommodations, open year-round. For reservations and information from 7:30 AM to 10:30 PM daily, call: 650-728-7177. The site is also a state park; day visitors are requested to visit the hostel office first.

JAMES V. FITZGERALD MARINE RESERVE: *Foot of California Ave., Moss Beach.* The James V. Fitzgerald Marine Reserve is one of the richest intertidal areas in California; 25 species new to science have been discovered here. Abundant marine life at the reserve includes giant green anemones, limpets, chitons, barnacles, spiny purple sea urchins, sea palms, surfgrass, feather boa kelp, and several species of crabs and snails. Kelp greenling, cabezon, lingcod, rockfish, and red abalone are found in offshore kelp beds.

The marine reserve is a highly popular destination, and it could be loved to death; enjoy the close-up view of marine creatures and plants, but do not pry animals off the rocks, move shells or vegetation, or take anything away. Watch your step around tidepools. For information, call: 650-728-3584. The tidelands of the Fitzgerald Marine Reserve, created in 1969 and managed by the San Mateo County Parks Department, are encompassed within the boundaries of the Montara State Marine Reserve designated by the California Department of Fish and Game.

At the seaward end of California Ave., turn right on N. Lake St. to the marine reserve parking area; a ramp to the beach is planned. A loop trail begins opposite the foot of California Ave. and leads south to Seal Cove.

SEAL COVE: *Foot of Cypress Ave. at Beach Way, Moss Beach.* A stairway leads down the bluff to a sandy beach; the James V. Fitzgerald Marine Reserve is offshore. Do not disturb tidepool animals, plants, or rocks; maintain a distance of at least 300 feet from marine mammals. There is no parking at Seal Cove; instead, walk five minutes from the Fitzgerald Marine Reserve parking area.

PILLAR POINT BLUFF TRAILS: *Off Airport St., 1 mi. S. of Cypress Ave., Pillar Point area.* Park in the lot next to the industrial buildings on Airport St. and explore a two-mile-long system of trails, including the Jean Lauer Trail. In summertime, pink farewell-to-spring and golden lizard tail bloom on the bluff. Dogs on leash OK. No beach access.

WEST BEACH TRAIL: *Off West Point Ave., Princeton Harbor.* From the point, a large exposed reef is visible at low tide, but any surfers who might be at the offshore Mavericks break are largely out of view. The Pillar Point Air Force Tracking Station atop the cliff is closed to the public.

PILLAR POINT HARBOR: *W. of Hwy. One and Capistrano Rd., Princeton-by-the-Sea.* The harbor contains a popular municipal fishing pier. There are 228 commercial and 141 recreational berths. Facilities include a six-lane boat ramp (launching fee), fuel dock, guest dock, and pumpout facilities. Fresh fish is available to the public off the boats. For harbor information, including surf and weather report, call: 650-726-5727. Sport-fishing and whale-watching trips are available from vendors in Pillar Point Harbor.

EAST BREAKWATER: *W. of Hwy. One, .5 mi. S. of Capistrano Rd., Half Moon Bay.* Popular fishing access. Parking area is off Hwy. One; fee applies. RV camping in self-contained vehicles is available at the adjacent, private Pillar Point RV Park; call: 650-712-9277.

RANCHO CORRAL DE TIERRA: *E. of Hwy. One, N. of Montara.* This 4,200-acre property was added to the Golden Gate National Recreation Area in 2011. Planning for public use is on-going; hiking and horseback riding, along with habitat improvements, are likely. For information, call: 415-561-4323.

The story of the aptly named Devils Slide is, like Highway One itself, long, convoluted, and in the end, even profound. Two decades after the Ocean Shore Railroad gave up trying to maintain a rail line across the slide in the early 1900s, Highway One was built there in the mid-1930s. The problems of erosion and a frequently sliding roadbed, expensive maintenance, and the constant threat of a multi-year closure if the nearby San Andreas Fault took out the entire slide made the vision of a replacement route off the slide plane an attractive option for highway engineers.

The most often-cited alternative in the 1950s and 1960s was a Devils Slide bypass, over the mountain and behind the slide. Unfortunately it was designed to 1950s freeway mentality, which, along with a major push for freeways everywhere, led to the freeway revolt in the 1960s. The bypass became one of the casualties of this revolt and the growing environmental movement; in fact, Caltrans was only weeks away from starting construction of the bypass when the relatively new environmental law, the National Environmental Policy Act (NEPA), and a court injunction halted construction. In contesting the lawsuit, the state argued that plans for the freeway were made before NEPA was made law and thus were exempt; however the U.S. District Court ruled on Dec. 6, 1972, in favor of environmentalists.

Caltrans moved the bypass to the back burner until the 1980s, and in the meantime, the California Dept. of Parks and Recreation purchased the area surrounding the highway corridor (formerly McNee Ranch, now part of Montara State Beach). After a lengthy Highway One closure in 1983 the bypass concept was resuscitated, emergency federal funds were secured, an Environmental Impact Report completed, and plans submitted to the California Coastal Commission. Although the bypass was heavily overdesigned, violated many Coastal Act policies, and would have virtually destroyed the McNee Ranch addition to the State Park system, after several denials the Coastal Commission approved a modified bypass. Further litigation immediately ensued. Area activists then expanded their efforts and pushed for a tunnel as a permanent solution. The tunnel was placed on the ballot for a San Mateo County-wide voter initiative, and voters, apparently tired of the stalemate over the bypass, overwhelmingly passed the measure.

After it passed, Caltrans agreed to pursue the tunnel alternative, and tunnel construction commenced in 2007. As an appropriate footnote to this story, the environmental activists and Caltrans engineers literally got up together on stage singing "Kumbaya" at a local celebration for the tunnel commencement.

Devils Slide

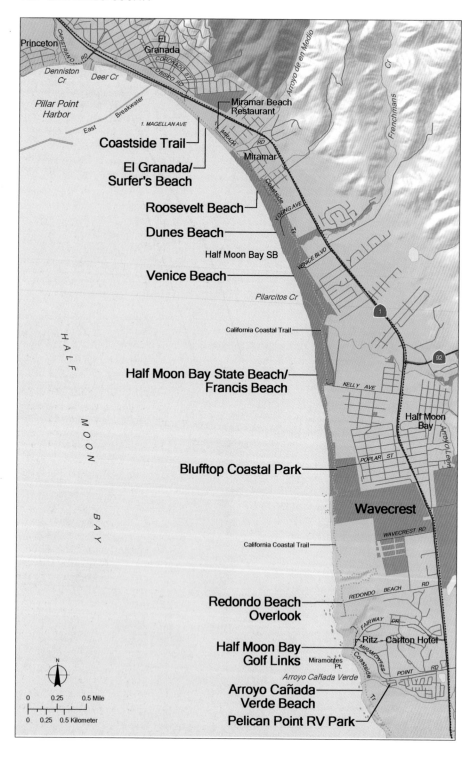

Princeton

El Granada

CAPISTRANO RD

CORONADO ST

Obispo Rd

Denniston Cr

Deer Cr

Arroyo de en Medio

Frenchmans Cr

Pillar Point Harbor

Breakwater

Miramar Beach Restaurant

East

1. MAGELLAN AVE

MIRADA RD

Coastside Trail

Miramar

Coastside Tr

El Granada/ Surfer's Beach

YOUNG AVE

Roosevelt Beach

Dunes Beach

Half Moon Bay SB

VENICE BLVD

Venice Beach

Pilarcitos Cr

1

California Coastal Trail

92

Half Moon Bay State Beach/ Francis Beach

KELLY AVE

Half Moon Bay

Arroyo Leon

POPLAR ST

Blufftop Coastal Park

Wavecrest

WAVECREST RD

California Coastal Trail

REDONDO BEACH RD

Redondo Beach Overlook

FAIRWAY DR

Ritz - Carlton Hotel

Half Moon Bay Golf Links

Miramontes Pt.

MIRAMONTES

Coastside

POINT RD

Arroyo Cañada Verde

Arroyo Cañada Verde Beach

Coastside Tr

Pelican Point RV Park

H A L F   M O O N   B A Y

N

0   0.25   0.5 Mile

0   0.25   0.5 Kilometer

Half Moon Bay

	Sandy Beach	Rocky Shore	Trail	Visitor Center	Campground	Wildlife Viewing	Fishing or Boating	Facilities for Disabled	Food and Drink	Restrooms	Parking	Fee
Coastside Trail			•				•			•		
El Granada/Surfer's Beach	•	•								•	•	•
Roosevelt Beach	•	•					•			•	•	•
Dunes Beach	•	•					•			•	•	•
Venice Beach	•	•			•		•			•	•	•
Half Moon Bay State Beach/Francis Beach	•	•	•	•			•			•	•	•
Blufftop Coastal Park	•	•								•	•	
Wavecrest		•				•				•		
Redondo Beach Overlook		•								•		
Half Moon Bay Golf Links									•	•	•	•
Arroyo Cañada Verde Beach	•	•					•		•	•		
Pelican Point RV Park					•				•	•	•	•

COASTSIDE TRAIL: *Pillar Point Harbor to Purisima Creek, Half Moon Bay.* A scenic blufftop trail, some nine miles long and part of the California Coastal Trail, spans the city of Half Moon Bay. The trail is suitable for pedestrians and bicyclists (some portions are paved and wheelchair accessible), as well as limited equestrian use. The Coastside Trail can be reached from beach parks and from many streets west of Hwy. One, including Mirada Rd., Young Ave., Kelly Ave., Poplar St., and Miramontes Point Road.

EL GRANADA/SURFER'S BEACH: *Between East Breakwater and Mirada Rd., Half Moon Bay.* A wide, sandy beach popular with surfers lies south of Pillar Point Harbor. A fee parking lot with restrooms is located at the foot of the East Breakwater, one-half mile south of Capistrano Road. A second, no-fee parking lot is located inland of Hwy. One off Obispo Road. Cross busy Hwy. One on foot only at the Coronado St. stoplight.

A paved link in the Coastside Trail runs south from Coronado St. to Magellan Avenue. From there, turn seaward and follow the shoreline. Limited public beach parking is available in one lot behind the Miramar Beach Restaurant. Beach access is also available at the end of Mirada Rd. (very limited street parking), off Hwy. One about one-half mile south of Magellan Avenue.

ROOSEVELT BEACH: *Foot of Young Ave., Half Moon Bay.* Roosevelt Beach is the northernmost unit of two-mile-long Half Moon Bay State Beach. Turn right (north) at the end of Young Ave. The wide sandy beach is backed by dunes. Facilities include picnic tables, restrooms, and plenty of parking. Fee for entry. Call: 650-726-8819.

DUNES BEACH: *Foot of Young Ave., Half Moon Bay.* From Young Ave., turn left to reach Dunes Beach; state park fee applies. Restrooms are adjacent. A paved segment of the Coastside Trail extends a mile and a half to the north and three-quarters of a mile to the south. An equestrian trail east of the parking lot runs from Dunes Beach south to Francis Beach. Horse rentals are available at two stables west of Hwy. One between Young Ave. and Venice Boulevard.

VENICE BEACH: *Foot of Venice Blvd., Half Moon Bay.* Venice Beach has parking located close to beach level; farther south, Half Moon Bay beaches are backed by a high bluff. The Sweetwood group campsite is situated in a grove of cypress trees. Facilities include picnic tables, barbecue grills, and restrooms. Parking and overnight fee applies.

HALF MOON BAY STATE BEACH/FRANCIS BEACH: *Foot of Kelly Ave., Half Moon Bay.* Amenities include a visitor center, picnic area, beach shower, 52-site campground, beach wheelchair, and a long stretch of white sand. Leashed dogs allowed in the campground and picnic area. Call: 650-726-8819.

BLUFFTOP COASTAL PARK: *Foot of Poplar Ave., Half Moon Bay.* Beach access is available via a steep dirt path down the bluff from a paved parking area. Dogs on leash OK. Maintained by the city of Half Moon Bay; call: 650-726-8297.

WAVECREST: *End of Wavecrest Rd., Half Moon Bay.* Once slated for development, the property has been acquired by the Peninsula Open Space Trust, a nonprofit group. Near the parking area are baseball fields and horseshoe courts. To the north of the playfields are informal trails that lead one-quarter mile across the coastal terrace toward the shoreline. The open grasslands and tall trees provide habitat for raptors, such as hawks, that prey upon small animals. From the bluff edge, there are delightful views of the sea and coastline, but no beach access.

REDONDO BEACH OVERLOOK: *Foot of Redondo Beach Rd., Half Moon Bay.* An unimproved parking area with fine coastal views is at the end of Redondo Beach Road. No beach access. The Coastside Trail continues south toward the Ritz-Carlton Hotel.

HALF MOON BAY GOLF LINKS: *Two Miramontes Point Rd., Half Moon Bay.* Two 18-hole golf courses, both available for public play, are located on scenic ocean bluffs near the Ritz-Carlton Hotel. The pro shop carries rental equipment, and there is a restaurant. Call: 650-726-1800.

ARROYO CAÑADA VERDE BEACH: *Off Miramontes Point Rd., .6 mi. W. of Hwy. One, Half Moon Bay.* A gorgeous cove beach is located below the high bluff at the mouth of Arroyo Cañada Verde. A 15-car public parking lot (no fee) is located south of the Ritz-Carlton Hotel. Walk west on a paved wheelchair-accessible path toward the beach; restrooms are located en route. Along the way, turn left across the creek and proceed downcoast through the golf greens. Or, continue west toward the beach stairway. The paved trail also heads north toward the Ritz-Carlton Hotel and beyond.

Additional public parking for users of the coastal trail is available in the Ritz-Carlton's parking structure on a no-fee basis; ask at the entrance kiosk for instructions and a trail map. The blufftop trail runs seaward of the hotel, offering lovely views, but steep bluffs prevent beach access.

PELICAN POINT RV PARK: *Off Miramontes Point Rd., Half Moon Bay.* The RV park contains 75 recreational vehicle campsites; tent camping also permitted. Laundry facilities, small store, and restrooms. Overnight fee applies. For reservations, call: 650-726-9100.

Roosevelt Beach

The Ocean Shore Railroad was founded in 1905 by a group of high-profile investors with a grand plan to connect San Francisco and Santa Cruz via the coast, but soon the 1906 earthquake sent trains and newly-laid track into the ocean. The company rebuilt, but switched double tracks for electric trains to a more economical single track for steam engines. To earn revenue, trains started running north from Santa Cruz (in 1906) and south from San Francisco (in 1907), even though the two ends did not meet.

However, problems continued. Landslides caused track closures at notoriously unstable Devils Slide in San Mateo County. The little railway encountered aggressive competition from the mammoth Southern Pacific Railroad. Trucks began taking away the Ocean Shore's business of hauling produce, lumber, and other goods.

The railroad met the great engineering challenges of building a tunnel at San Pedro Point in present-day Pacifica, trestles over numerous creeks and canyons, and miles of rails on steep cliffs high above the shoreline. Using its "Reaches the Beaches" slogan, the Ocean Shore ran popular "picnic trains" from San Francisco to San Mateo County beaches, with riders enjoying stunning scenery along the way.

And then there were the lofty plans. Coastside hotels, resorts, and elegant stations were designed and sometimes actually built. The affiliated Shore Line Investment Company enticed people to visit land on the coast that was marketed as future beautiful suburbs for commuters. Streets were laid out for new towns with alluring names ("Granada," "Miramar") and real estate speculation took off for a time.

Population growth on the coast was slow, however, and the Ocean Shore Railroad lacked the capital to ever finish the 26-mile gap between Tunitas Creek south of Half Moon Bay and Swanton in northern Santa Cruz County. Following an employee strike in 1920, the money-losing railroad finally tore up tracks to sell as scrap metal and sold off trains. New investors later tried to rebuild the railroad, and even without trains, the Ocean Shore Railroad Company continued as a business, involved in lawsuits for decades over rights-of-way and other land holdings.

Today several Ocean Shore stations remain standing, including Vallemar Station in Pacifica at Reina del Mar Ave. and Highway One. Ocean Shore School in Pacifica bears its name. A ledge graded for tracks remains visible at Tunitas Creek. But the biggest reminder is probably Highway One itself. The state of California ultimately took over much of the Ocean Shore's right-of-way, and the highway now follows the coastline as the railroad once did; while trains may have struggled for ridership, driving along the coast instead has proved to be much more popular.

Former Ocean Shore Railroad, Vallemar Station, Pacifica

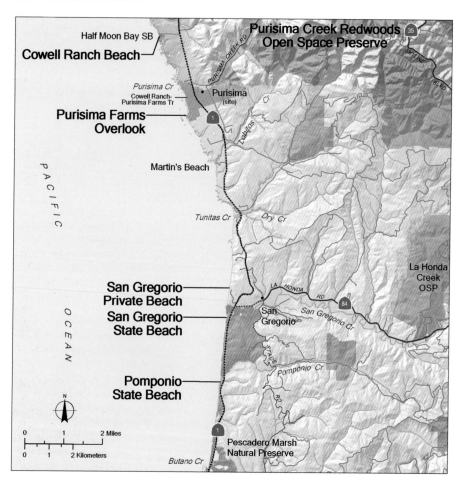

Pomponio State Beach

Cowell Ranch to Pomponio State Beach

	Sandy Beach	Rocky Shore	Trail	Visitor Center	Campground	Wildlife Viewing	Fishing or Boating	Facilities for Disabled	Food and Drink	Restrooms	Parking	Fee
Cowell Ranch Beach	•		•							•	•	
Purisima Farms Overlook			•					•		•	•	
Purisima Creek Redwoods Open Space Preserve			•					•		•	•	
San Gregorio Private Beach	•										•	•
San Gregorio State Beach	•					•	•			•	•	•
Pomponio State Beach	•						•			•	•	•

COWELL RANCH BEACH: *W. of Hwy. One, .5 mi. S. of Miramontes Pt. Rd.* An 18-car parking lot is located next to Hwy. One. A gravel trail, one-half mile long, leads to a blufftop viewing area. Stairs descend to a sandy beach. A new link in the California Coastal Trail, opened in 2011, extends south from Cowell Ranch Beach a distance of three miles to the Purisima Farms Overlook.

PURISIMA FARMS OVERLOOK: *W. of Hwy. One, 2 mi. S. of Cowell Ranch Beach parking area.* A 17-car parking area equipped with restrooms is located among actively farmed fields. A public trail easement leads west to an ocean overlook. From there, a public blufftop trail leads north to Cowell Ranch Beach. The path, also known as the Cowell Ranch-Purisima Farms Trail, is wheelchair accessible and is open to pedestrians and bicyclists; no dogs or horses allowed. The trail does not provide access to beaches. The coastal terrace remains in agricultural use; stay on the path, obey posted signs, and re-spect adjacent farm operations. Occasional closure of the overlook trail may occur when spraying of the fields is underway.

PURISIMA CREEK REDWOODS OPEN SPACE PRESERVE: *From the end of Purisima Creek Rd. to Skyline Blvd. (Hwy. 35), San Mateo Co.* Red-wood-forested canyons and a 21-mile-long network of trails are found in this preserve. The Purisima Creek trailhead with a 10-ve-hicle parking area is at the end of Purisima Creek Rd., 3.7 miles east of Hwy. One. The Purisima Creek Trail climbs some 1,600 feet in elevation to Skyline Blvd. At Skyline Blvd., located six and one-half miles south of Hwy. 92, there is parking, a picnic area, and the wheelchair-accessible Redwood Trail. Yet another trailhead on Skyline Blvd. is located four and one-half miles south of Hwy. 92. Dogs not allowed on the trail. For information about the preserve, call: 650-691-1200. Hiking trails continue eastward from Skyline Blvd. down the slope of the ridge onto additional open space lands, in-cluding the Phleger Estate unit of the Gold-en Gate National Recreation Area.

SAN GREGORIO PRIVATE BEACH: *Off Hwy. One, .1 mi. N. of La Honda Rd./Hwy. 84, San Gregorio.* The beach is located at the end of an unpaved toll road, which can be identi-fied by the white gate located among trees. Entrance fee applies. Clothing optional. The beach is usually open on weekends, de-pending on the weather.

SAN GREGORIO STATE BEACH: *Hwy. One, .1 mi. S. of La Honda Rd./Hwy. 84, San Gregorio.* A large parking area on the bluff overlooks a large sandy beach strewn with driftwood. A path and stairs lead from the parking lot down to the shore, where surf fishing for rockfish and surfperch is popular. Amenities include picnic tables, barbecue grills, and restrooms. A bronze plaque commemorates the 1769 Portolá expedition's camp that was located at an Ohlone village near the mouth of San Gregorio Creek. Highly eroded bluffs; dangerous rip currents. Day-use hours are 8 am to sunset; entrance fee applies. Leashed dogs allowed in the picnic area, but not on the beach. Beach fires are prohibited; please do not take driftwood, shells, or other natu-ral features. Call: 650-879-2170.

San Gregorio State Beach

The San Gregorio Creek estuary and fresh-water marsh extend both east and west of Hwy. One. Water-associated birds such as herons and egrets inhabit the marsh. Silver salmon, steelhead trout, and Pacific lam-prey spawn upstream in gravel beds. The beach is an overwintering area for plovers and other shorebirds. Surrounded by rolling hills, the tiny town of San Gregorio is about a mile inland from the beach; the town was a popular resort at the turn of the 20th century before the redwoods were logged out. Stage Rd., a present-day scenic route between San Gregorio and Pescadero, was the old stage-coach road from 1865 until 1905.

POMPONIO STATE BEACH: *Hwy. One at Pomponio Creek, Pescadero.* A sandy beach ex-tends for miles below the sandstone bluffs. Facilities include picnic tables, barbecue grills, and restrooms. Day use hours are 8 AM to sunset; fee applies. Fires prohibited; dogs not allowed. Call: 650-879-2170.

Pomponio Creek is named for a Native American known as Pomponio who at-tacked Spanish settlers and repeatedly escaped from the missions. His mountain hideout was at the headwaters of Pomponio Creek, where he made a desperate stand against the takeover of Indian-occupied lands.

A road sign. A creek name. A 19th cen-tury cemetery. Eucalyptus trees nearly 200 feet tall, planted in the 1870s. These are all that remain of the once-thriving town of Purisima. Traveling south four miles from Half Moon Bay along Hwy. One, one would never guess that 140 years ago, just inland of the highway at Purisima Creek, there was a general store and dance hall, hotel, school-house, a wagon and harness shop, blacksmith, shoemaker, and the two-story, 17-room mansion of Henry Dob-bel, whose 1,000-acre ranch produced wheat, barley, and potatoes.

Dobbel had come by sea via Cape Horn to California from the Schleswig-Holstein region of Germany just before the gold rush of 1849. He had amassed enough wealth by 1868 to sell his ranch in the Mt. Eden area of what is now Hayward east of San Francisco Bay and buy the ranchland at Purisima from John Purcell. Together with several oth-er hard-working farmers and merchants who owned land nearby, he helped develop a bustling town that by 1872 was considered the hub of a promising district rivaling Spanishtown (renamed Half Moon Bay in 1874).

But as fate and nature would have it, Purisima's future would be brief. During the 1880s it became obvious that Half Moon Bay had a superior location, providing a crossroad east to San Mateo on San Francisco Bay as well as a north-south route along the coast. A nation-wide economic recession ensued from 1882–5, including the Panic of 1884, during which banks across the county halted investments and called in outstanding loans. As in other parts of the country, the effects in California and the San Francisco region were significant. In 1885, a severe gale caused major damage along the coast and destroyed the wooden loading chute near the mouth of Tunitas Creek, just south of Purisima, where local lumber and agricultural products were shipped. Another economic recession in 1887–8, coupled with several successive years of crop failures and bad business decisions left Henry Dobbel no choice but to mortgage all of his land to the wealthy landowner Henry Cowell, and in 1890 Dobbel lost it all in foreclosure proceedings. A year later he died, and within several more years other prin-

cipal residents of the town had also passed on, leaving Purisima to begin its decline into history. Deserted by the 1930s, the townsite is marked now only by non-native trees planted on the site of the Dobbel estate and the overgrown pioneer cemetery.

The Dobbel Ranch became known as the Cowell Ranch and, fortunately for the public, was acquired by the Peninsula Open Space Trust (POST) in 1986 when the Cowell Foundation decided to sell the property. In order to permanently protect the land from development, POST then donated beach access and sold conservation easements to the State of California. The California Department of Parks and Recreation opened the agricultural view trail and public access path to Cowell Ranch Beach in 1995. Hikers can now view the northern coastal parcels of the former Dobbel Ranch as they look south from the trail heading west to the overlook and beach stairway. Parking for the Cowell Ranch Beach trail is west of Hwy. One, three-quarters of a mile south of Miramontes Rd.

Town of Purisima ca. 1870s, Residence, Ranch & Property of Henry Dobbel

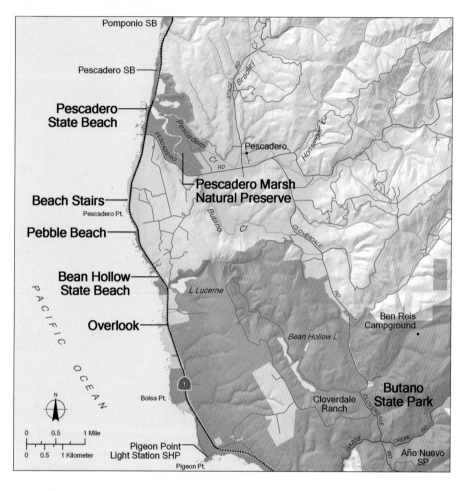

Pescadero State Beach

Pescadero State Beach to Butano State Park

	Sandy Beach	Rocky Shore	Trail	Visitor Center	Campground	Wildlife Viewing	Fishing or Boating	Facilities for Disabled	Food and Drink	Restrooms	Parking	Fee
Pescadero State Beach	•	•	•			•	•			•	•	•
Pescadero Marsh Natural Preserve			•			•						
Beach Stairs	•	•				•						
Pebble Beach	•	•								•	•	
Bean Hollow State Beach	•	•	•				•			•	•	
Overlook			•			•					•	
Butano State Park			•		•	•			•	•	•	

PESCADERO STATE BEACH: *Along Hwy. One from 1 mi. N. of Pescadero Rd. to .75 mi. S. of Pescadero Road.* A wide sandy beach, large active sand dunes, and some gorgeous rocky shoreline make up Pescadero State Beach. The park also includes the Pescadero Marsh Natural Preserve inland of Hwy. One. As is true along much of the San Mateo County coast, the glimpses of beach and ocean available to travelers on Hwy. One almost pale in comparison to the strikingly beautiful scenes on the shoreline itself. Access to beaches and bluff trails is easy at many locations along the county's spectacular coast.

Three parking lots serve Pescadero State Beach. One is located at the end of Pescadero Rd., and it provides access to sandy coves and rocky areas. A second parking lot is located two-tenths of a mile north of Pescadero Rd.; trails lead from that parking area to the blufftop where there are stunning views of offshore rocks and a harbor seal haulout. Access down to the sand is not easy from the steep bluffs. The third, and northernmost, parking lot is one mile north of Pescadero Rd., and it offers easy foot access to a half-mile-long, fine-sand beach. The beach is divided by the mouth of Pescadero Creek. A parking fee applies at the northern parking lot only; restrooms are located at each of the three parking areas.

On the flat sandy beach, western gulls, California gulls, Heermann's gulls, and shorebirds such as sandpipers, dowitchers, godwits, and willets are abundant seasonally. Large sand dunes spread inland of the beach up to the Hwy. One shoulder. Among the dunes, leaf litter of coastal scrub vegetation provides sandy habitat for the rare globose dune beetle. Among the tidepools at Pescadero State Beach, poke-poling for monkey-face eels is popular. Dogs and beach fires are prohibited at Pescadero State Beach; parking lots are open from 8 AM to sunset. For information, call: 650-879-2170.

PESCADERO MARSH NATURAL PRESERVE: *E. of Hwy. One, N. of Pescadero Road.* Inland of Hwy. One is a 510-acre wildlife sanctuary that includes the largest coastal marsh between San Francisco Bay and Elkhorn Slough. The preserve includes both tidal estuary and freshwater marsh habitats, along with riparian woodland and northern coastal scrub. The preserve provides important habitat for a variety of animals, such as deer, raccoons, foxes, skunks, white-tailed kites, yellow-throated warblers, Allen's hummingbirds, and overwintering dabbling and diving ducks. More than 200 species of birds have been recorded in the marsh, including more than 60 that nest there. The best birding is during the late fall and early spring.

Endangered or threatened species in Pescadero Marsh include the San Francisco garter snake, California red-legged frog, tidewater goby, steelhead trout, and coho salmon. One trail leads along the northern perimeter of the marsh, starting opposite the northernmost parking lot at Pescadero State Beach; use extreme caution in crossing the busy highway. Another trail, somewhat overgrown, starts at a small dirt pull-out on Pescadero Rd. just east of Hwy. One. Dogs are prohibited in the preserve at all times. For information, call: 650-879-2170.

Volunteer docents with the San Mateo Coast Natural History Association lead nature walks into Pescadero Marsh Natural Preserve on the first Sunday of each month at 10 AM and on the third Sunday at 1 PM. Meet at the middle parking lot of Pescadero State Beach, just south of the Pescadero Creek bridge. Tours last about two hours; bring water and binoculars and be prepared for changeable weather.

BEACH STAIRS: *Off Hwy. One, 1.1 mi. S. of Pescadero Road*. An unsigned portion of Bean Hollow State Beach is located between Pescadero State Beach and Pebble Beach. There are two small pull-outs and short paths that lead to a beach made up of pebbles, sand, and rocky reef; no facilities.

PEBBLE BEACH: *Off Hwy. One, 1.6 mi. S. of Pescadero Road*. Like other California beaches bearing the same name, San Mateo County's Pebble Beach is strewn with small rounded stones. From the signed parking lot, stairs lead to a cove where you can examine the pebbles. Also seen at Pebble Beach are examples of honeycomb-like rocks called tafoni. Picnic tables and restrooms are near the parking lot.

There are tidepools south of Pebble Beach, and fossils can be seen in the cliffs. A blufftop self-guided nature trail starts at the parking lot and extends south about a mile to the main Bean Hollow State Beach entrance. The trail provides great opportunities for taking photos of the rocky shore and of spring wildflowers that include blue iris, seaside daisy, and California poppy. Dogs are permitted, but must be on a leash no more than six feet long. Part of Bean Hollow State Beach; call: 650-879-2170.

A major resort hotel, known as "Coburn's Folly," was located near Pebble Beach during the 1890s. The hotel's developer anticipated tourists who would arrive via the Ocean Shore Railroad that was planned to connect San Francisco and Santa Cruz. The line never reached as far as Pebble Beach, however, and the hotel was a financial failure.

Pescadero Marsh Natural Preserve

BEAN HOLLOW STATE BEACH: *Along Hwy. One, .9 mi. S. of Pebble Beach.* Picnic tables equipped with barbecue grills are sited on the bluff overlooking the rocky shore. There is easy access from the small parking area to adjacent sandy beaches. Tidepools are at the north end of the beach. Surf fishing for rockfish is popular. Leashed dogs are permitted. For information, call: 650-879-2170.

OVERLOOK: *10257 Cabrillo Hwy., Pescadero.* A ten-foot-wide path leads from the Hwy. One frontage road to a rocky bluff and scenic overlook. Look for the opening in the guardrail eight-tenths of a mile south of Bean Hollow State Beach, then turn north on narrow frontage road. Do not block driveway; respect adjacent private property.

BUTANO STATE PARK: *Cloverdale Rd., 5 mi. S. of Pescadero and 3 mi. E. of Hwy. One.* This inland state park includes over 2,000 acres of canyons and hills vegetated with redwoods, mixed evergreen forests, oaks, and chaparral. The land was selectively logged during the 1880s but second-growth woods remain. There are 30 miles of hiking trails and campsites for both car camping and walk-in camping. Overnight and day-use fees apply. Special hiker/bicyclist group camping is available. Summertime nature walks and campfire programs are offered. Leashed dogs are allowed in the campground and developed park areas, but not on trails. For camping reservations, call: 1-800-444-7275; for park information, call: 650-879-2040.

Pebble Beach

The pebbles at San Mateo County's Pebble Beach consist mostly of chert, but take on a variety of colors, including red, tan, green, and white due to various impurities. The origin of all of these chert pebbles is a mystery, since none of the rocks on the west side of the San Andreas Fault (as is this site) contain chert like this. These pebbles could have come from the Franciscan rocks found from Pacifica to the Marin Headlands. But why are they found nowhere between Pacifica and Bean Hollow State Beach, and why do they make up such a preponderance of the pebbles found at Pebble Beach? Perhaps the pebbles came from an ancient river bed that swung down to these latitudes during the last Ice Age, when sea level was some 400 feet lower than it is now.

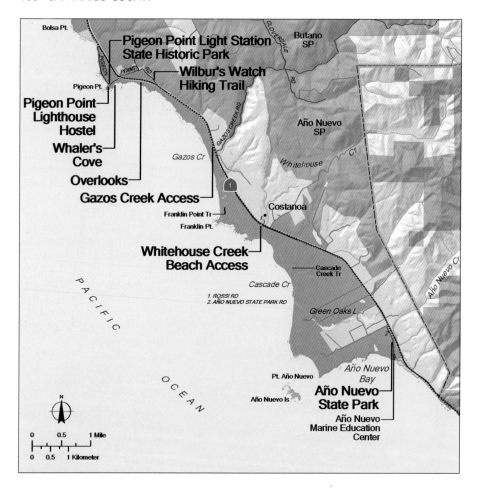

Bolsa Pt.

Pigeon Point Light Station
State Historic Park

Butano
SP

CLOVERDALE

Wilbur's Watch
Hiking Trail

PIGEON

POINT RD.

Pigeon Pt.

GAZOS CREEK RD

RD.

Pigeon Point
Lighthouse
Hostel

Whaler's
Cove

Overlooks

Gazos Creek Access

Año Nuevo
SP

Gazos Cr

Whitehouse   Cr

Costanoa

Franklin Point Tr

Franklin Pt.

Whitehouse Creek
Beach Access

Cascade
Creek Tr

P A C I F I C

Cascade Cr

1. ROSSI RD
2. AÑO NUEVO STATE PARK RD

Green Oaks L

Año Nuevo Cr

O C E A N

N

Pt. Año Nuevo

Año Nuevo
Bay

Año Nuevo Is

Año Nuevo
State Park

0   0.5   1 Mile

Año Nuevo
Marine Education
Center

0   0.5   1 Kilometer

Whaler's Cove

Pigeon Point to Año Nuevo

	Sandy Beach	Rocky Shore	Trail	Visitor Center	Campground	Wildlife Viewing	Fishing or Boating	Facilities for Disabled	Food and Drink	Restrooms	Parking	Fee
Pigeon Point Light Station State Historic Park	•	•	•						•	•		
Pigeon Point Lighthouse Hostel	•								•	•	•	
Whaler's Cove	•	•								•		
Wilbur's Watch Hiking Trail			•							•		
Overlooks		•				•				•		
Gazos Creek Access	•	•					•	•	•	•		
Whitehouse Creek Beach Access	•	•	•							•		
Año Nuevo State Park	•	•	•	•		•		•	•	•	•	

PIGEON POINT LIGHT STATION STATE HISTORIC PARK: *Pigeon Point Rd., W. of Hwy. One.* In 1853, the Boston clipper ship *Carrier Pigeon* drifted aground on the headland then known as Punta de la Ballena, or Whale Point; after the wreck the headland became known as Pigeon Point. A whaling station was located on the point during the late 1800s, and lumber and produce were shipped from Pigeon Point Wharf until the 1920s. After numerous shipwrecks, a steam-operated fog signal with a 12-inch whistle was installed on the bluff in 1871. The 115-foot-high brick lighthouse was built the following year; it is the tallest functioning lighthouse on the West Coast. Although the brick lighthouse survived the 1906 San Francisco and 1989 Loma Prieta earthquakes, portions of the structure's cornice fell to the ground in 2002, causing closure of the lighthouse to the public. The grounds are open for viewing, and docents lead free half-hour-long history walks on Fridays, Saturdays, and Sundays from 10 AM to 4 PM; rain cancels. Facilities are not wheelchair accessible. For information, call: 650-879-2120.

North of the lighthouse, Pigeon Point Rd. runs along the top of a low bluff. There is informal access down dirt paths to the shoreline; this is a good place for beautiful late-afternoon views of the lighthouse, with the sun at a low angle.

Pigeon Point Light Station State Historic Park

PIGEON POINT LIGHTHOUSE HOSTEL: *Pigeon Point Rd., W. of Hwy. One*. A Hostelling International facility, the hostel offers private and shared rooms in the restored lighthouse keeper's quarters. Amenities include kitchens with dining areas, lounges, ocean-view hot tub, beach access, satellite Internet, and free WiFi. Call: 650-879-0633.

WHALER'S COVE: *E. of the Pigeon Point Lighthouse*. A circular blufftop seating area with commemorative plaques honoring local conservation leaders overlooks a sandy cove located just east of the Pigeon Point Lighthouse. A stairway leads down to the shoreline, which is sheltered by the point.

WILBUR'S WATCH HIKING TRAIL: *Inland of Hwy. One, near the southern intersection of Pigeon Point Rd. and Hwy. One*. The trail begins on Pigeon Point Rd. and leads a mile uphill, where the view encompasses the coast from Pigeon Point to Point Año Nuevo. The parking lot holds six vehicles; open daily from dawn to dusk. The site is managed by the Peninsula Open Space Trust (POST); call: 650-854-7696.

OVERLOOKS: *Along Hwy. One, S. of Pigeon Point Rd.* The blufftop south of the lighthouse has unimproved dirt pullouts and nice views of the rugged shoreline. The property is co-owned by San Mateo County and POST. No facilities.

GAZOS CREEK ACCESS: *Hwy. One, N. of Gazos Creek Rd.* A wheelchair-accessible path leads to the sandy beach, where surf fishing for rockfish and surfperch is popular. Facilities include parking and restrooms.

WHITEHOUSE CREEK BEACH ACCESS: *Hwy. One, .1 mi. S. of Rossi Road.* A dirt parking area near Whitehouse Creek marks a trail leading to a rocky cove beach, part of Año Nuevo State Park. At the cove, look for a porthole-size opening in the rock that frames a lovely shoreline view to the south. Additional beach access paths from Hwy. One include the Franklin Point Trail, located one-half mile north of Whitehouse Creek and the Cascade Creek Trail, one-half mile south of Whitehouse Creek. A blufftop trail overlooks the shoreline.

AÑO NUEVO STATE PARK: *Off Hwy. One, 27 mi. S. of Half Moon Bay.* Punta del Año Nuevo, "New Years Point," was named by the chaplain of Spanish explorer Sebastián Vizcaíno, who sighted it on January 3, 1603. At that time the region was occupied by Ohlone Indians whose first contact with Europeans did not occur until much later, in 1769, when the Portolá Expedition explored the area. When Vizcaíno wrote of Punta del Año Nuevo, he made no mention of the offshore island that now lies nearly one-half mile from the mainland. Indeed, it appears that what is now Año Nuevo Island was at

Whitehouse Creek Beach

Año Nuevo State Park and Año Nuevo Island at upper right

that time part of the mainland, linked to it by an extension of the dune field that now covers the tip of the point. The dunes have since eroded away, isolating the island in one of the most dramatic examples of coastal erosion in central California.

Point Año Nuevo is crossed by at least five active faults, together making up the San Gregorio Fault system. The primary faults are the Coastways Fault, seen in the sea cliff 1.2 miles southeast of the mouth of Año Nuevo Creek, and the Frijoles Fault, exposed 0.4 miles northwest of the creek. The latter is easily reached from the viewpoint near the "staging area," about one-half mile from the parking lot. Stairs provide access to the beach. The Frijoles Fault, here consisting of a zone of "fault gouge" some 200 feet wide, juxtaposes 9–14,000-year-old sediments deposited by Año Nuevo Creek southeast of the fault with the five-million-year-old Purisima Formation siltstone to the northwest.

Año Nuevo has had many owners including the mountain man Isaac Graham, Daniel Boone's cousin, who was an archetypical western frontiersman. In 1862 the Steele Brothers dairy empire was established and soon became famous throughout the west. Several historic structures remain, including the restored 1880s Flora Dickerman Steele dairy barn, which houses the Año Nuevo Marine Education Center (open daily from 8:30 AM to 4:30 PM) and a bookstore/gift shop (generally open fewer hours).

During the elephant seal breeding season, from December 15 to March 31, docent-led tours provide the only access to the breeding area. Reservations recommended, and separate fee applies; call: 1-800-444-4445 or see http://anonuevo.reserveamerica.com. The walks are three miles long and cover sloping terrain. For required reservations for disabled-access tours via boardwalk, available on weekends from January through March, call: 650-879-2033. During most of the remainder of the year, visitors may explore the trails without a docent, but a visitor permit must be obtained first from park staff. From December 1 to 14 there is no public access to the elephant seal viewing area. East of Hwy. One, Año Nuevo State Park includes a 225-acre Cultural Preserve that contains the remains of a village occupied by the Ohlone people.

No pets are allowed in the state park, including in vehicles in the parking lot. Parking fee applies. Visitor hours vary by season; for recorded park information, call: 650-879-0227.

Northern elephant seals (*Mirounga angustirostris*) are the largest of the true seals; females are up to 12 feet long and weigh 900 to 1,800 pounds, while males reach 16 feet in length and weigh up to 5,000 pounds. Elephant seals, like harbor seals, cannot turn their hind flippers forward, and are able only to wriggle on their bellies when on land. By contrast, sea lions (the "seals" seen in circus shows) and fur seals have hind flippers that make the animals more agile when out of the water. Elephant seals are powerful swimmers, however; they can dive to tremendous depths in the ocean, between 1,000 and 2,000 feet and occasionally reaching nearly a mile below the surface. Elephant seals feed on fish, squid, and octopus. In turn, the seals are prey for white sharks and for orcas, also called killer whales.

Elephant seals were slaughtered in large numbers during the 19th century for their oil-rich blubber. At the low point of their population, only a few dozen elephant seals remained on Guadalupe Island off Baja California. During the 20th century, the number of elephant seals grew, and the animals established rookeries on the Channel Islands, Año Nuevo Island, Southeast Farallon Island, and on the mainland.

The largest colonies of elephant seals are found at San Nicolas and San Miguel Islands, south of Point Conception; northern elephant seals are estimated to number 175,000 worldwide.

Females give birth from the end of December through February. After pups are weaned, the mothers depart, leaving their offspring to teach themselves how to swim. Adult males also leave the land, spending the next few months feeding at sea. During the spring and summer, adults and juveniles of both sexes return for a month or so to the beaches to molt, then once again take to the ocean to feed. In the fall, the seals haul out on the shore, first the youngest, followed by the mature males at the end of November and females ready to give birth in mid-December. An individual female elephant seal spends a total of two months per year on land, while a male spends four months on land. Elephant seals can be seen along the shore nearly year-round.

When male elephant seals fight for dominance, they move surprisingly fast. Do not place yourself in the path of one of these animals that weighs as much as a pickup truck. Elephant seals are protected by law; it is also dangerous to approach or harass the animals.

Male elephant seal at Año Nuevo State Park

Page opposite: Yellow Bank Beach, Santa Cruz County

Santa Cruz County

Santa Cruz County

THE CITY OF SANTA CRUZ is by far the largest urban area in the county, but its walkable downtown streets and Victorian-era buildings offer a picture of small-town America. The city's Main Beach and Cowell Beach offer sand, scenery, and recreation, along with the convenience of close-by lodgings and dining options. The famous Santa Cruz Beach Boardwalk amusement park is one of the few like it still operating on the California coast.

Northwest of Santa Cruz is a succession of beaches, some narrow and some wide, but all beautiful. Gorgeous sandy strands, some of them just out of sight of travelers on Hwy. One, are backed by colorful sandstone walls festooned with hanging gardens of wildflowers. The names of beaches are as vivid as the scenery: Sharktooth, Yellowbank, Four Mile, and Three Mile (the latter two referring to their distance from the edge of Santa Cruz).

East of Santa Cruz along the shore of Monterey Bay are expansive beaches that include New Brighton State Beach, Seacliff State Beach, and Sunset State Beach. Access to the sand is easy, and the wide stretch of beach seems endless. The bay's waters are more sheltered and swimmable than are the ocean waters along the north coast of the county.

The fertile coastal terraces of Santa Cruz County's north coast produce much of California's Brussels sprouts, while the Pajaro Valley is noted for crops of lettuce, strawberries, artichokes, and cut flowers. Farm stands are open seasonally near Davenport, Watsonville, and elsewhere, and numerous farmers markets offer local products. The downtown Santa Cruz Farmers Market takes place at Cedar and Lincoln streets every Wednesday afternoon, year-round. At Davenport, the American Abalone farm raises red abalone in tanks for sale; open to the public from 10 AM to 2 PM on Saturdays at 245 Davenport Landing Road.

North of the city of Santa Cruz are the rugged Santa Cruz Mountains, which contain beautiful upland forests of coastal redwoods, *Sequoia sempervirens*. These forests have been logged since the 19th century, but some old-growth redwood groves remain. A popular hiking trail that passes through redwood groves in Big Basin Redwoods State Park is the scenic 30-mile-long Skyline-to-the-Sea Trail that extends from Castle Rock State Park to the ocean at Waddell Creek Beach.

For visitor information, contact the Santa Cruz Area Chamber of Commerce: 831-457-3713, or the Capitola Chamber of Commerce: 831-475-6522.

Surf shops in Santa Cruz include:

Beach area: O'Neill, 400 Beach St., 831-459-9230; Shoreline Surf Shop, 125 Beach St., 831-471-7873; Cowell's Beach Surf Shop, 30 Front St., 831-427-2355.

Downtown: Cove Water Paddle Surf, 831-600-7230; Pacific Wave, 1502 Pacific Ave., 831-458-9283; Patagonia Santa Cruz, 415 River St. #C, 831-469-1945.

West side: Haut Surf and Sailboards, 345 Swift St., 831-426-7874; Arrow Surf and Sport, 2322 Mission St., 831-423-8286.

Pleasure Point area: Billabong Santa Cruz, 4105 Portola Dr., 831-476-7873; Santa Cruz Surf Shop, 753 41st Ave., 831-464-3233; Freeline Design Surf Shop, 821 41st Ave., 831-476-2950.

La Selva Beach: La Selva Beach Surf Shop, 308 Playa Blvd, 831-684-0774.

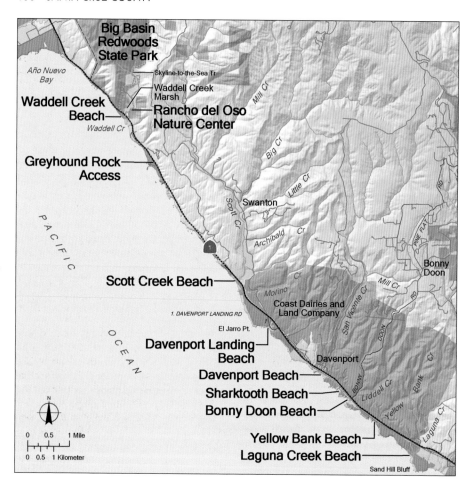

- Big Basin Redwoods State Park
- Año Nuevo Bay
- Skyline-to-the-Sea Tr
- Waddell Creek Marsh
- Waddell Creek Beach
- Rancho del Oso Nature Center
- Waddell Cr
- Mill Cr
- Big Cr
- Greyhound Rock Access
- Little Cr
- Scott Cr
- Swanton
- Cr
- Archibald Cr
- PINE FLAT RD
- PACIFIC
- Bonny Doon
- Scott Creek Beach
- Molino Cr
- Mill Cr
- 1. DAVENPORT LANDING RD
- Coast Dairies and Land Company
- San Vicente Cr
- DOON RD
- El Jarro Pt.
- OCEAN
- Davenport Landing Beach
- Davenport
- Davenport Beach
- Bonny Cr
- Liddell Cr
- Bank Cr
- Sharktooth Beach
- Bonny Doon Beach
- Yellow Cr
- Laguna Cr
- N
- Yellow Bank Beach
- Laguna Creek Beach
- 0   0.5   1 Mile
- 0   0.5   1 Kilometer
- Sand Hill Bluff

Waddell Creek Beach

Santa Cruz County North

	Sandy Beach	Rocky Shore	Trail	Visitor Center	Campground	Wildlife Viewing	Fishing or Boating	Facilities for Disabled	Food and Drink	Restrooms	Parking	Fee
Big Basin Redwoods State Park	•	•	•	•	•	•		•	•	•	•	•
Waddell Creek Beach	•	•			•	•	•			•	•	
Rancho del Oso Nature Center				•		•				•	•	
Greyhound Rock Access	•	•	•			•	•	•		•	•	
Scott Creek Beach	•	•				•	•			•		
Davenport Landing Beach	•	•				•	•		•	•	•	
Davenport Beach	•	•	•			•	•				•	
Sharktooth Beach	•	•	•			•					•	
Bonny Doon Beach	•										•	
Yellow Bank Beach	•	•	•								•	
Laguna Creek Beach	•	•	•								•	

BIG BASIN REDWOODS STATE PARK: *Main entrance on Hwy. 236, 14 mi. N.W. of Santa Cruz.* Over 18,000 acres of old-growth redwoods, numerous waterfalls, and a variety of wildlife are features of Big Basin Redwoods State Park. There are 80 miles of hiking trails, an equestrian trail and camp, 35 walk-in tent cabins, and five backpacker trail camps. Campgrounds lack trailer hookups; trailer dump station is located at Huckleberry Campground. Park headquarters and the Nature Lodge museum, on Big Basin Way, are nine and one-half miles west of the community of Boulder Creek. Call: 831-338-8860. On the inland side of Hwy. One from Waddell Creek Beach is Waddell Creek Marsh. The marsh provides habitat for avocets, stilts, herons, and egrets. Coho salmon and steelhead trout can be found seasonally in Waddell Creek. Nature trails lead through thick riparian vegetation. The Skyline-to-the-Sea Trail runs from the coast over 30 miles inland through Big Basin Redwoods State Park and beyond. Leashed dogs are allowed only on designated trails in Big Basin Redwoods State Park.

WADDELL CREEK BEACH: *Hwy. One, 1 mi. S. of San Mateo County line.* Kitesurfing and windsurfing are popular at this wide, often-breezy beach. A rocky area holds tidepools; ranger-led walks are held on some weekends. Packed earth parking area. No dogs allowed on the beach, which is part of Big Basin Redwoods State Park. Gulls, waterfowl, and shorebirds such as the marbled godwit, willet, and sanderling overwinter at the sandy beach and dune area near the mouth of Waddell Creek. To the south is a harbor seal rookery.

RANCHO DEL OSO NATURE CENTER: *Old Coast Rd., .25 mi. from Hwy. One, Big Basin Redwoods State Park.* Turn inland from Hwy. One, south of Waddell Creek, to reach the Rancho del Oso Nature Center, which occupies a former ranch house. There are historical and natural history exhibits and occasional guided nature tours. Open weekends from noon to 4 PM. Call: 831-427-2288.

GREYHOUND ROCK ACCESS: *Hwy. One, 1.2 mi. S. of Waddell Creek.* This popular fishing spot includes a steep, paved pedestrian path that leads to a sandy, sheltered cove beach. The beach is dotted with sea rocks, including the large rock that provides the site's name. There are also tidepools to explore. Atop the bluff are parking, picnic tables, and a disabled-accessible viewing platform. Dogs are allowed on the beach. A Santa Cruz County park facility; call: 831-454-7901.

SCOTT CREEK BEACH: *Hwy. One, 2.9 mi. N. of Davenport.* Fishing, kitesurfing and kite-flying are among the popular activities at this half-mile-long sandy beach. There are low dunes at the south end, and at the north end, Scott Creek flows into the sea beneath a bluff. Improved parking along the highway shoulder; use caution crossing the road. A wheelchair-accessible viewing platform and bicycle rack are available. Call: 831-454-7901.

DAVENPORT LANDING BEACH: *Davenport Landing Rd. off Hwy. One, 1.4 mi. N. of Davenport.* Davenport Landing Rd. is a loop off Hwy. One; enter only via the southern end. A short, level path leads to a sandy beach bounded by rocks. Shoulder parking, restrooms, picnic tables, and barbecue grill. Popular with kite and windsurfers.

DAVENPORT BEACH: *Across Hwy. One from Davenport, 9 mi. N. of Santa Cruz.* From a dirt parking lot an unimproved trail leads southward to a sandy beach. Nice views of offshore rocks, part of the California Coastal National Monument; gray whales may be spotted from November through May, and perhaps a humpback whale in summer or fall.

SHARKTOOTH BEACH: *Off Hwy. One, .5 mi. S. of Davenport.* A 200-yard-long trail leads from the dirt shoulder of the highway southward to the bluff edge. A rough trail leads down to a pocket beach bordered by towering rocks, some with ocean-carved tunnels.

BONNY DOON BEACH: *W. of Hwy. One at Bonny Doon Rd.* Look for improved parking spaces along the southbound shoulder of Hwy. One; there is a left-turn lane for northbound vehicles. An informal trail at the north end of the parking area leads 200 yards to a broad sandy beach. No dogs allowed on the beach. Call: 831-454-7901.

YELLOW BANK BEACH: *W. of Hwy. One, 1 mi. S. of Bonny Doon Rd.* Park along a dirt frontage road, seaward of Hwy. One, and look at the north end of the parking area for a short dirt trail to the beach.

Exposed in the sea cliff is Santa Cruz Mudstone, intruded by sandstone of the Santa Margarita Formation. While still soft, the sandstone was injected into the mudstone from below by the weight of the overlying sediments. Petroleum then migrated into fingers of the most porous sandstone staining portions of it dark gray. Later still, percolating waters brought iron into the sandstone, which weathers into the mineral limonite that is bright orange or yellow, giving the beach its name.

LAGUNA CREEK BEACH: *W. of Hwy. One, 2.2 mi. S. of Bonny Doon Rd.* A broad sandy beach dotted with rocks and tidepools is at the mouth of Laguna Creek; a gradually sloping dirt path provides easy access. Small parking area on the inland side of Hwy. One; use extreme caution crossing the road.

Scott Creek Beach

Andrew Putnam Hill was a painter-turned-photographer in San Jose when in 1899 he was assigned to photograph redwood trees in Santa Cruz County. After getting into an argument with a private landowner who demanded his images, he became inspired to achieve public ownership of the redwoods. In 1900 he and some friends convened a meeting of respected community members at Stanford University, where the group learned about the possibility of preserving giant redwoods at Big Basin (named for being in a wide, bowl-shaped depression). After traveling there to explore the area and finding themselves awed by the ancient trees that were endangered by nearby logging, group members formed the Sempervirens Club, dedicated to saving *Sequoia sempervirens*, the coast redwood. "What words can describe the beauty, the grandeur, the solemn stillness, the wonderful fascination of this forest?" wrote Carrie Stevens Walter, the Club's first secretary. "They can be understood only by one who has visited it."

Creating a public park took a great deal of political work, negotiating, and help from many influential people. San Francisco attorney D. M. Delmas spoke to the California State Assembly in 1901 about the impressive old-growth redwoods and their impending danger: "A sense of humility overwhelms you as you gaze upon these massy pillars of Nature's temple, whose tops, lost amid the clouds, seem to support the vault of the blue empyrean." He continued, "As you behold their lofty foliage stirred by the ocean breeze, you seem to hear them murmur a prayer to be saved from . . . desecration. . . . In one universal accord the inhabitants of California call upon you . . . to prevent the work of destruction. Legislators of California,

guardians of her material interests, but custodians no less of her physical beauty, will you turn a deaf ear to these appeals?"

Soon after, Governor Henry Gage signed a bill authorizing the use of $250,000 to purchase 2,500 acres of forest (despite the opinion of some that $100 per acre was too expensive). The Big Basin Timber Company turned over another 1,300 acres of land, and the 3,800-acre Redwood State Park became California's first state park in 1902; it has since been expanded greatly and renamed Big Basin Redwoods State Park in 1927. The appointed California Redwood Park Commission has now evolved into the California Department of Parks and Recreation. Visitors enjoy hiking trails, waterfalls, campsites, redwood trees that are 1,500 years old and 300 feet high, and the Founders Monument at the base of Slippery Rock, where the Sempervirens Club was created and California's state park system has its earliest roots.

Big Basin Redwoods State Park

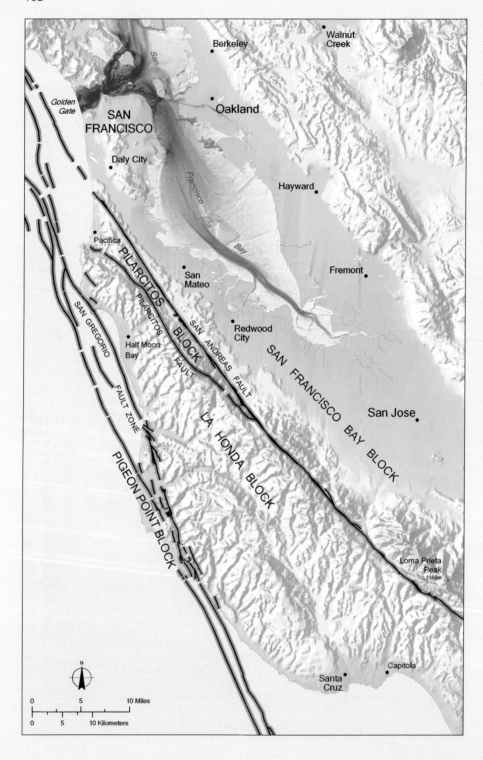

Berkeley

Walnut
Creek

Oakland

SAN
FRANCISCO

Golden
Gate

Daly City

Hayward

San
Francisco

Pacifica

Fremont

San
Mateo

PILARCITOS BLOCK

Redwood
City

SAN GREGORIO

PILARCITOS
FAULT

SAN ANDREAS FAULT

SAN FRANCISCO BAY BLOCK

Half Moon
Bay

FAULT ZONE

LA HONDA BLOCK

San Jose

PIGEON POINT BLOCK

Loma Prieta
Peak
1160m

Capitola

Santa
Cruz

N

0   5   10 Miles

0   5   10 Kilometers

Geology of the Santa Cruz Mountains

THE SANTA CRUZ MOUNTAINS form the backbone of the San Francisco Peninsula and extend south of the Peninsula proper to their transition with the Gabilan Range in northern Monterey County. The highest peak of the Santa Cruz Mountains is Loma Prieta, 3,806 feet high and located south of San Jose. This peak lent its name to a major earthquake that occurred on October 17, 1989, likely on the San Andreas Fault (or, possibly, on a nearby fault in the same system), and had an epicenter near Loma Prieta. The San Andreas Fault and other faults divide the San Francisco Peninsula into a number of geologic blocks, which have wildly varying origins.

The most prominent faults on the Peninsula are the San Andreas, San Gregorio, and Pilarcitos faults. All of these are primarily strike-slip faults belonging to the San Andreas Fault system, and, with the exception of the Pilarcitos, all appear to be active. A "strike-slip fault" results in primarily horizontal motion of blocks on either side of the fault. By contrast, a "thrust fault," also common in the Santa Cruz Mountains, results in compression and shortening due to vertical motion on a dipping fault plane. The crustal blocks defined by these faults are the San Francisco Bay Block, lying east of the San Andreas Fault; the Pilarcitos Block, lying between the San Andreas and Pilarcitos Faults; the La Honda Block, lying between the Pilarcitos and San Gregorio Faults; and the Pigeon Point Block, lying west of the San Gregorio Fault. Some geologists recognize additional smaller blocks, but these four are the most distinct. The "basement rocks," that is, the rocks underlying the sedimentary sequences making up the younger rocks of these blocks, vary across the faults, demonstrating their diverse origins.

The basement rocks of the San Francisco Bay Block are the 65-to-200-million-year-old Franciscan Complex. These rocks are particularly well exposed to view along the sea cliffs of San Francisco. The Franciscan Complex rocks have been divided into a number of "terranes" based on rock types and their separation by fault boundaries. These rocks formed in the deep sea, from sediments derived from both sea and land, and they have been thrust onto the North American Plate. Rock types include basalt, serpentine, chert, shale, limestone, and sandstone. Overlying these rocks are a series of sedimentary rocks ranging from about 5 to 50 million years in age. Especially prominent is the sandstone-dominant Whiskey Hill Formation. The resistant marine sandstones of this unit form prominent ridges on the eastern side of the Santa Cruz Mountains.

The Pilarcitos Block also contains basement rocks of the Franciscan Complex. The Pilarcitos Block is the only area in northern California where the Franciscan Complex is found on the west side of the San Andreas Fault. This fact has led most geologists to conclude that the Pilarcitos Fault, which makes up the western boundary of the block, represents the former active trace of the plate boundary now represented by the San Andreas Fault. Younger rocks that are not offset by the fault indicate that the abandonment of the Pilarcitos Fault probably occurred between three and four million years ago. The Franciscan Complex basement is overlain by thinly interbedded sandstones and shales that are well exposed at Point San Pedro and at Devils Slide south of Pacifica. These beautifully banded rocks are very weak, and they are responsible for the slippery nature of Devils Slide, which has caused problems for transportation routes over the last century.

The granite that forms the basement of the La Honda Block is well exposed at Montara Mountain and in the roadcuts just south of Devils Slide along Hwy. One. This granite is analogous to that found north and south along the coast as the basement of the Sa-

Santa Cruz Mudstone bluffs, Old Cove Landing Trail, Wilder Ranch State Park

linian Block, leading geologists to the conclusion that the La Honda Block is merely a subset of that much larger terrane. Overlying the granite is an immense sequence of sediments that together are over 47,000 feet thick. The oldest of these units, the Butano Sandstone, is especially widespread and represents sandstones and mudstones deposited in deep sea fan deposits in the La Honda Basin. As the basin filled with sediments, it shallowed, and younger deposits are mainly shallow-marine sandstones and silica-rich sandstones deposited on the continental shelf. Two of these deposits are especially prominent on the coast. The Purisima Formation makes up the bluffs of much of San Mateo and Santa Cruz Counties, and it contains abundant fossil clams, burrows, and even skeletons of marine mammals. Burrows and clams are well exposed in the bluffs at San Gregorio State Beach, and careful examination at low tide of the boulders below Depot Hill in Capitola will usually reward the observer with fragments of whale skeletons. The overlying Santa Cruz Mudstone forms bluffs in northern Santa Cruz County, such as at Wilder Ranch State Park. Despite its name, the Santa Cruz Mudstone is fairly resistant to erosion and forms numerous sea caves developed along fractures in the rock.

The basement rocks beneath the Pigeon Point Block, which lies west of the San Gregorio Fault, are unknown. The oldest rocks that are exposed, however, are marine conglomerates, sandstones, and shales of the Pigeon Point Formation. These were once thought to be part of the Salinian Complex, but they are now known to correlate with the Atascadero Formation, found about 100 miles to the south, in southern Monterey County. These beautiful rocks represent deep marine submarine canyon fill and submarine fan deposits that are about 65 to 70 million years old and are well exposed at Pigeon Point, north of the lighthouse. Overlying the Pigeon Point Formation are sandstones that may correlate with the Vaqueros Formation, also from south-central California, and the finely bedded siliceous mudstones of the Monterey Formation. The latter are complexly folded in the sea cliffs and offshore of Seal Cove at the Fitzgerald Marine Reserve, where the folds are well exposed at low tide. These folded rocks also form the offshore surf break known as Mavericks, located off Pillar Point, where big-wave surfers from around the world gather when conditions are just right.

Rocks of the four main blocks originated in very different environments in areas probably separated by hundreds of miles. They have been juxtaposed by the faults of the San Andreas Fault system. Rocks that originated at the plate margin are now found well inland, as blocks slid into place from the south. All of these rocks, however, were deposited in marine environments—many of them, in fact, in deep marine settings. How then, did these rocks end up 3,000 or more feet in the air? Furthermore, aside from the origin of the rocks, what is the origin of the mountains themselves? The answer lies in the active geology of the California coast.

Unlike many mountains in the eastern U.S., the mountains of coastal California are for the most part made up of rocks that are not very resistant to erosion. Rather, California's coastal mountains are prominent because tectonic forces are actively uplifting them. The Santa Cruz Mountains are no exception. They owe their origin to a subtle bend in the San Andreas Fault south of San Jose. Because blocks on either side of the fault are sliding past each other, any bend in the fault causes either compression or extension, depending on the direction of the bend. It is that bend, in conjunction with the strike-slip nature of the sliding along the fault that has caused compression and uplift of the Santa Cruz Mountain range. Also, because of the bend, there are numerous thrust faults in the southern part of the range, in addition to the more common strike-slip faults that define the region. With each earthquake on these faults, the mountains gain a bit in height. During the Loma Prieta Earthquake of 1989, the southern Santa Cruz Mountains grew in height by almost a foot.

Monterey Formation mudstones exposed at extreme low tide in Seal Cove near Moss Beach, San Mateo County

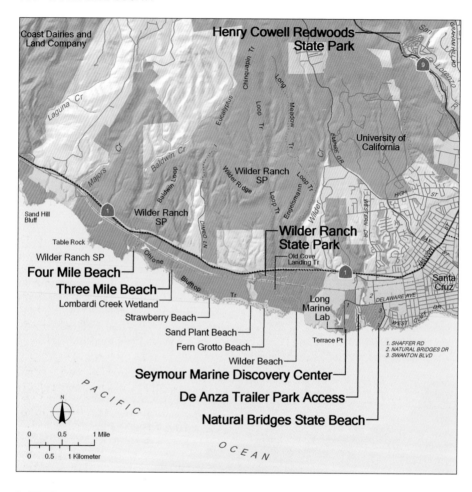

Fields of Brussels sprouts adjacent to Three Mile Beach, Wilder Ranch State Park

Wilder Ranch to Natural Bridges

	Sandy Beach	Rocky Shore	Trail	Visitor Center	Campground	Wildlife Viewing	Fishing or Boating	Facilities for Disabled	Food and Drink	Restrooms	Parking	Fee
Four Mile Beach	•		•							•	•	
Three Mile Beach	•	•	•							•		
Wilder Ranch State Park	•	•	•	•	•	•		•	•	•	•	
Henry Cowell Redwoods State Park			•	•				•	•	•	•	•
Seymour Marine Discovery Center		•	•	•		•		•	•	•	•	
De Anza Trailer Park Access	•		•									
Natural Bridges State Beach	•	•	•	•	•	•		•		•	•	

FOUR MILE BEACH: *Off Hwy. One, 2.1 mi. W. of Wilder Ranch State Park entrance.* Park on the seaward side of Hwy. One on the dirt; a five-minute walk on a sloping dirt path brings you to a long sandy beach, one-quarter mile long. Chemical toilets are located along the beach access path; no other facilities. Part of Wilder Ranch State Park; northern terminus of the Ohlone Blufftop Trail. For information, call: 831-423-9703. A blufftop loop trail is located just north of Four Mile Beach; highway shoulder parking.

In *Santa Cruz Coast: Then and Now* University of California at Santa Cruz geologist Gary Griggs and architect Deepika Shrestha Ross document in photographs the sometimes rapidly evolving California coastline. A photo taken in 1969 shows a massive unbroken promontory at the south end of Four Mile Beach. A photo taken in 1987 shows the large arch that had been carved in only a couple of decades by wave action, and a third photo taken in 1995 shows that the arch had collapsed entirely, leaving a prominent sea stack at one end.

THREE MILE BEACH: *Off Hwy. One, 1.4 mi. W. of Wilder Ranch State Park entrance.* A small pull-out seaward of Hwy. One can accommodate only a few vehicles. A one-third-mile-long trail leads straight to the bluff edge. From there, a steep trail leads down to a sandy beach at the mouth of Lombardi Creek. At the north end of the beach are rocky areas with tidepools and beautiful views of offshore rocks. Intensively used

agricultural land is adjacent to the beach access path; do not trespass. To reach the Ohlone Blufftop Trail that leads south to the main part of Wilder Ranch State Park, follow the railroad tracks south to skirt the Lombardi Creek wetland, and then follow the bluff edge. Call: 831-423-9703.

WILDER RANCH STATE PARK: *Hwy. One, 2 mi. W. of Santa Cruz.* The Old Cove Landing Trail begins on the east side of the parking area. The gravel path leads through a coastal meadow with little hint of the scenic riches to come. At the coast, the trail overlooks a series of gorgeous coves enclosing some of California's most beguiling beaches. The first one you see, Wilder Beach, is a large expanse of white sand backed by an extensive wetland; access to this entire area is off-limits to visitors in order to protect the western snowy plover. Walk a few minutes farther along the blufftop and you will overlook honey-colored sandstone walls surrounding crescent-shaped beaches of sparkling sand. In spring, the bluffs are ablaze with pink beach aster and golden lizard tail; red-footed pigeon guillemots nest in rocky crevices.

Some of the steep-sided beaches are inaccessible on foot, only heightening their allure. Fern Grotto beach can be reached by an easy path, and seeps nourish wildflowers on the bluff face. There is also foot access to sheltered Sand Plant Beach, located one and one-quarter miles from the trailhead at the Wilder Ranch parking area. Private farmland lies inland of Sand Plant Beach;

state park visitors must return to the starting point via the same route. Alternatively, intrepid hikers or bicyclists may continue west along the Ohlone Bluff Trail as far as Four Mile Beach.

The Wilder Ranch was operated intensively for a century by five generations of the Wilder family, beginning in the 1870s. Horses, cows, chickens, and other animals were raised; Santa Cruz County's first butter was produced at a creamery established here in 1895. Historic houses in the Cultural Preserve part of the park include a Gothic-style farmhouse built in the 1850s and an 1897 Victorian house. Before the Wilders took possession, the land was part of a Spanish land grant, subsequently known as Rancho del Refugio. Russian-born José Antonio Bolcoff jumped ship in Monterey and married Maria Candida Castro, who inherited the property; the Bolcoff adobe still stands on the property. Even earlier, the

Ohlone people made their home in the area. A visitor center with exhibits on the area's history and a small gift shop are next to the historic buildings; pick up a brochure for a self-guided walking tour.

The old Wilder Ranch houses and barns were located on old Hwy. One; most of the state park lies inland of modern Hwy. One. Trails that lead under Hwy. One link to a trail network that continues some seven miles inland, rising to an elevation of 1,800 feet. Near Dimeo Ln. off Hwy. One is an equestrian staging area with six first-come, first-served equestrian campsites. For access, call: 831-423-9703. Equestrians are welcome on all park trails inland of Hwy. One; bicyclists may use 35 miles of multi-use trails located throughout the park.

Wilder Ranch State Park is open daily from 8 AM to 5 PM. Dogs are not allowed in the state park. Call: 831-423-9703.

Three Mile Beach, Wilder Ranch State Park

Natural Bridges State Beach

HENRY COWELL REDWOODS STATE PARK: *Hwy. 9, 3 mi. N. of Santa Cruz.* The Redwood Grove natural trail winds through tall trees; the wide trail is wheelchair accessible. Nature center open from 10 AM to 4 PM on weekends and holidays year-round, from 10 AM to 4 PM on summer weekdays, and from 11 AM to 3 PM on winter weekdays. There is also a gift shop. Dogs are allowed on the Meadow Trail, Pipeline Rd., and the Graham Hill Trail as well as in the day use area off Hwy. 9 and the campground on Graham Hill Road.

SEYMOUR MARINE DISCOVERY CENTER: *Delaware Ave. and Shaffer Rd., Santa Cruz.* Aquarium displays, touch tanks, interactive exhibits, and a bookstore are at the Discovery Center, next to Long Marine Laboratory of the University of California at Santa Cruz. Tours and children's programs are offered. Public trails loop through restored coastal prairie around the Discovery Center. A blue whale skeleton is said to be the world's largest on display. The Discovery Center is open from Tuesday to Saturday, 10 AM to 5 PM, and on Sunday from noon to 5 PM; call for holiday schedule. Fee for entry. Docent-led tours are offered twice a month to Younger Lagoon, including to an untouched sandy beach not otherwise publicly accessible; for

information and required reservations, call: 831-459-3800.

DE ANZA TRAILER PARK ACCESS: *2395 Delaware Ave., Santa Cruz.* A one-third-mile-long path leads from Delaware Ave. through the mobile home community to a pocket beach.

NATURAL BRIDGES STATE BEACH: *2531 W. Cliff Dr., Santa Cruz.* The park is named for the wave-carved rock arches that have been a visitor attraction since the early days of Santa Cruz; some bridges that were prominent in historic photos have since collapsed, and only one remains. Natural Bridges State Beach is also a destination for migrating monarch butterflies. The butterflies congregate in the park's eucalyptus groves from October to March; a visitor center is open daily during that period. A wheelchair-accessible walkway leads through the butterfly grove. Amenities at Natural Bridges State Beach include a sandy beach, tidepools, dramatic offshore rocks, and picnic facilities. Vehicle entrance (fee applies) is at the end of Natural Bridges Dr.; a free short-term parking area allows visitors to take in the view. Dogs are not allowed in the park. For information or to borrow a beach wheelchair, call: 831-423-4609.

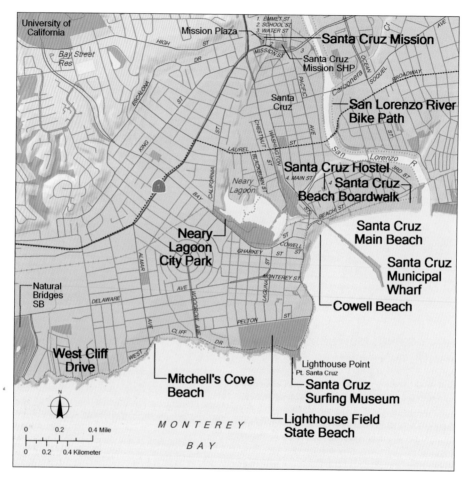

West Cliff Drive

Santa Cruz Central

	Sandy Beach	Rocky Shore	Trail	Visitor Center	Campground	Wildlife Viewing	Fishing or Boating	Facilities for Disabled	Food and Drink	Restrooms	Parking	Fee
West Cliff Drive		•	•			•					•	
Mitchell's Cove Beach	•	•										
Lighthouse Field State Beach		•	•			•	•			•	•	
Santa Cruz Surfing Museum				•						•	•	
Cowell Beach	•						•			•	•	
Neary Lagoon City Park			•			•	•			•	•	
Santa Cruz Municipal Wharf						•	•	•	•	•	•	•
Santa Cruz Beach Boardwalk				•			•		•	•	•	
Santa Cruz Main Beach	•						•		•	•	•	
Santa Cruz Mission				•						•		
San Lorenzo River Bike Path			•									
Santa Cruz Hostel									•	•	•	

WEST CLIFF DRIVE: *From Natural Bridges State Beach to Cowell Beach, Santa Cruz.* A three-mile-long oceanside bicycle-pedestrian path follows West Cliff from Natural Bridges to the Santa Cruz Wharf. Numerous scenic overlooks of Monterey Bay with parking bays and benches are located along the route: just upcoast of Lighthouse Point (Its Beach); just downcoast of the Point at the end of Pelton Ave.; and at the end of Monterey Street. Coastal bluffs are highly eroded; tidal rocks are slippery when wet. The intertidal between Swift and Fair avenues contain calcium carbonate–rich formations that are remnants of deep-water seep systems formed when these rocks were submerged.

MITCHELL'S COVE BEACH: *W. Cliff Dr. at Almar Ave., Santa Cruz.* Stairs to a cove are at the end of Almar Avenue. Dogs under voice control are allowed off leash before 10 AM and after 4 PM.

LIGHTHOUSE FIELD STATE BEACH: *Along W. Cliff Dr. at Point Santa Cruz.* The park includes open uplands and a scenic viewpoint overlooking the renowned surfing spot Steamer Lane. Parking, trails, picnic tables, free parking bays. Leashed dogs are allowed in the lighthouse area. Call: 831-429-2850.

SANTA CRUZ SURFING MUSEUM: *Mark Abbott Memorial Lighthouse, Lighthouse Point, Santa Cruz.* Historic surfboards and old-time surfing photos are on display, and there is a large collection of books about surfing. A plaque documents the introduction of surfing to Santa Cruz in 1885 by three young Hawaiian princes. Gift shop. The museum is open Thursday to Monday, noon to 4 PM; call: 831-420-6289. The brick lighthouse was donated to the public by the family of young Mark Abbott, who drowned in 1965 off Santa Cruz.

COWELL BEACH: *Between W. Cliff Dr. and the Municipal Wharf, Santa Cruz.* Cowell Beach is located on the west side of the Municipal Wharf. The wide expanse of sand is highly popular for beach recreation, sunbathing, and surfing. At the foot of the wharf is a small overlook plaza with restrooms and beach shower and a very small parking lot. There is also metered street parking in the area. A nice viewpoint above Cowell Beach is located on W. Cliff Dr. between Cowell and Gharkey streets.

Lifeguard towers on Cowell Beach and Santa Cruz Main Beach are staffed daily during the summer and spring break and also on

Santa Cruz Main Beach

spring and fall weekends. A ramp and beach wheelchair are available at Tower #1 during the summer, from 10 AM to 5 PM daily; for a reservation, call: 831-420-6015, extension 6. For recorded information on beach water quality, call: 831-454-3188. Gas and charcoal grills are allowed on the beach; used coals must be fully extinguished and removed from the sand (there is a disposal station at 3rd St. adjacent to the Beach Boardwalk). Dogs are not allowed on Cowell Beach.

NEARY LAGOON CITY PARK: *Off California St., N. of Bay St., Santa Cruz.* Boardwalks and wheelchair-accessible paths lead around this freshwater nature refuge. Good birding. Tennis courts, children's play equipment, parking, and restrooms are located on California St. at Bay St., where there is a trailhead. Additional entry points and street parking are located at the ends of Chestnut and Blackburn Streets, off Laurel Street.

SANTA CRUZ MUNICIPAL WHARF: *End of Washington St. at Beach St., Santa Cruz.* The present wharf, more than one-half mile long and constructed in 1913, is the fifth and longest of the wharves built in Santa Cruz. The first wharf, built in 1853 by the Renfield Brothers, was located at the foot of Bay Street. The wharf is now a tourist attraction with its many restaurants and shops; boat rentals and fishing equipment are available.

The wharf accommodates bicycles, pedestrians, and cars; fee applies for vehicle entrance. Open all year; no dogs are allowed on the wharf. Santa Cruz Boat Rentals has motor boats for hire; call: 831-423-1739. At the Monterey Bay National Marine Sanctuary Exploration Center, opened in 2012 near the foot of the municipal wharf, visitors can view video footage created deep in the Monterey Bay Submarine Canyon and other exhibits.

The fishing pier at the end of the wharf attracts many anglers, who catch flounder, bonita, blue shark, lingcod, halibut, and crab. Sea lions haul out on the timbers below the wharf. There is an open anchorage area for visiting boats, next to the wharf, and a public dinghy landing on the wharf.

SANTA CRUZ BEACH BOARDWALK: *400 Beach St. E. of Municipal Wharf, Santa Cruz.* One of California's few remaining seaside amusement parks, the Santa Cruz Beach Boardwalk has been updated regularly with new attractions in its century of operation, while old favorites remain. Ride high above the beach and bay on the Giant Dipper wooden roller coaster, built in 1924. The classic carousel features animals carved in 1911 by famed designer Charles Looff; riders on the outside grab for steel rings and try to toss them in the clown's mouth. Newer thrill rides include the Tsunami, the Hurricane, and the Wipeout. Younger visitors enjoy the Kiddie Speed Boats, Jet Copters, and Red Baron rides.

The Beach Boardwalk, which has free admission and free summer entertainment, is open daily from Memorial Day through Labor Day and also on most weekends and holidays during the spring and fall months. Some attractions are open year-round, including the Casino Arcade, Neptune's Kingdom restaurant and game area, and a bowling alley. For information about hours and ride packages, call: 831-426-7433.

SANTA CRUZ MAIN BEACH: *E. of Municipal Wharf, Santa Cruz.* Beachgoers flock to the wide beach of soft sand located between the lively attractions of the Beach Boardwalk and the sheltered waters of Monterey Bay. For beach wheelchair information, call: 831-420-6015 extension 6. For recorded information on beach water quality, call: 831-454-3188. During the summer months, volleyball standards and nets are provided and ramps for wheelchair access are set up on the sand. Dogs are not allowed on the beach.

SANTA CRUZ MISSION: *Emmet St. and High St., Santa Cruz.* In 1791, Franciscan Father Fermín Francisco de Lasuén founded a mission at the lower end of the San Lorenzo Valley. To protect against flooding, the mission was relocated in 1793 to a mesa above the San Lorenzo River. The new church was built from native stone and adobe, with other buildings added as needed, forming an open square. The mission church and priests' quarters were sited on what is now High Street. The earthquake of 1857 caused the mission to collapse; in 1931 a replica was built on Emmet St. identical in proportions, but half the size of the original structure.

The site of the original mission is within Santa Cruz Mission State Historic Park on School St. off Mission Plaza. One original building, the Neary-Rodriguez Adobe built in 1791, survives; open Thursday to Saturday from 10 AM to 4 PM; to confirm hours, call: 831-425-5849.

SAN LORENZO RIVER BIKE PATH: *Along San Lorenzo River, Santa Cruz.* A bike path runs along both sides of the San Lorenzo River levee from just inland of Hwy. One to the river mouth at Santa Cruz Main Beach.

SANTA CRUZ HOSTEL: *321 Main St., Santa Cruz.* The hostel is a short walk from the Santa Cruz Boardwalk and Municipal Wharf. Guest rooms are located in quaint, nicely remodeled buildings, known as the Carmelita Cottages, among pleasant landscaping. Each cottage has a common living area, and there is also a shared kitchen. Linens and towels are provided by the hostel. For information, call: 831-423-8304.

Santa Cruz Beach Boardwalk

Santa Cruz Beach Boardwalk

DURING the Spanish colonization of California in the 18th century, both a Catholic mission (founded in 1791 and named Santa Cruz, or "holy cross") and a town, or pueblo, (founded in 1797 and named Villa de Branciforte) were established near the mouth of the San Lorenzo River. Mission Santa Cruz was located on the west side of the river and Branciforte on the east side. The mission was secularized by Governor Figueroa in 1834, and the church was destroyed by earthquake in 1857. Today's mission church is a small-scale replica built of concrete in 1931. As for Branciforte, it was absorbed into the growing city of Santa Cruz. Meanwhile, Santa Cruz saw the establishment of industries that included a tannery (circa 1850) that processed hides from ranches in the area as well as from South America, a sawmill built around 1846 at Soquel, an iron foundry established in 1848, and a gunpowder factory established in 1861.

Santa Cruz became a visitor destination early on. As early as the 1860s public bathhouses were built on the Santa Cruz shoreline. By 1893, these simple shelters for changing into bathing attire had been augmented by the Miller-Leibbrandt Plunge, which featured a heated saltwater swimming pool, billiard parlor, card room, and café. By the 1880s, the Southern Pacific Railroad was bringing visitors from the San Francisco Bay Area. A succession of attractions were devised, including the Venetian Water Carnivals that began in 1895 and featured gondola rides on the San Lorenzo River.

In the late 19th century, "beach bathing" meant just that. Visitors changed into beach attire in dressing rooms set up on the sand, then went straight into the bay for a dip. Sunbathing was not part of the equation; in fact, to lounge in your bathing costume on the sand was prohibited. Women wore long black stockings and heavy flannel outfits, which, when wet, must have threatened to pull the wearer under. Beach bathing was

Santa Cruz Beach and Boardwalk

Sea Swings ride

an occasional pastime for most visitors and did not warrant purchasing a wardrobe for the occasion; visitors typically rented their bathing suits at the beach, as unlikely as that sounds today. And for those beach visitors who didn't care to get into the water, the expected attire was much the same, to our eyes at least, as what might be worn to church: long dresses and elaborate hats for women, and suits and ties for men.

Fashions in clothing come and go, but a beach resort has always been a place to show off one's physical charms. Santa Cruz was the site in 1924 of the first Miss California beauty pageant. Daredevil swimmers, divers, and acrobats performed regularly at Santa Cruz. Duke Kahanamoku, the Hawaiian swimmer who won Olympic gold medals at Stockholm in 1912 and Antwerp in 1920, performed in an aquatic show at Santa Cruz's beachfront plunge in 1938. Photos of pioneering surfers, including Duke Kahanamoku, who helped popularize the sport in California, are on view at the Santa Cruz Surfing Museum at Lighthouse Field State Beach.

Fred Swanton of Santa Cruz was one of 20th century California's indefatigable boosters. Long before he became mayor of Santa Cruz in 1927, Swanton promoted a series of ventures to entertain beach visitors. Economical lodgings took the form of a "Tent City" that was built in 1903 near the beach, soon to be replaced by a "Cottage City" of small bungalows. In 1904, the Neptune Casino opened, attended by great publicity. The term "casino" referred to various forms of recreation, not including gambling. After the Neptune Casino burned in 1906, Swanton and his Santa Cruz Beach Company rebuilt the attraction in an even grander fashion. The new casino held a large theater and ballroom, a restaurant, and private dining rooms. The adjacent plunge, also known as a "natatorium," housed heated saltwater pools and slides. A "Pleasure Pier" extended bayward from the plunge, offering visitors a place to enjoy a stroll or board a tour boat. The Pleasure Pier also supported a seawater intake pipe that fed the saltwater swimming pools.

Fred Swanton pursued many projects, some tourism-oriented and some not, including telephone technology, theatrical events, and a local professional baseball team. He operated a "Palace of Pharmacy" that dispensed pharmaceutical products, toiletries, and, reportedly, whiskey. Among Swanton's more visible efforts were a series of booster railroad trains that toured inland communities as far afield as Reno, Nevada. The trains carried fireworks and musicians who paraded through town, along with a stock of brochures that touted the joys of a Santa Cruz visit. Some of Swanton's projects were less financially successful than others, and by 1915 his Beach Company had gone bankrupt. One of his failed schemes was a subdivision that he sold to the state and that became what is now Natural Bridges State Beach.

Management of the casino and associated attractions was taken over by the Santa Cruz Seaside Company, which still operates the evolving attractions of what is now known as the Santa Cruz Beach Boardwalk. Some attractions are much the same as ever, including the carousel built in 1911 by famed designer Charles I. D. Looff. The Giant Dipper rollercoaster, built in 1924 by Looff's son, Arthur, is also still in happy operation. During the mid-20th century, the Beach Boardwalk's casino was renamed as the Cocoanut Grove, and in that venue beach visitors once danced to the music of Benny Goodman's big band. In the 1960s, entertainers at the Cocoanut Grove included Sonny and Cher. The Cocoanut Grove remains, but the Plunge closed in 1962, and its building was converted into Neptune's Kingdom entertainment center.

Santa Cruz Beach Boardwalk

Sea Beach Hotel ca. 1904

What is a seaside resort without inviting hostelries? Santa Cruz had its grand Sea Beach Hotel, which once overlooked Main Beach from a hilltop on the inland side of Beach Street. The original structure on the site dated from the 1870s; it was later enlarged and renamed. By the turn of the 20th century, the hotel was a five-story shingle-style hotel, with conical "witch's cap" turrets, somewhat in the vein of the Hotel Del Coronado in southern California. The hotel grounds included decorative gardens planted with colorful pelargoniums. Sadly, the Sea Beach Hotel burned in 1912 and was not rebuilt.

The Casa del Rey Hotel was built just north of the Boardwalk in 1911. Converted to a retirement home later on, the building was still in use until it was damaged in the 1989 Loma Prieta earthquake and then demolished. The Casa del Rey Apartments, somewhat altered, still maintain a bit of period architecture–flavor in the Boardwalk neighborhood.

Santa Cruz has all the attributes of a classic beach resort. Its warm, south-facing setting on Monterey Bay, sandy beaches, surf breaks, and nearby redwood forests have made Santa Cruz a natural destination for tourists. For Northern Californians growing up in the mid-20th century, a summer trip to "the lake" implied Tahoe; "the river" meant the Russian; and "the beach"? Well, where else but Santa Cruz?

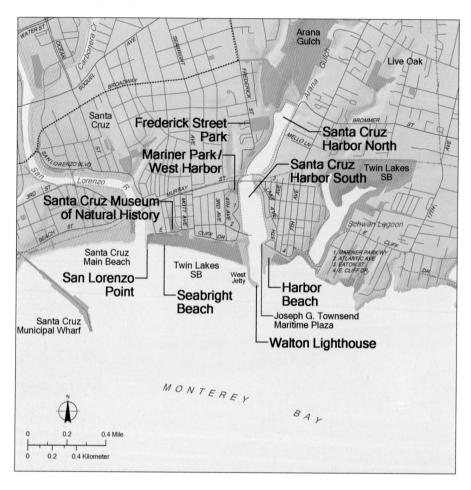

Seabright Beach

Santa Cruz Harbor

	Sandy Beach	Rocky Shore	Trail	Visitor Center	Campground	Wildlife Viewing	Fishing or Boating	Facilities for Disabled	Food and Drink	Restrooms	Parking	Fee
San Lorenzo Point											•	
Seabright Beach	•									•	•	
Santa Cruz Museum of Natural History				•						•	•	•
Walton Lighthouse						•	•					
Mariner Park/West Harbor			•			•	•		•	•	•	•
Frederick Street Park										•	•	
Santa Cruz Harbor North			•		•		•		•	•	•	•
Santa Cruz Harbor South						•	•		•	•	•	•
Harbor Beach	•						•		•	•	•	

SAN LORENZO POINT: *Foot of E. Cliff Dr. off Murray St., Santa Cruz.* The rock promontory on the east side of the San Lorenzo River mouth is not accessible to visitors, but adjacent to it is a grassy overlook with a picnic table and benches. There are grand views of the Beach Boardwalk, Monterey Bay, and Seabright Beach. A small parking area is located on E. Cliff Dr. off Murray Street.

SEABRIGHT BEACH: *E. Cliff Dr., San Lorenzo Point to Seabright Ave., Santa Cruz.* Spacious Seabright Beach extends from San Lorenzo Point to Santa Cruz Harbor. Seabright Beach is also called Castle Beach for the fortress-like resort that once stood on the shore opposite the current site of the Santa Cruz Museum of Natural History. A passenger drop-off zone is at the foot of Mott Ave.; a paved walkway runs along the blufftop both west and east from Mott Avenue. There are restrooms on the sand near the Mott Ave. entrance. Street parking on E. Cliff Drive is very limited; there are a few pull-in spots at the end of 3rd Avenue. Dogs on leash are allowed on Seabright Beach, which is part of Twin Lakes State Beach. For beach information or to borrow a beach wheelchair, call: 831-427-4868.

Once a beach of fluctuating width, depending on the season, Seabright Beach is now hundreds of feet wide year-round. The change is due to construction in 1962 of the jetty at the mouth of Santa Cruz Harbor; beach sand is trapped between the jetty and the rock headland at San Lorenzo Point.

SANTA CRUZ MUSEUM OF NATURAL HISTORY: *1305 E. Cliff Dr., Santa Cruz.* The museum's permanent collections focus on biology, Native American culture, and history of the Santa Cruz area. Past traveling exhibitions have highlighted California's sea otters, the impacts of plastics in the marine environment, and tropical forests in Panama. Summer camps and programs for young people are offered.

Open from Memorial Day through Labor Day on Wednesday through Sunday and the remainder of the year on Tuesday through Saturday, from 10 AM to 5 PM. Fee applies for adult admission; those under 18 enter free. For information, call: 831-420-6115.

WALTON LIGHTHOUSE: *West Jetty, Santa Cruz Harbor.* A level sandy path leads to the lighthouse, constructed in 2001 at the mouth of Santa Cruz Harbor. Popular fishing and viewing spot; no facilities. Approach on foot from Seabright Beach, or park at Mariner Park on the west side of the harbor.

MARINER PARK/WEST HARBOR: *Mariner Park Way off Atlantic Ave., Santa Cruz.* Santa Cruz Harbor is relatively narrow but nearly one mile long. A paved pedestrian and bicycle path rings the harbor at water level.

Santa Cruz Harbor

While surrounding through streets are located mainly on the blufftop above the harbor, streets from the west (Atlantic Ave.), north (Brommer St.), and east (Lake Ave. and 5th Ave.) provide dead-end access to the harbor. At the harbor there are metered parking spaces and restrooms.

Mariner Park on the west side of the harbor can be reached via Atlantic Ave. and Mariner Park Way. The park has lawns and benches overlooking the boats in the harbor. There is a restaurant nearby.

A launch ramp for hand-carried kayaks and other craft is located at the north end of Mariner Park Way, near the Murray St. bridge. A stairway next to the Santa Cruz Yacht Club on 4th Ave. overlooking the harbor leads down the bluff into Mariner Park.

FREDERICK STREET PARK: *Frederick St., off Soquel Ave., Santa Cruz.* On the northwest side of Santa Cruz Harbor is Frederick Street Park, a pleasant spot with lawns, volleyball nets, playground equipment, picnic tables, barbecue grills, and restrooms. There is also a designated off-leash area for dogs. Street parking only. A stairway leads down the bluff to North Harbor. Frederick St. is a

dead-end street; approach Frederick Street Park from Soquel Ave. or Broadway.

SANTA CRUZ HARBOR NORTH: *Brommer St. off 7th Ave., Santa Cruz.* The North Harbor has 600 boat berths and dry storage area for several hundred vessels. There are also picnic tables, metered public parking, and fish cleaning tables. Twelve self-contained RV camping spots are available; for reservations, call: 831-475-3279. Also at North Harbor is an RV dump station.

A loop trail for hikers links North Harbor with the City of Santa Cruz's Arana Gulch open space preserve, located due north of the boat dry storage area. On the east side of North Harbor, a pedestrian path and stairway lead from the end of Mello Lane off 7th Ave. down to the harbor.

SANTA CRUZ HARBOR SOUTH: *Off Eaton St., Santa Cruz.* Murray St. crosses over the harbor and becomes Eaton St. on the east side. There is pedestrian access, via stairs, from the Murray St. Bridge down to the harbor. Santa Cruz Harbor was created out of Woods Lagoon, one of the coastal lagoons known originally as the "Twin Lakes" (Schwan Lagoon is the other one).

For vehicle access to South Harbor, turn onto Lake Ave. from Eaton Street. Most of the harbor's main attractions, including shops, restaurants, and marine services, are located here. Fresh fish is often available off the boats. The Joseph G. Townsend Maritime Plaza contains a compass rose and indicates the distance to maritime destinations around the world.

South Harbor contains 400 boat berths, and there is a four-lane concrete public boat launch, open 24 hours; launch fee applies. Also available is a half-ton boat hoist and a 60-ton travel lift at the boat yard, open from 8 AM to 5 PM. A fuel dock is open from 6:00 AM to 4:30 PM; call: 831-476-2648. Boat sales and repair and marine services are available from several vendors. Transient vessels must report to the harbor office at the southeast corner of the harbor for berth assignments, which are available on a first-come, first-served basis. Santa Cruz Harbor is operated by the Santa Cruz Port District; for information, call: 831-475-6161.

Metered public parking is available off Eaton St.; meters operate daily from 8 AM to 10 PM. On peak days, parking spaces fill up quickly. Additional parking is available at North Harbor on Brommer St.; a shuttle van service to the South Harbor operates on weekends. There is also a water taxi that links the North and South Harbors on weekends and holidays from Memorial Day through Labor Day, 10 AM to 6 PM, and on certain Thursday evenings during beach barbecue events.

HARBOR BEACH: *East of harbor jetty to 5th Ave. at E. Cliff Dr., Santa Cruz.* Harbor Beach, part of Twin Lakes State Beach, is located on the east side of Santa Cruz Harbor. Catamarans are stored on the sand, and there are beach volleyball nets and fire rings. Dogs on leash are allowed. For state beach information, call: 831-427-4868. A ramp and beach wheelchair are available at The Kind Grind; call: 831-476-9136.

Harbor Beach

Sport fishing, scenic tours, and boat rentals are offered at the harbor:

Captain Jimmy Charters, 831-662-3020;

Chardonnay Sailing Charters, 831-423-1213;

Lighthall Yacht Charters, 831-429-1970;

Monterey Bay Charters, 831-818-8808;

Pacific Yachting and Sailing, 831-423-7245;

Reel Sport Fishing, call: 831-212-1832;

Santa Cruz Sport Fishing, 831-426-4690;

Stagnaro Whale Watching & Fishing, 831-427-0230;

Surf City Catamarans, call: 831-359-5918;

Kayak Connection, call: 831-479-1121.

O'Neill Yacht Charters offers sailing aboard a 65-foot catamaran; on the same vessel, the Sea Odyssey program, founded by noted surfer Jack O'Neill, offers schoolchildren an up-close look at marine resources in Monterey Bay. A shore-side lesson follows; call: 831-475-1561.

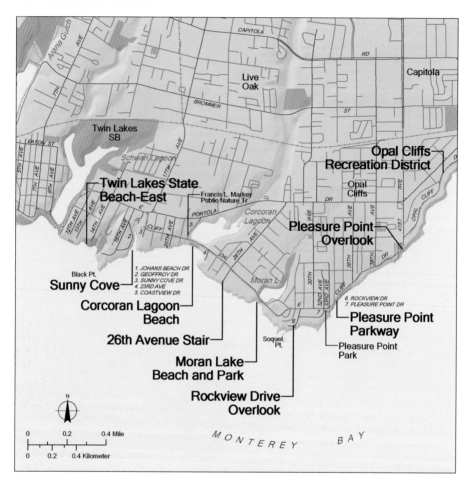

Capitola

Live
Oak

Twin Lakes
SB

Opal Cliffs
Recreation District

Twin Lakes State
Beach-East

Opal
Cliffs

Francis L. Markey
Public Nature Tr

Pleasure Point
Overlook

Black Pt.

1. JOHANS BEACH DR
2. GEOFFROY DR
3. SUNNY COVE DR
4. 23RD AVE
5. COASTVIEW DR

Sunny Cove

6. ROCKVIEW DR
7. PLEASURE POINT DR

Corcoran Lagoon
Beach

Pleasure Point
Parkway

26th Avenue Stair

Soquel
Pt.

Pleasure Point
Park

Moran Lake
Beach and Park

Rockview Drive
Overlook

MONTEREY   BAY

0   0.2   0.4 Mile

0   0.2   0.4 Kilometer

Twin Lakes State Beach-East

Santa Cruz East

	Sandy Beach	Rocky Shore	Trail	Visitor Center	Campground	Wildlife Viewing	Fishing or Boating	Facilities for Disabled	Food and Drink	Restrooms	Parking	Fee
Twin Lakes State Beach-East	•								•	•		
Sunny Cove	•					•						
Corcoran Lagoon Beach	•					•						
26th Avenue Stair	•										•	
Moran Lake Beach and Park	•					•	•		•	•		
Rockview Drive Overlook		•									•	
Pleasure Point Parkway	•		•				•		•			
Pleasure Point Overlook	•	•	•				•		•	•		
Opal Cliffs Recreation District	•									•	•	

TWIN LAKES STATE BEACH-EAST: *From 5th to 14th Avenues, Live Oak.* Twin Lakes State Beach includes the shoreline along E. Cliff Dr. as well as nearby Schwan Lake. There is shoulder parking along E. Cliff Dr. with easy access to the sand opposite 9th Avenue. Restrooms and a beach shower are located off 7th Ave. and E. Cliff Drive.

Beach stairways maintained by the County of Santa Cruz are located at the end of 12th Ave. and near the end of 13th Avenue. At the end of 14th Ave. there is pedestrian access to the beach as well as restrooms and beach volleyball standards. Leashed dogs are allowed on Twin Lakes State Beach east of Harbor Beach. Schwan Lake is a refuge for waterfowl; there is no access to the lake, but there are nice views from 9th Ave. near E. Cliff Drive.

Parking is limited to the street shoulders near the beach in Live Oak, which is the unincorporated community located between the cities of Santa Cruz and Capitola. Along or near E. Cliff Dr., between 5th and 41st Avenues, street parking is regulated and is subject to purchase of either a day-use or seasonal pass, from late spring through Labor Day, on Saturday, Sunday, and holidays, between the hours of 11 AM and 5 PM. Affected areas are signed. For information on the Live Oak parking restrictions and seasonal parking passes, call: 831-454-2990.

SUNNY COVE: *Foot of Johans Beach Dr., Live Oak.* Sunny Cove is a sheltered pocket beach with access from Johans Beach Drive. Informal beach access is also available down the bluffs from Geoffroy Dr. on the west side of the cove and from Sunny Cove Dr. on the east side. About 50 yards upcoast from the cove there is access to a flat rock shelf that is popular with fishermen as well as surfers. Parking is very limited in the area.

CORCORAN LAGOON BEACH: *Between 20th and 23rd Avenues, Live Oak.* The beach is seaward of E. Cliff Dr. and the lagoon; there is easy access on foot from the road onto the sand. The west end of the beach is accessible from a stairway at the end of 20th Avenue. Call: 831-454-7901.

Inland of the beach is Corcoran Lagoon. The Francis L. Markey Public Nature Trail starts at Coastview Dr. near E. Cliff Dr. and extends a couple of hundred yards along the lagoon. From the flat, packed-earth trail there are nice views of the wetlands, home to a variety of wildfowl.

26TH AVENUE STAIR: *Foot of 26th Ave., Live Oak.* A public stairway leads down the bluff to the sandy beach; there is on-street parking. Call: 831-454-7901.

MORAN LAKE BEACH AND PARK: *23000 block of E. Cliff Dr., Live Oak.* The wide sandy beach is south of Moran Lake. The beach is

Pleasure Point beach and seawalls

accessible to wheelchairs via a ramp from E. Cliff Drive. Parking and restrooms are located inland of E. Cliff Dr., next to the lake. A wide, dirt nature trail runs along the west side of the lake for about one-half mile. Birds seen year-round in the area include snowy egrets, black-crowned night herons, and killdeer; migratory species include sandpipers, dunlins, and dowitchers.

ROCKVIEW DRIVE OVERLOOK: *Foot of Rockview Dr., Pleasure Point.* Excellent ocean view; popular spot to watch surfers. There is a picnic table at the overlook, and a short blufftop walkway leads to the west. Informal access from the picnic table leads down to a rock ledge and a small seasonal beach. There is on-street parking nearby. Stairs just east of 18 Rockview Dr. and just east of 2970 Pleasure Point Dr. provide access to seasonal sandy beaches and surf areas.

PLEASURE POINT PARKWAY: *E. Cliff Dr., from 32nd to 41st Avenues, Pleasure Point.* Soquel Point, near the foot of Rockview Ave., has come to be known as "Pleasure Point." The name perhaps stems from the 1920s, when the area gained a reputation for speakeasies and other places of entertainment. Then, as now, the area was outside any city limits. Today Pleasure Point means shoreline recreation. The half mile or so of coastline is a destination renowned among surfers for its consistency. Sunbathers, bodyboarders, tidepoolers, and anglers also enjoy the area.

Major new coastal access facilities at Pleasure Point, along with new concrete seawalls, have been completed. A pedestrian and bicycle path equipped with benches runs along the edge of the bluff, offering views of scenic Monterey Bay and surfing activity. There are stairs at the foot of 33rd, 36th, 38th, and 41st Avenues. Sandy beaches at the base of the bluff are generally narrow and dependent on tidal conditions. Viewing benches and shady trees are found at Pleasure Point Park at 32nd Ave. and E. Cliff Drive. Restrooms are located at 33rd Ave. and also in the parking area at the end of 41st Avenue.

PLEASURE POINT OVERLOOK: *E. Cliff Dr. at 41st Ave., Pleasure Point.* Known as an overlook, this is also a shoreline access point. A stairway leads down the bluff to a narrow beach just west of 41st Avenue. Inland of E. Cliff Dr. is a parking area equipped with restrooms and beach shower. Offshore is the well known surf spot known as the "Hook."

OPAL CLIFFS RECREATION DISTRICT: *4500 block of Opal Cliffs Dr., Pleasure Point.* A stairway leads to a narrow sandy beach that is popular with surfers. Keys to the locked gate are sold each year at Freeline Design Surf Shop, located at 821 41st Avenue. There are six off-street parking spaces plus street parking.

Pleasure Point stairs at 41st Ave.

The state of California owns all tidelands, submerged lands, and the beds of inland navigable waters, holding them for "public trust" uses that include fishing, navigation, commerce, nature preserves, swimming, boating, and walking. Tidelands consist of the area on a beach or rocky coastline that is between the mean high tide line and the mean low tide line. The public has the right to use all lands seaward of the mean high tide line. In addition, portions of the privately owned dry sandy beach are available for some public uses, because of legal public access easements and deed restrictions.

Members of the public using tidelands should exercise caution when there is a potential for encroaching on private land, just as private land owners should be cautious in questioning the public's right to be on areas of the beach covered by public rights.

Shore Protection in Santa Cruz

T HE COAST of northern Santa Cruz County consists largely of rocky cliffs and occasional sandy pocket beaches, while along the county's southern coast there are wide sandy beaches that stretch for miles. Santa Cruz beaches have undergone dramatic changes due to both natural processes and human activities. One type of shoreline change, known as "accretion," is the enlargement of a beach area. Accretion can be caused by both natural and artificial means. Natural beach accretion occurs when sand or sediments are deposited by water or wind. Artificial beach accretion is a similar build-up of material on the shore, but caused by human activity. The construction of breakwaters, jetties, or groins that retain sand and slow its movement away from a section of coast can result in artificial accretion. Artificial accretion also occurs through "beach nourishment," the placement of beach fill by mechanical means.

In contrast to accretion, "erosion" is the wearing away of land by natural forces, including wave action, water currents, and the wind. Erosion is primarily a natural phenomenon. Nevertheless, erosive conditions can be created or exacerbated by human activities that reduce the amount of sand reaching the beach or divert it away from the beach. Studies by the U.S. Geologic Survey have found that when shoreline conditions are averaged over approximately 100 years of observations, most of Santa Cruz County's beaches have accreted. However, during the second half of the 20th century, most beaches east of the Santa Cruz Yacht Harbor extending almost to Capitola, with the exception of Twin Lakes State Beach and Capitola City Beach itself, have eroded.

Where beach accretion has been observed in the Santa Cruz area, it has been due to both the natural abundance of sand in the Santa Cruz "littoral cell" and the construction of two major sand retaining structures along the coast: the jetties at the Santa Cruz Harbor and the groin at Capitola. A littoral cell is the region that encompasses most

Accretion of sand at Seabright Beach upcoast of the Santa Cruz Harbor Jetty

Artificial accretion through "beach nourishment" dredge pipe at Harbor Beach, part of Twin Lakes State Beach

natural features that affect the transport of sand and other sediment. Sand and sediments within a littoral cell generally move from mountains and inland sources toward the sea, borne by rivers and streams, and then move along the coast, carried by longshore ocean currents. Some sand moves on and off the beaches on a seasonal basis, being eroded during winter storms and carried landward during the summer. Eventually, the sediment is lost from the littoral cell, off the edge of the continental shelf or into a deep submarine canyon.

Careful examination of the littoral cell that includes the shoreline located just upcoast of Santa Cruz Harbor shows an unusual combination of steep bluffs with wide beaches. Until the construction of the harbor jetties in 1963, in fact, the beaches were typically much narrower than they are now, and waves regularly attacked the base of the bluffs. After the jetties were built, they trapped sand upcoast of the harbor. A wide beach, now known as Seabright Beach, developed at the toe of the bluffs, providing a much-used recreational area for the region and a buffer from wave energy for the bluffs.

As at Santa Cruz Harbor, the beach upcoast of the groin at Capitola has accreted, contributing to the size of the recreational beach at the Capitola Pier. The accretion at Capitola is the result of both the groin that has helped to hold sand on the beach and a nourishment effort that has added sand to this beach area.

Despite the occurrence of beach accretion in some areas, long stretches of the Santa Cruz County coast remain subject to erosion. "Shoreline armoring" is the general term applied to methods for slowing erosion and for protecting structures, roads, and other development located landward of the shoreline. One type of armoring is the revetment, which is made of piled boulders, called riprap. Revetments protect the back shore by absorbing much of the wave energy and reducing the wave forces that reach inland of the structure. If waves are high enough to overtop the revetment, of course, then erosion of the back shore can still occur. Erosion and gullying of the exposed bluff or area inland of the revetment can also occur due to the action of rain and surface runoff.

Revetments are common in Santa Cruz County. Many of them were installed prior to the adoption in 1976 of the California Coastal Act, and such revetments underwent little regulatory review for their impacts to coastal resources, including public access to the beach. Several other revetments that were constructed after passage of the California Coastal Act were allowed by emergency permits during particularly stormy winters such as the El Niño events of 1982–83, and again, they underwent little regulatory review. Public discussion about the future of these revetments has taken place, including consideration of options to convert or change them eventually to vertical seawall structures in the style of those built at Pleasure Point.

Another type of shoreline armoring is a concrete seawall with a more or less vertical face toward the ocean. A vertical seawall is an engineered structure, often constructed out of concrete or wood with either a straight vertical face or a sloping and undulating face that attempts to mimic a natural bluff. This type of wall gets its strength and stability either by being anchored deeply into the lower bedrock (a cantilevered wall), by being anchored into the back bluff a (tied-back wall), or through its own mass and bulk (a gravity wall).

An alternative to both the revetment and the vertical seawall, and one that does not involve shoreline armoring, is beach nourishment. The process of beach nourishment places sand on the beach or in the nearshore area, with the intent of widening the existing beach so it can provide either more recreational area or a greater buffer from wave attack.

Although construction of a revetment is relatively inexpensive when compared with either construction of a vertical seawall or beach nourishment, revetments require regular maintenance. The stones that form the revetment can be dislodged during storms, requiring maintenance that involves the use of heavy equipment. A study by Kim Fulton-Bennett and Gary Griggs found that the one-time cost of maintaining a

Shoreline rock revetment near West Cliff Dr. and Lighthouse Field State Beach

revetment following a storm event with an expected recurrence of roughly once every ten years can be as much as 20 to 40 percent of the structure's initial cost, belying the "inexpensive" nature of revetments. Furthermore, one of the public costs of a revetment is the loss of beach due to the area that the rocks occupy. A typical revetment is 50 to 100 percent wider than it is tall, and if the revetment is not well-maintained, dislodged stones can expand the footprint to several times its initial size.

The Santa Cruz area is one coastal area where improving the appearance of seawalls has been of particular concern. A good example of this treatment is the seawall at Pleasure Point on the east side of Santa Cruz. For years, the shoreline was littered with scattered rock and rubble that provided little protection from shoreline erosion. A 2009 project by the city of Santa Cruz and the U.S. Army Corps of Engineers has opened up the beach area by removing all the rock debris and providing shore protection with a colored and texturized vertical seawall. The wall obtains its stability through a system of tiebacks that anchor the wall to the existing natural bluff. Shotcrete, a material consisting of cement, sand, small gravel, and water that is sprayed onto the bluff face, has been installed over the engineered wall, and this facing has been stained and sculpted to look like the natural bluffs. Small "goat paths" have even been installed in the wall to help people escape from the surf if they get trapped on the beach during a high tide. These walls do not avoid the inherent problem of seawalls, namely that they protect the back shore while doing nothing to improve or maintain the beach seaward of the wall. But at least they take up much less space on the beach than revetments and greatly improve the visual quality of the area where shoreline armoring is an appropriate option for protecting roads and structures.

Pleasure Point seawall and stairway

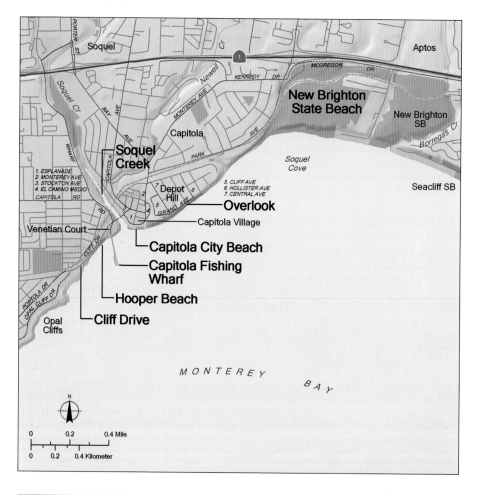

Capitola City Beach and Capitola Fishing Wharf

Capitola to New Brighton State Beach

	Sandy Beach	Rocky Shore	Trail	Visitor Center	Campground	Wildlife Viewing	Fishing or Boating	Facilities for Disabled	Food and Drink	Restrooms	Parking	Fee
Cliff Drive			•								•	
Hooper Beach	•					•	•				•	
Capitola Fishing Wharf						•	•		•	•	•	
Capitola City Beach	•						•		•	•	•	
Soquel Creek			•		•							
Overlook			•									
New Brighton State Beach	•		•	•	•		•	•		•	•	•

CLIFF DRIVE: *Along the bluff, W. of Capitola.* A bluff edge sidewalk with metered parking bays runs along Cliff Dr. as it descends to Capitola Village. Just before the first building on the bay side, a stairway winds down the steep bluff to Hooper Beach.

HOOPER BEACH: *W. of Capitola Fishing Wharf, Capitola.* Hooper Beach is the section of sandy beach upcoast of Capitola Wharf. There is limited small boat storage on the beach. Sand ramp at the base of the wharf.

CAPITOLA FISHING WHARF: *Foot of Wharf Rd., Capitola.* The wharf provides free public fishing access; anglers catch flounder, sole, sanddabs, and halibut. Amenities on the pier include boat and kayak rentals, fishing equipment sales and rentals, and a restaurant. Daily fishing licenses are available at the bait and tackle shop; call: 831-462-2208. Public restroom. The wharf is open from 5 AM to midnight. Very limited parking at the foot of the wharf; stairway to the beach at the same location.

Next to the wharf is the Venetian Court, one of California's earliest condominium-type subdivisions, now operated as the Capitola Venetian Hotel. With its 1920s-style pastel stucco construction, tiled roofs, and ornate decorations, the Venetian Court is a unique architectural site and in 1987 was listed on the National Register of Historic Places.

Capitola Fishing Wharf

CAPITOLA CITY BEACH: *S. of Esplanade and Monterey Ave., Capitola.* Capitola City Beach is a popular swimming area; surfers gather off the jetty. Lifeguard towers on the sand are staffed from late May to September and on weekends into October. Volleyball standards and nets are on the beach. The Capitola Village Esplanade, which backs the beach, offers restaurants, shops, and beach equipment rentals. There is limited metered parking on nearby streets. A free shuttle operates on summer weekends and holidays from a parking lot at the intersection of Monterey and Park Avenues; take the Park Ave. exit from Hwy. One. For recorded information on beach water quality at Capitola and other Santa Cruz County beaches, call: 831-454-3188. Dogs are not allowed on the beach. For a beach wheelchair, call: 831-462-3125.

SOQUEL CREEK: *E. of Wharf Rd., Capitola.* A trail runs a couple of hundred yards along the east side of Soquel Creek, upstream from Stockton Avenue. Soquel Creek is a perennial stream that supports an important steelhead run. Adult fish enter the creek during winter and spring storms in order to reproduce and can sometimes be spotted from the Stockton Ave. bridge. Young fish spend a couple of years in the lower creek or lagoon before heading to sea and points as far away as Alaska or Baja California. The

Capitola Ave., Capitola

Said to be the oldest seaside resort on the Pacific Coast, Capitola was founded in 1869 by a local lumberman named F.A. Hihn and was incorporated in 1950 with a population of 1,848. Previously, the site was occupied by Ohlone Indians, then became part of two Mexican land grants; later, Soquel Landing at the mouth of Soquel Creek was used for shipping lumber and ranch products. Hihn named the resort "Camp Capitola" hoping to convince the State Legislature to move from Sacramento to the coast. Historic sites in Capitola Village include the "Six Sisters," six Victorian houses built in a row along the Esplanade behind Capitola Beach.

The Capitola Begonia Festival has been held annually for decades. There is a parade of begonia-covered floats on Soquel Creek, boat races, a sand sculpture contest, and concerts. The festival takes place on Labor Day weekend; for information, write: P.O. Box 501, Capitola CA 95010-0501.

creek is also habitat for the tidewater goby, a small native fish that thrives in water of low salinity, such as that found at the mouth of Soquel Creek.

OVERLOOK: *Along Grand Ave., Capitola.* A blufftop path leads about four blocks along the top of Depot Hill, above the bay. Climb the stairway from El Camino Medio St. to Cliff Ave., then follow the bluff edge as far as Hollister Avenue. There are fine views of Monterey Bay and surfers off the jetty.

NEW BRIGHTON STATE BEACH: *1500 Park Ave., Capitola.* New Brighton State Beach includes both sandy shore and upland areas. There is day-use parking near beach level, along with restrooms and beach shower; on the forested bluff there is a 111-site campground including hike/bike camping area. Some sites are wheelchair accessible. There is a camp host, a visitor center, and an RV dump station.

Beach fires are allowed only in provided fire rings and must be attended at all times. Dogs are allowed in picnic and campground areas; dogs must be on a six-foot leash and cannot be left unattended. A beach wheelchair is available; for information, call: 831-685-6500. The beach was once known as China Beach, after a Chinese fishing village that stood here from the 1870s until about 1890. The village was built of scrap lumber and driftwood. Fishermen went into the bay to fish, and dried their catch on the sand.

Surf shops in the Capitola area include:

Arrow Surf and Sport, 831-475-8960

O'Neill Surf Shop, 831-475-4151.

New Brighton State Beach

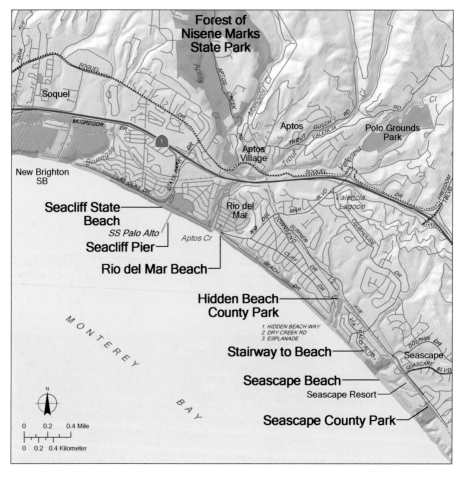

Rio del Mar Beach, Aptos Dr. entrance

Aptos and Rio del Mar

	Sandy Beach	Rocky Shore	Trail	Visitor Center	Campground	Wildlife Viewing	Fishing or Boating	Facilities for Disabled	Food and Drink	Restrooms	Parking	Fee
Seacliff State Beach	•	•	•	•		•	•		•	•	•	•
Seacliff Pier						•	•	•		•		
Forest of Nisene Marks State Park			•						•	•	•	
Rio del Mar Beach	•		•				•		•	•	•	
Hidden Beach County Park	•									•	•	
Stairway to beach	•									•		
Seascape Beach	•									•		
Seascape County Park			•							•	•	

SEACLIFF STATE BEACH: *Foot of State Park Dr., Aptos.* Seacliff State Beach includes nearly two miles of shoreline. The wide sandy beach lies below steep sandstone cliffs. There is ample parking in a large lot on the bluff, and additional parking at beach level. Near the Seacliff Pier are picnic areas, restrooms with beach shower, the Beach Shack café, and a visitor center and gift shop (open Tuesday through Sunday, from 10AM to 4 PM). A paved pedestrian/bicycle path runs both up and downcoast.

Camping at Seacliff State Beach is available for self-contained RVs and trailers only. For reservations, call: 1-800-444-7275; overflow spaces are also available and are assigned through a lottery system at the park entrance. Campsites have picnic tables, barbecue grills, electricity, and water; restrooms have showers.

Beach fires are not allowed at Seacliff State Beach. Dogs are allowed in picnic and campground areas; dogs must be on a six-foot leash and cannot be left unattended. For recorded information on beach water quality at Seacliff State Beach and other locations, call: 831-454-3188. A beach wheelchair can be reserved; call: 831-685-6500.

SEACLIFF PIER: *Foot of State Park Dr., Aptos.* The wooden pier is 500 feet long and popular with anglers who fish for perch, flounder, sole, and halibut. A California fishing license is not required to fish from the pier, al-though Department of Fish and Game catch limits apply. At the end of the pier is the old concrete ship *Palo Alto*, which sits grounded in the intertidal zone and is closed to visitors. The pier is wheelchair accessible.

FOREST OF NISENE MARKS STATE PARK: *Aptos Creek Rd. off Soquel Dr., Aptos Village.* Covering nearly 10,000 acres, the Forest of Nisene Marks is one of the largest state parks in central California. Previously owned and extensively logged by the Loma Prieta Lumber Company during the 40-year lumber boom (1883–1923), the property was sold in the 1950s to the Marks family, a prominent Salinas Valley farming family. In 1963 the three Marks children donated the land to the State of California in memory of their mother, Nisene. As specified in the deed, the park is managed as a semi-wilderness; redwood trees once again stand tall there.

Park facilities are limited to picnic areas, barbecue grills, basic restroom facilities, and 30 miles of hiking trails. Aptos Creek flows through the park, bordered by lush ferns and moss. The Old Growth Loop Trail begins near the entrance station and leads to a grove of redwood trees with oddly twisted trunks and to a colony of tiger lily plants. Dogs on leash are allowed in picnic areas and on Aptos Creek Rd. as far as the Porter Picnic area.

RIO DEL MAR BEACH: *End of Rio del Mar Blvd., Rio del Mar.* The southern end of Seacliff State Beach; linked to the rest of the state beach by a paved pedestrian/bicycle path, which spans the mouth of Aptos Creek. Restrooms and beach showers; no-fee parking in a small lot at the end of Rio del Mar Blvd. that also serves nearby businesses. Additional parking (fee applies) is three-quarters of a mile south along Beach Drive. Dogs are not allowed on the beach.

HIDDEN BEACH COUNTY PARK: *End of Cliff Dr. and Hidden Beach Way, Rio del Mar.* This hard-to-find park, with very limited parking, is reached via Cliff Dr., off Rio del Mar Boulevard. Or walk in from Sumner Ave. east of Dry Creek Road, crossing under the railroad trestle. The shady park includes a children's play area. Leashed dogs allowed on the beach. Maintained by Santa Cruz County; call: 831-454-7901. A second pathway to this beach is located on the west side of the arroyo. It is accessed from Hidden Beach Way, just past Cliff Drive.

STAIRWAY TO BEACH: *Via Palo Alto, off Clubhouse Dr., Rio del Mar.* A long stairway leads to the sandy beach. On-street parking; no facilities.

SEASCAPE BEACH: *Sumner Ave. and Seascape Resort, Seascape.* There are two access-ways through the Seascape Resort to the sandy beach: a dirt path at the north end of the resort and a paved pathway in the middle of the resort. A separate dirt path located outside the resort property also leads to the same beach from Sumner Ave., starting at a point opposite Dolphin Drive. Cross under the old railroad trestle; no facilities. Dogs allowed on the beach. No fires, alcohol, or glass containers. There are designated public parking spaces within the Seascape Resort lot for beachgoers. Call: 831-454-7901.

SEASCAPE COUNTY PARK: *Sumner Ave. and Seascape Blvd., Seascape.* The blufftop park includes broad lawns and children's play equipment. Small parking area and restrooms; popular dog-walking area. At the north end, a blufftop path runs past the Seascape Resort and connects to a paved beach access path.

Seacliff Pier at Seacliff State Beach

A ship made of concrete? An odd idea, perhaps, but one that once had more than a few proponents. During World War I the idea of concrete ships was explored as a way of quickly replacing vessels lost in combat. After all, a concrete ship would be fireproof, corrosion-proof, and bug-proof, as well as speedy to build and easy to repair. And, yes, a concrete ship can float.

The concrete *Palo Alto*, designed as an oil tanker, was launched in the Oakland Estuary in 1919. The ship's steel-reinforced walls were four inches thick. The concrete poured into forms was a mixture of one part Portland cement (produced at Davenport in Santa Cruz County) and two parts aggregate. But by the time the *Palo Alto* was afloat, World War I had come to an end. And the collision in 1920 on the Eastern Seaboard of a different concrete ship with a steel cargo vessel laden with granite highlighted a dramatic drawback of the design; the concrete ship broke up in as little as three minutes, sank to the bottom, and took 19 crew members with it.

No one seemed to want a concrete oil tanker. The *Palo Alto* ended up in the old "Mothball Fleet" parked in Suisun Bay, near Benicia. With its engine and bronze propeller removed, the *Palo Alto* was sold in 1929 to the Seacliff Amusement Corporation, towed to Seacliff Beach, and sunk at the end of the wooden pier, with its bow facing into Monterey Bay. For a couple of years, the ship served as a pleasure pier, with a restaurant, dancehall, swimming pool, and amusement arcade. In the summer of 1930, ferryboats carried revelers from the Santa Cruz Wharf to dine and dance on "The Ship."

Hard times came, and the Seacliff resort failed. The State of California later acquired Seacliff Beach for use as a state park and paid one dollar for the *Palo Alto*. Stripped of all its mechanical equipment, the concrete shell of the old ship became a popular fishing pier. It enabled shore anglers to reach deep water nearly 1,000 feet offshore. But winter storms broke the brittle ship in two, and since the 1980s it has been closed to the public. Fish now glide through the ship's submerged chambers, and cormorants perch on the deck, drying their wings in the sea breeze.

Concrete ship *Palo Alto* at Seacliff State Beach

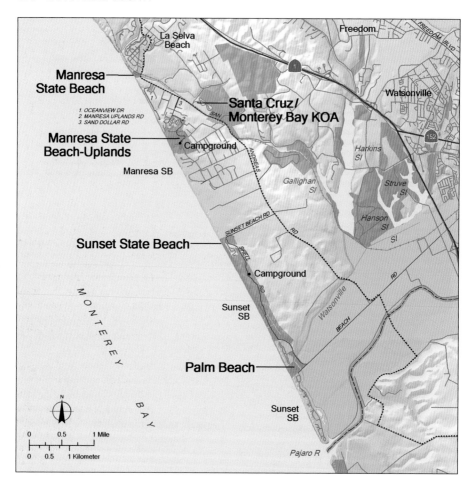

Manresa State Beach

Santa Cruz County South

	Sandy Beach	Rocky Shore	Trail	Visitor Center	Campground	Wildlife Viewing	Fishing or Boating	Facilities for Disabled	Food and Drink	Restrooms	Parking	Fee
Manresa State Beach	•	•		•	•	•			•	•	•	
Manresa State Beach-Uplands	•			•		•			•	•	•	
Santa Cruz/Monterey Bay KOA				•		•		•	•	•	•	
Sunset State Beach	•	•		•		•	•			•	•	
Palm Beach	•					•	•			•	•	

MANRESA STATE BEACH: *San Andreas Rd. at Union Pacific track, La Selva Beach.* The main day-use entrance to Manresa State Beach is off San Andreas Rd. near the small community of La Selva Beach. A large parking area, picnic tables, and restrooms are situated on a bluff. A stairway and a wheelchair-accessible paved ramp lead down to a broad sandy beach. Dogs on leash are allowed on the beach upcoast of the Manresa State Beach-Uplands campground. For park information, call: 831-761-1795.

An additional informal access to Manresa State Beach is located off Oceanview Dr., which intersects San Andreas Rd. one-quarter mile south of the main day-use entrance. Road-side parking; no facilities. A dirt trail leads down the bluff to the sand.

The bluff and adjacent border of the coastal terrace supports a narrow band of coastal sage scrub vegetation, including coyote brush, California sagebrush, and lizardtail, and provides habitat for such wildlife as the Allen's hummingbird, lesser goldfinch, spotted towhee, and brush rabbit. The intertidal area of the beach is inhabited by such marine invertebrates as the sand crab, purple olive snail, beach hopper, and Pismo clam. Sea otters swim and feed offshore. During their migration, California gray whales can also be seen.

MANRESA STATE BEACH-UPLANDS: *Manresa Uplands Rd. off San Andreas Rd., La Selva Beach.* A day-use area and a campground are located in the southern section of Manresa State Beach. Turn off San Andreas Rd. on Sand Dollar Dr., then left on Manresa Uplands Rd. to the entrance kiosk. Picnic tables and restrooms are at the parking area, and a packed-earth path leads to a long stairway to the beach. Fee for day use.

Campsites for tents only are dispersed on a pleasant blufftop meadow and are equipped with picnic tables and firepits. Campers may unload their gear at their sites, then must park in a central lot. A campground host is stationed at the parking area.

SANTA CRUZ/MONTEREY BAY KOA: *1186 San Andreas Rd., La Selva Beach.* Private campground with swimming pool, game room, bicycle rentals, free Wi-Fi, laundry, and showers; provides over 230 overnight sites, including cabins, tent sites, and RV spaces, many with full hookups. Open all year; camping fee applies. Pets on leash allowed. For reservations, call: 831-722-0551.

SUNSET STATE BEACH: *End of Sunset Beach Rd., south Santa Cruz County.* Day use and camping are offered at this state park unit, which has seven miles of beachfront (including Palm Beach). A picnic area is located on the bluff behind the beach; in March and April poppies and bush lupine bloom in the surrounding meadows. A paved ramp leads down to the sand. A second day-use area with restrooms and beach showers is located a mile past the entrance station. High dunes support a diverse coastal strand community of plants, including mock heather, sea rocket, sand verbena, and beach sagewort. Several rare endemic plants, including Monterey paintbrush, robust spineflower, and the endangered coast wallflower, grow here; the California legless lizard also uses the dunes. Popular fishing spot; surf perch, sardines, and the occasional striped bass are caught. Hazardous swimming. Dogs not allowed on the beach. Call: 831-763-7062.

The wooded Sunset State Beach campground has 90 sites, including group and wheelchair-accessible sites. Amenities include picnic tables, barbecue grills, and showers. A campground host staffs the site.

PALM BEACH: *End of Beach Rd., south Santa Cruz County.* No palms, but miles and miles of sand. Huge dunes separate the parking area from the beach, requiring a somewhat difficult walk through loose sand. There is a picnic area under the trees. Palm Beach is part of Sunset State Beach, which extends almost to the mouth of the Pajaro River. Dogs are allowed in the picnic area; must be on a six-foot leash and attended at all times.

The California coast offers outstanding opportunities for both recreational and serious bicyclists. The Pacific Coast Bicycle Route, inaugurated in 1976 in honor of the nation's bicentennial, includes over 1,000 miles of streets, roads, and bikeway segments all along the coast that provide not only spectacular views but also access to many beaches, parks, and coastal towns. The terrain, riding conditions, and available services vary from place to place and season to season, enabling cyclists of all abilities to enjoy either leisurely paced or more challenging rides.

The Capitola-to-Watsonville route is a particularly good example of a cycling experience for all levels of enthusiasm. Traditionally, bicyclists ride from north to south in order to take advantage of prevailing northwesterly winds. The route covers approximately 16.5 miles between Capitola and Watsonville. Most fit riders will need between one and two hours of riding time to complete the distance, and tourists with heavily laden bicycles should plan for at least a two-hour ride. The terrain includes stretches of flat marine terrace, rolling coastal hills punctuated by coastal streams and estuaries, and no steep mountainous sections or sustained difficult climbs. This is a mixed urban and rural ride for cyclists who are supplied with adequate water and food and prepared to perform roadside repairs if needed; an eight-mile section in southernmost Santa Cruz County has no roadside services available.

The ride begins at the beachfront Esplanade in Capitola and proceeds with a brief mild climb inland (north) on Monterey Ave., approximately one-quarter mile long, to Park Avenue. Turn right (northeast) on to Park Ave. and ride approximately one-and-a-half miles to McGregor Drive. Take in the view downcoast from Park Ave. as it follows the 80-foot-high bluff above Soquel Cove, just west of New Brighton State Beach. Watch for campers and other large vehicles as another right turn (east) onto McGregor Dr. takes you past the entrance to the campground at New Brighton State Beach.

Proceed downcoast approximately one-and-a-half miles along McGregor Dr. to State Park Dr., where a right turn towards the coast takes you down to Seacliff State Beach and Las Olas Drive. Watch your speed as you descend the switchbacks from the marine terrace 200 feet or so past the state park campground to the beach. Follow Las Olas Dr. southeast along the beach approximately one-quarter mile to the Esplanade at Rio Del Mar, where a brief stop at the Rio Market or Pixie Deli may be in order. Continue southeast about one-quarter mile up Rio Del Mar Blvd. onto the marine terrace and into the community of Rio Del Mar. Proceed three-tenths of a mile farther inland on Rio Del Mar Blvd. to Sumner Avenue. Turn right (southeast) on Sumner Ave. and continue riding downcoast adjacent to the former Santa Cruz Railroad right-of-way about a mile and three-quarters to the village of Seascape.

Watch for the street signs, and turn left (inland) on Seascape Blvd.; continue through Seascape approximately eight-tenths of a mile to San Andreas Road. Turn right at San Andreas Rd. and head south about a mile and one-half towards La Selva Beach.

Pedaling south along San Andreas Rd. past Manresa State Beach, riders will experience a more rural feeling. Rolling hills blanketed with lettuce and strawberry fields dominate the landscape. Scenic creeks and wetlands provide important corridors for wildlife of many forms. After crossing Watsonville Slough, turn left at Beach Rd. and continue inland about three miles into the City of Watsonville. Cross Main St. and finish the ride at City Plaza Park, a fitting place to relax, eat a snack or have lunch, and savor your accomplishment.

Bike path in village of Seascape

Monterey Submarine Canyon

ONE of the most striking features of the sea floor off the Central Coast of California is the presence of numerous submarine canyons that cut into the continental slope, connecting the continental shelf with the deep-sea "abyssal plains." By far the largest is Monterey Submarine Canyon, the largest submarine canyon along any coast of North America, and probably the best studied submarine canyon in the world. Comparable in size to the Grand Canyon of Arizona, the canyon is nearly 300 miles long and has a maximum depth (from rim to floor) of over 5,500 feet. The canyon extends from shallow waters just off Moss Landing to a depth of over 11,000 feet at the edge of the abyssal plain, where the canyon discharges sediment to form a huge submarine fan.

Soquel Canyon is a major tributary canyon on the north side of the main submarine canyon, and Carmel Canyon branches off to the south. The San Gregorio Fault, a major component of the San Andreas Fault system, cuts across the canyon, and Carmel Canyon is aligned along the fault, as are smaller tributary canyons to the north. The head of Monterey Submarine Canyon is aligned along a more minor fault, the Monterey Canyon Fault. The Monterey Bay Fault system, which is a complex system of poorly understood features, crosses the canyon at right angles, parallel to and east of the San Gregorio Fault. Along these faults, fluids percolate from the sea floor, forming "cold seeps," depositing calcium carbonate, and providing a unique habitat for an unusual ecosystem.

Monterey Submarine Canyon

Remotely operated vehicle (ROV) *Ventana* launched by Monterey Bay Aquarium Research Institute (MBARI)

Submarine canyons were long thought to have been created simply by the incising action of rivers during the Last Glacial Maximum, some 18,000 to 20,000 years ago, when sea level was about 400 feet lower than it is today (much of the Earth's water was locked up then in polar ice caps). But where are the valleys that could be expected to cross the continental shelf? Although Monterey Submarine Canyon does come very near shore off Moss Landing, many other submarine canyons do not. And although Elkhorn Slough discharges today into the head of Monterey Submarine Canyon, it is hard to believe that its tiny watershed could have been responsible for creating such a gigantic feature. In any case, Monterey Submarine Canyon lies entirely west of the San Andreas Fault, and thus the canyon must have been carried for hundreds of miles to the northwest of its place of erosion, if it is a feature of any great age, as its scale would suggest. Perhaps the ancestral Sacramento and San Joaquin rivers, which are known to have flowed south through the Central Valley before discharging to the sea, could have had something to do with the canyon's creation. The current alignment of the canyon with Elkhorn Slough may be more coincidence than evidence of causation.

Ever since 1929, when sediment discharged by the 1929 Grand Banks earthquake off Labrador sequentially broke a series of underwater cables at different times after the earthquake, scientists have known that a discharge of sediment could travel with a velocity of 60 miles per hour or more in a dense flow known as a "turbidity current." Turbidity currents, whose deposits are now recognized in the geologic record, must have tremendous erosive capacity, and they undoubtedly play a major role at least in sculpting submarine canyons, if not creating them. Indeed, a large turbidity current was detected in Monterey Submarine Canyon on December 20, 2001, by Monterey Bay

Aquarium Research Institute (MBARI) scientists. They determined that the flow started in water less than 1,000 feet deep. After the event, a core sample collected from the center of the canyon at a depth of 4,200 feet was shown to contain fresh, green organic material, suggesting that it was deposited by the turbidity flow. The evident trigger was only moderately high surf.

Studies continued, and the U.S. Geological Survey and the Naval Postgraduate School have measured *in situ* turbidity currents in the canyon, the first time this has been done directly in any submarine canyon. One event measured by MBARI scientists carried an estimated 2.8 million cubic yards of material approximately 1,800 feet down the canyon. These large events clearly contribute to the carving of the canyon.

Meanwhile, researchers at California State University–Monterey Bay have performed repeated high-resolution sonar scans of upper Monterey Submarine Canyon. Their precision surveys have revealed the presence of enormous sand waves that carry sediment down the canyon. Repeated surveys show changes in the shape of these waves as they migrate down-canyon. The surveys also reveal areas of erosion and deposition. The heads of the tributary canyons are actively eroding, as are canyon walls, especially at narrow bends. Deposition is occurring mostly in an area between minor tributary heads near the entrance to Moss Landing Harbor. Perhaps this accumulation of sediment will cascade down the canyon someday as a turbidity flow following some triggering mechanism such as an earthquake or heavy surf.

Due to its complex configuration, depth, and proximity to shore, Monterey Submarine Canyon supports a wide variety of unique marine species. Located a short distance from the head of Monterey Submarine Canyon, scientific research institutions such as Monterey Bay Aquarium Research Institute, Moss Landing Marine Lab, and Hopkins Marine Station are strategically located to plumb the depths of the canyon and shed some light on these mysterious organisms. The canyon serves both as a tremendous source of biological discovery and a testing ground for the new technologies, instruments, and equipment needed to make these discoveries. Because the canyon is so inhospitable to humans, undersea exploration into its depths often requires the use of specially designed manned and unmanned submersible vehicles (including remotely operated vehicles, or ROVs, that are guided from above and autonomous underwater vehicles, or AUVs, that move independently). New marine species, ecological phenomena and even entirely new ecosystems are encountered on many of the journeys these vehicles make into the canyon.

One remarkable deep-sea ecosystem that has been discovered in Monterey Submarine Canyon is associated with the "cold seeps" that exist at depths of over 3,000 feet on the canyon walls and floor. A cold seep is an area on the sea floor where naturally occurring methane and sulfide-rich fluids leak out of the substrate at temperatures around 35 degrees Fahrenheit. Similar to their super-heated counterparts, hydrothermal vents, cold seep areas have given rise to communities of animals and microorganisms that derive energy from the chemicals within the seeping fluid. Cold-seep communities in Monterey Submarine Canyon are notable both for their ability to persist and thrive in an extremely high sulfide environment that would be toxic to most animal species (hydrogen sulfide is known to inhibit an organism's ability to absorb oxygen) and because they exist totally independent from the solar energy that forms the basis for the majority of life on Earth. In addition to large mats of free-living bacteria, Monterey Submarine Canyon's cold-seep communities predominantly support vesicomyid clams and vestimentiferan tube worms.

Found exclusively on the lightless deep-ocean floor, the **vesicomyid clam** is represented in Monterey Submarine Canyon by six species, *Calyptogena kilmeri, C. pacifica, C. packardana, C. phaseoliformis, Vesicomya stearnsii,* and *V. gigas.* These species are able to withstand the toxic levels of sulfide that characterize many cold seeps. Instead of killing the vesicomyid clam, the sulfide actually provides an indirect source of nutrients for it, thanks to a symbiotic relationship that the clam has developed with a specialized type of chemoautotrophic bacteria. The vesicomyid clam supports large numbers of these bacteria within its body and uses its long, flexible foot to extract sulfide from sediments. The bacteria are able to feed themselves and their host clam by oxidizing sulfide and producing organic carbon and energy.

Vesicomyid clam, *Calyptogena pacifica*

Common to many hydrothermal vent communities, the **vestimentiferan tube worm** (*Lamellibrachia barhami*) has also been found in some of Monterey Submarine Canyon's cold seep communities. Like vesicomyid clams, these marine tube worms make use of a symbiotic relationship with sulfide-loving bacteria to obtain nutrients. The vestimentiferan tube worm can grow to almost five feet in length and shelters these bacteria—an estimated 285 billion per ounce of tissue—in a specialized organ called a trophosome. The trophosome is made up of spongy tissue that the worm bathes in sulfide and oxygen-rich fluid to provide its resident bacteria with the chemical compounds it requires to produce the organic carbon used to fuel the growth of both organisms.

Vestimentiferan tube worms with anemones

Giant sea spiders (class *Pycnogonida*), up to 20 inches in length, are sometimes seen during submersible voyages to the bottom of Monterey Submarine Canyon. Although not true spiders, these ancient relatives of land spiders, scorpions, and horseshoe crabs are known to exist both in shallow and deep waters. Like many organisms with closely related species that inhabit such a diverse range, if the intertidal version is very small, its deep-sea counterpart may be substantially larger—a phenomenon known as "abyssal gigantism." *Pycnogonids* found at depths of over 9,000 feet are often much larger than their tide pool–dwelling counterparts.

Giant sea spider

Pom-pom anemone

Pom-pom anemones (*Liponema brevicornis*), a frequent food source for the giant sea spiders of Monterey Submarine Canyon, have often been called the "living tumbleweeds" of the deep ocean. Unlike many of their sedentary relatives, these animals do not attach to rocks and instead roll around with the currents on the soft, muddy seafloor at depths from a few hundred to a few thousand feet, and accumulate next to boulders, submerged wood, and whale skeletons. The pom-pom anemone reaches a size of about ten inches across and feeds on plankton, krill, and other tiny creatures that are unlucky enough to drift into its stinging tentacles.

Vampire squid

With a name as memorable as its appearance, the **vampire squid** (*Vampyroteuthis infernalis*—literally "vampire squid from hell") is a remarkable inhabitant of the Monterey Submarine Canyon. The animal has dark red skin, webbed arms, and dozens of sharp claws on its tentacles. Although it is found in several of the world's oceans, it is unique in several ways. Technically, it is neither an octopus nor a squid but has traits of both and is classified in an order all its own. The vampire squid is the only known cephalopod with the ability to squirt not ink but clouds of glowing bioluminescent particles and mucus in order to distract would-be predators. For its size, the vampire squid has the largest eyes of any known animal—nearly an inch across on a body that is only about the size of a football.

Pacific hagfish

The **Pacific hagfish** (*Eptatretus stoutii*), a jaw-less fish, has the ability to excrete protein slime from its skin, often fouling undersea scientific equipment and assuredly foiling the attempts of would-be predators (one scientist estimated that a hagfish could fill an entire barrel with slime in little over an hour). The Pacific hagfish grows about two feet long and relies on its sense of smell to seek out dead animals that sink to the sea floor. Hagfish are often the first to colonize "whale falls," sunken whale carcasses that are a source of nutrients. When feeding, the hagfish has been known to literally tie itself into a knot; it uses its eel-like body to gain the purchase needed to remove a mouthful of food since it does not have the jaws required to bite.

Page opposite: Northern Big Sur, Monterey County

Monterey County

PACIFIC

OCEAN

MONTEREY

SANTA CRUZ

SANTA CLARA

MERCED

SAN BENITO

SAN LUIS OBISPO

Monterey Bay

Pajaro R
Zmudowski SB
Moss Landing SB
Salinas River SB
Salinas R
Castroville
Elkhorn Sl
Moro Cojo Sl
Marina SB
Marina
Fort Ord Dunes SB
Monterey SB
Monterey SHP
Pt. Pinos
Asilomar SB
Cypress Pt.
Pescadero Pt.
Carmel River SB
Point Lobos SNR
Garrapata SP
Fort Ord
RESERVATION RD.
Sand City
Seaside
Monterey
Carmel
Salinas
Carmel R
Carmel Valley
CARMEL
RIVER
RD
VALLEY RD
Gonzales
Soledad
Greenfield
Salinas R
Seco R
ELM AVE
CENTRAL AVE
Little Sur R
Pt. Sur
Point Sur SHP
Big Sur R
Big Sur
Andrew Molera SP
Pfeiffer Big Sur SP
Los Padres NF
Ventana Wilderness
Julia Pfeiffer Burns SP
John Little SNR
Los Padres NF
ARROYO SECO RD
Arroyo
King City
Lopez Pt.
Lucia
Limekiln SP
NACIMIENTO-FERGUSSON RD
MISSION RD
JOLON RD
Hunter Liggett Military Reservation
San Antonio Res
INTERLAKE
Cape San Martin
Nacimiento Res
Paso Robl
Pt. Piedras Blancas
Hearst San Simeon SHM
To Cayucos

To San Jose
101
152
152
25
156
156
183
68
101
146
25
5
Los Ba
San Luis Re
Coalin
1
9
17
1

N

0   10   20 Miles
0   10   20 Kilometers

Monterey County

THE COAST of Monterey County occupies a prominent place in California's history and among the state's natural and scenic marvels. The Ohlone, or Costanoan, Native Americans occupied the Monterey Bay area for at least 10,000 years prior to Spanish settlement. The Big Sur Coast was occupied by the Ohlone, Salinan, and Esselen Indians, the latter one of California's smaller indigenous societies and the first to become extinct. Juan Rodríguez Cabrillo, in the service of Spain, sighted the Monterey Peninsula in 1542, and Monterey Bay was apparently entered by Sebastián Rodríguez Cermeño, a Portuguese explorer who made his way south along the coast in a small boat in December 1595, after his galleon *San Agustín* was wrecked on Point Reyes. Sebastián Vizcaíno, who had accompanied Cermeño, returned in 1602 to make a landing on the shores of Monterey Bay, a harbor that he described as so magnificently sheltered that later Spanish explorers had trouble recognizing it. In 1769, Juan Gaspar de Portolá's pioneering overland expedition set out from San Diego to find Monterey Bay, but went past it, encountering San Francisco Bay before heading back south. The following year, Portolá and Padre Junípero Serra returned to establish the Presidio of Monterey and the second California mission, San Carlos Borromeo, at Carmel.

The county's coast offers some of the world's best-known coastal attractions. Beaches include the unbroken stretch of sand along the great arc of Monterey Bay, the brilliant white sand of Carmel, and the scattered beaches of Big Sur, some made inaccessible by the sheer cliffs of the Coast Range. Monterey pine and cypress trees, sculptured by wind in their dramatic settings, grow naturally on a tiny band of California coast centered on the Monterey Peninsula, but are now planted widely around the globe. The sea otters of the Monterey County coast are winsome, but feisty, marine mammals. Other mammals sighted on wildlife trips on Monterey Bay include gray, humpback, and blue whales; orcas, also known as killer whales; and several species of dolphins.

Coastal communities in Monterey County vary dramatically, reflecting their settings. Monterey overlooks its sheltered bay, while Carmel and Pacific Grove are towns built in the forest, and Marina is a town in the dunes. Big Sur is not really a town at all, but a thinly settled patch of mountain and shore with a reputation built on its mix of dramatic scenery and personal exploration.

Monterey-Salinas Transit serves Monterey-area communities and Hwy. One to Big Sur, with stops at key beaches. The seasonal MST Trolley links downtown Monterey, Pacific Grove, and the Monterey Bay Aquarium. The Monterey Transit Plaza is at Munras Ave. and Alvarado St.; call: 831-899-2555.

The Monterey County Visitor Center, open for drop-ins, is at Camino El Estero and E. Franklin Street. For information by telephone, call: 888-221-1010.

The Carmel Visitor Center is on San Carlos St. between 5th and 6th Avenues, or call: 831-624-2522.

Monterey Peninsula Chamber of Commerce, 831-648-5360.

Moss Landing Chamber of Commerce, 831-633-4501.

Pacific Grove Chamber of Commerce, 831-373-3304.

Big Sur Chamber of Commerce, 831-667-2100.

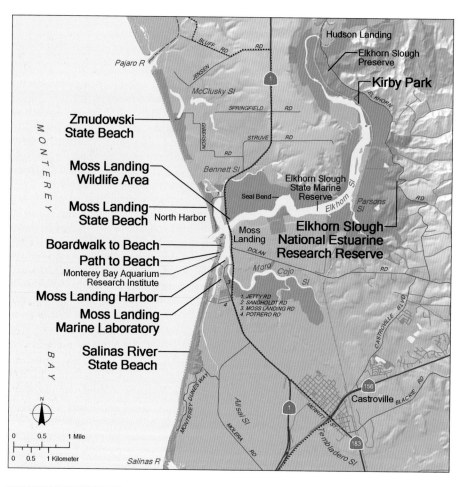

Hudson Landing

Elkhorn Slough
Preserve

Kirby Park

Pajaro R

McClusky Sl

SPRINGFIELD   RD

Zmudowski
State Beach

STRUVE   RD

RD

Moss Landing
Wildlife Area

Bennett Sl

Elkhorn Slough
State Marine
Reserve

Seal Bend

Parsons
Sl

RD

Moss Landing
State Beach   North Harbor

Moss
Landing

Elkhorn Slough
National Estuarine
Research Reserve

Boardwalk to Beach

DOLAN

Path to Beach

Moro Cojo
Sl

RD

Monterey Bay Aquarium
Research Institute

Moss Landing Harbor

1. JETTY RD
2. SANDHOLDT RD
3. MOSS LANDING RD
4. POTRERO RD

Moss Landing
Marine Laboratory

Salinas River
State Beach

156

Castroville

BLACKIE   RD

MONTEREY
BAY

N

1

MERRITT ST

0   0.5   1 Mile

0   0.5   1 Kilometer

Salinas R

183

Moss Landing Harbor

Northern Monterey County

	Sandy Beach	Rocky Shore	Trail	Visitor Center	Campground	Wildlife Viewing	Fishing or Boating	Facilities for Disabled	Food and Drink	Restrooms	Parking	Fee
Zmudowski State Beach	•					•	•			•	•	
Kirby Park			•			•	•	•		•	•	
Elkhorn Slough National Estuarine Research Reserve			•	•		•		•		•	•	•
Moss Landing Wildlife Area			•			•						
Moss Landing State Beach	•					•	•			•	•	
Boardwalk to Beach	•						•				•	
Path to Beach	•											
Moss Landing Harbor				•		•	•	•	•	•	•	
Moss Landing Marine Laboratory				•								
Salinas River State Beach	•		•			•	•			•	•	

ZMUDOWSKI STATE BEACH: *End of Giberson Rd., 3 mi. N. of Moss Landing.* From Hwy. One, turn west on Struve Rd., then continue on Giberson Rd. two miles through farm fields. Zmudowski State Beach offers an undeveloped expanse of dunes and a beach popular for surf fishing and beachcombing. A slough to the north of the parking area can be viewed from an adjacent boardwalk. On the beach, marbled godwits feed along the surf line, and brown pelicans fly low over the ocean. Zmudowski State Beach is part of the miles-long crescent, backed by dunes, that forms the eastern shore of Monterey Bay. It is possible to hike along the wet sand all the way to the harbor entrance at Moss Landing. The parking area is open from sunrise to sunset. Portable toilets. Day use only; no dogs or fires allowed. Horses are permitted on the wet sand only. Call: 831-649-2836.

KIRBY PARK: *Elkhorn Rd., N.E. of Moss Landing.* A public fishing access is located at the northeast end of the slough. There is a ramp and floating pier; this is one of the few places (Moss Landing Harbor is another) to launch a boat or kayak into Elkhorn Slough. Portable restrooms and barrier-free access to the waterfront for fishing. A mile-long paved wheelchair-accessible trail runs north along the slough. Open from 5 AM to 10 PM daily. Managed by the Moss Landing Harbor District; call: 831-633-2461.

ELKHORN SLOUGH NATIONAL ESTUARINE RESEARCH RESERVE: *1700 Elkhorn Rd., N. of Castroville.* The 1,700-acre reserve protects wetlands and uplands for scientific research, public education, and visitor enjoyment. The visitor center near the main entrance features a bookstore and interpretive displays with larger-than-life models of a fat innkeeper worm and other mudflat creatures. Entrance to the visitor center and outdoor picnic area is free. The reserve is open from 9 AM to 5 PM, Wednesday through Sunday. No pets allowed.

Several trails, one wheelchair accessible, lead from the visitor center through stands of coast live oak trees and grasslands to viewpoints overlooking wetland fingers and the main channel of Elkhorn Slough. Docents lead nature walks on weekends at 10 AM and 1 PM; a birding walk takes place on the first Saturday of each month at 8:30 AM. At the Parsons Slough overlook, 116 bird species were seen on a single day in October 1982, setting a North American record. Fee charged for using the trails into the reserve; entry is free with a California hunting or fishing license, although hunting and fishing are prohibited within the reserve boundaries. There is no boating access to Elkhorn Slough. The Elkhorn Slough National Estuarine Research Reserve is managed cooperatively by the California Department of Fish and Game in partnership with the National Oceanic and Atmospheric Administration, with support from the nonprofit Elkhorn Slough Foundation. Call: 831-728-2822.

MOSS LANDING WILDLIFE AREA: *N. of Elkhorn Slough, E. of Hwy. One, Moss Landing.* Watch carefully for the abrupt turn-off from Hwy. One, marked by a brown sign with a binocular icon. Park to the east of the boat repair shop. The wildlife area protects nesting sites for the western snowy plover and roosting grounds for other birds. A dirt trail leads to an overlook; in summer, watch for brown pelicans cruising low over the water.

MOSS LANDING STATE BEACH: *Jetty Rd., W. of Hwy. One.* Fishing, surfing, strolling, and horseback riding are popular on this narrow spit between the ocean and Bennett Slough. Along Jetty Rd., there are three pull-outs, each with limited parking, restrooms, and a short path to the beach. Yellow and pink sand verbena can be seen growing in the dunes. Strong rip currents make the ocean unsafe for swimming. For picnickers, the dunes provide some shelter from afternoon winds.

The end of Jetty Rd. is a good place to view birds, including surf scoters, brown pelicans, sanderlings, killdeers, and marbled godwits. Sea otters feed in the narrow entrance channel, and pigeon guillemots rest on the water; harbor seals haul out on the sand. Moss Landing State Beach offers day use only; no fires. Call: 831-649-2836.

BOARDWALK TO BEACH: *7544 Sandholdt Rd., Moss Landing.* A wheelchair-accessible boardwalk to the sandy beach is located on the north side of a Moss Landing Marine Laboratory building. Parking; no facilities.

PATH TO BEACH: *N. of 7700 Sandholdt Rd., Moss Landing.* A half-hidden path located between a marine laboratory building and Phil's Fish Market leads 200 feet to the beach. Loose sand path; no facilities.

MOSS LANDING HARBOR: *Sandholdt Rd., W. of Hwy. One, Moss Landing.* The harbor is used for commercial and sport fishing, research vessels, and pleasure boating, and is considered to be an extremely safe refuge. Facilities include slips and dry storage, fuel dock, pumpout station, supplies, bait and tackle, restaurants, showers, and restrooms. The mouth of Elkhorn Slough separates the harbor into two parts. The North Harbor has a public viewing wharf, a boat

Moss Landing Harbor

dock for visiting boats, and a four-lane boat ramp; fee charged. Kayaks can be launched into the slough from here. The South Harbor includes parking and fishing and is the site of the harbor office; call: 831-633-2461. The privately operated Moss Landing RV Park offers 46 RV spaces with hookups, cable TV, and free Wi-Fi; call: 877-735-7275. The Monterey Bay Aquarium Research Institute is located in the harbor area; no public facilities.

MOSS LANDING MARINE LABORATORY:
8272 Moss Landing Rd., Moss Landing. This facility serves marine researchers and students and is open to the public only by appointment or during annual open house days; call: 831-771-4400.

SALINAS RIVER STATE BEACH: *W. of Hwy. One, Moss Landing.* There are two miles of sandy beach and three parking areas. One is located at the south end of Sandholdt Rd., near Moss Landing Harbor. A short, loose-sand trail leads through vegetated dunes to a steep beach, which is part of the seemingly endless curve of Monterey Bay shoreline. A second parking area and path are located at the end of Potrero Rd. These two parking lots are linked by a trail, overlooking the slough that was once a part of the Salinas River. Watch for brush rabbits moving warily through the dunes, or white-crowned sparrows feeding in groups.

A third beach-access point in Salinas River State Beach is reached via Molera Rd. and Monterey Dunes Way. A quarter-mile-long sandy path leads to a steep beach that is popular for fishing, clamming, and hiking. The large paved parking area is suitable for horse trailers, and equestrians use this as a starting point for riding along the shore; riders are limited to the beach and the trail through the dunes. Fires not allowed. For information, call: 831-649-2836.

Captain Charles Moss, with his partner Cato Vierra, a whaler from the Azores, built a wharf and pier in 1866. Whales, highly prized for their oil, were originally processed on board whaling ships; with the development of land-based facilities, such as those at the settlement known as Moss, processing moved to shore. The blubber was rendered for lamp oil, meat was processed into animal feed, baleen was used for women's corsets and stays, and bones were ground into bone meal.

Kerosene lamps, and later electricity, began to replace whale oil lamps, and the whale boom collapsed. Beginning in 1918, the whaling industry revived briefly as ships began to hunt farther from shore; captured whales were inflated with air and then towed to shore for processing. By 1927 all whale processing at Moss Landing had ended.

Following the 1906 earthquake, which destroyed Moss and Vierra's original wharf and pier, the Pacific Coast Steamship Company moved its offices to Moss Landing to oversee shipments to the San Francisco Bay Area of food and supplies for rebuilding. Sardines packed at canneries at Moss Landing were shipped to soldiers overseas during both world wars. Most of the canneries closed with the collapse of the sardine industry, but five fish processing plants still operate today in Moss Landing, and the Monterey Bay Aquarium Research Institute (MBARI), the research arm of the world-famous aquarium, now sits on land once occupied by a cannery.

One of Moss Landing's new industries is tourism; excursion boats regularly take visitors into Monterey Bay to catch sight of blue, gray, humpback, and other species of whales. Sanctuary Cruises offers whale-watching trips from Moss Landing, call: 831-917-1042. Kayak rentals and sport fishing trips are also available at Moss Landing Harbor.

Elkhorn Slough

ELKHORN SLOUGH, located at the midpoint of the Monterey Bay shoreline, is one of about 30 National Estuarine Research Reserves, six of which are on the West Coast. (National Estuarine Research Reserves are the product of a partnership between the National Oceanic and Atmospheric Administration and coastal states, intended to promote public education, water-quality monitoring, and research.) While much smaller than San Francisco Bay, Elkhorn Slough is one of central California's major estuaries. Estuaries are ecosystems at the boundary between coastal rivers and the ocean, where fresh and salt water mingle. More than 340 bird species, 100 fish species, and over 500 species of aquatic invertebrates live in the slough or visit it for part of the year. The sheltered areas provide nursery spots for juvenile marine fish. Leopard sharks cruise the channels, harbor seals haul out on the banks, and southern sea otters rest and groom while floating together in groups known as "rafts." Elkhorn Slough is a complex tapestry of tidal saltmarsh and intertidal mudflats transected by a meandering tidal channel and tidal branches. The main tidal channel follows a sinuous route some seven miles inland from Moss Landing.

Elkhorn Slough is accessible by both land and water. Moss Landing Harbor and the Hwy. One bridge are near the ocean end of Elkhorn Slough. Public access is available to the shoreline on both sides of the ocean entrance; watch carefully for sea otters feeding in the channel. Northeast of the Hwy. One bridge are acres of former salt ponds where ocean waters were held within diked areas and salt was harvested after the water evaporated. The old salt flats are visible from the Moss Landing Wildlife Area; the endangered western snowy plover nests on the flats in spring and summer. Inland along the east-west channel of Elkhorn Slough is a point called Seal Bend. About a mile inland of Seal Bend the main channel veers north, paralleling the Union Pacific railroad

Elkhorn Slough

tracks. Kirby Park and the Estuarine Research Reserve Visitor Center are located along the north-south segment of the Slough. Hudson Landing, also known as Watsonville Landing, is located at the head of the estuary.

There is archaeological evidence that the Costanoan Indians occupied the area around Elkhorn Slough at least 8,000 years before present. There would have been large expanses of pickleweed on the saltmarshes, an abundance of oysters in the upper estuary, shorebirds feeding on the mudflats, fish and otters in the tidal channels, and possibly elk in the upland areas. The region provided a cornucopia for the coastal Indians, as indicated by the abundance of oyster shells, fish skeletons, and bone fragments in the many middens found around the slough.

When the Costanoans occupied the area, they set fire to the marshes in the fall in order to maintain grasslands and possibly to flush game. When non-Indian settlers first came to the Elkhorn Slough area in the 19th century, they apparently were shocked by this practice and discontinued it. The fire-free regime that followed allowed the conversion of grasslands to scrublands and forests. The new settlers also introduced agriculture to the estuary area, building dikes around marshlands and draining the plots so the land could support crops. The slough has been reduced in size by almost 50 percent through human-caused modifications.

Elkhorn Slough has experienced many hydrologic changes over the years. Based on the disparity between the relatively small size of the Elkhorn Slough watershed and the immense size and depth of the Monterey Submarine Canyon, geologists speculate that the rivers of California's great Central Valley once drained to the ocean through Elkhorn Slough. Until 1908 the slough joined the Salinas River before flowing into Monterey Bay at a point a few miles north of Moss Landing. Then, during a series of winter storms, the river mouth migrated south about five miles; it has been maintained in this location ever since. The loss of the Salinas River's flow reduced one of the main sources of sediment to the slough. The Pajaro River, to the north, is a sporadic sediment source for the slough, such as during the floods of 1995, when the river overflowed its banks and flowed into the slough. The greatest change to the slough in recent years, however, has been the construction of jetties and a fixed channel opening at Moss Landing Harbor in 1946-7.

During the early settlement of the Elkhorn Slough area by farmers, large areas of the wetlands were planted with row crops or used for grazing, or were severed from the main estuary by roads or the railroad. In the second half of the 20th century, Elkhorn Slough experienced rapid changes to habitat due to subsidence and loss of sediment. The loss of marsh in the main part of the slough has amounted to about three acres per year, or more than 200 acres since 1931 due to conversion of marsh to open water at the edges of channels and to the die-off of marsh vegetation elsewhere. Channel banks have eroded at about 1.3 to 2.0 feet per year in the upper slough and about 1 foot per year in the lower slough. Channels widened from 8 to 40 feet from 1930 to 2003. The tidal prism, or daily flow of water in and out, has almost tripled since the first measurements in 1956; maximum tidal velocities have increased from 1.4 to 3.4 miles per hour in the main channel. Despite these changes, the slough remains a wonderful location for nature trips, birdwatching, canoeing, and kayaking. The staff of the Estuarine Research Reserve are studying ways to reduce physical changes to the slough without reducing the quality of its waters or reducing its biodiversity. As a complex system, however, the slough is subject to a range of effects from any and all management actions—even no action.

Sea lettuce

There are at least ten species of **sea lettuce** (*Ulva* spp.) that grow worldwide, all of which occur along the California coast. With thin, fragile, somewhat translucent green blades, sea lettuce and other macroalgae form the basis of the food web at Elkhorn Slough. Not only does sea lettuce take in carbon dioxide and release oxygen into the environment, it also provides habitat for a variety of intertidal creatures. Nevertheless, large mats of sea lettuce can be indicative of poor water quality, as algal growth is stimulated by eutrophication (nutrient enrichment), such as from agricultural runoff. In addition, large algal blooms can shade and choke out important aquatic vegetation, such as eelgrass. Due to increased tidal erosion sea lettuce has been increasing in Elkhorn Slough over the past 20 years.

Taylor's sea hare

Not a rabbit at all, **Taylor's sea hare** (*Phyllaplysia taylori*) is a sea slug. Its two rabbit-ear-like appendages (called rhinopores) and its rounded body shape make it look like a sitting hare underwater. It can be found in the low intertidal zone, grazing on diatoms and other small organisms among blades of eelgrass. The sea hare's stomach contains a set of hardened teeth to grind up food, and because diatoms are made of hard silica that wears the teeth down, new teeth form every couple of days. Taylor's sea hare is usually bright green with black and white stripes that camouflage it against the blades of eelgrass. Measuring two to three inches long, it is the smallest sea hare in California.

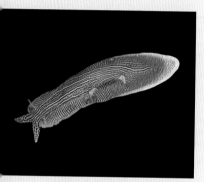

Pacific gaper clam

The **Pacific gaper clam** (*Tresus nuttalli*) and its more northern cousin, the fat gaper (*T. capax*), live in firm sandy-mud bottoms in estuaries and bays and are highly sought after by recreational clammers during extreme low tides. The gaper is so named because its large muscular siphon prevents the shell from closing. These deep-burrowing bivalves often occur at densities up to 20 per square foot. Gaper clams are taken recreationally in a part of Elkhorn Slough just east of Moss Landing Harbor. Clamming is also popular on shoals in Tomales Bay and other coastal bays. A taste for clams is not new. Evidence from Native American middens shows that clams have been part of the human diet for at least seven thousand years. At Elkhorn Slough sea otters dine on gapers too.

The low intertidal mudflats of Elkhorn Slough provide important nursery and foraging habitat for the **leopard shark** (*Triakis semifasciata*). Female leopard sharks generally enter the shallow slough waters in March to give birth to live young, which are approximately eight inches long at birth. Adult sharks average four to five feet in length. Eelgrass beds provide shelter and food for the young pups. Leopard sharks eat a variety of benthic prey, but in Elkhorn Slough their primary food is the fat innkeeper worm. The sharks can live for 30 years and tend to remain in a localized area for much of their lives. Due to their small teeth and timid nature, these sharks are not harmful to humans.

Leopard shark

The **California red-legged frog** (*Rana draytonii*) is the largest native frog found west of the Rocky Mountains. It can be recognized by the "ridge," called a dorsolateral fold, that runs along both sides of its upper body. The frog mostly occupies freshwater wetland habitats where there is a permanent source of water, including streams, ponds, and marshes, but it can travel remarkable distances; some have been known to travel nearly a mile overland. The California red-legged frog was once described as *Rana aurora draytonii* and thought to be closely related to the northern red-legged frog (*Rana aurora aurora*), but genetic studies suggest they are biologically distinct species. The California red-legged frog eats insects, mollusks, and occasionally small vertebrates such as fish, mice, and tree frogs.

Red-legged frog

During the spring and summer, you may be treated to the sight of **Caspian terns** (*Sterna caspia*) plunging into estuarine waters for anchovies, topsmelt, and other small to medium-sized fish. There is no mistaking this largest of all terns, due to its massive coral-red bill and harsh call. The Caspian tern frequents all the continents except Antarctica. In the Americas, it winters along the southern coasts of the U.S. and Mexico, the West Indies, and northernmost South America. Breeding takes place from April through August at scattered coastal and inland sites in the U.S. and Canada, including San Francisco Bay. In 1992, a breeding colony established itself in the Elkhorn Slough South Marsh, but nesting has been sporadic, apparently limited by severe predation, especially by raccoons.

Caspian tern

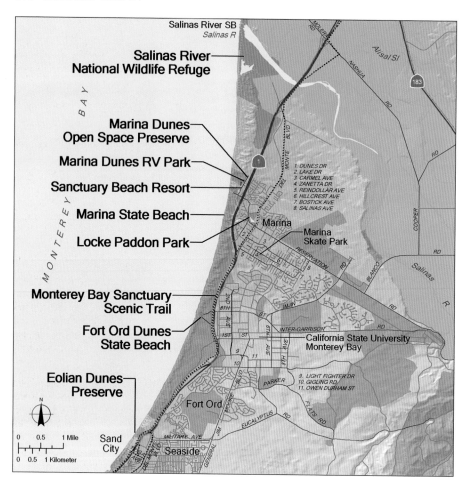

Salinas River SB
Salinas R

Salinas River—
National Wildlife Refuge

Marina Dunes—
Open Space Preserve

Marina Dunes RV Park—

Sanctuary Beach Resort—

Marina State Beach—

Locke Paddon Park—

1. DUNES DR
2. LAKE DR
3. CARMEL AVE
4. ZANETTA DR
5. REINDOLLAR AVE
6. HILLCREST AVE
7. BOSTICK AVE
8. SALINAS AVE

Marina

Marina
Skate Park

Monterey Bay Sanctuary—
Scenic Trail

Fort Ord Dunes—
State Beach

California State University
Monterey Bay

9. LIGHT FIGHTER DR
10. GIGLING RD
11. OWEN DURHAM ST

Eolian Dunes—
Preserve

Fort Ord

Sand
City

Seaside

0   0.5   1 Mile
0   0.5   1 Kilometer

BAY

MONTEREY

Marina State Beach

Salinas River to Sand City

	Sandy Beach	Rocky Shore	Trail	Visitor Center	Campground	Wildlife Viewing	Fishing or Boating	Facilities for Disabled	Food and Drink	Restrooms	Parking	Fee
Salinas River National Wildlife Refuge	•		•			•	•			•		
Marina Dunes Open Space Preserve	•		•			•						
Marina Dunes RV Park				•			•		•	•	•	•
Sanctuary Beach Resort	•		•							•		
Marina State Beach	•		•				•	•		•	•	
Locke Paddon Park			•		•			•		•	•	
Monterey Bay Sanctuary Scenic Trail	•		•					•				
Fort Ord Dunes State Beach	•		•				•	•		•	•	
Eolian Dunes Preserve	•		•							•		

SALINAS RIVER NATIONAL WILDLIFE REFUGE: *N.W. of Hwy. One, 3 mi. S. of Castroville.*
This is an excellent spot for fishing, hiking, photography, and wildlife observation. Leave Hwy. One at Del Monte Blvd. (exit 412) and head north one mile on the dirt access road between artichoke fields; do not trespass. An unpaved parking area is the trailhead for a level mile-long path leading west and north to the ocean. Adjacent to the coastal dune ridge, the native vegetation includes species such as live-forever, colorful Indian paintbrush, and the threatened Monterey spineflower. The endangered Smith's blue butterfly feeds and nests on two species of buckwheat in the sand dunes. To protect plant and animal resources, stay on the trail. Avocets and black-necked stilts nest in the marsh north of the path, and red-necked phalaropes gather during migration. Caspian terns flock here in the summer, hoarsely crying what sounds for all the world like *maybe they are . . . maybe they are.*

The Salinas River mouth attracts California brown pelicans, gulls, and wintering ducks. The river flows from its headwaters in San Luis Obispo County, 170 miles southeast of this point. The Salinas River is unusual in that most of its water is out of sight, flowing beneath its bed. Once you reach the shore, you can hike several miles north along the strand into the neighboring Salinas River State Beach, except when storm waves breach the dune barrier and the river flows to the sea. At the wildlife refuge, beach anglers take striped bass, starry flounder, sand sole, surfperch, steelhead, jacksmelt, and small sharks. Hunting for waterfowl is also allowed. No facilities; dogs and horses prohibited. Call: 510-792-0222.

MARINA DUNES OPEN SPACE PRESERVE: *N. end of Dunes Dr., Marina.* On the site of a former sand mine is a dune preserve revegetated with native plants. A one-third-mile-long gently sloping path leads from the end of Dunes Dr. to an overlook above the shoreline. The first part of the path is well packed, and the seaward end is loose sand. Stay on the path to protect the revegetation efforts. Typical dune species of the area include the Monterey spineflower, beach sagewort, and sand verbena. The California legless lizard may also be present in the dunes. The sandy beach extends for miles in both directions, uninterrupted by natural barriers. To the north, private property separates the Marina Dunes from public lands near the mouth of the Salinas River. To the south, the beach is open past Fort Ord Dunes State Beach and beyond. Streetside parking; no facilities. Dogs on leash are allowed. Managed by the Monterey Peninsula Regional Park District; call: 831-372-3196.

MARINA DUNES RV PARK: *3330 Dunes Dr., Marina.* Use the Reservation Rd. exit off Hwy. One, and turn north on Dunes Dr., just

before the Marina State Beach entrance. The private campground offers more than 60 RV sites, some wheelchair accessible, with patios, picnic tables, barbecue grills, fireplaces, and free Wi-Fi. Individual and group tent campsites are also available. The park includes a playground, laundry, gift shop, and fitness room. Pets allowed. Fee applies; reservations recommended. For information, call: 831-384-6914.

SANCTUARY BEACH RESORT: *3295 Dunes Dr., Marina.* A public path and boardwalk lead 500 feet over a dune to the steep sandy beach. Upon entering the resort property, skirt to the right of the entrance building, and then turn left to park; walk seaward between the buildings to the beach path, which is open during daylight hours only.

MARINA STATE BEACH: *W. end of Reservation Rd., Marina.* Marina State Beach is located on high dunes, some of the tallest along Monterey Bay. Popular with picnickers, anglers, and surfers, the beach is not good for swimming due to strong currents. The elevated and breezy site makes this a popular spot for hang-gliders, paragliders, and model airplane enthusiasts.

The main park entrance on Reservation Rd. leads to a paved overlook with parking, picnic tables, and bike racks. The beach is adjacent. Restrooms with running water are east of the parking lot. Across the entrance road from the restrooms is a boardwalk, parts of which may be inundated by sand, leading south about one-half mile along the crest of the dunes. Markers describe typical plants and animals of the Monterey Bay dunes, including the endangered Menzies wallflower, blooming bright yellow in the summer. Dogs, horses, and fires are not allowed at Marina State Beach. For information, call: 831-649-2836.

Another accessway to Marina State Beach is located at the west end of Lake Drive. A loose sand path, one-third mile long, leads to the beach, up and over the 150-foot-high dunes. Loose sand makes this a more challenging access point, but the high elevation offers an attractive launch spot for hang-gliders. Pilots must first register at the Reservation Rd. parking lot and use appropriate safety equipment.

LOCKE PADDON PARK: *Reservation and Seaside roads, Marina.* This park includes a fresh-

Marina Dunes Open Space Preserve

Fort Ord Dunes State Beach

water pond that attracts waterfowl. There are a wheelchair-accessible overlook and a pedestrian dirt path leading along the edge of the wetland. Picnic tables and restrooms are available, and nature walks and educational programs are offered. From the east side of the park, bicyclists and hikers can access the Monterey Bay Sanctuary Scenic Trail, which runs along Del Monte Blvd. south to Monterey and Pacific Grove. Locke Paddon Park is maintained by the City of Marina; call: 831-884-1253.

MONTEREY BAY SANCTUARY SCENIC TRAIL: *Along Monterey Bay, from Santa Cruz to Pacific Grove.* The Monterey Bay Sanctuary Scenic Trail, which incorporates variously named trail segments in different communities, is planned to ring Monterey Bay, connecting Santa Cruz and Monterey Counties. The trail offers hikers and bicyclists a safe off-road route to reach parks and beaches along the bay or to connect to other spur trails. A major purpose of the trail is to offer visitors views of the Monterey Bay National Marine Sanctuary, just offshore from the planned trail route. Call: 831-883-3750.

A half-mile east of the trail, which runs along Del Monte Blvd. near the Marina city hall, is the Marina Skate Park, 304 Hillcrest Ave.

near Zanetta Dr. The park is free and open daily; helmets and safety pads required.

FORT ORD DUNES STATE BEACH: *Shoreline of Monterey Bay, Fort Ord.* Exit Hwy. One at Light Fighter Dr. and head inland, then turn north on 2nd Avenue. Turn left again (west) on 1st St., also signed as Divarty Street. Cross under the freeway and turn right; follow directional signs to the paved parking area. A sandy path leads between towering dunes to the beach.

Part of former Fort Ord is now occupied by California State University Monterey Bay (CSUMB). Camp SEA Lab ("Science, Education, and Adventure") at CSUMB offers summer programs for K–12 students about the marine environment and its stewardship; call: 831-582-3681.

EOLIAN DUNES PRESERVE: *W. ends of Tioga Ave. and Bay St., Sand City.* Two public street ends provide shoulder parking and informal access to the beach and windblown, or "eolian" dunes. The Monterey Peninsula Regional Park District manages scattered park holdings in the dunes, mixed among undeveloped private parcels of land. The sandy beach extends south through Monterey State Beach into the heart of Monterey. Call: 831-372-3196.

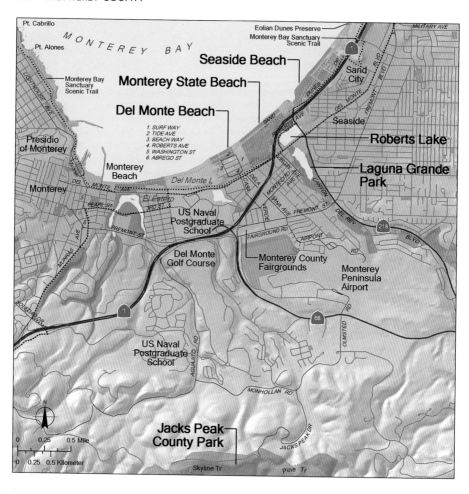

Pt. Cabrillo
MONTEREY BAY
Pt. Alones

Eolian Dunes Preserve
Monterey Bay Sanctuary Scenic Trail
MILITARY AVE

Monterey Bay Sanctuary Scenic Trail

Seaside Beach

Monterey State Beach

Sand City

Del Monte Beach

Seaside

1. SURF WAY
2. TIDE AVE
3. BEACH WAY
4. ROBERTS AVE
5. WASHINGTON ST
6. ABREGO ST

Presidio of Monterey

Roberts Lake

Monterey Beach

Del Monte L

Laguna Grande Park

Monterey

DEL MONTE AVE

PEARL ST

3RD ST

El Estero

US Naval Postgraduate School

FAIRGROUND RD

AIRPORT

218

MUNRAS AVE

FREMONT ST

Del Monte Golf Course

Monterey County Fairgrounds

RD

BLVD

1

Monterey Peninsula Airport

68

US Naval Postgraduate School

AGUAJITO RD

OLMSTED RD

MONHOLLAN RD

N

0   0.25   0.5 Mile
0   0.25   0.5 Kilometer

Jacks Peak County Park

JACKS PEAK DR

Skyline Tr

Pine Tr

Monterey Bay Sanctuary Scenic Trail

Seaside to Monterey

	Sandy Beach	Rocky Shore	Trail	Visitor Center	Campground	Wildlife Viewing	Fishing or Boating	Facilities for Disabled	Food and Drink	Restrooms	Parking	Fee
Seaside Beach	•	•					•			•	•	
Monterey State Beach	•	•					•			•	•	
Del Monte Beach	•	•					•			•	•	
Roberts Lake		•			•					•		
Laguna Grande Park		•			•	•			•	•		
Jacks Peak County Park		•			•	•			•	•		

SEASIDE BEACH: *Sand Dunes Dr., W. of Hwy. One, Seaside.* A unit of Monterey State Beach is located on the north side of the Beach Resort Monterey. Paved parking, picnic tables, a sandy path to the beach, and boardwalks through a small area of vegetated dunes. Portable restrooms. Call: 831-649-2836.

MONTEREY STATE BEACH: *Sand Dunes Dr., W. of Hwy. One, Seaside.* This unit of Monterey State Beach, known as Houghton M. Roberts Beach, is located at the south end of Sand Dunes Dr. It has parking, restrooms, and access down the sloping dune to the sandy beach.

DEL MONTE BEACH: *N. of Del Monte Blvd., Monterey.* Turn off Del Monte Blvd. toward the bay at the stoplight at Casa Verde and bear right on Roberts Ave., then left on Surf Way to the beach. This park, maintained by the City of Monterey, offers broad vistas of Monterey Bay and the wooded Monterey Peninsula from its elevated site, which slopes gently down to the water's edge. A wheelchair-accessible boardwalk leads through the dunes, and benches are placed to take advantage of the views. Restrooms located at the south end of Tide Ave. at Beach Way. Street parking; wheelchair-accessible parking at end of Beach Way.

Del Monte Beach

The California Department of Parks and Recreation is the state's premier supplier of coastal recreation. More than a quarter of the 1,270-mile California coastline, some 320 miles of shore, is encompassed within the state park system. The state park system draws 80 million visitors annually; of the ten most-visited California state park units, nine are sandy beaches.

On a coast with a growing population, state parks provide unparalleled natural scenery, recreation from sunset viewing to surfing the ultimate wave, and even solitude. Coastal plant and animal communities, including many that are rare statewide, are well represented in state park units. More than one-third of the species listed by the state and federal government as threatened or endangered can be found in the state park system. The protection of habitat is the primary goal for most of the land and water in state parks and reserves, but recreational opportunities are abundant. Most state park units protect cultural resources as well as natural resources. At San Mateo County's Año Nuevo State Park and Santa Cruz County's Wilder Ranch State Park, historic farm buildings look much as they did in the 19th century. State marine parks include underwater areas that can be explored by divers.

Interpretive programs and campfire talks are offered at many locations. Thousands of volunteers help staff the parks; at Point Lobos State Natural Reserve, docents are available to point out the dusky-footed wood rat nests tucked almost out of sight among the Monterey cypress trees. At Pescadero State Beach docents lead tours into the Pescadero Marsh Natural Preserve. From Marin to Monterey County, more than 30 state park units are enjoyed by visitors. Many facilities are accessible to those with impaired mobility.

Affordable overnight accommodations overlooking the beach or set in a forest are provided by many state parks. For visitors arriving without a vehicle, hike or bike campsites have especially low fees; equestrian campsites are available in some locations. Environmental campsites offer simple facilities in natural settings, away from cars and crowds. Enroute camping, for those with a self-contained recreational vehicle, is available at many locations, and others offer trailer or RV hookups. Some campsites are available to those who arrive first, while others can be reserved up to seven months in advance; call: 1-800-444-7275.

The Golden Poppy Annual Day Use Parking Pass provides one year of unlimited access to 97 state park units, although not to certain locally managed or high-demand parks such as Hearst Castle. Other pass programs provide a discount for disabled persons and certain military veterans and low-income persons. To learn more about pass programs, call: 1-800-777-0369 ext. #3. For information about state parks, see the department's website at www.parks.ca.gov, or call: 916-653-6995. Due to budget cuts, not all parks are open all the time; check ahead for hours and restrictions.

California poppies

ROBERTS LAKE: *Roberts Ave. and Canyon Del Rey, Seaside.* Roberts Lake and Laguna Grande were once a single brackish lagoon with an outlet to Monterey Bay. Over the years, filling for development and transportation purposes divided the lake and cut off tidal action from the formerly estuarine complex. The reeds on the west side of Roberts Lake, opposite a small grassy picnic area, are habitat for green herons and pied-billed grebes. The lake is also a popular model boat racing area. Parking on Roberts Ave. The site adjoins the Monterey Bay Sanctuary Scenic Trail. Call: 831-899-6825.

LAGUNA GRANDE PARK: *Off Del Monte Ave., along Canyon Del Rey Blvd., Seaside, and Virgin Ave., Monterey.* Laguna Grande is a freshwater lake that is lined with tules and cattails, a habitat for red-winged blackbirds. A paved path around Laguna Grande crosses the lake via a bridge; grassy picnic areas have barbecue pits, and a playground has volleyball nets for rent. Restrooms and parking are available on both east and west sides. Free blues concerts are offered on Sunday afternoons in late summer. The portion of the park along Canyon Del Rey Blvd. is maintained by the city of Seaside; call: 831-899-6825. On the other side of the lake, off Virgin Ave., the city of Monterey manages park facilities; call: 831-646-3866.

JACKS PEAK COUNTY PARK: *Jacks Peak Dr., Monterey.* Although it lies inland from the coast, the high ridge on which Jacks Peak County Park is located offers magnificent views of the ocean and Monterey Bay. Views are filtered by the native Monterey pine forest, which cloaks the peak.

There are eight miles of hiking and equestrian trails, picnic areas with tables and barbecue grills, and restrooms. The Skyline self-guided nature trail leads visitors through an area of Miocene-epoch fossils; descriptive brochures are available at the entrance station. Open daily; hours vary by season. Vehicle entrance fee. Managed by Monterey County Parks Department; for information, call: 888-588-2267. Jacks Peak County Park is named for Scottish immigrant David Jacks, whose local dairies produced "Monterey Jack" cheese, a California creation.

Del Monte Beach

Started in 1958, the Monterey Jazz Festival is the world's longest-running event of its kind. The festival takes place annually in September at the Monterey County Fairgrounds, off Hwy. 68 and Fairground Rd. The Next Generation Festival, featuring young jazz performers, takes place during the spring season at venues in downtown Monterey. For festival information, call: 831-373-3366.

In 1967 the Monterey County Fairgrounds was the site of the three-day Monterey Pop Festival, which featured such performers as Janis Joplin, Jefferson Airplane, and the Grateful Dead. The festival marked a turning point in rock music as it introduced Jimi Hendrix to America and was the nation's first huge outdoor rock concert.

Monterey Bay Dunes

DUNES have been a part of the Monterey Bay landscape for at least the last million years. The Aromas sand, which is approximately one million years old, is widespread east of Monterey Bay and is the geologic record of a sheet of sand that was primarily blown here by the wind. This sandy geologic formation has been overridden south of the Salinas River by a series of dunes, the oldest of which were formed well before the latest period of rapid sea level rise, called the "Flandrian Transgression," roughly 18,000 to 6,000 years ago. These so-called pre-Flandrian dunes have been stabilized by vegetation and are much more subdued in expression than their younger counterparts, but are still quite recognizable. The depressions between dunes collect water and commonly host wetlands. Soils generally are well developed on these older sands and can be very productive—for example, the Monterey Bay area is considered to be the artichoke capital of the world.

The pre-Flandrian dunes are in turn overridden by more recent dunes that formed during and after the Flandrian Transgression. These younger dunes are scarcely stabilized by vegetation, and are parabolic in shape, with the open end pointing seaward. They are on the move, and particular dunes may come and go as the sand is blown away. As the younger dunes are stripped away, the older, more resistant pre-Flandrian dunes are left behind, protected by their soil crust.

Dunes of all ages are, however, susceptible to erosion by waves. As sea level has slowly risen, marine erosion has carved away at the dunes, leaving a bluff that may reach heights of as much as eighty feet. Because the loose sand of the dunes is so easily eroded, some of the greatest long-term erosion rates measured along the California shoreline occur in the southern Monterey Bay area. The eroding dunes provide a source of sand to the marine environment. Much of the sand ends up back on the beaches, where it is susceptible to being picked up once more by the wind, to form dunes once again. Abrasion and weathering of the sand grains that occur in the beach environment serve to remove the softer and less durable components, leaving young dunes of almost pure quartz, which is resistant to weathering and abrasion. This pure quartz sand is a highly attractive resource for the manufacture of glass. Sand of less pure quality is still eagerly sought for use in making concrete. Mining of both commodities has been greatly curtailed in the past decade due to concerns over the loss of dune habitat and sand supply to the beach.

Artichoke field and Monterey Bay dunes

Monterey spineflower (*Chorizanthe pungens* var. *pungens*) is a soft, hairy, low-growing herb endemic to coastal areas in southern Santa Cruz and northern Monterey Counties. Monterey spineflower is a member of the buckwheat family (*Polygonaceae*) and is in a genus of wiry annual herbs that inhabit dry, sandy soils. Because of the patchy and limited distribution of such soils, many species of *Chorizanthe* tend to be very localized in their distributions. Portions of the coastal dune and coastal scrub communities that support Monterey spineflower have been eliminated or altered by recreational use, industrial and urban development, and military activities. This is one reason that this species is listed as threatened, pursuant to the Federal Endangered Species Act.

Monterey spineflower

Menzies wallflower (*Erysimum menziesii*), a low-growing succulent herb, is a member of the mustard family. This species produces dense clusters of bright yellow, four-petaled flowers from February to April. The characteristic fleshy, spoon-shaped rosette leaves distinguish this coastal species from other wallflowers. Menzies wallflower is restricted to foredunes and dune scrub communities. Due to habitat degradation by commercial and residential development, off-road vehicle use, trampling by hikers and equestrians, and sand mining, the Menzies wallflower is listed as endangered by the U.S. Fish and Wildlife Service and the California Department of Fish and Game. Look for this beautiful showy wildflower at Asilomar dunes, where the California Department of Parks and Recreation has restored historic dune habitat.

Menzies wallflower

Monterey manzanita (*Arctostaphylos montereyensis*), also known as Toro manzanita, is a beautiful shrub species with evergreen leaves, slick reddish bark, and flowers that are tiny, sweet-smelling, and bell-shaped. This plant reaches a maximum height of three to seven feet and is a member of the heather family. It is endemic to Monterey County. Monterey manzanita is an indicator species of maritime chaparral, a habitat type that is limited to sandy soils. Manzanita berries are an important food source for birds and small mammals. The Spanish called the tiny red fruit of this coastal shrub *manzanita*, meaning "little apple."

Monterey manzanita

Eastwood's goldenbush

Eastwood's goldenbush (*Ericameria fasciculata*), also known as mock heather, is a compact, evergreen shrub, one to three-and-a-half feet tall, in the *Asteraceae*, or sunflower, family. It is endemic to the Monterey County dunes and sandy areas near the coast. Eastwood's goldenbush has resinous herbage, peeling bark, and green leaves clustered on the stem. The radiating, pale yellow flowers sit in terminal clusters of two to six flowers. The plant blooms from August to November and is ranked by the California Native Plant Society as extremely rare. When you walk in the dunes in the late summer or fall and spy a yellow-flowering shrub, it may be Eastwood's goldenbush.

Beach-primrose

Beach-primrose (*Camissonia cheiranthifolia*) has lovely flowers that are delicate in appearance, although the plant is adapted to a harsh environment. The beach and dunes hold precipitation poorly, and the sand on which beach-primrose grows can be alternately chilly and, on a bright day, blazing hot. The hairy, grayish leaves help to reflect solar rays. A central rosette of leaves hugs the strand. Prostrate stems spread out, allowing the sand beneath to shift. The petals, about half an inch long, bloom yellow and sometimes change to red as they age. The flowers close at night, providing an alternate name of beach evening primrose.

Smith's blue butterfly

Smith's blue butterfly (*Euphilotes enoptes smithi*) spends its entire life in association with two buckwheat plants in the genus *Eriogonum*. Emerging in late summer and early autumn, the adult butterflies mate and lay eggs on the flowers of these host plants. The eggs hatch shortly thereafter, and the larvae feed on the flowers of the plant. After several weeks of feeding and development, the larvae build cocoons, beginning a ten-month period of transformation. The next spring, when the buckwheat plants flower again, the adult butterflies emerge from the cocoons. Due to increasing automobile and foot traffic along the coast and the invasion of introduced plants, habitat for the Smith's blue butterfly has been degraded. This species was listed as endangered by the federal government in 1976. This butterfly is only about one inch across. The male's upper wings are vivid blue and the female's are dark brown with an orange band. Both sexes are pale and spotted underneath.

The **yellow-rumped warbler** (*Dendroica coronata*) is among the most common warblers in North America. Two forms are found in the continental U.S., the western Audubon's warbler (*auduboni* ssp.) and its eastern counterpart, Myrtle's warbler (*coronata* ssp.). The Audubon's warbler has a yellow throat, while the Myrtle's has a white throat. Yellow-rumped warblers occur in a wide variety of habitats including coastal dunes. Their main diet consists of insects, although they rely heavily on berries when insects are not available. They can be spotted picking at insects on washed-up seaweed at the beach.

Yellow-rumped warbler

Kangaroo rats are not related to the typical rat that most people imagine. The **Salinas kangaroo rat** (*Dipodomys heermanni goldmani*) occurs in maritime chaparral habitat with sandy soils. The kangaroo rat has big hind feet and a long tail to help it balance when it jumps along at night, gathering seeds. The kangaroo rat places the seeds into fur-lined pouches inside its cheeks and later deposits them in a storage area called a cache. The short forefeet have strong claws for digging burrows in the sand. Kangaroo rats construct elaborate burrow systems where they spend the day out of the heat, protected from predators. When they are done foraging at night and return to their burrows, they push up a little plug of sand in front of the burrow opening to deter intruders. The next time that you take a hike at Fort Ord look for a small burrow hole that appears to have been filled in, and you may be lucky enough to find the home of a Salinas kangaroo rat.

Salinas kangaroo rat

The **California legless lizard** (*Anniella pulchra*) is a burrowing reptile that looks like a snake and is about the size of a pencil. However, it is actually a lizard that has adapted to a legless condition to allow it to live a subterranean life in loose, sandy soil. The black morph of the legless lizard, formerly considered a separate subspecies and named *A. pulchra nigra*, lives in the dune habitat where there is moisture, warmth, loose material to burrow in, and plant cover. The legless lizard usually forages at the base of shrubs or other vegetation, either on the surface or just below it in leaf litter or sandy soil. It feeds mainly on insects, insect larvae, and spiders.

California legless lizard

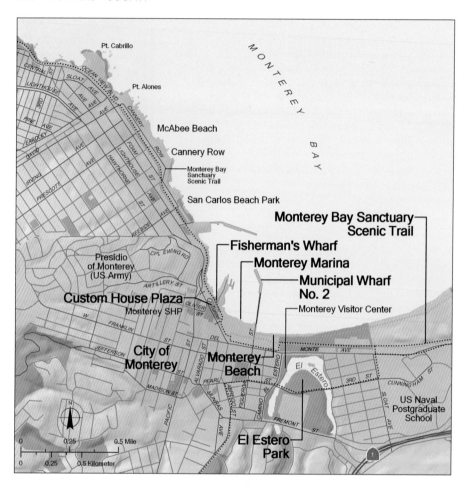

Pt. Cabrillo

Pt. Alones

McAbee Beach

Cannery Row

Monterey Bay
Sanctuary
Scenic Trail

San Carlos Beach Park

Monterey Bay Sanctuary Scenic Trail

Fisherman's Wharf

Presidio
of Monterey
(US Army)

Monterey Marina

Municipal Wharf No. 2

Custom House Plaza

Monterey SHP

Monterey Visitor Center

City of Monterey

Monterey Beach

US Naval Postgraduate School

El Estero Park

0   0.25   0.5 Mile

0   0.25   0.5 Kilometer

Monterey Bay Sanctuary Scenic Trail

Monterey Central

	Sandy Beach	Rocky Shore	Trail	Visitor Center	Campground	Wildlife Viewing	Fishing or Boating	Facilities for Disabled	Food and Drink	Restrooms	Parking	Fee
Monterey Bay Sanctuary Scenic Trail	•	•	•			•		•	•	•	•	
El Estero Park			•			•	•	•	•	•	•	
Monterey Beach	•		•				•	•		•	•	
Municipal Wharf No. 2							•	•	•	•	•	•
Monterey Marina							•	•				
Fisherman's Wharf						•	•	•	•	•	•	•
City of Monterey	•	•	•	•	•	•	•	•	•	•	•	
Custom House Plaza			•	•				•		•	•	

MONTEREY BAY SANCTUARY SCENIC TRAIL: *Parallel to waterfront, Monterey.* A paved bicycle path and trail runs along the old Southern Pacific Railroad right-of-way, from Marina and Seaside to Lovers Point in Pacific Grove; a link to Santa Cruz County is planned. The wheelchair-accessible trail runs near many of Monterey's most popular attractions.

EL ESTERO PARK: *Del Monte Ave. and Camino El Estero, Monterey.* A grassy city park inland of Del Monte Ave. features pedal boats on a lake and picnic areas. Dennis the Menace Playground contains a steam locomotive, a climbing wall, a pint-size maze, and other unusual play equipment. El Estero attracts ducks and other migratory birds; do not feed the birds. There is lake fishing from a pier off 3rd St.; no license required for anglers under 16. The Monterey Skate Park is located north of the ball field, next to the lake. For information, call: 831-646-3866.

MONTEREY BEACH: *Shoreline E. of Municipal Wharf No. 2, Monterey.* A broad sandy beach popular with sunbathers and kayakers. Sand volleyball courts, picnic facilities, and the Monterey Bay Sanctuary Scenic Trail are adjacent to the beach. A beach wheelchair is available at Monterey Bay Kayaks; call: 831-373-5357. The city of Monterey has expanded the Monterey Bay Waterfront Park along Del Monte Ave. as part of a project known as the Window on the Bay. The park offers fine views of Monterey Bay. For information, call: 831-646-3866.

MUNICIPAL WHARF NO. 2: *Foot of Figueroa St., Monterey.* An active commercial fishing operation is located at Municipal Wharf No. 2; sanddab, sole, squid, shrimp, salmon, rockfish, northern anchovy, and Pacific herring are unloaded here. Public facilities include restaurants, snack bar, and restrooms; metered parking. A three-ton capacity token-operated public boat hoist is available 24 hours a day; hoist use requires training. A 700-foot fishing promenade is on the east side of the wharf; no fishing license required for sport fishing. For information about the wharf, call: 831-646-3950.

MONTEREY MARINA: *Between Fisherman's Wharf and Municipal Wharf No. 2, Monterey.* The Municipal Marina has 413 slips up to 50 feet in length. Visiting boats may rent slips on a no-reservation basis; call the Harbormaster: 831-646-3950. Two public launch

Monterey Beach

Fisherman's Wharf

Kayak rentals, instruction, and wetsuit rentals are available on Monterey Beach, east of Municipal Wharf No. 2.

Sailboat rentals, fishing boat charters, and wildlife-watching trips are available from several vendors on Fisherman's Wharf.

Several shops in the downtown area rent bicycles and other recreational equipment.

The Monterey Sports Center at 301 E. Franklin St. has a swimming pool with water slide, gymnasium, tennis courts, locker rooms, café, and pro shop; fee for facility use. Call: 831-646-3700.

ramps are located next to the Harbormaster's office; no fee required. Metered parking is available for vehicles with boat trailers. The Monterey Harbor and Marina are open daily, 24 hours a day.

FISHERMAN'S WHARF: *Foot of Alvarado St., Monterey.* A wharf was constructed on the site in 1870 by the Pacific Coast Steamship Company, which provided passenger and freight service along the west coast of North America. In 1913, the city took over the facility, which came to be called Fisherman's Wharf. Sardines were big business; on some days, 10,000 or more cases of the canned fish were shipped from the wharf. Visitor-oriented uses came to predominate after World War II, when the sardine fishery collapsed due to overfishing. Fisherman's Wharf features restaurants, gift shops, art galleries, and tackle and bait shops. Harbor cruises and fishing and whale-watching trips can be arranged on the wharf. Fee parking.

CITY OF MONTEREY: *20 mi. S.W. of Salinas.* Monterey was California's political and social center until the gold rush of 1849, when San Francisco became the major port of trade. Once a port for New England hide and tallow traders, Monterey was also the site of a Portuguese shore whaling operation, a Chinese fishing village, and later, a world-renowned sardine canning industry. Tourism is the biggest industry now, and Monterey offers a wide range of visitor attractions.

CUSTOM HOUSE PLAZA: *Foot of Fisherman's Wharf, Monterey.* Custom House Plaza has been a focus of activity in Monterey since the city's early days; the Custom House was built in 1827. In the historic building now are the Pacific House Museum and the Monterey Museum of the American Indian. Open variable hours; call: 831-649-7118.

The Museum of Monterey, at 5 Custom House Plaza, holds the Allen Knight Collection of ship memorabilia and models. It has the Fresnel lens used for 90 years at Point Sur Lighthouse. Museum gift shop includes ship models. Open daily except Monday from 10 AM to 5 PM; for information, call: 831-372-2608. Fee for entry.

In August 1879, Scottish writer Robert Louis Stevenson took up residence in a boarding house in Monterey. Stevenson, then in his mid-20s, came to town in order to be near Fanny Vandegrift Osbourne, a married woman with whom he had commenced an affair several years earlier. The couple had met in France, where she was studying painting and he was pursuing the Bohemian life of a writer, rather than the career in engineering or law that his father might have preferred.

His journey from Scotland to Monterey provided material for Stevenson's strong storytelling skill and acute powers of observation. *Treasure Island*, his adventure story involving a buried fortune and a band of murderous, if comically inept, buccaneers, hints at a California connection. The reader is given to suppose that the locale is somewhere off South America, the area known by British pirates as the Spanish Main. But consider the words of Jim Hawkins, the story's youthful protagonist: "I have never seen the sea quiet round Treasure Island. The sun might blaze overhead, the air be without a breath, the surface smooth and blue, but still these great rollers would be running along all the external coast, thundering and thundering by day and night; and I scarce believe there is one spot in the island where a man would be out of earshot of their noise." Then compare to excerpts from a travel essay by Stevenson about Monterey: ". . . from all round, even in quiet weather, the low, distant, thrilling roar of the Pacific hangs over the coast and the adjacent country like smoke above a

battle." And—". . . go where you will, you have but to pause and listen to hear the voice of the Pacific."

In *Treasure Island*, Jim Hawkins remarks upon rattlesnakes and sea lions, both characteristic of the Monterey Peninsula but not native to the Caribbean, or Scotland. He describes unfamiliar vegetation: "Then I came to a long thicket of these oaklike trees—live, or evergreen, oaks, I heard afterwards they should be called—which grew low along the sand like brambles, the boughs curiously twisted, the foliage compact, like thatch." Elsewhere, Stevenson writes about Monterey: "The crouching, hardy, live oaks flourish singly or in thickets—the kind of wood for murderers to crawl among..." In short, the island of the novel, published several years after Stevenson visited California, sounds less like the palmy, tropical isles of the Caribbean than the pine-forested hills of Monterey.

Following her divorce, Fanny married Robert in 1880, and they settled eventually on the Pacific isle of Upolu, in Samoa. There Robert continued to write, and there he died in 1894. His grave lies on a luxuriantly forested promontory, above the little harbor town of Apia, facing the Monterey Peninsula across the wide Pacific Ocean. The early-19th-century adobe house where Stevenson stayed is at 530 Houston Street, part of the Monterey State Historic Park; call: 831-649-7118.

Stevenson House

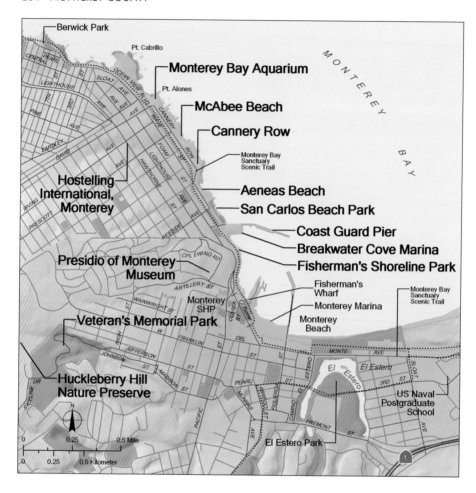

Berwick Park

Pt. Cabrillo

Monterey Bay Aquarium

M O N T E R E Y

Pt. Alones

McAbee Beach

Cannery Row

Monterey Bay
Sanctuary
Scenic Trail

B A Y

**Hostelling
International,
Monterey**

Aeneas Beach

San Carlos Beach Park

Coast Guard Pier

Breakwater Cove Marina

**Presidio of Monterey
Museum**

Fisherman's Shoreline Park

CPL EWING RD

ARTILLERY ST

Fisherman's
Wharf

Monterey Bay
Sanctuary
Scenic Trail

WAINWRIGHT ST

Monterey
SHP

Monterey Marina

Veteran's Memorial Park

W. FRANKLIN ST

Monterey
Beach

JEFFERSON ST

MONTE AVE

JOHNSON ST

El Estero

El Estero

3RD ST

SLOAT

**Huckleberry Hill
Nature Preserve**

PEARL ST

US Naval
Postgraduate
School

N

PACIFIC AVE

FREMONT ST

0   0.25   0.5 Mile

El Estero Park

0   0.25   0.5 Kilometer

1

Sea lions off Coast Guard Pier breakwater

Monterey and Cannery Row

	Sandy Beach	Rocky Shore	Trail	Visitor Center	Campground	Wildlife Viewing	Fishing or Boating	Facilities for Disabled	Food and Drink	Restrooms	Parking	Fee
Fisherman's Shoreline Park			•			•		•				
Breakwater Cove Marina							•	•	•	•	•	•
Coast Guard Pier						•	•	•	•	•	•	
San Carlos Beach Park	•					•	•		•	•		
Aeneas Beach	•											
Cannery Row	•	•	•			•		•	•	•	•	
McAbee Beach	•											
Monterey Bay Aquarium				•		•		•	•	•		•
Hostelling International, Monterey								•	•	•	•	
Presidio of Monterey Museum				•				•	•	•		
Veteran's Memorial Park					•			•	•	•		
Huckleberry Hill Nature Preserve		•				•						

FISHERMAN'S SHORELINE PARK: *Between the Coast Guard Pier and Fisherman's Wharf, Monterey.* Benches and viewpoints are located along a narrow coastline park that incorporates part of the Monterey Bay Sanctuary Scenic Trail. Look for harbor seals and sea lions in the harbor waters.

BREAKWATER COVE MARINA: *32 Cannery Row, Monterey.* Located on the downtown side of the Coast Guard Pier is a marina with 80 slips, a boat hoist, boat storage, and boat repair facility. Guest boat slips available. There is a restaurant and deli overlooking the water; diving equipment and kayak rentals are also found here. Call for marina information, Monday to Friday, 8 AM to 12 PM and 1 to 5 PM: 831-373-7857. Fuel dock open every day; call: 831-647-9402.

COAST GUARD PIER: *S.E. end of Wave St., Monterey.* The Coast Guard Pier is part wharf and part breakwater that shelters the Monterey Marina. The pier is home port for Coast Guard vessels; public access is permitted from sunrise to sunset. Fishing is permitted on the north side of the breakwater. At the foot of the breakwater is a launch ramp for trailered boats and other small craft; a boat hoist for larger boats is available at the ad-

jacent Breakwater Cove Marina. Restrooms and showers are located at the foot of the breakwater. Facilities open daily. A change machine at the entrance provides coins for the parking meters. The rock jetty extension of the 1,700-foot-long breakwater serves as a haul-out for hundreds of seals and noisy sea lions. Adjacent San Carlos Beach provides a popular sandy beach entry point for divers.

SAN CARLOS BEACH PARK: *Foot of Reeside Ave., Monterey.* At the east end of Cannery Row is a pleasant park with green lawns, picnic tables, and access to the sandy beach by stair and ramp. Restrooms and an out-

Monterey Bay Sanctuary Scenic Trail

door shower are available. Metered parking is adjacent. A popular beach and entry point for divers. At the west end of the beach, there is a public viewing deck overlooking the sea at the Monterey Bay Inn.

AENEAS BEACH: *400 Cannery Row, Monterey.* This sandy beach with rocky areas and tidepools can be reached by a stairway at the east end of the Monterey Plaza Hotel. A large public terrace, part of the hotel development, overlooks the beach, where divers sometimes enter the water. There is also access to a rocky promontory viewpoint via a walkway under the Chart House Restaurant, on the west side of the hotel. A public walkway, located on the ocean side of the hotel, connects the beach on the east with the viewpoint on the west.

CANNERY ROW: *Between David Ave. and Coast Guard Pier, Monterey.* The area was once the center of a thriving sardine canning industry started by Frank Booth, who built the first fish-packing plant near Fisherman's Wharf in 1902. In 1905 Knut Hovden from Norway modernized packing methods and developed a system for steam-cooking sardines that revolutionized the industry. Pietro Ferrante from Sicily introduced the lampara net in 1911, which greatly increased the sardine catch. Sardines were canned almost exclusively for human consumption until the end of World War I, when the price fell so low that an additional use was developed

Kayak trips from Cannery Row: A B Seas Kayaks, 1-800-979-3370.

Kayak and bicycle rentals: Adventures by the Sea, 831-372-1807.

by Booth. Sardine by-products, previously considered waste, were reduced to fish meal for animal feed, and oil for manufacturing soap, tires, paint, vitamins, and glycerine. As a result of this more efficient use of the fish, and the introduction of the purse seiner boat in 1928, the annual sardine catch jumped from 3,000 tons in 1916 to 250,000 tons in 1945.

The sardine industry peaked in 1945—the same year that John Steinbeck's novel *Cannery Row* was published; at that time 23 canneries and 19 reduction plants occupied nearly one mile of shoreline. The "silver harvest" continued, despite warnings of overfishing, until the sardines virtually disappeared in 1951. Too many fish were taken, but the plunge in sardine numbers appears also to be part of a natural up-and-down cycle lasting some 30 to 40 years, during which ocean temperatures and other conditions fluctuate. Pacific sardines are once again abundant, and the wild-caught fish are listed as a "best choice" on the Monterey Bay Aquarium's Seafood Guide.

Sea otters diving, Monterey Harbor

MCABEE BEACH: *Foot of Prescott Ave., Monterey.* The sandy beach where divers enter the water is reached by a stairway from Steinbeck Plaza and at either side of Spindrift Inn. Spindrift Inn provides a public outside shower on the bay side of the building.

MONTEREY BAY AQUARIUM: *Cannery Row at David Ave., Monterey.* The Monterey Bay Aquarium offers a unique introduction to the marine ecosystems of the bay and ocean. The internationally acclaimed aquarium contains numerous habitat displays, touch tanks, hands-on exhibits, an outdoor plaza overlooking Monterey Bay, a restaurant, a gift shop, and more. Fully wheelchair accessible. The aquarium is a nonprofit organization supported by entry fees and member contributions. Open daily except Christmas; for information, call the 24-hour information line at 831-648-4888. A free public viewpoint overlooking the bay is located next to the aquarium entrance, through the middle of the building. Offshore Point Cabrillo, the Edward F. Ricketts State Marine Conserva-

Monterey Bay Aquarium

Monterey Bay Aquarium, Kelp Forest exhibit

Cannery Row

tion Area limits the take of living marine resources and is one of several marine protected areas extending west past Point Pinos.

HOSTELLING INTERNATIONAL, MONTEREY: *778 Hawthorne St., Monterey.* The hostel is located in a renovated historic carpenter's union hall, four blocks from Cannery Row. Self-serve kitchen; dorm and private rooms offered. Groups welcome. Bicycle rentals and free Wi-Fi available; wheelchair-accessible facilities; free parking. For information, call: 831-649-0375.

PRESIDIO OF MONTEREY MUSEUM: *Corporal Ewing Rd. near Artillery St., Presidio of Monterey.* The city of Monterey manages a 26-acre park on the grounds of the historic Presidio of Monterey. The original Presidio, whose ruins are located downtown off Church and Figueroa Streets, was built in 1770; it was one of four major Spanish military forts built in California between 1769 and 1797. El Castillo was a fortification built in 1792 on a hill overlooking Monterey Bay to protect the Presidio. The present Presidio was built by the U.S. Army in 1902 on the site of El Castillo.

The military history of the area is the focus of the Presidio of Monterey Museum, locat-

ed on Corporal Ewing Rd. near Artillery St. and operated by the city of Monterey. Open Monday, 10 AM to 1 PM; Thursday to Saturday, 10 AM to 4 PM; and Sunday, 1 to 4 PM. Free admission. Call: 831-646-3456.

VETERAN'S MEMORIAL PARK: *W. end of Jefferson St., Monterey.* This delightful city park set high on a hill above downtown Monterey offers picnic areas and children's play equipment set among expansive lawns and a 40-site campground for tents or RVs up to 21 feet long. Hike or bike campers welcome. One campsite is wheelchair accessible. Restrooms, showers, and RV dump station available. Family campsites are first-come, first-served; youth group campsites and group picnic areas can be reserved in advance. Fee for camping. A park attendant resides in the park; call: 831-646-3865.

HUCKLEBERRY HILL NATURE PRESERVE: *Presidio of Monterey, W. of Veteran's Memorial Park.* Enter this city-run open space area through adjacent Veteran's Memorial Park. The 80-acre open space area, leased by the city of Monterey from the U.S. Army, contains hiking trails through Monterey pine forest and maritime chaparral. Fine filtered views of Monterey Bay through the trees. Call: 831-646-3865.

Between Point Alones (Abalone Point), where the Monterey Bay Aquarium now stands, and nearby Point Cabrillo (formerly called China Point), on a cove with a sandy beach suitable for hauling shallow boats, was once the biggest Chinese fishing village in the Monterey Bay region. This community was first settled in the 1850s by Chinese immigrants and at its largest was home to several hundred people.

Taking advantage of the abundance of sea life off Monterey's shores, the residents of the Point Alones village gathered, dried, packaged, and exported many tons of seafood, thereby pioneering Monterey's renowned commercial fishing industry. While they fished for a wide variety of species, they found a niche in squid. They hunted them from their boats at night, using small fires to lure the squid to the water's surface. Local residents enjoyed watching the fires on the water after dark, and the present-day lit boat parade at Pacific Grove's annual Feast of Lanterns festival echoes that spectacle.

Fishermen who brought their wives from China were helped by their family members. While it was illegal for Chinese immigrants to become American citizens, their American-born offspring had U.S. citizenship, and so children born at Point Alones were some of California's first Chinese Americans. The Point Alones fishermen also gathered abalone, and some fellow Chinese fishers near 17-Mile Drive sold abalone shells to tourists at roadside stands, foreshadowing the souvenir shops now common in the area.

Because it resembled an authentic Chinese village, the Point Alones settlement itself became a tourist attraction. But despite Lunar New Year celebrations and gifts enjoyed by neighboring Caucasians, the village was not popular in the community, due to anti-Chinese sentiment and the very strong, fishy odor that came from seafood drying on racks, roofs, and other available surfaces. Residents were finally told they had to leave by the Pacific Improvement Company, the village's landowner and a subsidiary of the Southern Pacific Railroad, which had tracks running through the site. Then in May 1906, as residents were resisting moving, a fast-moving fire burned the village down. Despite speculation that it was purposely set, no evidence was discovered to officially determine the cause.

For another year, some strong-willed residents stayed in the few buildings that had not burned, until finally they were allowed to relocate their community to nearby McAbee Beach. But that Chinatown never grew as large, and the number of fishermen dropped considerably. The site occupied by the Point Alones village now belongs to Stanford University's Hopkins Marine Station.

Children at Chinese fishing village near Point Alones ca. 1900

Monterey Bay Aquarium

TANKS of shimmering anchovies, ethereal jellies, and shape-changing octopuses provide a glimpse into the world within Monterey Bay and the Pacific Ocean. The richness of life in the sea along California's Central Coast, and beyond, is on display at the Monterey Bay Aquarium. The fascination of learning about plants and animals that few will ever see in their native habitat is matched, for many of us, by astonishment at the brilliant colors and unexpected forms of the organisms on display.

When it opened in 1984, the Monterey Bay Aquarium was an instant hit; by 2010, more than 48 million visitors had viewed its varied exhibits. Founders Lucile and David Packard provided funds for initial construction, and subsequent expansion projects have made room for many more displays. The aquarium occupies a site on Monterey's Cannery Row on which a major fish cannery once stood. Opened in 1916 by Knut Hovden, the cannery processed sardines here until 1973. In the peak years of the 1940s, the sardine industry in Monterey processed 250,000 tons of fish each year.

The Monterey Bay Aquarium is a world leader in marine education and conservation. The aquarium has won awards for its exhibits and has many innovations to its credit, including the first living kelp forest display in an aquarium. Unlike many old-style aquariums, the Monterey Bay Aquarium displays fish, invertebrates, plants, and other organisms in contexts that match their origin, rather than divided by species among separate tanks. The million-gallon Open Sea exhibit, in the space formerly devoted to the Outer Bay, displays a world of marine life that is in constant motion. Long-distance migrators, such as green sea turtles, can be viewed along with deep-sea stingrays and enormous ocean sunfish, known as mola mola. A thick sheet of acrylic plastic measuring 15 by 54 feet—the largest window in the world when installed in 1996—provides a clear view of ocean resources found off California's coast. The Mission to the Deep

Bubble windows offer a unique perspective on sea life in the Monterey Bay Habitats exhibit.

Visitors can watch three daily feeding and training sessions at the sea otter exhibit.

exhibit has highlighted research efforts of the Monterey Bay Aquarium Research Institute among the strange life forms found at the bottom of the Monterey Bay Submarine Canyon. In another special exhibit, vibrantly colored coral reefs and hot pink flamingos have helped tell the story of global climate change.

There are more than 550 species on display at the Monterey Bay Aquarium, in nearly 200 galleries and exhibits. A constant stream of sea water is pumped through the aquarium's displays, filtered during the day to keep the exhibits as clear as possible, and unfiltered at night to provide the plankton and larvae that are food sources for many of the aquarium's inhabitants and that colonize the exhibit rockwork, contributing to its natural appearance. The water is kept at temperatures that match those of the habitats of the species on display.

Southern sea otters, with a population in the wild of fewer than 3,000 animals, are among the aquarium's most popular residents. Most are pups that were rescued after becoming accidentally separated from their mothers in the wild. Sea otters at the Monterey Bay Aquarium have the appearance, and sometimes the behavior, of furry rascals: they have unscrewed or unbolted parts of their exhibit, scratched the acrylic windows with shells, and tucked toys in water pipes. The aquarium's Sea Otter Research and Conservation program has rehabilitated injured sea otters and returned them to the wild.

As extensive as the aquarium's collections are, some notable species are not included. Whales, dolphins, and sea lions may be seen outside the aquarium, often not far from its ocean-view decks overlooking Monterey Bay.

The aquarium's very informative website, at www.montereybayaquarium.org, includes an on-line field guide, with photos and information on hundreds of species that inhabit

Kids get suited up to become "Underwater Explorers" during a summer program at the aquarium.

the deep sea, the sea floor, coastal wetlands, rocky shore, and other habitats. Selected past exhibits at the aquarium are still viewable on the website. Video cameras stream live action from several current exhibits, which in the past have featured sharks, penguins, and the kelp forest, as well as from Monterey Bay itself. The aquarium's popular Seafood Watch program provides recommendations to diners about the sustainability of various market fish; a smartphone application enables users to tag restaurants that serve ocean-friendly seafood.

Learning resources available on the aquarium's website include activities that families and schoolchildren can do in conjunction with a visit, or in place of a visit. The very popular Underwater Explorers program offers aquarium visitors ages 8 to 13 an opportunity to accompany staff on a "dive" using SCUBA equipment in the aquarium tide pool. Other adventure programs include sailing excursions on Monterey Bay. Family sleepovers allow visitors to enjoy an evening film followed by a night spent in front of a favorite aquarium exhibit.

The aquarium conducts research in conjunction with Stanford University's Hopkins Marine Station, located nearby in Pacific Grove. Research subjects include tuna in the world's oceans and white sharks, which inhabit the waters off California as well as many other places around the world. In addition to paid staff, the nonprofit aquarium relies on the efforts of more than 1,000 volunteers.

The aquarium's independent sister institution, the Monterey Bay Aquarium Research Institute (www.mbari.org), was founded in 1987 by David Packard with a mission to carry on a range of research projects related to ocean science. The institute's studies address marine biology, the geology of the deep sea, climate studies, and new techniques for observing conditions in the deep ocean, among other topics. One research project has investigated the effects of increasing carbon dioxide in the atmosphere, while another has studied the dynamics of the coastal upwelling phenomenon along

California's coast that brings nutrients from the deep sea to the surface. The Monterey Bay Aquarium Research Institute is located at Moss Landing.

The Monterey Bay Aquarium opens every day at 9:30 AM during the summer months and on holidays and at 10 AM the rest of the year; closing time varies seasonally from 5 PM to 8 PM. Closed on December 25. Fee for entry. Same-day tickets are available at the aquarium; advance tickets are recommended during the summer and on holidays. Call the 24-hour information line at 831-648-4888 for information in English or Spanish. All exhibits are accessible to visitors with disabilities; a wheelchair may be borrowed from the information desk. A free trolley provided by Monterey-Salinas Transit links the Monterey Bay Aquarium to Fisherman's Wharf and downtown Monterey during the summertime and on holidays; a second summertime trolley route connects the Aquarium with downtown Pacific Grove. For information, call: 831-899-2555.

Leopard sharks cruise a wetland pool in the Coastal Wetland to Sandy Shore exhibit in the Ocean's Edge wing.

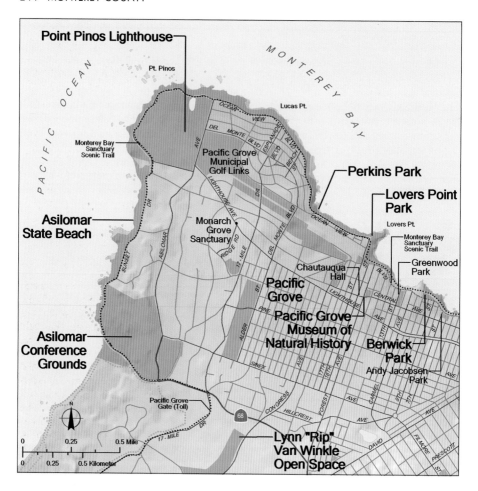

Point Pinos Lighthouse

PACIFIC OCEAN

MONTEREY BAY

Pt. Pinos

Lucas Pt.

Monterey Bay
Sanctuary
Scenic Trail

Pacific Grove
Municipal
Golf Links

Perkins Park

Lovers Point
Park

Lovers Pt.

Asilomar
State Beach

Monarch
Grove
Sanctuary

Monterey Bay
Sanctuary
Scenic Trail

Greenwood
Park

Chautauqua
Hall

Pacific
Grove

Pacific Grove
Museum of
Natural History

Berwick
Park

Asilomar
Conference
Grounds

Andy Jacobsen
Park

Pacific Grove
Gate (Toll)

68

Lynn "Rip"
Van Winkle
Open Space

0   0.25   0.5 Mile

0   0.25   0.5 Kilometer

Pelicans off Pacific Grove shore

Pacific Grove

	Sandy Beach	Rocky Shore	Trail	Visitor Center	Campground	Wildlife Viewing	Fishing or Boating	Facilities for Disabled	Food and Drink	Restrooms	Parking	Fee
Pacific Grove	•	•	•	•		•	•	•	•	•	•	
Berwick Park		•	•									
Lovers Point Park	•	•	•				•	•	•	•	•	
Perkins Park	•	•	•								•	
Pacific Grove Museum of Natural History				•				•		•	•	
Point Pinos Lighthouse				•	•						•	
Asilomar State Beach	•	•	•		•			•		•	•	
Asilomar Conference Grounds				•				•	•	•	•	•
Lynn "Rip" Van Winkle Open Space		•				•				•		

PACIFIC GROVE: *N.W. of the city of Monterey.* This residential community was founded as a Methodist retreat and tent city in 1875 and incorporated in 1889. The first Chautauqua in the West was organized here in 1879—a nationwide summer educational program with lectures and entertainment; Chautauqua Hall at 16th St. and Central Ave. is a State Historical Landmark and is still used for dances and other events. A Victorian Home Tour is held each October; call: 831-373-3304. The Pacific Grove Municipal Golf Links, at 77 Asilomar Ave., is an oceanfront 18-hole course, with white water views, pro shop, restaurant, and more affordable fees than other Monterey Peninsula courses; for information, call: 831-648-5775.

Monarch butterfly

Beginning in October, thousands of monarch butterflies overwinter in Pacific Grove in native Monterey pine trees and introduced eucalyptus trees, collectively called "butterfly trees." The number of monarchs arriving each fall has declined since the 1990s, due perhaps to loss of habitat and of milkweed plants, a prime food source. Monarch viewing areas include a city-owned sanctuary off Ridge Rd. near Lighthouse Ave. and George Washington Park at Alder St. and Pine Ave.; the park also has a picnic area, restrooms, children's play facilities, and a baseball field.

The community of Pacific Grove is proud of its scenic shoreline. A series of city parks follow the blufftop above the town's rocky coast. The paved Monterey Bay Sanctuary Scenic Trail, serving bicyclists and pedestrians, connects sites around Monterey Bay and runs through Pacific Grove as far west as Lovers Point. From there to Point Pinos and beyond, the shoreline is publicly owned and bordered by a shorefront path. Stairs at several locations allow access to Pacific Grove's pocket beaches. Offshore waters are part of the Monterey Bay National Marine Sanctuary. Blue-jacketed volunteer docents from Bay Net, a Sanctuary affiliate, are often present along the Monterey Bay Sanctuary Scenic Trail, where they provide information to visitors about marine resources.

BERWICK PARK: *Along Ocean View Blvd. between Carmel Ave. and 9th St., Pacific Grove.*

In 1542, Juan Rodríguez Cabrillo may have landed at the nearby point, now named for him. Part green lawn and part native plant landscaping, this small city park offers dramatic vistas of Monterey Bay and Pacific Grove's rocky shoreline. A paved pedestrian and bicycle path extends through the park, with benches scattered along it. Street parking. Two nearby city parks, both located on the inland side of Ocean View Blvd., offer additional open space and views: Andy Jacobsen Park is at the foot of 7th St. and Greenwood Park is at the foot of 13th St.

LOVERS POINT PARK: *End of 17th St. at Ocean View Blvd., Pacific Grove.* A grassy blufftop park dotted with Monterey cypress trees is situated on this rocky point. Paths along a seawall overlook the water. A short concrete pier structure on the east side of the point separates two small, protected sandy beaches, accessible by stairs. These beaches provide one of the few safe swimming areas along Monterey County's shoreline and are extremely popular. Other park activities include picnicking, sunning, fishing, surfing, and diving. Facilities include benches, picnic tables, barbecue grills, and restrooms. A sand volleyball court and children's swimming pool are also provided, and there is a restaurant and snack bar. Kayak and bicycle rentals available in the park. Parking at the corner of Ocean View Blvd. and 17th St. The park is managed by the city of Pacific Grove; call: 831-648-5730.

PERKINS PARK: *Along Ocean View Blvd., N.W. of Lovers Point, Pacific Grove.* Perkins Park occupies the shoreline to the west of Lovers Point. Paths wind through the colorful, but nonnative, ice plant. Benches are sited to take in the wonderful views of surf, rocky coast, and bay. Mostly street parking; there is a small parking lot at the foot of Beach St. and another at the foot of Asilomar Ave., where there are picnic tables and grills. Four stairways provide access to small pocket beaches. Undeveloped Esplanade Park is located at Esplanade and Ocean View Boulevards.

PACIFIC GROVE MUSEUM OF NATURAL HISTORY: *Forest Ave. at Central Ave., Pacific Grove.* The museum features the natural history of the Monterey area, with exhibits on wildlife, local geology, and the history of the area's indigenous peoples. A California native garden features plants of local ecosystems, including coastal scrub, chaparral, and oak woodland. The museum includes a volunteer-staffed gift shop. For information, call: 831-648-5716. Open Tuesday through Sunday, from 10 AM to 5 PM, except major holidays. Donation suggested.

Pacific Grove

POINT PINOS LIGHTHOUSE: *Asilomar Ave., S. of Ocean View Blvd., Pacific Grove.* Point Pinos, or Pine Point, is the rocky, low-lying northerly tip of the Monterey Peninsula. Sea stars, snails, black abalone, and marine algae inhabit the tidepools; whales and pelagic birds can be seen from the point. The Asilomar State Marine Reserve, designated by the California Department of Fish and Game, prohibits the take of all living marine resources from Point Pinos to Asilomar State Beach. Offshore rocks, islets, and exposed reefs off Point Pinos and elsewhere along the state's coast are part of the California Coastal National Monument.

Point Pinos Lighthouse, built in 1885, is the oldest continuously operating lighthouse on the West Coast. The Fresnel lens of the third order, meaning of medium size and focal length, was manufactured in France in 1853. At first, the light source was a lantern fueled by whale oil, followed by lard oil and later kerosene. The lamp is now a 1,000-watt electric bulb that produces a beacon visible up to 17 miles at sea. Open Thursday through Monday, from 1 to 4 PM. Donation requested; for information, call: 831-648-3176.

ASILOMAR STATE BEACH: *W. of Sunset Dr., Pacific Grove.* Asilomar State Beach includes rugged rocky shore, tidepools, sandy beach, and dunes. Inland of the dunes is Monterey pine forest; look for acorn woodpeckers among the trees. Past practices of livestock grazing and uncontrolled public access caused significant damage to the sand dune environment. The area has been revegetated by the Department of Parks and Recreation, and a wheelchair-accessible boardwalk has been installed to lead visitors through the dunes without damage to the habitat.

On Asilomar Beach, the distinctive white sand comes from local granodiorite rocks, which are weathered and broken down by the surf. A free beach wheelchair for use on the sand and boardwalk may be reserved in advance; call: 831-372-8016. Do not disturb plants or creatures in the tidepools. No fires on the beach; dogs must be on a six-foot leash. Parking areas are spaced along Sunset Dr. For state beach information, call: 831-646-6440.

ASILOMAR CONFERENCE GROUNDS: *Asilomar Ave. at Sunset Dr., Pacific Grove.* Asilomar means "refuge by the sea," and this state park conference center is a popular retreat destination. The facility began as a Young Women's Christian Association (YWCA) camp, with Arts and Crafts–style structures designed by Julia Morgan, a renowned California architect and designer of Hearst Castle. In 1951, the property became a unit of the state park system. Meeting rooms and overnight lodging are available for group events; guest rooms and meals are also available to individuals. Guest rooms are simple, but have private baths; some have fireplaces. For reservations, call: 888-635-5310.

LYNN "RIP" VAN WINKLE OPEN SPACE: *Congress Ave. between Sunset Dr. and Forest Lodge Rd., Pacific Grove.* This open space park contains native Monterey pine, Monterey cypress, and coast live oak trees. Walking paths through the trees; dogs allowed off-leash. Street parking. From the Open Space, there is free pedestrian access to the Del Monte Forest and 17-Mile Dr. via the Country Club Gate.

Asilomar State Beach

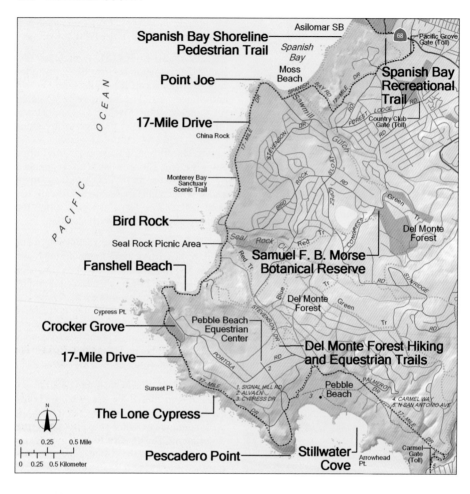

Fanshell Beach

17-Mile Drive

	Sandy Beach	Rocky Shore	Trail	Visitor Center	Campground	Wildlife Viewing	Fishing or Boating	Facilities for Disabled	Food and Drink	Restrooms	Parking	Fee
Spanish Bay Recreational Trail			•									
Spanish Bay Shoreline Pedestrian Trail	•	•	•									
Point Joe		•	•			•					•	
17-Mile Drive	•	•	•			•	•		•	•	•	•
Bird Rock		•				•	•		•	•		
Fanshell Beach	•					•				•		
Crocker Grove										•		
The Lone Cypress		•								•		
Pescadero Point		•								•		
Stillwater Cove	•						•		•	•		
Del Monte Forest Hiking and Equestrian Trails			•									
Samuel F. B. Morse Botanical Reserve			•			•				•		

SPANISH BAY RECREATIONAL TRAIL: *Sunset Dr. and Asilomar Ave., Pacific Grove.* A pedestrian and bicycle path starts at Sunset Dr. and Asilomar Ave. and extends into the Del Monte Forest, connecting with 17-Mile Dr. The trail passes through native Monterey pine forest inland of the Inn at Spanish Bay; picnic tables are located along the way. Where the trail merges with 17-Mile Dr., bicyclists may continue along the road, a designated bicycle route. No entrance fee to the 17-Mile Dr. for pedestrians and bicyclists.

SPANISH BAY SHORELINE PEDESTRIAN TRAIL: *Sunset Dr., W. of Asilomar Ave., Pacific Grove.* A pedestrian boardwalk runs seaward of the Spanish Bay golf course, starting at Asilomar State Beach; shoulder parking. From the boardwalk, short paths provide access to the broad, fine-grained sandy beach known as Moss Beach. To protect native dune vegetation, stay on the boardwalk. At the Spanish Bay picnic area on 17-Mile Dr., the boardwalk turns into a packed path and continues south along the shoreline as far as the Seal Rock picnic area. The path offers many scenic vistas of pocket beaches and offshore rocks. At the Spanish Bay picnic area and at Seal Rock Creek, the trail connects with the Del Monte Forest Hiking and Equestrian Trail network, which continues inland.

POINT JOE: *S.W. of Moss Beach, 17-Mile Dr.* Point Joe marks the south end of Spanish Bay. The site of several shipwrecks, the area directly offshore here experiences unusual wave patterns and turbulence resulting from ocean bottom topography and the meeting of ocean swells and currents. Two parking areas with viewing areas; a packed-earth path parallels the shore. Brandt's cormorants and other seabirds roost on nearby offshore rocks.

17-MILE DRIVE: *Between Pacific Grove and Carmel, Del Monte Forest.* This famous scenic drive traverses the edge of the Monterey Peninsula, past well-known attractions. The privately owned 17-Mile Dr. and Del Monte Forest have five entrance gates where a toll is charged for vehicles; pedestrians and bicyclists enter free. Overlooks, picnic areas, and trails along the 17-Mile Dr. are available for public use, and several golf courses and the Pebble Beach Equestrian Center are open to the public for a fee. Call: 831-647-7500.

The privately held Pacific Improvement Company opened a road in 1881 for use by guests at Monterey's Del Monte Hotel, now the Naval Postgraduate School. Horse-drawn coaches made a 17-mile round trip from Monterey along the coast of Pacific Grove, south to the Carmel Mission, and back over Carmel Hill to Monterey. The wooded area between Pacific Grove and Carmel became known as the Del Monte Forest. A stop on the tour was Pebble Beach, site of the famous golf course that opened to the public in 1919. Today's 17-Mile Dr. is part of the original sightseeing route.

Samuel F. B. Morse, the grandnephew of the inventor of Morse code, acquired the Del Monte Forest in 1919. Morse subdivided the land while preserving much of the Monterey pine and Monterey cypress tree forest. Today, the Del Monte Forest is a private community managed by the Pebble Beach Company and developed with elaborate homes of many styles, golf courses, and hiking and equestrian trails.

BIRD ROCK: *S. of Point Joe, 17-Mile Dr.* Bird Rock and neighboring Seal Rock are hauling-out grounds for harbor seals and California sea lions. The nearshore rocks also provide summer roosting sites for brown pelicans and nesting areas for Brandt's cormorants. The Seal Rock picnic area, overlooking the ocean and nearshore rocks, has tables and restrooms. A wheelchair-accessible path runs along the shoreline from Seal Rock Creek north to the Spanish Bay picnic area.

FANSHELL BEACH: *Signal Hill Rd. and 17-Mile Dr.* Sea otters frequent the crescent-shaped cove offshore from this sandy beach, and harbor seals give birth to their young here in the spring. The Fanshell Beach overlook is closed during the harbor seal pupping season, from April 1 to June 1. Pink sand verbena and the endangered Menzies wallflower occur on the dunes, which provide habitat for the black legless lizard.

CROCKER GROVE: *S.E. of Cypress Point, 17-Mile Dr.* Native Monterey pine and Monterey cypress trees can be viewed from the margin of this 13-acre reserve; a small parking area is located on 17-Mile Dr. The nearby Cypress Point lookout offers a well-known, but somewhat constricted, view across Carmel Bay.

THE LONE CYPRESS: *S.E. of Cypress Point, 17-Mile Dr.* A solitary Monterey cypress tree clinging to a granite headland is a highly popular attraction for photographers and artists. Perhaps the best view is from the observation platform at the southeast end of the viewing area.

PESCADERO POINT: *1.5 mi. S.E. of Cypress Point, 17-Mile Dr.* Pescadero Point, a blufftop overlook with a rocky shore and tidepools below, marks the northern tip of Carmel Bay. Just north of the point is the Ghost Tree, a Monterey cypress named for its bleached-white twisted trunk and gnarled branches shaped over time by wind and sea spray. Author Robert Louis Stevenson described Monterey cypress trees as "ghosts fleeing before the wind." No fishing or picnicking allowed at the viewpoint.

STILLWATER COVE: *End of Cypress Dr., off 17-Mile Dr., Del Monte Forest.* A small sandy beach and pier are located near the Lodge at Pebble Beach. Stillwater Cove Beach pro-

Pebble Beach ca. 1910

Bird Rock

vides diving access to Stillwater Cove, which is protected from northwest swells by Pescadero Point. The rocky substrate of the cove supports giant kelp, puffball sponges, sunflower stars, and sea hares.

Entrance to the beach is through the parking lot of the private Beach and Tennis Club at the foot of Cypress Drive. Divers or visitors with hand-launched boats may drive into the designated loading area in the Beach and Tennis Club to drop off or pick up equipment only; public parking is available nearby. As you approach the Beach and Tennis Club on Cypress Dr., turn right and park along the hedge. Ten spaces are available at no charge for public beach parking. Occasional special events may limit road access; call: 831-625-8536. An additional six parking spaces for beach users are located in the surface lot next to the tennis courts on Palmero Way, and more spaces for beach users are located in the parking structure next to Casa Palmero. West (upcoast) of the Lodge at Pebble Beach, a public access path leads to a blufftop overlook with sweeping views of Stillwater Cove and the Pebble Beach Golf Links.

DEL MONTE FOREST HIKING AND EQUES-TRIAN TRAILS: *Off 17-Mile Dr., Del Monte Forest.* A 25-mile network of riding and hiking trails leads through the forest. The color-coded trails are marked by wooden posts or small "blazers" mounted on trees; the longest trail, marked with green, loops from the Spanish Bay picnic area uphill to the Samuel F. B. Morse Botanical Reserve and back to the shoreline. Ask at a Del Monte Forest entrance gate for a trail map, or inquire at the Pebble Beach Equestrian Center, Portola Rd. near Stevenson Dr. Open from 8:30 AM to 5:30 PM; call: 831-624-2756.

SAMUEL F. B. MORSE BOTANICAL RESERVE: *Bird Rock Rd. and Congress Rd., Del Monte Forest.* The forest on Huckleberry Hill includes native Monterey pine trees, growing here in an unusual association with bishop pines, and the endangered Gowen cypress, which occurs naturally only at this location and at Point Lobos State Natural Reserve. Huckleberry Hill is an ancient marine terrace, some 800 feet above sea level, containing poorly drained claypan soils that support a stunted community, or "pygmy forest," of bishop pine and Gowen cypress. The reserve is maintained primarily to protect endangered native plants, but several hiking trails start at Congress Rd. near Bird Rock Rd. and lead through the two parcels of land that make up the reserve. The forest is a hazardous fire area; no smoking or campfires of any kind are permitted. Managed by the Del Monte Forest Foundation; call: 831-373-1293.

Monterey Pine Forest

MONTEREY PINES have been planted widely in many parts of the state and around the world. The significance of the native Monterey pine forest on California's Central Coast is somewhat obscured by the everyday appearance of the trees. Furthermore, the natural beauty of the Monterey pine forest in its grand coastal setting tends to overshadow its importance as a "gene bank" and a key component of a unique web of plant and animal life. On the Monterey Peninsula, the Monterey pine forest is associated with at least 19 plant species and 17 wildlife species that are designated as having special status, due to their rarity or significance.

The Monterey pine forest grows on the Monterey Peninsula, which enjoys a cool, maritime climate influenced by onshore breezes and the upwelling of cold ocean waters from arms of the deep Monterey Submarine Canyon that hug the peninsula. The area's modest rainfall of 15 to 20 inches per year occurs mostly in the winter months, but summertime fog drip provides significant additional precipitation. Monterey pine trees, and the Monterey cypress trees that also grow on the Monterey Peninsula, once occupied a much wider territory. When the California coast became hotter and drier between 8,000 and 4,000 years ago, Monterey pines persisted in three locations: the Monterey Peninsula, Año Nuevo Point near the San Mateo/Santa Cruz County line, and Cambria in San Luis Obispo County. Monterey pines are also found on two islands off the coast of Baja California.

The Monterey pine is a closed-cone conifer, meaning that its seeds are held closely on the cones, sometimes for years, until released by very hot weather or a fire. Following a light ground fire, pine seedlings sprout readily after being watered by winter rains. As development of homes and golf courses in the Monterey pine forest has taken place, fires have been suppressed, and reproduction of the native trees has suffered.

As restricted as it is, the Monterey pine forest found on the Monterey Peninsula has at least 11 distinct subtypes differentiated in part by soil type, including marine terrace deposits, dunes, alluvial deposits, and soils over shale and granite bedrock. On the Monterey Peninsula there are six marine terraces, and Monterey pines are found on all of them. The first terrace, the one closest to the shoreline, is the youngest. Farther from the shoreline, the terraces are progressively older and higher. This configuration of landforms is known as an "ecological staircase." Sand dunes, also of varying age, have accumulated on parts of the first, second, third, and fourth marine terraces, and Monterey pine trees occur on parts of these dunes. On the fifth marine terrace at an elevation of 320 to 540 feet, Monterey pines are somewhat stunted in size and mixed with coast live oak and stands of bishop pine forest. The Monterey pine trees grow to their fullest size locally, 80 to 100 feet tall, on the shale and granitic bedrock soils. Some researchers think that the forest subtypes are disjunctive and correspond to the marine terraces, whereas others see a simple gradient in forest characteristics. In any event, the Monterey pine forest is remarkably variable in growth characteristics and understory associations.

Monterey pine, called radiata pine or New Zealand pine in the timber industry, is a major commercial species in New Zealand, Australia, Chile, Spain, Kenya, South Africa, and elsewhere. There are nearly 10 million acres of commercial stands of the pine, which is the world's most-planted conifer. Monterey pine trees planted in New Zealand reach close to 200 feet tall. Artificially selected trees attain heights of over 100 feet in little more than 20 years, and trees reach maturity in less than 30 years. Given ample moisture and the warm temperatures of the tropics or subtropics, Monterey pines grow year-round and exhibit wood that lacks annual rings. The commercial appeal of the species comes from its rapid growth, large size when growing conditions are ideal, and high-quality lumber. Monterey pine plantations are a mixed blessing in the countries where they are grown. On the one hand, they probably have prevented the lumbering of many thousands of acres of native forests; on the other hand, they are exotic invaders of those same forests.

The world's commercial forests of Monterey pine trees differ from the few relict, native stands in California and Baja California not only in their appearance, but also in the fact that the farmed stands are restricted genetically, having been propagated selectively for fast, tall growth. The tree farms thus lack the genetic variability of the native Monterey pine forest. The preservation of a bank of different strains of Monterey pines is all the more important because of the challenge presented by pine pitch canker, a fungal disease that attacks Monterey pines and for which there is no available treatment. Since 1992, the forest on the Monterey Peninsula has been attacked by pine pitch canker. Some trees appear to be tolerant of the disease, however, suggesting that the genetic diversity of the native Monterey pine trees may one day help provide solutions for this and other tree diseases in Monterey and around the world.

Monterey pine forest community, Samuel F. B. Morse Botanical Reserve

Monterey pine

The **Monterey pine** (*Pinus radiata*) is closely related to bishop pine and knobcone pine, however it is distinguished from the former by having needles in groups of threes, and from both by having blunt scales on the cone. All three of these pine species are known as closed-cone pines. The cones of Monterey pine remain closed until opened by the heat of a forest fire; the abundant seeds are then discharged and begin a new forest. The cones may also burst open, with a snapping sound, in hot weather. The Monterey pine can be seen at many locations on the Monterey Peninsula. Point Lobos State Reserve is a great place to hike in a Monterey pine forest.

Monterey cypress

The **Monterey cypress** (*Cupressus macrocarpa*) occurs naturally in only two groves near Monterey. These native groves are protected within the Point Lobos State Reserve and the Del Monte Forest at Cypress Point. The trees grow on the exposed rocky headlands along the ocean. If you take a walk along the coast at Point Lobos you will see that the cypress trees, subjected to the constant sea breeze and salt spray, grow in a unique twisted and contorted fashion. The Costanoan Indians were known to make a decoction of Monterey cypress foliage to treat rheumatism. Although the Monterey cypress is widely planted as a landscape tree, the California Native Plant Society considers this a rare species, based on its limited natural occurrence.

Yadon's rein orchid

Yadon's rein orchid (*Piperia yadonii*), also known as Yadon's piperia, was first collected in 1925 in open pine forest near the town of Pacific Grove. At that time, it was identified as *Piperia unalascensis*. In a recent taxonomic analysis of the genus, two new species were identified. One of these, *P. yadonii*, was named after Vern Yadon, former director of the Museum of Natural History in Pacific Grove. As with other orchids, germination of Yadon's rein orchid seeds likely involves a symbiotic relationship with a fungus. One to several years after germination, orchid seedlings produce their first basal leaves. Yadon's rein orchid is found within Monterey pine forest and maritime chaparral communities in northern coastal Monterey County. This lovely orchid is listed as endangered under the federal Endangered Species Act.

Like most owls, the **great horned owl** (*Bubo virginianus*) is active at night and is almost silent in flight. This majestic and stately bird has large tufts of feathers on its head that look like horns. These feathers are sometimes referred to as "ear tufts," but they have nothing at all to do with hearing. The eyes, like those of all birds, are fixed in place, but the great horned owl can swivel its head more than 180 degrees in either direction. Great horned owls prey on birds, rabbits, and other small mammals, sometimes including animals larger than the owls themselves. They often build their nests in the hollows in old trees. Listen for the great horned owl when you take a night hike in the Monterey pine forest. You are likely to hear its distinctive call, a series of muffled hoots: *hoo hoodoo hoooo hoo.*

Great horned owl

The **dusky-footed wood rat** (*Neotoma fuscipes*) is a type of "packrat." The wood rats build large cone-shaped houses, two to five feet high, out of sticks and leaves. A house or den is usually located at the base of a tree, but sometimes the wood rats locate the house up in the tree's branches. The wood rat builds a nest inside the house, using shredded grass, leaves, and other materials. A single den is often the result of work by several generations of wood rats. The dusky-footed wood rat caches food such as leaves, berries, and nuts in chambers inside its nest. Sometimes the cache chambers may provide a home for other small mammals, frogs, and invertebrates. Point Lobos State Natural Reserve is a good place to look for wood rat nests.

Dusky-footed wood rat, *N. fuscipes annectens*

The **gray fox** (*Urocyon cinereoargenteus*) resembles a small dog with a big, bushy tail. It has a silvery gray mantle, conspicuous reddish or buffy patches on the throat and belly, and a black tip on the end of the tail. It is generally nocturnal and very shy, but occasionally it may be seen during the day hunting for food or "mousing." The gray fox feeds on small rodents, birds, berries, insects, and fungi. Gray foxes are unique among canids in their ability to climb trees. They have strong, hooked claws that allow them to get sufficient grip to scramble up trees. This unusual skill allows them to escape enemies, eat fruits or other foods found in trees, or just lounge in the comfort of the tree's canopy.

Gray fox

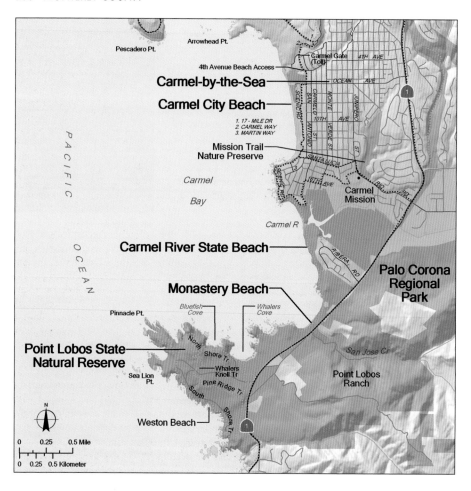

Carmel City Beach

Carmel Area

	Sandy Beach	Rocky Shore	Trail	Visitor Center	Campground	Wildlife Viewing	Fishing or Boating	Facilities for Disabled	Food and Drink	Restrooms	Parking	Fee
Carmel-by-the-Sea	•	•	•					•	•	•	•	
Carmel City Beach	•							•		•	•	
Carmel River State Beach	•	•	•			•		•		•	•	
Monastery Beach	•	•						•		•	•	
Point Lobos State Natural Reserve	•	•	•	•		•		•		•	•	•
Palo Corona Regional Park			•			•						

CARMEL-BY-THE-SEA: *Off Ocean Ave., W. of Hwy. One, 2 mi. S. of City of Monterey.* An utterly charming community in a forest. In Carmel, the post office serves as a town meeting-place; home mail delivery is not possible because houses bear name plaques rather than street numbers. The Great Sand Castle Contest held annually in the fall is serious business; the event is sponsored in part by the local chapter of the American Institute of Architects. The long-running summertime Carmel Bach Festival presents concerts at the Carmel Mission church and elsewhere; call: 831-624-1521.

CARMEL CITY BEACH: *Foot of Ocean Ave., Carmel.* The fine white sand beach, composed of quartz and feldspar from eroded granite, is extremely popular. Parking at the end of Ocean Ave. can be very tight on weekends. The north end of Carmel Beach can be reached on foot west of 4th Ave. along a residential driveway, boardwalk, and stair. Along Scenic Rd. a blufftop trail extends south from 8th Ave. to Martin Way. Street parking; eight stairways and a ramp provide access to the beach. Volleyball court on back beach. Dogs allowed on the beach under voice control; pick up after your pet. Beach

Carmel-by-the-Sea

fires permitted only south of 10th Avenue. Call: 831-620-2010. Non-wheelchair-accessible restrooms are at the end of Ocean Ave.; wheelchair-accessible portable toilets located on Scenic Rd. at Santa Lucia Avenue.

CARMEL RIVER STATE BEACH: *Scenic Rd. at Carmelo St., Carmel.* A splendid mile-long crescent of fine white sand lies at the mouth of the Carmel River. The beach is bounded by rock outcroppings to the north and the jagged profile of Point Lobos to the south, with forested slopes rising in the distance. Beach access, from the parking lot on Scenic Rd., has been complicated in recent years by the natural meandering of the Carmel River. When the river mouth moves north, there is sometimes only a narrow strip of sand connecting the parking lot to the beach.

The lagoon and wetlands near the mouth of the river are a bird sanctuary. In summer, great flocks of California brown pelicans rest on the sandbar, cruising low over the water to the nearby ocean. On a still afternoon, the enormous wings of the birds sound like sheets of canvas flapping in the breeze. Gulls and shorebirds rest and feed along the lagoon, and steelhead trout spawn upstream in the river. Divers use the beach for access to the nearby underwater kelp forest, where the rocky bottom supports sea lemons and strawberry anemones. Ocean swimming and wading are dangerous here. Restrooms with running water are located next to the parking lot. Another access point to Carmel River State Beach is located south of the Carmel River, off Hwy. One at the end of Ribera Road.

The Carmel River forms the northern boundary of the California Sea Otter Game Refuge, which extends south to San Luis Obispo County. The central California coast is one of only two remaining areas in which sea otters are found; the other is in Alaska. The best place to see the otters close up is at the Monterey Bay Aquarium; the animals can also be seen in the waters around the Monterey Peninsula, at Point Lobos, or at the mouth of Elkhorn Slough.

MONASTERY BEACH: *Off Hwy. One, 1.5 mi. S. of Rio Rd. intersection, Carmel.* Monastery Beach, part of Carmel River State Beach, offers fine views of Carmel and Point Lobos

Carmel River State Beach

Carmel River

and is a popular diving beach. Upwelling of nutrients from the nearby Carmel Submarine Canyon supports a rich marine life; a marine protected area designation by the California Department of Fish and Game provides special protection to marine resources in Carmel Bay; for information, call: 831-649-2870. The deep canyon also contributes to extremely dangerous surf conditions at this steep, coarse-grained beach, which is unsafe for swimming. The best diving access is from the north end of the beach near rocks and the adjoining kelp forest. Restrooms and roadside parking available; call: 831-649-2836.

Opposite Monastery Beach the California Department of Parks and Recreation has acquired the Point Lobos Ranch property, which includes stands of native Monterey pine forest and maritime chaparral. The area is not available for public use, pending necessary planning, facility development, and staffing; call: 831-649-2836.

POINT LOBOS STATE NATURAL RESERVE: *Off Hwy. One, 2.2 mi. S. of Rio Rd. intersection, Carmel.* The significance of the natural resources on this forested rocky headland is fully matched by the grandeur of the setting. Monterey cypress and Gowen cypress trees grow naturally only in the Point Lobos State Reserve and in the Del Monte Forest; the reserve also contains one of the world's few native stands of Monterey pine. Wrentits and white-crowned sparrows nest in coastal scrub vegetation, and yellow-rumped warblers winter here. Bobcats, black-tailed deer, and dusky-footed wood rats also inhabit the reserve. Look for wintering monarch butterflies along the Whalers Knoll Trail. Offshore, sea otters raft in large stands of giant kelp, which shelter rockfish, cabezon, and lingcod; Pacific loons may be seen in winter.

Point Lobos State Natural Reserve is a unit of the state park system and is maintained as a pristine area where all plants, rocks, wood, seashells, and animal life are protected and may not be disturbed, removed, or collected. Trails and picnic areas are available; docents and park rangers lead walks and answer questions. The reserve is open daily from 8 am until sunset. When full, the reserve allows vehicle entry only on a one-out, one-in basis; no trailers allowed, and vehicles over 20 feet in length are not allowed during busy periods. No pets; fee for entry. Call: 831-624-4909.

Diving and snorkeling is permitted only in Whalers and Bluefish Coves and is limited to 15 pairs of divers per day by permit only, available at the entrance gate. Advance diving or kayak reservations recommended, and for weekends, essential; call: 831-624-8413. Within the Point Lobos State Marine Reserve surrounding Point Lobos, the take of all living marine resources is prohibited.

PALO CORONA REGIONAL PARK: *E. of Hwy. One, S. of Carmel River Bridge.* This 4,350-acre park is open to visitors by advance permit only. Reservation requests are taken on a first-come, first-served basis and should be submitted no fewer than two days, and no more than 30 days, in advance of a planned visit. Up to 13 permits per day (one permit per vehicle) are issued. The park is managed by the Monterey Peninsula Regional Park

District. Call: 831-372-3196, or for a permit application, see: www.mprpd.org.

Public acquisition of the Palo Corona property was supported by the Wildlife Conservation Board, the State Coastal Conservancy, the California Department of Parks and Recreation, and the Monterey Peninsula Regional Park District. Funding came from Proposition 40, approved by California voters in 2002; the Big Sur Land Trust; and the Nature Conservancy. Palo Corona Regional Park and the adjacent Carmel River State Beach are links in a chain of protected areas that extend south some 70 miles through Garrapata State Park and the Los Padres National Forest into San Luis Obispo County. Palo Corona Regional Park includes stands of native Monterey pine trees and old-growth redwood forest, and habitat for the California condor, black bear, mountain lion, tiger salamander, Smith's blue butterfly, and steelhead trout.

Point Lobos State Natural Reserve

The splendor of the rocky coast of Point Lobos owes much to its geology. Two rock types make up the Point Lobos peninsula. One is an igneous unit, a granodiorite, and the other is a sedimentary unit, the Carmelo Formation, that is made up of sandstone, conglomerate, and shale.

Granodiorite is an intrusive igneous rock similar to granite; that is, it cooled from a molten state several miles below the earth's surface. Because it was insulated by the overlying rocks, it cooled slowly over several million years and formed large, interlocking crystals of feldspar, quartz, and lesser amounts of dark-colored minerals. This particular body of granodiorite has been dated at 100–110 million years old.

A large gap in time separates the cooling of the granodiorite and the deposition of the overlying Carmelo Formation, which is about 60 million years old. The younger rocks were not simply deposited horizontally on top of the granodiorite, but against it in what is known as a "buttress unconformity." In three dimensions, a canyon can be seen to be carved into the granodiorite. The Carmelo Formation fills this canyon.

At Sea Lion Point the Carmelo Formation consists of alternating conglomerate and sandstone layers. These coarse rocks indicate that they were deposited by strong water currents. Very sparse fossils found in these units indicate that they are marine deposits.

At Weston Beach the Carmelo Formation consists of alternating beds of fine sandstone and shale known as "turbidites," the deposit left by a "turbidity flow." Turbidity flows represent the sudden release of a sediment mass, which quickly incorporates large amounts of water and moves downslope as a density-driven, fluid mass. When the mass loses energy at the base of a slope, it leaves a characteristic sequence reflecting the decelerating flow.

The buttress unconformity and outcrop pattern of the Carmelo Formation strongly suggest that the unit represents the fill of a submarine canyon cut into the basement granodiorite at Point Lobos. The coarse conglomerates exposed at Sea Lion Point record the highest current velocities encountered within the formation. This suggests that the axis of the main channel of the canyon must have crossed near here. As one moves southeast toward Weston Beach, the grain size decreases, suggesting that one is moving away from the main channel.

The Point Lobos peninsula preserves the convergence of two submarine canyons. In fact, the canyon system is remarkably similar in scale and in orientation to the modern Monterey–Carmel Submarine Canyon system, which lies just offshore. By looking at the submarine canyon deposits preserved on Point Lobos, visitors get a dry look at conditions on the floor of the Monterey Submarine Canyon.

Interbedded sandstone and shale of the Carmelo Formation

Whalers Cove, Point Lobos, *original print sized 13.5 x 19 inches*

Rocky Shore

BETWEEN the high and low tide marks lies a strip of shoreline that is regularly covered and uncovered by the advance and retreat of the tides. This meeting ground between land and sea is called the intertidal. The plants and animals inhabiting this region are hardy and adaptable, able to withstand periodic exposure to air and the force of the pounding surf. Intertidal communities occur on sandy beaches, in bays and estuaries, and on wharf pilings, but the communities of rocky shorelines are perhaps the most diverse and densely populated. Rock faces, crevices, undersides of rocks, and tidepools each support an array of species.

The plants and animals of the intertidal are subject to a range of conditions not encountered in the relative stability of the deep ocean. Three factors—substrate, wave shock, and exposure to drying—are important in determining the types of organisms found in a given intertidal community. Sessile, or attached, organisms are typical of rocky shores, in contrast to sandy or mud substrates, which support an abundance of burrowing animals. Wave action on rocky headlands and exposed outer coasts can be tremendous, and only the most tenacious organisms survive. The most important factor in determining where marine organisms occur in the intertidal, however, is the ability to withstand desiccation and overheating while exposed to air by low tides.

The extent to which an organism is exposed to air is largely determined by its vertical position in the intertidal region and the pattern of the tides. On the California coast, there are two daily high tides and two low tides, of varying magnitude, so that each day there is a higher high tide, followed by a lower low tide, a lower high tide, and a higher low tide. The mean high tide level is the average of all daily high tides.

The intertidal can be divided into vertical zones based on the frequency and duration of exposure to water or air. A model proposed by Ed Ricketts and Jack Calvin in *Between Pacific Tides* divides the rocky shore into four zones characterized by different species of algae and animals. The location of these zones varies with exposure; strong wave action tends to widen the zones, whereas in sheltered areas of quiet water, the zones are narrow.

The uppermost horizon is the area above the mean high tide level and includes the splash zone that only receives spray from waves. Almost always exposed to air, the splash zone is covered with a thin sheet of black photosynthetic bacteria—"blue-green algae"—and the species found here are quite specialized. Below the splash zone is the second zone, the high intertidal, extending to the mean higher low tide level. Less harsh than the splash zone, this zone is home to a larger diversity and number of plants and animals. Large algae occur here, providing shelter for small animals and a food source for herbivores.

The middle intertidal, the third zone, extends to the mean level of the lower low tide— the zero tidal datum of the tide tables (average sea level is about +3 feet relative to this reference level). This zone is covered and uncovered by the tides twice a day and it teems with life, including mussels, barnacles, and anemones. The low intertidal, by far the richest and most densely populated zone, is the lowest of the four zones, extending from tidal datum to the level of the lowest low tide. This zone is uncovered only at "minus" tides, and it is habitat for sponges, nudibranchs, sea stars, and sea urchins. Many species would thrive lower in the intertidal than they are normally found, but are confined to higher levels by competitors, predators, or herbivores. For example, acorn barnacles are capable of living over a wide vertical range, but in the middle intertidal, the predatory rock snail eats juvenile barnacles that settle there. In the high intertidal, where the rock snail cannot survive, the barnacles flourish.

Acorn barnacle

Acorn barnacles (*Balanus* sp.) are abundant in the high intertidal zone of exposed and semi-exposed rocky shores. Acorn barnacles are crustaceans, closely related to shrimp. However, barnacles bear little similarity to their shrimp cousins. Each barnacle secretes its own calcareous, cone-shaped fortress, cemented to the rocky substrate. From within its shell, the acorn barnacle extends feathery "feet" with which it collects plankton and detritus from the churning water. When the tide goes out, the barnacle closes the opening of its shell to conserve moisture. Even with a protective shell, the acorn barnacle has a number of predators, including several marine snails and sea stars.

Opalescent nudibranch

During low tides, it is possible to find **opalescent nudibranchs** (*Hermissenda crassicornis*) in the kelp, generally in the low intertidal zone. The opalescent nudibranch is one of the most abundant nudibranchs, or "sea slugs," found on the Pacific Coast. It ranges from Kodiak Island, Alaska, to Punta Eugenia, Mexico. Opalescent nudibranchs feed on hydroids and other invertebrates. Their bright coloration serves as a warning to predators that the "cerata," or finger-like projections on their backs, are tipped with small, stinging structures called nematocysts that they obtain from their hydroid prey. Like acorn barnacles and most other sea slugs, opalescent nudibranchs are hermaphroditic. Therefore, reproduction can occur between any two individuals.

Monkeyface eel

Monkeyface eels (*Cebidichthys violaceus*) are not true eels, but rather are members of the prickleback family. Their distorted faces are a bit grotesque and give them an eel-like appearance. They act like eels as well, slithering into crevices under rocks and seaweed. This long slender fish, about one to two feet long, has the unfishlike ability to breathe and survive out of water temporarily. Typical habitat for monkeyface eels includes rocky areas with ample crevices, such as high and low intertidal tidepools, jetties and breakwaters, and relatively shallow subtidal areas, particularly kelp beds. Monkeyface eels do not move around much, seldom traveling more than 15 feet from their home. If you see someone with a long bamboo pole in the rocky intertidal, it is probably a "poke-poler" in search of monkeyface eels.

The **sea lemon** (*Archidoris montereyensis*) is a large, flattened sea slug, up to seven inches long, with two horn-like projections at one end and a tuft of gills at the other. The mantle is sprinkled with black dots. The sea lemon primarily feeds on encrusted sponges, especially *Halichondria* and *Haliclona* spp. It uses its radula (a flexible, tongue-like organ having rows of tiny teeth on the surface) to scrape the sponge off the substrate and then ingest it. Unlike other sea slugs, the sea lemon cannot store the toxins of its prey. However, with its bright coloration, it may be mimicking other sea slugs that have that ability and are therefore poisonous to predators. The sea lemon can be found in subtidal, shaded areas where sponges grow.

Sea lemon

The adult **Heermann's gull** (*Larus heermanni*) is one of the most beautiful and easily recognized North American gulls. With its dark gray upper parts, white head with a bright red, black-tipped bill, it is like no other species. Heermann's gulls are almost exclusively coastal, ranging only a few dozen miles out to sea to forage. They feed on small pelagic fish such as sardines and anchovies, and occasionally on crustaceans, mollusks, and other marine organisms scavenged from the beach and kelp beds. This medium-sized gull species can be quite aggressive, and is often seen harassing other birds to make them drop food items. Heermann's gulls nest primarily on islands in the Gulf of California.

Heermann's gull

The **ruddy turnstone** (*Arenaria interpres*) is a short-legged shorebird that is about seven inches in length. It has a short, dark bill that is slightly upturned at the end and striking black-and-white markings on its head. These small birds nest solely in the high arctic tundra, where they feed mainly on flies. In winter, the ruddy turnstone can be found in a variety of habitats, including mudflats, beaches, and the rocky intertidal, along the Pacific coast of the Americas from central California southward and also on Atlantic shores. The turnstone gets its name from its habit of turning over stones when it looks for food. It is also known as the seaweed bird, because it often feeds among the kelp at low tide. The ruddy turnstone's diet includes invertebrates, small fish, carrion, and sometimes the eggs of other bird species.

Ruddy turnstone

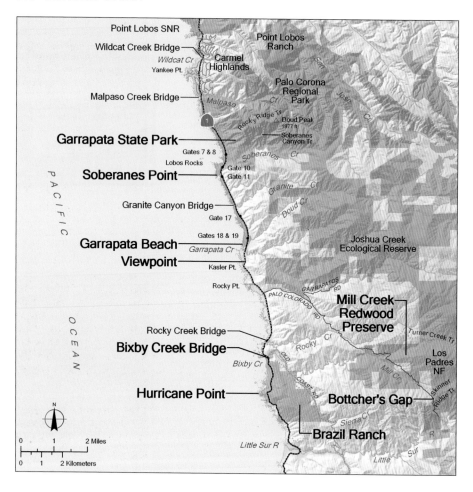

Point Lobos SNR
Wildcat Creek Bridge
Wildcat Cr
Yankee Pt.
Carmel Highlands
Point Lobos Ranch
Malpaso Creek Bridge
Malpaso
Palo Corona Regional Park
San
Jose
Cr
Rocky Ridge Tr
△ Doud Peak 1977 ft
Soberanes Canyon Tr
Garrapata State Park
Gates 7 & 8
Lobos Rocks
Soberanes   Cr
Soberanes Point
Gate 10
Gate 11
Granite   Cr
Doud Cr
Granite Canyon Bridge
Gate 17
Gates 18 & 19
Joshua Creek Ecological Reserve
Garrapata Beach
Garrapata Cr
Viewpoint
Kasler Pt.
Rocky Pt.
GARRAPATOS RD
PALO COLORADO RD
Mill Creek Redwood Preserve
Turner Creek Tr
Rocky Creek Bridge
Rocky   Cr
Los Padres NF
Bixby Creek Bridge
Bixby Cr
OLD   COAST RD
Mill Cr
Skinner Ridge Tr
Hurricane Point
Bottcher's Gap
Sierra Cr
Brazil Ranch
Little Sur R
Little   Sur   R

PACIFIC   OCEAN

N

0   1   2 Miles
0   1   2 Kilometers

View from Hurricane Point

Big Sur North

	Sandy Beach	Rocky Shore	Trail	Visitor Center	Campground	Wildlife Viewing	Fishing or Boating	Facilities for Disabled	Food and Drink	Restrooms	Parking	Fee
Garrapata State Park	•	•	•			•			•	•		
Soberanes Point		•	•			•				•		
Garrapata Beach	•	•	•							•		
Viewpoint		•								•		
Bixby Creek Bridge										•		
Hurricane Point		•								•		
Brazil Ranch		•										
Mill Creek Redwood Preserve			•			•						
Bottcher's Gap			•	•						•	•	•

GARRAPATA STATE PARK: *Hwy. One, 3.3 mi. S. of Point Lobos State Natural Reserve.* A little advance planning will make a visit to Garrapata State Park more rewarding. This day-use-only park stretches four miles along the seaward side of Hwy. One and more than two miles inland, but there are few facilities, and park entrances are limited to easily missed numbered roadside gates, next to pull-outs. Hwy. One traffic moves fast here; use caution when slowing to park along the highway. Look carefully for the trails, which are sometimes overgrown. Poison oak grows magnificently here, as do other native plants typical of the coastal bluffs.

At the north end of Garrapata State Park, four southbound pull-outs near the 67.0 milepost marker offer access to a steep bluff vegetated with spring wildflowers and sticky monkeyflower. There are good views of rocky shore but no safe access to the water. Near milepost 66.0 is roadside gate #7 and a steep path overlooking Soberanes Creek, where it cascades to a cobble beach. On the inland side of Hwy. One opposite gate #7, the Rocky Ridge Trail climbs five miles to the 1,977-foot summit of Doud Peak; bicycles are allowed on the trail. A couple of hundred yards south of gate #7 on Hwy. One, a hedgerow of Monterey cypress trees and pull-outs on both sides of the highway mark gate #8, leading to a blufftop with a particularly striking view of rocky shore. Opposite gate #8, the Soberanes Canyon Trail follows Soberanes Creek inland past a barn and up a long, narrow valley through a redwood grove, connecting to the Rocky Ridge Trail. Excellent views, and spring wildflowers, but the trail is steep and somewhat eroded; use caution. Pit toilet only; dogs not allowed. Call: 831-624-4909.

SOBERANES POINT: *Hwy. One, 4.9 mi. S. of Point Lobos State Natural Reserve.* Soberanes Point is marked by steep, cone-shaped Whale Peak, rising seaward of Hwy. One. Several small pull-outs provide parking. Gate #10 opens on two paths, the southerly one extending in a two-mile-long loop around the perimeter of Soberanes Point, and the northerly path leading to the 460-foot crest of Whale Peak, with striking views of rocky shore and offshore kelp forest. Watch for a wrentit or a buckeye butterfly among the dense growth of coffeeberry, ceanothus, and poison oak; gray whales may be sighted during winter months and humpback whales during the summer or fall. Sea lions rest and brown pelicans roost on Lobos Rocks, offshore from Soberanes Point. Part of Garrapata State Park; dogs not allowed on trails.

South of Soberanes Point, a pull-out marked with a brown Coastal Access sign is next to gate #11, where a short, steep path leads to an ocean-viewing bench inscribed with the words: "Into her arms he dove to begin his new journey." Gate #17 at milepost 64.0 south of the Granite Creek Bridge opens to a short, steep path leading to another bench with a fine view of the steep coastal terrace and rocky shore below.

GARRAPATA BEACH: *Hwy. One, 7.3 mi. S. of Point Lobos State Natural Reserve.* Garrapata Beach is one of the few publicly accessible sandy beaches between the mouth of the Carmel River and Andrew Molera State Park. Aquamarine ocean and a sweep of white sand are tempting to visitors, but the steep beach and rough surf make swimming unsafe and prohibited. Strolling, sunbathing, and solitude-seeking are popular here. Parking for the beach is in roadside pull-outs on both sides of Hwy. One; Monterey-Salinas Transit route signs mark the pull-outs. Paths lead seaward from half-hidden gates #18 and 19, on the north and south sides of Doud Creek, to the sandy beach and to a short north-south trail along the edge of the blufftop. At the south end of the beach, a stair accessible from gate #18 leads down

to the sand. Camping not allowed; dogs permitted on leash. No facilities; for information, call: 831-624-4909.

VIEWPOINT: *Hwy. One, .5 mi. S. of Garrapata Beach.* A view of rocky Otter Cove is available from a parking area on the west side of Hwy. One, north of Kasler Point.

BIXBY CREEK BRIDGE: *Hwy. One, 11 mi. S. of Point Lobos State Natural Reserve, Big Sur Coast.* The Bixby Creek Bridge is a major landmark of the Big Sur Coast. The bridge's completion in 1932 filled in one of the most challenging gaps in the construction of Hwy. One on the Big Sur coast. Before the bridge opened, Big Sur-bound travelers from Monterey headed east on the Old Coast Rd., which took an inland route to avoid the impassable canyons and steep cliffs at the mouth of Bixby Creek. The bridge deck is 260 feet high, exceeding the height above water of the Golden Gate Bridge by some 40 feet. There is a small southbound pull-out located on the north side of the bridge. The similar but smaller Rocky Creek Bridge,

Bixby Creek Bridge

Soberanes Point

also with a small view pull-out on the north side, is located a half-mile north of the Bixby Creek Bridge.

HURRICANE POINT: *Hwy. One, 1.3 mi. S. of Bixby Creek Bridge, Big Sur Coast.* Dramatic views are available from pull-outs on Hwy. One, which reaches an elevation at Hurricane Point of nearly 500 feet above sea level. Tufted puffins and common murres nest on the steep cliffs.

BRAZIL RANCH: *S. of Bixby Creek Bridge, E. and W. of Hwy. One, Big Sur Coast.* This 1,200-acre historic ranch property, including coastline between the Bixby Creek Bridge and Hurricane Point and inland redwood forest along Bixby and Sierra Creeks, has been acquired by the U.S. Forest Service for addition to Los Padres National Forest. The Old Coast Rd. borders part of the property; for information, contact the Monterey Ranger District: 831-385-5434.

MILL CREEK REDWOOD PRESERVE: *Off Palo Colorado Rd., E. of Hwy. One, Big Sur.* The five-and-a-half-mile, out-and-back Mill Creek Trail is accessible with an advance permit. Reservation requests are taken on a first-come, first-served basis and should be submitted no fewer than two days, and no more than 30 days, in advance of a planned visit. Up to eight permits per day are available, with five persons per permit. Managed by the Monterey Peninsula Regional Park District; call: 831-372-3196, or for a permit application, see: www.mprpd.org.

BOTTCHER'S GAP: *End of Palo Colorado Rd., 8 mi. E. of Hwy. One, Big Sur.* Bottcher's Gap is a day-use area, campground, and trailhead for hiking into the backcountry. There are 11 campsites with fire rings and barbecue grills among oak and madrone trees. Vault toilets; bring your own water. Fee for camping. Part of Los Padres National Forest; for information, call: 831-385-5434.

From Bottcher's Gap, the Skinner Ridge and Ventana Trails lead equestrians and backpackers some 21 miles into the Ventana Wilderness Area and to 4,853-foot-high Ventana Double Cone. Other trails lead to the upper watershed of the Little Sur River. South of Bottcher's Gap is Pico Blanco, a 3,709-foot mountain with a white top of metamorphosed limestone, or calcium carbonate.

Rivers and Streams

O N THEIR WAY to the ocean, California's coastal rivers and streams flow through the canyons and valleys of coastal mountains, linking forest, chaparral, grassland, and marsh. Riparian woodlands develop along stream banks and floodplains, and coastal wetlands and estuaries form where the rivers enter the sea. Rivers transport nutrients, sediments, and oxygen through the watershed, and life flourishes in their path.

Streams and the surrounding riparian woodlands support numerous animal species, including frogs, salamanders, snakes, and river otters. Western sycamore trees, alders, and willows grow along the stream banks and attract large numbers of resident and migratory birds. An entangling understory of shrubs, flowering plants, and vines provides sites for nesting, shelter, and shade for many animals. Algae and mosses proliferate in the water and on rocks. Leaves swept into the current decompose, adding nutrients and organic matter. Insects thrive here and in turn provide an abundant food source for invertebrates, fish, and birds. Anadromous fish such as salmon and steelhead migrate from the sea to fresh water to spawn, and depend on well-oxygenated streams and gravelly streambeds as spawning sites. River runoff, the amount of water discharged through surface streams, is determined by a combination of factors, including local geology, topography, drainage area, and rainfall patterns.

Limekiln Creek, Big Sur

The **California buckeye** (*Aesculus californica*) provides a perfect hideaway for summer naps, as the broad, pale green leaves provide a wonderful canopy to protect you against the heat of the sun. Each leaf has five leaflets, borne in a palmate arrangement. In May, the tree is covered with beautiful, fragrant flowering spikes of four- to five-petaled white flowers with long stamens. Although most of the flowers of this plant are pollinated, the tree aborts most of the young fruit. Its branches can only support a few of the heavy fruit. In the fall, big shiny chestnuts can be found on the ground at the base of the tree. The fruits are poisonous, and Native Americans poured an extract of the chestnuts into pools to stun and then catch fish. Buckeye trees grow next to springs and creeks in the coastal mountains.

California buckeye

The **western sycamore** (*Platanus racemosa*) is a deciduous, riparian tree, with five-fingered, star-shaped leaves. The most striking feature of this tree is the splotchy white and brown bark. Young greenish-gray bark exfoliates (peels off), leaving almost pure white inner bark; older bark is thicker, furrowed, and dark brown. This gives the sycamore a jigsaw puzzle-like appearance. Found not far from water, it can reach a height of 90 feet. The sycamore is home to the western tiger swallowtail butterfly. Offering shade from the summer sun, the tree affords protection and nutrients to the larva as the caterpillar becomes an adult.

Western sycamore

Coastal black gooseberry (*Ribes divaricatum*) is a deciduous, spiny shrub with beautiful flowers, edible fruit, fragrant foliage, and wonderful fall color. Gooseberries are loved by many birds including the hermit thrush and the American robin. Coastal black gooseberry plants have pendulous flowers that droop in bunches at the tips of branches from March to June. Each flower consists of a short tube, at the mouth of which are turned-back, greenish-red sepals and five white petals. Blackish berries covered in a gray-blue bloom replace flowers in late spring and summer. Despite the rather bland taste of the berries, Native Americans collected and ate them fresh.

Coastal black gooseberry

Belted kingfisher

The **belted kingfisher** (*Ceryle alcyon*) is unlikely to be confused with any other bird. Its huge bill, large head, shaggy crest, and coloring are distinctive. In addition, it has a characteristic call, consisting of a series of harsh, wooden, rattling notes of great carrying power. The belted kingfisher is bluish-gray above, with a white belly and a white ring around the neck. The belted kingfisher is one of only a few North American bird species in which the female is more colorful than the male. Females have a chestnut band across the belly that is absent in males. Belted kingfishers, as their name suggests, subsist mostly on fish. They typically sit at a waterside perch watching for prey, then they make steep dives headfirst into the water. Listen for the loud, rattle-like call of a belted kingfisher as it flies along the riparian corridor.

Green heron

The **green heron** (*Butorides virescens*) is a small, stocky wading bird common in riparian areas. However, while it may be common, it is generally difficult to see. Like other herons, it stands motionless waiting for small fish to approach within striking range. The green heron is known to drop bait onto the surface of the water to attract small fish that it then seizes with a jab of its bill. When afraid or in flight, the green heron may give an explosive alarm call that sounds like *skeow*. The green heron is a rather wary and solitary bird. When alarmed, it erects its short, reddish crest, straightens its neck, and nervously flicks its short tail. The bird usually goes unnoticed until it flushes from the edge of the water and flies off, uttering its sharp call.

Foothill yellow-legged frog

Foothill yellow-legged frogs (*Rana boylii*) frequent shallow, slow, gravelly streams and rivers. They are rarely encountered far from permanent water. Yellow-legged frogs are not smooth in appearance like other frogs; their skin is bumpy like a toad's. Foothill yellow-legged frogs may be brown, gray, or rust red in appearance. They rely heavily on camouflage for their survival. They sun themselves on the banks of rocky creeks and blend in with their surroundings. If you approach one, you may be in for a surprise when a stone leaps into the creek and swims away. The foothill yellow-legged frog is considered a species of special concern by the California Department of Fish and Game.

The **California roach** (*Lavinia symmetricus*) has a blue-gray body, rarely exceeding four inches in length, with a silvery underside. This highly adaptable fish is found in California's coastal streams, including intermittent ones, where it can tolerate dissolved oxygen levels as low as one or two parts per million and water temperatures ranging from near-freezing to warm. Its diet is also varied and consists of bottom-growing algae, tiny crustaceans, and aquatic insects. From spring into early summer, females seek shallow gravel bars on which to deposit small clusters of eggs, which are then fertilized by male fish.

California roach

The **Santa Lucia slender salamander** (*Batrachoseps luciae*) is a blackish-brown salamander measuring from one-quarter to nearly two inches in length from snout to vent. The salamander breathes through its smooth, moist, thin skin. It has short limbs, a narrow head, a slender body, and a long tail, giving this species a worm-like appearance. You may find the Santa Lucia slender salamander on wet nights when the temperature is mild. The salamander retreats underground when the soil dries or when the air temperature drops to near freezing. If you look under rocks or logs in moist areas, you may uncover one. It is thought that the Santa Lucia slender salamander may spend its entire lifespan in no more than a few square yards. This will not surprise you when you see how tiny its legs are.

Santa Lucia slender salamander

The **western tiger swallowtail** (*Papilio rutulus*) is one of our largest butterflies. Yellow and black tiger-striped markings adorn its wings, and it has long "tails" on its hind wings that resemble the long tail feathers of swallows. This beautiful butterfly is often observed gliding lazily along rivers and streams. When disturbed, however, it can flee quite rapidly. Next time you go on a streamside hike, look for the western tiger swallowtail in the wet sand or mud alongside the water. Butterflies sip water from the moist soil to obtain mineral salts and other nutrients that have leached from the surrounding soil and rocks. This is a phenomenon known as "puddling." Male butterflies do more puddling than females. It is thought that the male transfers the dissolved salts and minerals to the female during mating to give her the nutritional boost she needs to lay eggs.

Western tiger swallowtail

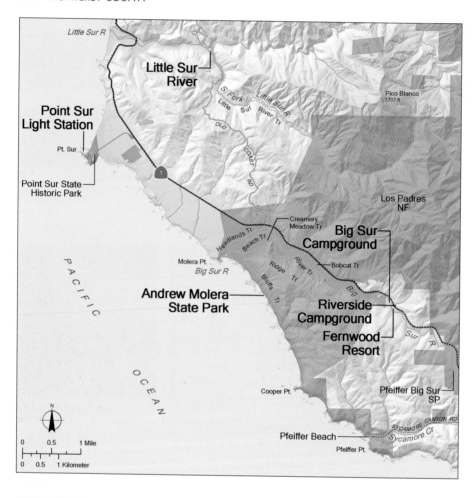

Little Sur R

Little Sur River

S. Fork Little Sur River Tr

Little Sur R

OLD COAST RD

Pico Blanco
△ 3707 ft

Point Sur Light Station

Pt. Sur

1

Point Sur State Historic Park

Los Padres NF

Creamery Meadow Tr

Big Sur Campground

Headlands Tr

Beach Tr

P A C I F I C

Molera Pt.

Big Sur R

Ridge Tr

River Tr

Bobcat Tr

Andrew Molera State Park

Bluffs Tr

Big Sur R

Riverside Campground

Fernwood Resort

O C E A N

Cooper Pt.

Pfeiffer Big Sur SP

N

0   0.5   1 Mile

0   0.5   1 Kilometer

Pfeiffer Beach

SYCAMORE CANYON RD

Sycamore Cr

Pfeiffer Pt.

Point Sur

Point Sur to Big Sur Valley

	Sandy Beach	Rocky Shore	Trail	Visitor Center	Campground	Wildlife Viewing	Fishing or Boating	Facilities for Disabled	Food and Drink	Restrooms	Parking	Fee
Point Sur Light Station			•						•	•	•	
Little Sur River			•									
Andrew Molera State Park	•	•	•	•	•	•	•	•	•	•	•	
Big Sur Campground					•				•	•	•	
Riverside Campground					•				•	•	•	
Fernwood Resort					•				•	•	•	•

POINT SUR LIGHT STATION: *Hwy. One at Point Sur, Big Sur Coast.* The light station was built in 1889 on the Point Sur headland, 270 feet above the ocean. The initial light source for its Fresnel lens, since removed, was a whale oil lantern. A modern beacon now operates at the station, which is within Point Sur State Historic Park and is open to visitors on a limited basis. Docent-led walking tours depart from the parking area off Hwy. One at 10 am on Saturday and Sunday, year-round, weather permitting; Wednesday afternoon tours are also offered, as are additional walks in summer and occasional moonlight walks. No reservations are taken; the tours depart promptly and last three hours, requiring a half-mile walk each way and considerable stair climbing. No pets, strollers, or picnicking allowed. Meet at the locked entrance gate on the west side of Hwy. One, one quarter-mile north of the former Point Sur Naval Facility. Limited parking; no large RVs. For information, call: 831-625-4419. Visitors to the light station can see surf, rocky coast, and perhaps a whale offshore, but there is no beach access; all the land surrounding Point Sur is private and closed to the public. Point Sur is an island of basaltic rock that is connected to the mainland by a large sandbar; this rare geologic formation is called a tombolo.

LITTLE SUR RIVER: *Off Old Coast Rd., 4 mi. N. of Hwy. One, Big Sur.* Steelhead trout spawn in the undammed Little Sur River. The headwaters of the river support a dense redwood forest. Off Old Coast Rd., a trail leads upstream through the trees into the Los Padres National Forest, beginning one half-mile south of the bridge where Old Coast Rd. crosses the south fork of the river. The private El Sur Ranch borders much of the lower reach of the Little Sur River, including the sandy beach at the river mouth; do not trespass.

ANDREW MOLERA STATE PARK: *Hwy. One, 8.3 mi. S. of Bixby Creek Bridge, Big Sur.* This large state park at the mouth of the Big Sur River offers walk-in camping, hiking on upland trails or along miles of sandy beach, surfing, and horseback riding. The park's vehicle entrance and parking lot are on the Hwy. One, or north, side of the river, while much of the park's land lies south of the river. Summertime plank bridges allow pedestrian crossing when the river's flow is low. The campground and trail to Molera Point are accessible all year, without the need to cross the river.

The campground is located in a meadow, a quarter-mile walk along a trail from the west end of the parking area. There are 24 family campsites, each accommodating up to four persons, with picnic tables, food storage lockers, and firepits. No reservations taken. Restrooms with running water are located near the campground. The campground can also be reached by footpath from a pull-out on Hwy. One, one-quarter mile west of the park's vehicle entrance.

Andrew Molera State Park boasts a spectacularly beautiful sandy beach, one of Big Sur's few surfing areas, located about a mile from the entrance parking area. Beachgoers

Andrew Molera State Park

can cross the Big Sur River near the parking area, then walk along the Beach or Creamery Meadow Trails to a 300-yard-long sandy beach strewn with driftwood and rocky shore farther south. Alternatively, hikers bent on getting to the coast can avoid the river crossing by heading west from the parking area past the campground to Molera Point, covered with wildflowers in spring, where elevated ground provides dramatic views. At Molera Point, however, you are separated from the main beach by the river mouth. Shorebirds such as willets, sanderlings, and red-necked phalaropes frequent the shallow lagoon. Private ranch land extends west from Molera Point; do not trespass.

Other trails in Andrew Molera State Park include the River Trail, which follows the south bank of the Big Sur River; the Ridge Trail, which climbs the spine of Pfeiffer Ridge; and the Bluffs Trail, which parallels the shoreline toward Cooper Point. The Bobcat Trail follows the Big Sur River on its north bank, starting at the entrance parking lot and also accessible from pull-outs on Hwy. One east of the park entrance. When hiking, watch out for poison oak and check for ticks. Fee for day use and camping; for information, call: 831-667-2315.

The nonprofit Big Sur Historical Society operates a visitor center at Andrew Molera State Park in a historic ranch house, staffed by volunteers and open usually on Saturday and Sunday, 11 AM to 3 PM. The Ventana Wildlife Society's Big Sur Discovery Center serves as the main hub for Society-led nature walks in the park, including bird and monarch butterfly walks, as well as California condor tours and eco-experiences. The Ventana Wildlife Society participates in the California condor recovery effort and offers summer nature camps for youth, condor wilderness camps, and condor presentations. The Discovery Center houses a condor exhibit and is open to the public free of charge; schedule varies. For information or to schedule a program/tour, call: 831-455-9514. Also at the park, guided horseback rides through western sycamore and redwood trees to the beach are available from Molera Horseback Tours; for information, call: 831-625-5486.

Spanish missionaries at Carmel Mission called the river draining the western slopes of the Santa Lucia Range El Rio Grande del Sur, "The Big River of the South." The Big Sur River Valley was homesteaded in the late 1860s by American settlers, including the Pfeiffers and the Posts. The community of Big Sur offers everything, and then some, that a world-famous resort area might be expected to have, from restaurants with ocean views to shops, galleries, and places of spiritual refuge. But a town center there is not; visitor services are strung along Hwy. One, with the largest concentration between Andrew Molera State Park and Pfeiffer Big Sur State Park, and others farther south. The Big Sur Valley is separated from the ocean by Pfeiffer Ridge, ensuring a moderate, sheltered summer climate among the redwoods. Big Sur's beaches are usually cooler than the Big Sur Valley during the summer; beaches are located at several state parks and sites within the Los Padres National Forest.

BIG SUR CAMPGROUND: *Hwy. One, 1.7 mi. N. of Pfeiffer Big Sur State Park, Big Sur.* Tent and RV campsites and cabins near the Big Sur River are available at this privately owned facility. RV sites have hookups; some cabins have kitchens and fireplaces. Hot showers, laundry, playground, and store. Fee for camping. Open all year; for reservations, call: 831-667-2322.

RIVERSIDE CAMPGROUND: *Hwy. One, 1.6 mi. N. of Pfeiffer Big Sur State Park, Big Sur.* This privately owned campground in the redwoods on the Big Sur River has 28 tent campsites with picnic tables and firepits and 14 sites with electrical and water hookups for RVs up to 34 feet long. Hot showers, laundry, and firewood available. Pets must be on a leash. Quiet time enforced after 10 PM. Cabins are also available. Fee for camping. Open all year, weather permitting. For reservations, call: 831-667-2414.

FERNWOOD RESORT: *Hwy. One, .7 mi. N. of Pfeiffer Big Sur State Park, Big Sur.* A privately owned facility on the Big Sur River. A 60-unit campground includes tent cabins, tent campsites, and RV campsites in the redwood forest next to the river. Hot showers available; RV sites have water and power hookups. Recreational facilities include a volleyball court and trails connecting to Pfeiffer Big Sur State Park. Also on the property are a motel, restaurant, general store, and tavern. Fee for camping. Open all year; for reservations, call: 831-667-2422.

Andrew Molera State Park

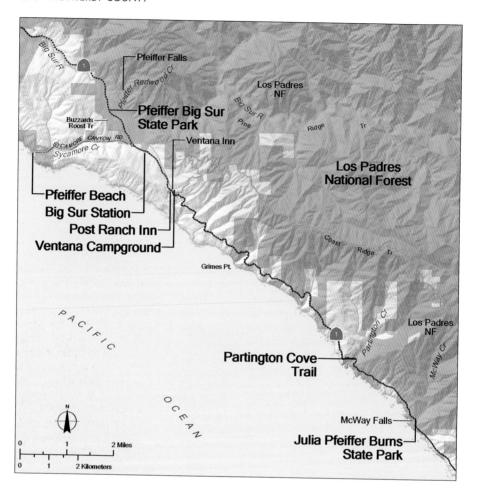

Big Sur R

Pfeiffer Falls

Pfeiffer Redwood Cr

Los Padres
NF

**Pfeiffer Big Sur
State Park**

Big Sur R

Pine

Ridge

Tr

Buzzards
Roost Tr

SYCAMORE CANYON RD

Sycamore Cr

Ventana Inn

**Los Padres
National Forest**

**Pfeiffer Beach
Big Sur Station
Post Ranch Inn
Ventana Campground**

Coast

Ridge

Tr

Grimes Pt.

Partington Cr

Los Padres
NF

PACIFIC

McWay Cr

OCEAN

**Partington Cove
Trail**

N

McWay Falls

0   1   2 Miles

0   1   2 Kilometers

**Julia Pfeiffer Burns
State Park**

Santa Lucia Range from Pfeiffer Big Sur State Park

Pfeiffer Beach to Julia Pfeiffer Burns State Park

	Sandy Beach	Rocky Shore	Trail	Visitor Center	Campground	Wildlife Viewing	Fishing or Boating	Facilities for Disabled	Food and Drink	Restrooms	Parking	Fee
Pfeiffer Beach	•	•					•		•	•	•	
Pfeiffer Big Sur State Park			•	•	•	•	•		•	•	•	
Big Sur Station				•	•		•		•	•		
Post Ranch Inn				•						•		
Ventana Campground					•				•	•	•	
Los Padres National Forest	•	•	•	•	•	•	•			•	•	
Partington Cove Trail		•	•									
Julia Pfeiffer Burns State Park	•	•			•		•			•	•	

PFEIFFER BEACH: *W. of Hwy. One, end of Sycamore Canyon Rd., Big Sur.* An unsigned highway turn-off leads to this beautiful beach; the intersection is six-tenths of a mile south of Big Sur Station. Narrow Sycamore Canyon Rd. parallels Sycamore Creek; private property is adjacent. At the end of the road is a beach surrounded by steep cliffs and sea stacks. Hazardous surf crashes spectacularly through natural arches in the rocks. Gusty winds are common; fires are prohibited. Day use only; fee charged. The beach, a unit of Los Padres National Forest, is open daily, 10 AM to 9 PM. Call: 831-385-5434.

PFEIFFER BIG SUR STATE PARK: *Along Hwy. One, 26 mi. S. of Carmel, Big Sur.* This popular state park includes 1,000 acres in the valley of the Big Sur River. The riparian forest includes coast redwood, western sycamore, black cottonwood, and big-leaf maple trees. Trails lead along the valley floor and up the adjacent steep slopes. Pfeiffer Falls on Pfeiffer Redwood Creek is a short walk from

Pfeiffer Beach

the park's nature center. West of Hwy. One, the Buzzards Roost Trail climbs steeply up a forested ridge, offering views of peaks in the Los Padres National Forest. Birds in the park include Steller's jays, canyon wrens, dark-eyed juncos, chestnut-backed chickadees, red-tailed hawks, and belted kingfishers. Coast horned lizards and western tiger swallowtail butterflies also inhabit the park. There is a self-guided nature trail, and walks and programs are given in the summer.

Pfeiffer Big Sur State Park has 200 family campsites plus tent-only sites, hike or bike sites, and group campsites; enroute camping is also allowed. Some sites are wheelchair-accessible. Trailers up to 27 feet long and RVs up to 32 feet long can be accommodated; RV dump station available. For campsite reservations, call: 1-800-444-7275. For park information, call: 831-667-2315. The Big Sur Lodge, with rooms and cabins, swimming pool and sauna, café, and gift shop, is located within the park; for reservations, call: 1-800-424-4787.

BIG SUR STATION: *E. of Hwy. One, .6 mi. S. of Pfeiffer Big Sur State Park entrance.* Rangers provide information on Big Sur state parks and the Los Padres National Forest. Fire permits, group picnic area reservations, and wedding permits are also available. A shop offers maps and books. The Pine Ridge Trail starts at the station; leashed dogs allowed on the trail. Open daily, 8 AM to 4:30 PM, with shorter hours during the winter; call: 831-667-2315. The Pine Ridge Trail starts at the station; leashed dogs allowed on the trail.

POST RANCH INN: *W. of Hwy. One, 2.4 mi. S. of Pfeiffer Big Sur State Park.* Private resort on ridge west of Hwy. One; entrance opposite Ventana Campground. An upland loop trail is open to the public on a permit basis; obtain a pass at the entry kiosk.

VENTANA CAMPGROUND: *E. of Hwy. One, 2.4 mi. S. of Pfeiffer Big Sur State Park.* This privately owned campground shares an entry with the Ventana Inn. Turn east off Hwy. One at the old red house, one-half mile south of the post office, then left to the campground. Ninety-two campsites with picnic tables and fire rings in the redwoods; running water and hot showers available.

Dogs on leash permitted. Campsites are for tents or for RVs up to 22 feet long; no generators allowed. Trails lead up the hill to the Ventana Inn, where there is a restaurant and gift shop. Campground closed in winter; for information, call: 831-667-2712.

Near the Ventana Inn is Cadillac Flat, a starting point for hikers and backpackers using the old Coast Ridge Rd. trail, which winds southeast along the mountains. Park at the vista point sign on the Ventana Inn access road and continue on foot, bearing right to the trailhead. From the Coast Ridge Rd. trail, connecting trails lead down the east side of the coastal range to campsites scattered along the Big Sur River, upstream from Pfeiffer Big Sur State Park.

LOS PADRES NATIONAL FOREST: *Big Sur Coast.* The Los Padres National Forest includes nearly two million acres of land in the Coast and Transverse Ranges. One part of the National Forest is in Monterey County, including the Big Sur area, and the other spans San Luis Obispo, Santa Barbara, Ventura, and Kern Counties. Ecosystems range from beaches to coastal redwood forests, from mixed evergreen forest to chaparral and oak woodlands. The National Forest includes two California condor sanctuaries, the Sisquoc Condor Sanctuary in Santa Barbara County and the Sespe Condor Sanctuary in Ventura County. Pictographs created by the Chumash indigenous people are found in caves and rock outcroppings. There are numerous picnic locations, campsites, and more than 1,200 miles of trails for day hikers and backpackers.

Wildfires are a concern, and permits are required for campfires or barbecues outside developed campgrounds. Camping outside designated campgrounds is allowed in some areas; contact a ranger station for more information. Pets must be leashed in developed recreation sites; follow posted regulations regarding horses and pack animals. California Department of Fish and Game rules regarding fishing and hunting apply within the National Forest. Off-road vehicles are allowed on designated trails only. Leave natural areas as you found them. Maps, fire permits, and information about Los Padres

National Forest are available at Big Sur Station, or call the National Forest office in King City: 831-385-5434.

PARTINGTON COVE TRAIL: *W. of Hwy. One, 1.8 mi. N. of entrance to Julia Pfeiffer Burns State Park.* At milepost 37.8 on Hwy. One is a trail that leads downhill, across Partington Creek, and through a 200-foot-long tunnel to a former doghole lumber port. (A doghole port, used by ships in 19th-century coastal commerce, is a cove just big enough for "a dog to turn around in.") Forest products, including tanbark and wooden shakes, were transferred to ships here. Partington Cove is now used by divers and sightseers. Park on the shoulder of Hwy. One.

JULIA PFEIFFER BURNS STATE PARK: *E. and W. of Hwy. One, 11 mi. S. of Pfeiffer Big Sur State Park.* Perhaps the most-photographed feature of this state park is the McWay waterfall, which cascades 80 feet onto the beach. Park east of Hwy. One; the Waterfall Trail leads seaward, beneath the road. Two environmental campsites are located on the headland; turn south from the Waterfall Trail just west of Hwy. One. Campers must register at Big Sur Station. For park information, call: 831-667-2315; for camping reservations,

call: 1-800-444-7275. The state park also includes hiking trails and picnic areas inland along wooded McWay Creek. Up a steeply rising trail is 4,099-foot Anderson Peak, located little more than two miles from the shoreline in the Los Padres National Forest.

California condor, Los Padres National Forest

Three miles southeast of the village of Big Sur, the Big Sur River makes a dramatic right-angle bend. The deep, steep canyon of Sycamore Creek is aligned with the canyon of the Big Sur River upstream of its bend. The canyon was carved by the Big Sur River when it flowed down a continuous straight canyon and entered the ocean at Pfeiffer Beach. The river was "captured" by the valley in which it now flows for its last six miles when a much smaller stream draining that valley eroded its headwaters closer and closer to the canyon of the Big Sur River. Eventually, the Big Sur River was diverted into the valley of the smaller stream and permanently shifted course. As it eroded deeper, the river left the downstream end of its former course—Sycamore Canyon—high and dry, later to be occupied by the small stream we see today.

Evidence for this story is provided by the brilliant pink sand, consisting of the mineral garnet, found at the present mouths of the Big Sur River and Sycamore Creek. Garnet is found in rocks in the Santa Lucia Range, but is entirely absent from the rocks drained by Sycamore Creek. The presence of pink garnet sand at Pfeiffer Beach indicates that the Big Sur River, currently bringing such sand to Andrew Molera State Park, formerly carried it to Pfeiffer Beach.

Colors of the Coast

While cool, gray fog is often associated with the coast of California, native plants and animals (and other prominent features) of California's coast display colors that are sometimes striking, sometimes subtle. Each has a story to tell.

Red

Stalked jellyfish, S. *Haliclystus* sp.

The **stalked jellyfish** (*Manania* sp. and *Haliclystus* sp., in the Order Stauromedusae) spend their lives attached to coralline and other red algae in low intertidal pools. While actually jellyfish, they have more in common with sea anemones; they cannot swim and they lead a "sessile," or permanently attached, lifestyle. Stauromedusae are small (less than one inch across), cryptic (well camouflaged) animals that are shaped like a funnel. While Stauromedusae cannot swim, they can move by turning "head-over-heels" and using their anchor tentacles to fix themselves temporarily as they flip over and then re-attach their adhesive disk.

San Francisco garter snake

The endangered **San Francisco garter snake** (*Thamnophis sirtalis tetrataenia*) has lost habitat to urban development, agriculture, and the altering of waterways. These habitat changes have also reduced populations of one of this snake's main food sources, the California red-legged frog (*Rana draytonii*). The remaining fragmented populations of this snake could be further threatened by collecting for the pet trade; San Francisco garter snakes are popular pets in Europe. The garter snake has toxins in its saliva which can be deadly to its prey, but although its bite might produce an unpleasant reaction, it is not considered dangerous to humans.

Orange

Golden Gate Bridge

The **Golden Gate Bridge**, named a Wonder of the Modern World by the American Society of Civil Engineers, is recognized as an iconic image of San Francisco. The orange color won out over the more standard carbon black and steel gray because its warm tones contrast with the bay setting and make the bridge more visible in the fog. Since it was built in the 1930s, the bridge has been painted a vermillion orange, named International Orange. A team of 17 ironworkers and 38 painters maintain the orange glow of the Golden Gate Bridge.

Although nearly all of the world's cone snail species are found in tropical waters, the one-and-a-half-inch-long **California cone snail** (*Conus californicus*) makes its home in the colder waters off California and ranges from Baja California, Mexico to San Francisco. The California cone snail feeds on other snails, worms, and small fish by either enveloping smaller animals with its body or shooting them with a special poison-tipped harpoon that it fires from its mouth. The harpoon itself is actually a type of tiny modified tooth that is hollow and barbed. When the California cone snail finds suitable prey, it aims its mouth, fills the modified tooth with potent venom, and contracts its muscles to fire the harpoon. The harpoon remains attached to the cone snail, and after the nerve toxin in the venom immobilizes or kills its prey, the cone snail retracts its harpoon, reels in the prey, and begins to feed.

California cone snail

Yellow

Yellow brain fungus (*Tremella mesenterica*) has a variety of common names, including "yellow brain," "golden jelly fungus," and "witches' butter." Yellow brain fungus is most frequently found on dead but attached or recently fallen tree branches parasitizing wood decay fungi in the genus *Peniophora*; that is, as a fungus that parasitizes yet another fungus. The gelatinous, orange-yellow fruit body of the yellow brain fungus has a winding or lobed surface that is slick or slimy when damp. It grows in crevices in bark, appearing during rainy weather. It then dries into a thin film or dried mass capable of reviving after a subsequent rain.

Yellow brain fungus

The **Santa Cruz garter snake** (*Thamnophis atratus atratus*) is an aquatic species seldom found far from its watery habitat, which includes streams, ponds, and lakes. The snake, which can be up to 40 inches long, preys on frogs, salamanders, and small fish. If threatened, the snake escapes into the water, and if caught, it strikes repeatedly while excreting feces and musk. The Santa Cruz garter snake bears its young alive during the summer months. Colorful markings include a dorsal stripe that is often bright yellow. The range of this garter snake includes the Santa Cruz Mountains and the southern San Francisco Peninsula.

Santa Cruz garter snake

Serpentine

Green

Serpentine, California's state rock, is primarily composed of one or more of the minerals lizardite, antigorite, and chrysotile. Chrysotile can take on a fibrous form and is the most common variety of asbestos. Serpentine is a metamorphic rock, derived from magnesium-rich igneous rocks. Most plants find the high levels of magnesium in serpentine-derived soils to be toxic, and "serpentine barrens" mark several parts of the coast. Some plants, however, such as San Francisco owl's clover, Marin dwarf flax, and Presidio clarkia, have evolved the capacity to deal with magnesium and have occupied this largely vacant ecological niche. Prominent outcroppings of serpentine are visible along the trail to Marshall's Beach in San Francisco.

Ohlone tiger beetle

The **Ohlone tiger beetle** (*Cicindela ohlone*) was scientifically named and described only in 1993 and added to the federal list of endangered species in 2001. The Ohlone tiger beetle's range consists of a very small portion of Santa Cruz County, on native-vegetation-dominated coastal-terrace prairies with sandy and clay soils. Unfortunately, this habitat is also highly sought after for residential development and agriculture. This species is an adept hunter—it uses its speed, agility, and large jaws, or mandibles, to chase down or ambush other insects. Although only a half-inch long, the Ohlone tiger beetle has a bright, metallic-green body with bronze markings that make this insect an easy one to identify.

California blue dorid

Blue

The **California blue dorid** (*Hypselodoris californiensis*), also called California's chromodorid, is a sea slug, or nudibranch. Nudibranchs are shell-less snails, or Gastropods, in the phylum Mollusca. Some people describe nudibranchs as the most beautiful animals in the ocean. The California blue dorid has a deep blue ground color, yellow spots arranged in rows down its back and down each side of its foot, and a band of cobalt blue along its back and foot. A defining feature of dorid nudibranchs is their gill plumes in the form of a circle on the posterior end of their body. The California blue dorid feeds exclusively on sponges.

A sighting of a bright blue snake in Central California is not uncommon, but what is seen is most likely not a snake at all, but rather a **Skiltons skink** (*Plestiodon skiltonianus skiltonianus*). A skink is a lizard, with generally stubbier legs, smoother scales, and a less prominent neck than other lizards. The Skiltons skink is well camouflaged, and often only its blue tail is spotted by predators. The non-essential tail detaches readily if grasped and will writhe afterward to divert attention from the skink while it escapes to safety. During the reproductive season males turn orange on the underside. Females lay from two to six eggs during June and July in nest chambers several centimeters deep in loose moist soil.

Skiltons skink

Violet

Purple nightshade (*Solanum xanti*) is a member of the Solanaceae family, which includes tomatoes, potatoes, petunias, peppers, tobacco, eggplant, and jimsonweed. This family of plants is infamous for poisonous alkaloids such as atropine and nicotine. In both *Romeo and Juliet* and *Macbeth*, belladonna, derived from deadly nightshade, is Shakespeare's poison of choice. Purple nightshade is a perennial plant found in sage scrub, chaparral, and oak woodland plant communities. Violet saucer-shaped flowers are about an inch across. The fruit is a purplish-black berry that is about one-quarter inch in diameter. Both the foliage and fruit of purple nightshade are toxic to humans.

Purple nightshade

The **Dungeness crab** (*Metacarcinus magister*) has certainly left its mark in waterfront communities such as San Francisco. Named after the town of Dungeness in Washington State, this species is the focus of a thriving commercial fishery on the north-central coast of California. The Dungeness crab can grow to nearly ten inches across and is equipped with powerful claws that can be used for defense as well as to capture prey and tear apart food. The Dungeness crab feeds on a variety of animals including fish, other crabs, clams, worms, and squid—essentially anything it can capture in its eelgrass-and-sandy-bottom habitat. The Dungeness crab's size and large, meaty claws make it the largest edible crab in California and a popular seafood item.

Dungeness crab

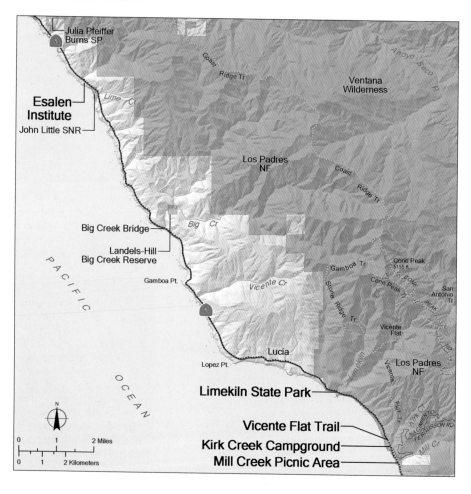

Limekiln State Park

Esalen to Mill Creek

	Sandy Beach	Rocky Shore	Trail	Visitor Center	Campground	Wildlife Viewing	Fishing or Boating	Facilities for Disabled	Food and Drink	Restrooms	Parking	Fee
Esalen Institute												•
Limekiln State Park	•	•	•	•		•	•		•	•	•	
Vicente Flat Trail			•							•		
Kirk Creek Campground	•	•		•	•				•	•	•	
Mill Creek Picnic Area	•	•	•				•		•	•		

ESALEN INSTITUTE: *W. of Hwy. One, 2.3 mi. S. of Julia Pfeiffer Burns State Park, Big Sur Coast.* The Esalen Institute offers workshops on subjects related to the body, mind, and spirit; personal retreats are also sometimes available. Fees are charged; most services, including massage and use of the natural hot-spring mineral baths, require advance reservations. Call: 831-667-3000.

Between the Esalen Institute and Gamboa Point is the Landels-Hill Big Creek Reserve, which includes 4,200 acres of mountainous terrain and is managed for research by the University of California at Santa Cruz. Very limited opportunities for public access include an annual open house day; for more information, call: 831-667-2543. Hwy. One pull-outs at the Big Creek Bridge and Gamboa Point offer sweeping views of rugged coast. In the Big Creek State Marine Reserve, off Gamboa Point, the take of all living marine resources is prohibited.

LIMEKILN STATE PARK: *Off Hwy. One, 2 mi. S. of Lucia.* Limekiln State Park has a sandy beach at the mouth of a steeply sided canyon. Twelve different plant communities, from coastal strand to alpine forest, can be found between the beach and the top of nearby Cone Peak, which rises sharply to an elevation of 5,155 feet. In the park's narrow canyon are 33 campsites, some overlooking the beach and others in a redwood grove by Limekiln Creek. All sites have picnic tables and fire rings. The narrow entrance road limits the creekside campsites to tent camping only; beach sites can accommodate RVs up to 24 feet long and trailers up to 15 feet. Restrooms have showers; firewood is sold at the entrance station. Leashed dogs allowed in campsites only. For camping reservations, call: 1-800-444-7275. From November 1 through mid-March, some campsites are available, on a first-come, first-served basis. For park information, call: 831-667-2403.

The sandy beach is bounded by steep cliffs; pelicans roost on offshore rocks. Surf fishing is popular, but rough water makes swimming inadvisable. Hikers can explore inland trails, each less than a mile long, to a 100-foot-high waterfall or a grove of some of Monterey County's largest redwood trees. The Kiln Trail leads to four historic limekilns constructed in the early 1880s. The kilns, made of stone and steel, were located to take advantage of a limestone deposit. The stone was processed, or "slaked," using heat produced by redwood cut nearby. The resulting lime, used in making cement, was packed and shipped from the mouth of the canyon, then known as Rockland Landing. Stay on trails to avoid poison oak.

VICENTE FLAT TRAIL: *E. side of Hwy. One, 3.9 mi. S. of Lucia.* This mountainous trail starts across Hwy. One from Kirk Creek Campground. Park at pull-outs on the highway; parking in Kirk Creek Campground is for campers only. As you reach an elevation of nearly 2,000 feet on the trail, the broad ocean seems to spread at your feet. The rigorous but scenic climb brings hikers to Vicente Flat, five miles from Hwy. One. Several well-spaced creek-side campsites have picnic tables and barbecue grills. Creek water must be filtered. The Vicente Flat Trail passes through grasslands dotted with spring wildflowers, groves of oak trees, and patches of redwood forest, continuing inland through canyons and to the top of Cone Peak. Primitive camps are located throughout the area. To explore inland trails, hikers can also drive east from Hwy. One for approximately seven miles on winding Nacimiento-Fergusson Rd., then turn north for four miles on unpaved Cone Peak Rd. to a junction with the Vicente Flat Trail. Call: 831-385-5434.

KIRK CREEK CAMPGROUND: *Off Hwy. One, 3.9 mi. S. of Lucia.* There are 33 campsites, including hike or bike sites, on a high terrace between Hwy. One and a rocky beach. Campsites have picnic tables and firepits; the campground host sells firewood. Fee for camping; trailers and RVs up to 30 feet in length allowed. Half the campsites can be reserved; the others are first come, first served. For campground information, call: 831-385-5434; for camping reservations, see: www.recreation.gov.

From the bluff there are dramatic vistas of the Big Sur coast. A rough path leads from the south end of the campground down the hundred-foot-high bluff to the narrow beach, where surf fishing is possible. Campers at Kirk Creek may use Forest Service–managed Sand Dollar Beach and Pfeiffer Beach with no additional charge. The Nacimiento-Fergusson Rd., which terminates south of the campground, provides a long, winding link to the southern Salinas Valley.

MILL CREEK PICNIC AREA: *W. of Hwy. One, 4.5 mi. S. of Lucia.* A handful of picnic tables with barbecue grills overlook the ocean; a steep path leads to the rocky shore, which is a diving area. Vault toilets. Open all year, 10 AM to 6 PM. Hang gliders who launch from Prewitt Ridge use the blufftop as a landing site. All hang gliders must register with the Pacific Valley Ranger Station; for information, call: 805-927-4211.

Vicente Flat Trail

Big Creek Bridge

A simple tree trunk spanning a creek probably ranks among the earliest examples of a bridge. Placement of intermediate supports allows longer bridges to be constructed. One of the great advances in bridge design arrived with the invention of the arch. The earliest extant example is a single arch bridge in the Greek Peloponnesus, built from stone in about 1300 BC, and probably built so that chariots could cross a small drainage channel. These early arches were formed out of stone blocks placed over a curved false-work form. The arch lacks stability until the center stone—the keystone—is placed. Pressure then radiates to the rest of the arch, forming a remarkably stable structure. Once the stone blocks are held together by friction and gravity, the false work can be removed. Over millennia, arches have become a common support element for bridges, and they are a unifying element of the bridges on Big Sur's coastal highway.

Until the 1930s, the Big Sur coast was one of the most remote areas of California, and travel along it was very slow. Even in 1930, a trip from Monterey to Point Sur might require four hours. Work had started in 1919 on California's new coastal road, designated as Hwy. One, but the section between Monterey and San Luis Obispo was especially challenging due to the steepness of the canyons that transected the Santa Lucia Mountain Range. The first bridge to be built as part of Hwy. One on the Big Sur coast was the Garrapata Bridge, a concrete arch bridge completed in 1931; the main arch span is almost 150 feet long and the entire bridge is 285 feet long. The second bridge, constructed over Bixby Creek, was one of the more challenging installations, and its location established the coastal focus of the highway. An inland tunnel coupled with a short bridge over the creek was considered, but highway engineers opted for a route closer to the ocean. As built, the coastal highway gives visitors a wonderful opportunity to experience the rugged coastal environment. Bixby Creek flows through a narrow, deep canyon into the sea, and the bridge over it is 714 feet long with a central arch 320 feet long. The highway surface is approximately 280 feet above the water. The length and height of the arch give the Bixby Bridge a very graceful appearance, and it is considered one of the most scenic bridges in the world.

Five other concrete arch bridges were constructed along the Big Sur coast between 1932 and 1935 at Big Creek, Granite Canyon, Malpaso Creek, Rocky Creek, and Wildcat Creek. Hwy. One between Monterey and San Simeon opened for through traffic in 1937. All the bridges except the one at Wildcat Canyon are of open-spandrel design, meaning no materials fill the area between the arches. This design gives these enormous structures an open feeling that allows then to blend into their surroundings. Along with providing connections to the communities of California's central coast, Big Sur's bridges are engineering marvels that let people connect to the splendor of the coast.

Rocky Creek Bridge

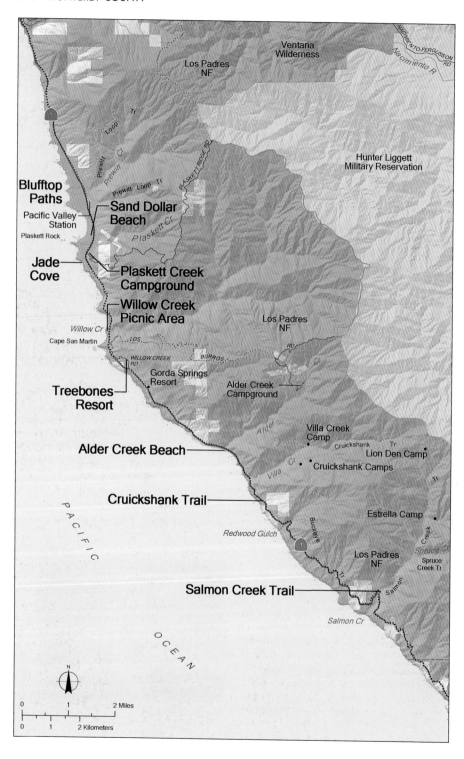

Ventana
Wilderness

Los Padres
NF

NACIMIENTO-FERGUSSON RD

Nacimiento R

Hunter Liggett
Military Reservation

Prewitt
Loop
Tr

Prewitt
Cr

Prewitt

Prewitt Loop Tr

PLASKETT RIDGE RD

**Blufftop
Paths**

Pacific Valley
Station

Plaskett Rock

**Sand Dollar
Beach**

Plaskett Cr

**Jade
Cove**

**Plaskett Creek
Campground**

**Willow Creek
Picnic Area**

Los Padres
NF

Willow Cr

Cape San Martin

LOS

RD

BURROS

Cr

WILLOW CREEK
RD

Gorda Springs
Resort

**Alder Creek
Campground**

**Treebones
Resort**

Alder

Villa Creek
Camp

Cruickshank   Tr

Alder Creek Beach

Lion Den Camp

Villa   Cr

Cruickshank Camps

Tr

Cruickshank Trail

Estrella Camp

P A C I F I C

Redwood Gulch

Buckeye

Los Padres
NF

Spruce Cr

Spruce
Creek Tr

Salmon Creek Trail

Tr

Salmon

Salmon Cr

O C E A N

N

0   1   2 Miles

0   1   2 Kilometers

Big Sur South

	Sandy Beach	Rocky Shore	Trail	Visitor Center	Campground	Wildlife Viewing	Fishing or Boating	Facilities for Disabled	Food and Drink	Restrooms	Parking	Fee
Blufftop Paths	•	•	•									
Sand Dollar Beach	•		•			•			•	•	•	
Plaskett Creek Campground			•		•				•	•	•	
Jade Cove		•	•									
Willow Creek Picnic Area	•	•				•	•		•	•		
Treebones Resort					•				•	•	•	•
Alder Creek Beach			•							•		
Cruickshank Trail			•		•					•		
Salmon Creek Trail			•		•					•		

BLUFFTOP PATHS: *W. of Hwy. One, 6.9 mi. S. of Lucia.* On the broad coastal terrace of Pacific Valley, within Los Padres National Forest, are several paths that lead to the bluff edge for views of the rugged shoreline or, in a few locations, descend to pocket beaches. Look along the shoulder of Hwy. One for stiles that allow hikers to cross the roadside fence. Several stiles are clustered between one and two miles north of Sand Dollar Beach, including one located opposite the U.S. Forest Service's Pacific Valley Station. Another stile is located one-quarter mile south of Sand Dollar Beach. Hikers bent on exploring inland canyons rather than the coast can use the Prewitt Trail; the better-maintained end of the loop trail starts one-half mile north of Pacific Valley Station, on the east side of Hwy. One.

SAND DOLLAR BEACH: *W. of Hwy. One, 11 mi. S. of Lucia.* This crescent-shaped strand is the longest accessible sandy beach on the Big Sur coast. High above the south end of the beach is a picnic area with eight tables and restrooms among Monterey cypress trees, and a paved path that leads across a grassy meadow to the edge of the bluff. A steep trail leads down to the shore. To the north, 5,155-foot-high Cone Peak can be seen rising above the Big Sur coast. Pacific sanddab, white croaker, and flounder inhabit the nearshore waters off Sand Dollar Beach. Gulls roost on offshore rocks at the south end of the bay. Hiking, surfing, and surf fishing are popular; this is also a hang glider landing area. The surf can be rough; use caution, as there is no lifeguard on duty. Pets must be leashed. Fee for day use. Part of Los Padres National Forest; for information, call: 831-385-5434.

The coastline north through Pacific Valley to Limekiln State Park and south past Willow Creek is all within Los Padres National Forest. Inland of Hwy. One there are scattered private land holdings among the public lands. National forest lands are open for hiking and exploration, although mountain biking and hang gliding are restricted in the Ventana Wilderness area.

PLASKETT CREEK CAMPGROUND: *E. side of Hwy. One, 11.7 mi. S. of Lucia.* The campground, set among Monterey pine trees, has 41 campsites with picnic tables, fire rings, and barbecue grills. Hike or bike sites and three group campsites are also available. There is drinking water, and restrooms have

On the southern Big Sur coast, visitor services are limited. Food and lodging are available at the hamlet of Lucia, near Limekiln State Park, and at Gorda Springs Resort, where gasoline is also available.

running water. Open all year; fee for camping. Half the campsites can be reserved; the others are first come, first served. For information, call: 831-385-5434; for camping reservations, see: www.recreation.gov.

JADE COVE: *W. of Hwy. One, .5 mi. S. of Sand Dollar Beach.* Look for the Los Padres National Forest sign on Hwy. One. Shoulder parking only; a steep trail leads down the serpentine cliff face to several rocky coves. A popular diving area; a two-ton jade boulder located underwater has been reported nearby. Call: 831-385-5434.

WILLOW CREEK PICNIC AREA: *W. of Hwy. One, 2.2 mi. S. of Sand Dollar Beach.* This day-use area is located where Willow Creek flows into the ocean. From the vista point at the southeast end of the Willow Creek Bridge, a steep paved road leads down to sea level. The shoreline is rocky to the south of the creek's mouth and sandy to the north. In spite of the rocks, surfers use the beach. Offshore kelp beds provide habitat for harbor seals and southern sea otters. Gulls and cormorants roost around Cape San Martin, a rocky point to the south of the beach. Vault toilets. Open all year, 10 AM to 6 PM.

TREEBONES RESORT: *E. of Hwy. One, off Willow Creek Rd., .9 mi. N. of Gorda.* The right fork of Willow Creek Rd. leads to the privately operated Treebones Resort, which offers five walk-in tent campsites, as well as furnished yurts, a heated swimming pool, and store; call: 877-424-4787. The left fork of Willow Creek Rd., also known as Los Burros Rd., winds inland eight miles to the Alder Creek Camp in the Los Padres National Forest. Two campsites are set among oak trees along the creek; picnicking and hiking are also possible. Bring your own water. Call: 831-385-5434.

ALDER CREEK BEACH: *W. side of Hwy. One, 2.5 mi. S. of Gorda.* An old road, now interrupted by rockfalls, leads to a rocky beach. A pull-out on Hwy. One offers views of seastacks and the rugged coast.

CRUICKSHANK TRAIL: *E. side of Hwy. One, 3.6 mi. S. of Gorda.* Small roadside pull-outs on both sides of Hwy. One are located at this trailhead; the trail sign, placed parallel to the

The scenic headland known as Plaskett Rock separates Sand Dollar Beach from Jade Cove. If you hike down to Jade Cove, you may be rewarded by finding pebbles of jade in the surf zone; the U.S. Forest Service prohibits collecting above the mean high tide line. The jade, consisting of the minerals jadeite and nephrite, is eroded out of the Franciscan Complex rocks that make up the bluffs in this area. These minerals form at very high pressures in the earth's crust, but at relatively low temperatures. Their presence is proof that parts of the Franciscan Complex rocks were shoved far below the surface during subduction of the Farallon Plate.

highway, is easy to miss. The Cruickshank Trail climbs sharply upward for the first mile, quickly reaching 1,500 feet in elevation, with spectacular views over the ocean. The trail also includes some gentle sections among trees; overall, the effort required here for a day hiker to explore a couple of miles inland may be somewhat less than on the Salmon Creek Trail, located a few miles farther south.

For backpackers, several campsites are located on the slopes above Villa Creek, within a few miles of Hwy. One. Lower Cruickshank and Upper Cruickshank camps have one site each, with picnic table and firepit. Villa Creek camp, located three miles from Hwy.

Plaskett Creek Campground

Jade Cove

One, is situated near the creek, with waterfalls and a forested setting. Water must be treated for drinking. The Cruickshank Trail continues inland to Lion Den camp and also connects to other trails, including the Buckeye Trail that leads north to Alder Creek and south to Salmon Creek. South of the Cruickshank Trail is Redwood Gulch, where the coast redwood tree reaches the southernmost limit of its natural range.

SALMON CREEK TRAIL: *E. side of Hwy. One, 8 mi. S. of Gorda.* At Hwy. One milepost 2.2, at a switchback in a steep ravine, is a trail that leads up the slope along the south bank of Salmon Creek. Cascades of water tumble down the stream course, bordered by ferns, alders, and California bay laurel trees. Views of the ocean can be glimpsed through the trees.

After a mile and a half of climbing, hikers on the Salmon Creek Trail reach the Spruce Creek Trail, where the two creeks come together. Spruce Creek camp, at the trail junction, offers a handful of scattered campsites in a forested setting, with swimming holes and waterfalls nearby. A mile and a half farther along the Salmon Creek Trail is Estrella

camp, set in a meadow with scattered oak trees. The Spruce Creek Trail leads to Dutra Flat, Turkey Springs, and San Carpoforo camps, the last one eight miles distant from the trailhead at Hwy. One.

Salmon Creek

Marble Cone from Pacific Valley, *original print 10.5 x 14 inches*

© 2012 Tom Killion

Protecting Coastal Resources

PROTECTING California's coast presents a challenge as never before. The state's population is ever-growing, and yet there are only so many miles of shoreline and only so many beaches. Coastal habitats, including wetlands, streams, and forests, are threatened. Even the ocean, once thought to be limitless in every respect, is now recognized to be highly vulnerable. Hundreds of millions of tons of waste, including debris from oil refineries, fruit canneries, and chemical plants, were once dumped in the Gulf of the Farallones off San Francisco. Between 1946 and 1970 some 47,800 containers of low-level radioactive waste were discarded near the Farallon Islands. Creation of the Gulf of the Farallones National Marine Sanctuary, along with other restrictions, has brought an end to dumping. However, plastic bags discarded by consumers, street debris that washes down storm drains, and toxic chemicals used in home gardens continue to pose a threat to ocean life.

Global Climate Change

Changes in climate associated with global warming are likely to alter many characteristics of the California coast. Temperature changes have been recorded already; a team of scientists from the National Aeronautic and Space Administration (NASA) and the Jet Propulsion Laboratory at the California Institute of Technology have observed an increase of 1.5 degrees Fahrenheit in average annual air temperature from 1950 to 2000 along the central California coast.

Greater variability can be expected in daily and seasonal temperature ranges, in precipitation amounts, and in other climate characteristics, resulting in unwelcome changes. Monterey pine trees, which occur naturally only on the Monterey Peninsula and at a few other California locations, may no longer seem to proliferate. While older trees survive, young trees are less able to get established. In the San Francisco Bay Area, alterations in precipitation have hastened the extinction of two populations of the checkerspot butterfly.

The link between climate change and sea level rise has been well-documented. With rising sea levels, we can expect greater erosion of beaches and coastal bluffs, increased inundation of low-lying coastal areas, drowning of existing wetlands, and shifts in areas of tidal influence. Other likely effects of climate change are the greater frequency and extent of forest fires; increased variability of precipitation, including extended periods of drought and flood events; and reduced storage of snow at high elevations coupled with earlier spring runoff.

Hydrocorals and Ocean Acidification

Water temperature, light levels, and other environmental factors in the deep ocean environment are much the same all the time. Many organisms there are dependent on those stable conditions. Creatures that are adapted to an unchanging environment experience stress or even a threat to their existence if conditions alter even slightly.

When we think of corals, we often think of warm, tropical waters, but both reef-building and solitary corals are found also in temperate and polar waters. Some corals live at depths of three miles or more. Corals, once settled and permanently attached, are animals that exist at the mercy of oceanic conditions. Corals and other species with skeletons or shells made of calcium carbonate are vulnerable to the process called ocean acidification. This phenomenon is associated with the rising level of atmospheric

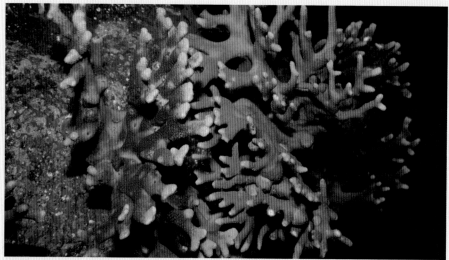

Hydrocoral *Stylaster californicus*

carbon dioxide (CO_2), itself associated with global climate change. An increase in CO_2 dissolved in the ocean changes the availability of minerals that are needed for shell formation, known as calcification. Higher acidity levels have been shown to sharply slow and diminish calcification in corals, sea urchins, clams, plankton such as pteropods, and corraline algae. The result is that organisms build weaker skeletons and shells, a process similar to osteoporosis in humans.

Creation of Marine Protected Areas

One way to offset the uncertainty associated with climate change is to designate marine protected areas, or "MPAs." Protecting marine life in key locations is a way to assure the survival of vulnerable organisms, especially those that are permanently attached, or "sessile," meaning that they cannot simply move to another location. California's Marine Life Protection Act was signed into law in 1999. The Act provides for a new statewide network of science-based marine protected areas with clear management and performance goals. Before 1999, marine reserves had been designated along the California coast, but typically on a piecemeal basis only, and sometimes without thorough evaluation of their resources or clear conservation objectives.

The Marine Life Protection Act created a public-private partnership that makes use of the best readily available science and the advice of resource managers, experts, fishermen, stakeholders, and members of the public. California's 1,271-mile-long coastline was divided into five separate study regions. In the first region, extending from Pigeon Point in San Mateo County to Point Conception in Santa Barbara County, 29 new marine protected areas encompassing 204 square miles were established in 2007. In the second region, from Alder Creek in Mendocino County to Pigeon Point in San Mateo County, including the Farallon Islands, 21 marine protected areas were designated in 2009, covering 153 square miles of nearshore and offshore waters. In December 2009, the public and stakeholder planning process for the south coast (Point Conception to the Mexican border) concluded; new MPA designations are anticipated for that area. The two remaining regions to be addressed include San Francisco Bay and the far North Coast, from the Oregon border to Alder Creek in Mendocino County.

Among the newly established marine protected areas between Marin County and Monterey County, fourteen areas have been provided the highest level of protection as "no-take" **marine reserves**. These reserves have especially fragile habitats such as rocky reefs, submarine canyons, estuaries, and offshore islands, and all marine life is protected. Sixteen **marine conservation areas** or **marine parks** have also been designated, allowing the catch of certain commercial or recreationally important species, with specified types of fishing gear. The regulations for each site are different, because each marine protected area was established with goals to protect certain unique species and habitats. Information about each of the marine protected areas, including exact locations and regulations, can be found at the California Department of Fish and Game website; see: http://www.dfg.ca.gov/mlpa.

Each California marine protected area has been designed to meet size guidelines—between three and eighteen square miles—and to contain particular habitats, in order to maximize the potential to protect and restore a diverse array of marine species. The spacing of each MPA along the coast was also carefully planned. Marine species such as lobster, shellfish, and kelp have a larval, or "planktonic," life stage lasting from several days to several months, allowing the animal to float freely and disperse away from the site at which it was born. Using information about the length of time most marine species in California spend floating as plankton, as well as about water currents, the scientific advisors for the MPA planning process developed guidelines for spacing so that species that originated in one reserve would be likely to settle in another reserve at the end of their larval growth period rather than becoming established in an area without protection.

In addition to collecting information on habitats and the presence of different species, the marine protected area planning effort has mapped the location and relative importance of commercial and recreational fishing grounds. This information was used, in conjunction with extensive feedback from the fishing community, to help ensure that marine protected areas could be sited in areas that would not result in the unacceptable loss of fishing grounds.

Although the implementation of California's landmark Marine Life Protection Act has been a contentious process that has required careful planning and negotiation among a wide variety of interest groups and ocean users, large-scale marine conservation planning is feasible. There is substantial evidence that marine protected areas will provide lasting benefits to marine species and habitats and contribute to the resilience of our coastal waters. California's process of designing and establishing a coordinated statewide network of marine reserves, marine conservation areas, and marine parks, based on the latest scientific understanding of marine ecological principles, conservation techniques and socio-economic considerations is one of the most comprehensive marine planning endeavors ever attempted in the United States.

A Wealth of Research Institutions

Along the coast from Marin County to Monterey County can be found one of the world's highest concentrations of marine science research centers. Each facility has developed its own unique research specialties over the years, with robust collaboration among biologists, ecologists, oceanographers, chemists, geologists, engineers, and students.

Since PRBO Conservation Science's founding in 1965 as the Point Reyes Bird Observatory at a site near Bolinas in Marin County, the nonprofit research organization has dedicated its efforts to conserving birds, other wildlife, and ecosystems through innovative scientific research and outreach. PRBO supports about 65 staff scientists, 55 seasonal biologists, and another 85 conservation biology interns that have helped justify the establishment of northern California's three national marine sanctuaries, the protection of vital bird breeding and migratory stopover sites, and the adoption of key fishing regulations and guidelines that have eliminated several known sources of mortality for sensitive seabird species.

Opened in 1978, the Long Marine Laboratory at the University of California at Santa Cruz provides work space for roughly 100 faculty members, researchers, graduate students, and support staff. Although its scientists are active in many fields, including nearshore ecology and ocean health, Long Marine Laboratory is especially well regarded for the research its staff has carried out with marine mammals. Significant advances in areas such as the diving physiology, physiological ecology, bioacoustics, and cognition of whales, seals, and other marine mammals have been achieved. The laboratory also houses the Seymour Marine Discovery Center, a public museum with a small aquarium that provides visitors with a better understanding of the role that research plays in the conservation of the world's oceans.

Near the shallow mouth of the Elkhorn Slough and the tremendous depths of the Monterey Submarine Canyon, the Moss Landing Marine Laboratories (MLML) are operated by a consortium of seven California State University campuses: Fresno, East Bay, Monterey Bay, Sacramento, San Francisco, San Jose, and Stanislaus. The laboratory's mission is to "provision the pioneers of the future" in the marine sciences through graduate and undergraduate-level education. At any one time, roughly 120 students are being trained or are carrying out field research in marine environments nearby.

Known as the research arm of the world-renowned Monterey Bay Aquarium, the Monterey Bay Aquarium Research Institute (MBARI) is a relative newcomer to the region's marine research community. Founded in 1987 by David Packard, MBARI has a mission to "achieve and maintain a position as a world center for advanced research and education in ocean science and technology, and to do so through the development of better instruments, systems and methods for scientific research in the deep waters of the ocean." MBARI is well positioned to carry out this mission due to its proximity to

Moss Landing Marine Laboratories, Monterey County

the Monterey Submarine Canyon. This mission is also complemented by the mechanical, electrical, and computer engineers represented on MBARI's staff of approximately 220. Since its early years, MBARI has distinguished itself as a unique institution due to the great strides its staff has made in developing innovative tools and methods for exploring difficult environments and research questions that were inaccessible to scientists using conventional technologies. MBARI's current efforts span eight research themes, including benthic (ocean floor) processes, mid-water research, upper ocean biogeochemistry, and remotely operated deep-sea vehicle enhancements.

Stanford University's Hopkins Marine Station is the oldest marine laboratory on the West Coast. Started in 1892 as a satellite to the main Stanford campus at Palo Alto, this facility has been located since 1917 at Cabrillo Point in Pacific Grove. Ten faculty members of the Department of Biology are typically housed at Hopkins Marine Station, and both undergraduate and graduate courses in marine biology and related topics are provided. In addition, research is carried out at the facility, often taking advantage of nearby access to marine plant and animal species and the adjacent state marine reserve, one of the oldest in California.

While it would be impossible to precisely quantify the advances that these five distinguished research institutions have inspired in the fields of marine science and engineering, or to count the number of current and future scientists that have passed through their doors, it is clear that their contributions to our understanding and conservation of the oceans has been immense. For over 100 years, California's central coast has supported a robust community of dedicated marine researchers and educators who have operated on the forefront of scientific understanding.

A deep-sea image of a yellow sponge covered with basket stars captured by the remotely operated vehicle (ROV) *Tiburon* is viewed at the surface by staff of the Monterey Bay National Marine Sanctuary in a joint research project with MBARI.

Afterword

In preparing this guide, we visited and researched all beaches, parks, and coastal accessways that are described here. We have incorporated comments and corrections supplied by various agencies and members of the public, who wrote to us regarding the information in previous California Coastal Commission publications. We also sought review of draft material by staff of parks departments, local governments, land trusts, and others. The book is accurate, to the best of our knowledge. Nevertheless, conditions on the coast are constantly changing, and there may be inaccuracies in this book. If you think something is incorrect or has been omitted, please let us know. The Coastal Commission intends to continue publishing revised guides in the future and would appreciate any additional information you can provide. Please remember, however, that this book includes only those beaches and accessways that are managed for public use.

Address all comments to:

Coastal Access Program
California Coastal Commission
45 Fremont Street, Suite 2000
San Francisco, CA 94105

or e-mail to: coast4U@coastal.ca.gov.

Shore crab at Ocean Beach, San Francisco

Acknowledgments

This book was funded in part with qualified outer continental shelf oil and gas revenues by the Coastal Impact Assistance Program of the Bureau of Ocean Energy Management, Regulation and Enforcement, U.S. Department of the Interior. The views and conclusions contained in this document are those of the authors and should not be interpreted as representing the opinions or policies of the U.S. Government. Mention of trade names or commercial products does not constitute their endorsement by the U.S. Government.

Additional writing and research:

Katie Butler

Dan Carl

Kelly Cuffe

Eli Davidian

Mark Delaplaine

Tami Grove

Ben Hansch

Ziad Hussami

John Prager

Larry Simon

Additional cartography:

Doug Macmillan

Darryl Rance

Principal Contributors, *California Coastal Access Guide* and *California Coastal Resource Guide*, from which selected material has been incorporated in this book:

Trevor Kenner Cralle

Linda Goff Evans

Stephen J. Furney-Howe

Jo Ginsberg

Michelle Jesperson

Christopher Kroll

Trish Mihalek

Don Neuwirth

S. Briggs Nisbet

Victoria Randlett

Sabrina S. Simpson

Pat Stebbins

Mary Travis

Jeffrey D. Zimmerman

Thanks to the following individuals and organizations for their invaluable assistance:

James Barry

Dominique D. Bruce

California Academy of Sciences

California Historical Society

California Natural Resources Agency

Matt Conens

Tim Duff

Christina V. Fidler

Kim Fulton-Bennett

Bill Gissel

Richard Hargrave

Susan Jordan

Tom Killion

Bonnie Lewkowicz

Monterey Bay Aquarium

Monterey Bay Aquarium Research Institute (MBARI)

National Oceanic and Atmospheric Administration

Office of Ocean and Coastal Resource Management

Oregon Dept. of Fish and Wildlife

Alena Porte

Chris Potter

Kirsten Ramey

Rebecca Roth

Solano Land Trust

State Coastal Conservancy

Julie Takata

Susan Zaleski

Photo and Illustration Credits:

© 2002–2010 Kenneth & Gabrielle Adelman, California Coastal Records Project, www.Californiacoastline.org, 23, 24, 186, 187, 268, 289

© Allen Andrews/Monterey Bay Aquarium Research Institute, 299

© Rinus Baak, 245

Bancroft Library, Oliver Family Photo Collection, 239

© Terry Blaine, 82

Stacy Boorn, 80

Ted Brown © California Academy of Sciences, 283c

California Dept. of Public Health, 53c

California Historical Society

   233, Robert Louis Stevenson House, Monterey California. Color postcard: E.H. Mitchell. Courtesy, California Historical Society, FN-36323

   250, Pebble Beach, 1910. Courtesy, California Historical Society, FN-36324

© Robert Campbell, 26

© Brandon Cole, 206c

© Phillip Colla, 52c, 79a, 296

Gerald and Buff Corsi © California Academy of Sciences, 255a, 265a

© Bob Cranston/SeaPics.com, 52a

T.W. Davies © California Academy of Sciences, 273c

© Jeremiah Easter, 282b

Kip Evans, 264a, 264c, 281

Lesley Ewing, 189

© Annie Kohut Frankel, 247

© Daniel Geiger, 283b

© John Gibbens/SeaPics.com, 78c

© David Graber, 227c

© Joyce Gross, 284b

© Scott Groth, 216c

© Matthew Hooge, 131a, 131b, 131c

Dr. Lloyd Glenn Ingles © California Academy of Sciences, 229b

© Alden Johnson, 255c

Mark Johnsson, 261

© Tom Killion, 10, 48, 74, 262, 294

© Neal Kramer, 104a, 228b, 254a, 254b, 285b

Dorothea Lange © The Dorothea Lange Collection, Oakland Museum of California, City of Oakland, Gift of Paul S. Taylor, 73

© Peter LaTourrette, 52b, 79b, 79c, 104c, 217c, 229a, 265b, 265c, 272a

© Sylvie B. Lee, 246

© William Leonard, 229c

© David Liebman, 228c

Linda Locklin, 176, 178, 180

© Valerie T. McCormick, 96

© Gary McDonald, 216a, 216b, 264b, 283a, 284c

© Thomas H. Mikkelsen, 14,16, 19, 25, 28, 29, 30, 32, 33, 42, 43, 44, 45, 47, 54, 55, 56, 60, 63, 66, 70, 72, 95, 98, 108, 110, 118, 119, 124, 128, 129, 130, 134, 137, 141, 142, 144, 148, 154, 158, 161, 169, 170, 174, 197, 200, 207, 214, 232, 237a, 244, 248, 251, 260, 269, 274

© Randy Morse/GoldenStateImages.com, 51b, 53a, 288b

© Monterey Bay Aquarium, 243

© Monterey Bay Aquarium/Randy Wilder, 241, 242

© Monterey Bay Aquarium/Rob Lewine, 240

© Monterey Bay Aquarium Research Institute (MBARI), 202 ©1998 MBARI, 203, 205b, 205c, 206a

© Aaron Nadig, 273a

© Gary Nafis, 217b, 272c, 273b, 285a

National Oceanic and Atmospheric Admin., 27a

© Doug Perrine/SeaPics.com, 51c

PRBO Conservation Science, 78b

© Kevin Raskoff, 53b

© Kim Reisenbichler © 1996 MBARI, 206b

© Andy Sallmon/Mondragonphoto.com, 217a

San Francisco Maritime National Historic Park, reproduced by permission, 85

© Rob Schell, 255b

© Annie Schmidt, 78a

Steve Scholl, 13,15, 22, 34, 35, 38, 39, 40, 41, 51a, 57, 59, 62, 65, 68, 69, 76, 77, 83, 84, 89, 92, 94, 97, 99, 106, 109, 111, 113, 115, 117, 125, 126, 127, 132a, 132b, 132c, 133a, 133b, 133c, 140, 146, 149, 150, 151, 152, 153, 155, 160, 164, 165, 166, 168, 172, 173, 175, 181, 182, 184, 185, 188, 190, 191, 192, 193, 194, 196, 198, 201, 212, 218, 220, 221, 222, 223, 224, 225, 226, 227b, 230, 231, 234, 235, 236, 237b, 238, 253, 256, 257, 258, 259, 266, 270, 271a, 271b, 276, 277, 278, 279, 282c, 284a, 285c, 286, 288a, 292, 293a, 293b, 298, 300

© Aaron Schusteff, 227a

Todd Sergot, 67

© Stephen Sharnoff, 37c

Doreen Smith, 254c, 271c

© Craig Stern, 46

Clyde Sunderland/courtesy of Pacific Aerial Surveys, a division of PhotoScience Inc. Oakland CA, 101

© Ian Tait, 272b

© Dean W. Taylor, 228a

US Fish and Wildlife Service, 105b

© Masa Ushioda/SeaPics.com, 105c

Jonathan Van Coops, 201

145, Engraving courtesy of Jonathan Van Coops, great-great-grandson of Henry Dobbel

Larry Wade/US Fish and Wildlife Service, 105a

© James Watanabe, 282a

© Doug Wirtz, 104b

© Lindsey Koepke Wise, 37a

© Ron Wolf, 37b

© David Wrobel/SeaPics.com, 205a

Whale Tail license plate designed by Elizabeth Robinette Tyndall and Bill Atkins, 17

Glossary

anadromous. Migrating from salt water to fresh water in order to reproduce.

annual. A plant that germinates, flowers, sets seed, and dies within one year or less.

basalt. A dark igneous rock of volcanic origin. Basalt is the bedrock of most of the world ocean.

bay. A partially enclosed inlet of the ocean.

beach. The shore of a body of water, usually covered by sand or pebbles.

bluff. A high bank or bold headland with a broad, precipitous, sometimes rounded cliff face overlooking a plain or a body of water.

brackish. Used to describe water that contains some salt, but less than sea water (from 0.5 to 30 parts per thousand).

coastal scrub. A plant association characterized by low, drought-resistant, woody shrubs; includes coastal sage scrub.

coastal strand community. A plant association endemic to bluffs, dunes, and sandy beaches, and adapted to saline conditions; includes coast goldenbush and sand verbena.

coastal terrace. A flat plain edging the ocean; uplifted sea floor that was cut and eroded by wave action. Synonymous with marine terrace.

cobble. A rock fragment larger than a pebble and smaller than a boulder, having a diameter in the range of 2.5 to 10 inches and being somewhat rounded or otherwise modified by abrasion in the course of transport.

conifer. A cone-bearing tree, usually evergreen, such as a pine or fir.

continental borderland. An area of the continental margin located between the shoreline and the continental slope that is topographically more complex than the continental shelf.

continental shelf. The shallow, gradually sloping area of the sea floor adjacent to the shoreline, terminating seaward at the continental slope.

crustaceans. A group of mostly marine arthropods; e.g., barnacles, shrimp, and crabs.

current. Local or large-scale water movements that result in the flow of water in a particular direction, e.g., alongshore, or offshore.

delta. A fan-shaped alluvial deposit at the mouth of a river.

dorsal. Pertaining to the upper surface or the back of an organism. A dorsal fin is a vertical fin arising from the back of a fish or cetacean (whales, dolphins, and porpoises). *Compare* ventral.

El Niño. A warming of the ocean current along the coasts of Peru and Ecuador that is generally associated with dramatic changes in the weather patterns around the world.

endangered. Refers specifically to those species designated by the California Dept. of Fish and Game or the U.S. Fish and Wildlife Service as "endangered" because of severe population declines.

endemic. A plant or animal native to a well-defined geographic area and restricted to that area.

erosion. The gradual breakdown of land by weathering, solution, corrosion, abrasion, or transportation, caused by action of the wind, water, or ice; opposite of accretion.

estivate. To pass the summer in a state of dormancy.

estuary. A semi-enclosed coastal body of water that is connected with the open ocean and within which seawater mixes with freshwater from a river or stream.

exotic. Any species, especially a plant, not native to the area where it occurs; introduced.

fault. A fracture or fracture zone along which displacement of the earth occurs resulting from seismic activity.

groin. A low, narrow jetty, constructed at right angles to the shoreline, that projects out into the water to trap sand or to retard shoreline erosion; a shoreline protective device.

habitat. The sum total of all the living and non-living factors that surround and potentially influence an organism; a particular organism's environment.

halophyte. A plant that is adapted to grow in salty soils.

haul-out. A place where pinnipeds emerge from the water onto land to rest or breed.

herb. Botanically, a plant that lacks a woody stem and whose above-ground parts last only a growing season. Medicinal and culinary herbs include plants of many growth forms, including shrubs and trees, whereas most botanical herbs are never found in the kitchen or in the pharmacy.

igneous rock. A rock that solidified from molten or partially molten material.

intertidal. Pertaining to the shoreline area between the highest high tide mark and the lowest low tide mark.

intrusion. In geology, the process of emplacement of molten rock in pre-existing rock.

invasive species. Weedy, generally non-native plants or wildlife species that invade and/or proliferate following disturbance or continued overuse.

invertebrate. An animal with no backbone or spinal column; 95 percent of the species in the animal kingdom are invertebrates.

jetty. An engineered structure constructed at right angles to the coast at the mouth of a river or harbor to help stabilize the entrance; usually constructed in pairs on each side of a channel.

krill. Any of numerous species of shrimp-like crustaceans. Krill occur in all the world's oceans, but are particularly abundant in polar waters, where they form enormous swarms that are a critical food source for many large animals, including many whales.

La Niña. A periodic cooling of surface ocean waters in the eastern tropical Pacific along with a shift in convection in the western Pacific, affecting weather patterns around the world.

lagoon. A body of fresh or brackish water separated from the sea by a sandbar or reef.

longshore current. A current flowing parallel to and near shore that is the result of waves hitting the beach at an oblique angle.

magma. Naturally occurring molten or partially molten rock material, generated within the Earth and capable of intrusion and extrusion, from which igneous rocks are derived through solidification and related processes.

marsh. General term for a semi-aquatic area with relatively still, shallow water—such as the shore of a pond, lake, or protected bay or estuary—and characterized by mineral soils that support herbaceous vegetation.

metamorphic rock. A rock formed by changes in the mineralogical, chemical, and structural character of a pre-existing rock resulting from changes in physical and chemical conditions imposed at depth, generally through burial.

mollusks. Soft-bodied, generally shelled invertebrates; for example, chitons, snails, limpets, bivalves, and squid.

Monterey Formation. A group of sedimentary rocks consisting of cherts, siltstones, sandstones, and shales deposited during the Miocene Epoch and exposed extensively in coastal California.

nearshore. The area extending seaward an indefinite distance from the shoreline, well beyond the breaker zone.

pectoral. Pertaining to the front side of an organism toward the head (the chest in humans). The pectoral fins are the paired fins on the lower front of fishes and correspond to the forelimbs of four-legged vertebrates.

pelagic. Pertaining to open ocean rather than inland waters or waters adjacent to land.

perennial. A plant that lives longer than a year.

pinnipeds. Marine mammals that have fin-like flippers, including seals, sea lions, and walruses.

plankton. Free-floating algae (phytoplankton) or animals (zooplankton) that drift in the water, ranging from microscopic organisms to larger species such as jellyfish.

predator. An animal that eats other animals; a carnivore.

pycnocline. A layer in an ocean or lake where water density changes abruptly.

reef. A submerged ridge of rock or coral near the surface of the water.

relict. In ecology, a genus or species from a previous era that has survived radical environmental changes resulting from climatic shifts.

revetment. A sloped retaining wall built of riprap or concrete blocks to prevent coastal erosion and other damage by wave action; similar to a seawall.

rip current. A narrow, swift-flowing current that flows seaward through the breaker zone at nearly right angles to the shoreline and returns water to the sea after being piled up on the shore by waves and wind.

riparian. Pertaining to the habitat along the bank of a stream, river, pond, or lake.

riprap. Boulders or quarry stone used to construct a groin, jetty, or revetment.

schist. Medium- to coarse-grained metamorphic rocks composed of laminated, often flaky, parallel layers of chiefly micaceous minerals.

seawall. A structure, usually a vertical wood or concrete wall, designed to prevent erosion inland or damage due to wave action.

sedimentary rock. Rocks resulting from the consolidation of loose sediment.

shale. A fine-grained sedimentary rock formed by the consolidation of clay, silt, or mud.

slough. A small marshland or tidal waterway that usually connects with other tidal areas.

species. A taxonomic classification ranking below a genus, and consisting of a group of closely related organisms that are capable of interbreeding and producing viable offspring.

subduction zone. A long narrow belt in which one lithospheric plate descends beneath another.

substrate. The surface on which an organism grows or is attached.

surf zone. The area affected by wave action, from the shoreline high-water mark seaward to where the waves start to break.

take. As defined by the Endangered Species Act, "to harass, harm, pursue, hunt, shoot, wound, kill, capture, or collect, or attempt to engage in any such conduct."

tectonic. Pertaining to the forces involved in the regional assembling of structural or deformational features of the Earth.

terrestrial. Living or growing on land, as opposed to living in water or air.

thermocline. The boundary zone in a body of water between significantly different temperature layers.

threatened. Refers specifically to those species designated by the California Dept. of Fish and Game or the U.S. Fish and Wildlife Service as "threatened" because of severe population declines.

tidal wave. The regular rise and fall of the tides; often misused for *tsunami*.

tide. The periodic rising and falling of the ocean resulting from the gravitational forces of the moon and sun acting upon the rotating earth.

tidepool. Habitat in the rocky intertidal zone that retains some water at low tide.

tsunami. A sometimes destructive ocean wave caused by an underwater earthquake, submarine landslide, or volcanic eruption; inaccurately called a tidal wave.

uplifted. Pertaining to a segment of the earth's surface that has been elevated relative to the surrounding surface as a result of tectonic activity.

upwelling. A process by which deep, cold, nutrient-rich waters rise to the sea surface.

ventral. Pertaining to the lower surface, front, or belly of an organism. *Compare* dorsal.

waterfowl. Ducks, geese, and swans.

wetland. General term referring to shallow water (less than six feet deep) and land that is tidally or seasonally inundated, including marshes, mudflats, lagoons, sloughs, bogs, swamps, and fens.

Selected State and Federal Agencies

California State Agencies:

California Coastal Commission
710 E St., Suite 200
Eureka, CA 95501
707-445-7833

California Coastal Commission
45 Fremont St., Suite 2000
San Francisco, CA 94105
415-904-5200

California Coastal Commission
725 Front St., Suite 300
Santa Cruz, CA 95060
831-427-4863

California Department of Fish and Game
Marine Region Main Office
20 Lower Ragsdale Dr., Suite 100
Monterey, CA 93940
831-649-2870

California Department of Fish and Game
1850 Bay Flat Rd.
P.O. Box 1560
Bodega Bay, CA 94923
707-875-4260

California Department of Parks and Recreation
1416 Ninth St.
Sacramento, CA 95814
1-800-777-0369
info@parks.ca.gov

California Department of Parks and Recreation
845 Casa Grande Rd.
Petaluma, CA 94954
707-769-5665

California Department of Parks and Recreation
2211 Garden Rd.
Monterey, CA 93940
831-649-2836

State Coastal Conservancy
1330 Broadway, Suite 1100
Oakland, CA 94612
510-286-1015

California State Lands Commission
100 Howe Ave., Suite 100 South
Sacramento, CA 95825
916-574-1900

Federal Agencies:

Cordell Bank National Marine Sanctuary
1 Bear Valley Rd.
Point Reyes Station, CA 94956
415-663-0314

Gulf of the Farallones National Marine
Sanctuary (headquarters)
991 Marine Dr., The Presidio
San Francisco, CA 94129
415-561-6622

Gulf of the Farallones National Marine
Sanctuary (satellite office)
625 Miramontes St.
Half Moon Bay, CA 94019
650-712-8948

Monterey Bay National Marine Sanctuary
299 Foam St.
Monterey, CA 93940
831-647-4201

U.S. Fish and Wildlife Service
2800 Cottage Way
Sacramento, CA 95825
916-414-6464

Bibliography

California Coastal Commission. *California Coastal Access Guide*. 6th ed. Berkeley: University of California Press, 2003.

_____. *California Coastal Resource Guide*. Berkeley: University of California Press, 1987.

Deland, C., C. B. Cameron, K. P. Rao, W. E. Ritter, and T. H. Bullock. "A taxonomic revision of the family Harrimaniidae (Hemichordata: Enteropneusta) with descriptions of seven species from the Eastern Pacific." *Zootaxa* 2408:1–30.

Delmas, Delphin Michael. *Speeches and Addresses*. San Francisco: A.M. Robertson, 1901.

Goodson, Gar. *Fishes of the Pacific Coast*. Stanford, CA: Stanford University Press, 1988.

Griggs, Gary, Kiki Patsch, and Lauret Savoy. *Living with the Changing California Coast*. Berkeley: University of California Press, 2005.

Griggs, Gary and Deepika Shrestha Ross. *Santa Cruz Coast: Then and Now*. San Francisco: Arcadia Publishing, 2006.

Hoover, Mildred Brooke, Hero Eugene Rensch, and Ethel Grace Rensch. *Historic Spots in California*. 3rd ed. Stanford, CA: Stanford University Press, 1966.

Kampion, Drew, ed. *The Stormrider Guide: North America*. Bude, Cornwall, UK: Low Pressure Ltd., 2002.

Klaas, M.D. *Clipper Across the Pacific*, in *Air Classics* magazine, Part One, Dec. 1989, p. 14 and Part Two, January 1990, p. 62.

_____. *Clipper to Honolulu: What it Would Have Been Like to Fly on the Boeing 314 Clipper*, in *Air Classics* magazine, Vol. 40, No. 5, 2004, p. 15.

London, Jack. *John Barleycorn*. 1913. Charleston: Forgotten Books, 2010.

Marinacci, Barbara and Rudy Marinacci. *California's Spanish Place Names: What They Are and How They Got Here*. San Rafael, CA: Presidio Press, 1980.

Morris, William, ed. *The American Heritage Dictionary of the English Language*. Boston: Houghton Mifflin Co., 1976.

Munz, Philip A. *Introduction to Shore Wildflowers of California, Oregon, and Washington*. Berkeley: University of California Press, 2003.

Nigmatullin, Ch. M., K. N. Nesis, and A. I. Arkhipkin. "A review of the biology of the jumbo squid *Dosidicus gigas* (Cephalopoda Ommastrephidae)." *Fisheries Research* 54: 9–19.

Santa Cruz Seaside Co. *The Santa Cruz Beach Boardwalk: A Century by the Sea*. Berkeley: Ten Speed Press, 2007.

Soulé, Frank, John H. Gihon, MD, and James Nisbet. *The Annals of San Francisco*. New York and San Francisco: D. Appleton and Co., 1855. As reprinted by Lewis Osborne, Palo Alto, CA, 1966.

Stuart, John D. and John O. Sawyer. *Trees and Shrubs of California*. Berkeley: University of California Press, 2001.

Taylor, Arthur A. *California Redwood Park*. Sacramento: State Printing Office, 1912.

Trautman, James. *Pan American Clippers: The Golden Age of Flying Boats*. Erin, Ont.: Boston Mills Press, 2007.

Twain, Mark. "Early Morning at the Cliff House," first published July 3, 1864 in the Golden Era, reprinted in *More San Francisco Memoirs 1852–1899: The Ripening Years*, compiled and introduced by Malcolm Barker. San Francisco: Londonborn Publications, 1996.

Wagner, Jack R. *The Last Whistle (Ocean Shore Railroad)*. Berkeley: Howell-North Books, 1974. Walter, Carrie Stevens. "The Preservation of the Big Basin." *Overland Monthly: An Illustrated Magazine of the West*. Oct. 1902: 354-361.

Zeidberg, Louis D. and Bruce H. Robison. "Invasive range expansion by the Humboldt squid, Dosidicus gigas, in the eastern North Pacific." *Proceedings of the National Academy of Sciences*: 12948–12950.

Suggestions for Further Reading

Bakker, Elna S. *An Island Called California: An Ecological Introduction to Its Natural Communities*. 2nd ed. Berkeley: University of California Press, 1985.

Bascom, Willard. *Waves and Beaches: the Dynamics of the Ocean Surface*. Garden City, NY: Anchor Press, 1980.

Cralle, Trevor. *Surfin'ary: A Dictionary of Surfing Terms and Surfspeak*. Rev. ed. Berkeley: Ten Speed Press, 2001.

Guisado, Raul and Jeff Klaas. *Surfing California: A Complete Guide to the Best Breaks on the California Coast*. Guilford, CT: Falcon Guide, 2005.

Harding, D. R. *California Geology*. Upper Saddle River, NJ: Prentice Hall, 1998.

Humann, Paul. *Coastal Fish Identification: California to Alaska*. Jacksonville, FL: New World Publications, 1996.

Jones, Ken. *Pier Fishing in California: The Complete Coast and Bay Guide*. 2nd ed. Roseville, CA: Publishers Design Group, 2004.

Love, Milton. *Probably More Than You Want to Know about the Fishes of the Pacific Coast*. Santa Barbara: Really Big Press, 1996.

McPeak, Ronald H., Dale A. Glantz, and Carole Shaw. *The Amber Forest: Beauty and Biology of California's Submarine Forests*. San Diego: Watersport Publications, 1988.

Mondragon, Jennifer, and Jeff Mondragon. *Seaweeds of the Pacific Coast: Common Marine Algae from Alaska to Baja California*. Monterey, CA: Sea Challengers, 2003.

Ricketts, Edward F., Jack Calvin, and Joel Hedgpeth. *Between Pacific Tides*. Rev. ed. Stanford, CA: Stanford University Press, 1992.

Starr, Kevin. *California: A History*. New York: Modern Library, 2005.

Yeats, R.S. *Living with Earthquakes in California: A Survivor's Guide*. Corvallis, OR: Oregon University Press, 2001.

Index

Bold numeral indicates photograph.

EXPERIENCE THE CALIFORNIA COAST

The Experience the California Coast guides are the authoritative resource for exploring California's magnificent coastline. Each lavishly illustrated regional volume describes all publicly accessible beaches and accessways, along with plants and wildlife to look for and points of geological and historical interest. Feature stories tell about coastal environments from upland forests to wetlands to the deep ocean. Short sidebars tell the tales of shipwrecks, lighthouses, and colorful personalities of the past. All listed beach access routes, hiking trails, and major bicycle routes are depicted on color topographical maps. Easy-to-use charts list key facilities and amenities at all sites. Each guide is fully indexed and includes a glossary of terms and suggestions for further reading.

Experience the California Coast:
A Guide to Beaches and Parks in Northern California

Counties included: Del Norte, Humboldt, Mendocino, Sonoma, Marin

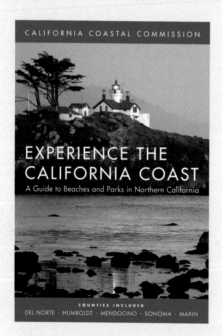

- More than 300 beaches, paths to the shoreline, coastal parks, and campgrounds

- Del Norte County's Smith River, Old Town Eureka, Humboldt County's Lost Coast, Pete's Beach, Mendocino, Bodega Bay, Tomales Point, Limantour Beach

- Redwood National and State Parks, Sinkyone Wilderness State Park, Point Reyes National Seashore, Sonoma Coast State Park

- Historic lumber industry, rock formations known as tafoni, pygmy forest, shipwreck of the *Brother Jonathan* and the *Tennessee*

- Where to find kayak rentals, horseback riding, surf shops

320 pages, 51 maps, published 2005
ISBN: 9780520245402

To order Experience The California Coast guides, visit www.ucpress.edu.

Beaches and Parks from Monterey to Ventura

Counties included: Monterey, San Luis Obispo, Santa Barbara, Ventura

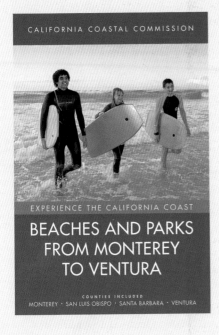

- More than 310 beaches, shoreline access paths, parks, campgrounds, nature preserves, and natural history museums

- Monterey Bay Aquarium, Stillwater Cove, Point Lobos, Big Sur, Hearst Castle, Morro Rock, Santa Barbara, Surfer's Point, Silver Strand Beach

- Pfeiffer Beach, Oceano Dunes, Channel Islands National Park, Santa Monica Mountains National Recreation Area

- Writer Robert Louis Stevenson's stay in old Monterey, geology of the Santa Lucia Range, the Santa Barbara oil spill of 1969, building California's coastal railroad

- Where to see elephant seals, rent a bicycle or surfboard, catch an ocean fishing trip

320 pages, 46 maps, published 2007
ISBN: 9780520249493

Beaches and Parks in Southern California

Counties included: Los Angeles, Orange, San Diego

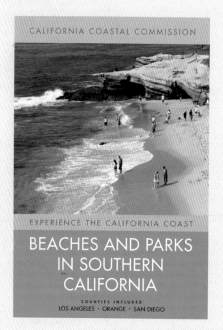

- More than 450 beaches, paths to the shoreline, parks, nature preserves, and aquariums

- Westward Beach, Santa Catalina Island, Sunset Beach, Newport Bay, Fisherman's Cove, Oceanside Pier, La Jolla, San Diego's Mission Bay Park

- Surfrider Beach, Crystal Cove State Park, Torrey Pines State Natural Reserve, Old Town San Diego State Historic Park

- Ports of Long Beach and Los Angeles, history of lifeguarding in Southern California, Palos Verdes Peninsula, wetland restoration in San Diego County, Kate Sessions and the creation of Balboa Park

- How to help keep ocean waters clean, where to find whale-watching trips, where to take your dog to the beach

352 pages, 50 maps, published 2009
ISBN: 9780520258525

To order Experience The California Coast guides, visit www.ucpress.edu.